IMPROVING READING

Quick Reference Guide

Children's 10 Rights to Excellent Reading Instruction

Children have a right to appropriate early reading instruction based on their individual needs. Children have a right to reading instruction that builds both the skill and the desire to read increasingly complex materials. Children have a right to well-prepared teachers who keep their skills up to date through effective professional development. Children have a right to access a wide variety of books and other reading material in classroom, school, and community libraries. Children have a right to reading assessment that identifies their strengths as well as their needs and involves them in making decisions about their own learning. Children who are struggling with reading have a right to receive intensive instruction from professionals specifically trained to teach reading. Children have a right to reading instruction that involves parents and communities in their academic lives. Children have a right to reading instruction that makes meaningful use of their first language skills. Children have the right to equal access to the technology used for the improvement of reading instruction. Children have a right to classrooms that optimize learning opportunities.

IMPROVING READING

Strategies and Resources

Third Edition

Jerry L. Johns
Northern Illinois University, Emeritus

Susan Davis Lenski
Illinois State University

KENDALL/HUNT PUBLISHING COMPANY
4050 Westmark Drive Dubuque, Iowa 52002

Book Team

President & Chief Executive Officer: Mark C. Falb
Vice President, Director of National Book Program:
 Alfred C. Grisanti
Editorial Development Supervisor: Georgia Botsford
Vice President, Production Editorial:
 Ruth A. Burlage
Production Manager: Jo Wiegand
Production Editor: Ellen Kaune
Design Manager: Jodi Splinter
Designer: Deb Howes

Books by Jerry L. Johns

Basic Reading Inventory (eight editions)
Spanish Reading Inventory (two editions)
Balanced Reading Instruction: Teachers' Visions and
 Voices (edited with Laurie Elish-Piper)
Secondary & College Reading Inventory (two editions)
Literacy for Diverse Learners (edited)
Handbook for Remediation of Reading Difficulties
*Informal Reading Inventories: An Annotated
 Reference Guide* (compiled)
Literacy: Celebration and Challenge (edited)

Books by Jerry L. Johns and Susan Davis Lenski

*Improving Writing: Resources, Strategies, and
 Assessments*
Early Literacy Assessments & Teaching Strategies
 (with Laurie Elish-Piper)
*Reading & Learning Strategies for Middle & High
 School Students* (with Mary Ann Wham)
Celebrating Literacy: The Joy of Reading and Writing
 (with June E. Barnhart, James H. Moss, and
 Thomas E. Wheat)
Language Arts for Gifted Middle School Students

Author Information for Correspondence and Workshops

Jerry L. Johns
Reading Consultant
2105 Eastgate Drive
Sycamore, IL 60178
E-mail: *jjohns@niu.edu*
815-895-3022

Susan Davis Lenski
Illinois State University
239 DeGarmo Hall
Normal, IL 61790-5330
E-mail: *sjlensk@ilstu.edu*
309-438-3028

Ordering Information

Address: Kendall/Hunt Publishing Company
 4050 Westmark Drive
 Dubuque, IA 52004

Telephone: 800-247-3458, Ext. 5

Web site: www.kendallhunt.com

Photos by JM©IMAGES

Copyright © 1994, 1997, 2001 by Kendall/Hunt Publishing Company

ISBN 0-7872-7614-6

Printed in the United States of America
10 9 8 7 6 5 4 3 2 1

Brief Contents

Contents

3 Identifying Words 125

4 Developing Fluency and Successful Oral Reading Behaviors 185

Resources 521

References 619

Index 627

Preface

Who Will Use This Book?

Preservice teachers, practicing teachers, and professionals who fulfill special resource roles will appreciate the user-friendly approach we have taken in *Improving Reading: Strategies and Resources*. This book is grounded on sound reading theory and emphasizes a balanced approach to the teaching of reading. *Improving Reading* will be useful in college and university courses for preservice and practicing teachers who are looking for practical ideas to help students improve their reading abilities. The book is ideal for school and district professional development programs.

What Are Some of the Unique Characteristics of This Book?

Improving Reading: Strategies and Resources is chock full of ideas for teachers who work with individual students or groups of students in reading. The book is divided into eight chapters. These eight chapters are main components of a reading curriculum. Within each chapter you will find 8 to 13 sections. These sections provide you with many teaching strategies, activities, and resources to help students with a specific reading problem.

What Grade Levels Do the Strategies Address?

This book is not written for distinct grade levels. The strategies may be used for students of any grade. Use the Quick Reference Guide to identify the problem, and then use the recommended strategy to address the problem.

Is This Book Easy to Use?

Absolutely! The format of *Improving Reading* allows you to quickly find teaching strategies, ideas, and resources that will help students learn.

How to Use This Book

You can use *Improving Reading* in two ways. If you want to strengthen your teaching of a particular area, look at the Contents. In the Contents you will find the names of skills and strategies that apply to that topic. You can develop a systematic approach to the teaching of comprehension, for example, by thinking about the components of comprehension listed in the Contents.

Sample of Contents

You also can use *Improving Reading* to help one or more students with a specific reading problem. For example, say a student has difficulty reading fluently. Check the Quick Reference Guide and look at the chapter on fluency. Under the chapter heading are several behaviors that a student could be exhibiting. Scan the list of behaviors to determine which one best describes the student's reading problem. Then turn to that section to use with the student.

Sample of Quick Reference Guide

You will see that most chapters are arranged in the same format:

- Overview
- Numbered section heading
- Boxed student learning goal behavior observed and anticipated outcome
- Background information
- Numbered teaching strategies

There is a **numbered section** heading (e.g., 5.3 Compound Words and Affixes).

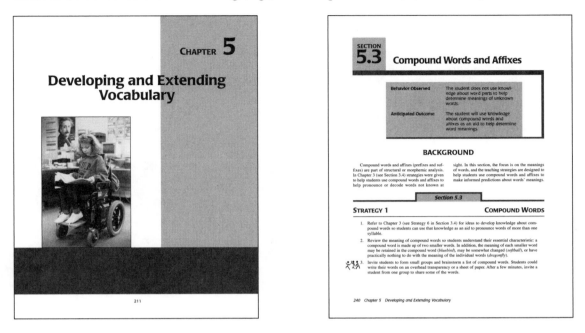

The **behavior observed** and **anticipated outcome** for the section are identified in the box.

Background information is given to aid in reaching the goal.

Teaching strategies form the heart of this book. These strategies are carefully described and use examples from various content areas. For each goal, you will find one or more strategies. Practice and reinforcement activities are also included.

Technology Resources

Throughout the book you will find **Technology Resources** listing web sites that will provide you with more background information or teaching ideas. Remember, though, that web addresses change without warning. Because of frequent web site changes, we cannot ensure their accuracy.

Appendices

The appendices provide easy reference to additional resources for the teacher of reading.

Appendix A: Books without Words includes a list of popular picture books.
Appendix B: Alphabet Books lists alphabet books that teachers have found useful.
Appendix C: Pattern Books contains ideas for teaching pattern books and a list of pattern books.
Appendix D: Literacy-Related Web Sites contains additional ideas and web sites about reading instruction.

Teacher and Student Resources

Includes student sheets (denoted by a student reading icon) and teacher resources (denoted by an apple icon) for the tracking of your students understanding of the important strategies introduced in each chapter.

Acknowledgments

We would like to thank the following individuals who shared ideas, compiled resources, edited our writing, and offered support and encouragement during the writing of this book.

Dawn Andermann
Jane Cheatham
Tara Cooper
Dawn Daily
Heather Davis
Rebecca Dunham
Linda Frank
Mary Grabenstetter
Janis Heck
Kathy Hultine
Patricia Ingram
Annette Johns
Rose Kamnikar
Eric Kingdon

Wendy Knudson
Constance Krabill
Amy Kupec
Michelle Laird
Jennifer Lawless
Fran Lenski
Joy McCombs
Stephanie Medler
Cathy Montgomery
Martha Oertle
Amy Pierce
Stacie Rada
Tracy Riebel

Patty Rieman
Marilyn Roark
Meghan Roberts
Amy Schmidt
Amy Shepard
Aileen Shorkey
Suzanna Sneeden
Bonnie Stiles
Susan Stumpf
D'Ann Urish
Viola Walker
Renee Wenger
Sally Whitcomb

About the Authors

Jerry L. Johns has been recognized as distinguished professor, writer, and outstanding teacher educator. He has taught students from kindergarten through grade eight and has held the position of reading teacher. Dr. Johns now serves as a consultant and speaker to schools and professional organizations. He is also an officer of the International Reading Association and will serve as president during 2002–2003.

Professor Johns is a past president of the Illinois Reading Council, College Reading Association, and Northern Illinois Reading Council. He has received recognition for outstanding service to each of these professional organizations and is a member of the Illinois Reading Council Hall of Fame. Dr. Johns has served on numerous committees of the International Reading Association (IRA) and was a member of the Board of Directors. He recently received the Outstanding Teacher Educator in Reading from IRA.

Dr. Johns has been invited to consult, conduct workshops, and make presentations for teachers and parents throughout the United States and Canada. He has also prepared nearly 300 publications that have been useful to parents and a diverse group of educators. His *Basic Reading Inventory,* now in an eighth edition, is widely used in undergraduate and graduate classes as well as by practicing teachers. Dr. Johns recently coauthored a book on writing instruction. A current project is focused on extending the scope of his Spanish Reading Inventory.

Susan Davis Lenski is an Associate Professor in Elementary Education at Illinois State University. Before joining the faculty at ISU, Dr. Lenski taught in public schools for 20 years. Her teaching experiences include working with children from kindergarten through high school. Dr. Lenski currently teaches undergraduate and graduate reading and language arts courses.

Professor Lenski has been recognized by several organizations for her commitment to education. Among her numerous awards, Dr. Lenski was presented with the Nila Banton Smith Award from the International Reading Association for her work in integrating content area subjects with reading instruction in secondary school. As an elementary school reading specialist, Dr. Lenski was instrumental in her school receiving an Exemplary Reading Program Award from the International Reading Association.

Professor Lenski's research interests are in improving reading and writing instruction in elementary and middle schools. She has conducted numerous inservice presentations and has presented at many state and national conferences. Dr. Lenski has written over 40 articles for professional journals. This is her sixth book.

CHAPTER 1

Motivating Students to Read

OVERVIEW

"If only my students were more motivated to read." Teachers of young children through young adults have the same goal: they desire their students to *want* to read. Teachers intuitively know what research bears out—that motivated readers are better readers (Guthrie et al., 1999). And because teachers want their students to be good readers, they also want their students to be motivated to read. The question for most teachers, however, is *how* to motivate students to read.

Reading motivation is a multifaceted combination of a student's personal goals, values, and beliefs interacting with topics, processes, and outcomes of reading (Guthrie & Wigfield, 2000). Motivated readers want to read. They find reading enjoyable and choose to read during some of their free time. Motivated readers recognize that they learn through reading. Reading is attractive to them because they find topics of interest in books and other types of printed material. Motivated readers set learning goals. They find ways to challenge themselves through reading. Motivated readers also read outside of the school setting. They not only choose to read in school, but they also read at home, in the library, and wherever they can take a book. Motivated readers, then, have a combination of personal qualities that make them motivated.

Because reading motivation is so complex, it is situational and often fragile. Cole (2000) has used the term "literacy personalities" to highlight the unique variety of motivators for students. Teachers find that activities that are motivational at the beginning of the school year sometimes lose their appeal by December. Furthermore, motivation can change in individual students. First-grade teachers frequently find almost all of their students highly motivated to read. However, reading motivation tends to decline in many students as they progress through school (Wigfield et al., 1997). Therefore, it's important that teachers recognize how motivation changes and flexibly apply a variety of strategies that will motivate their students to read.

Not every student will become an avid reader, but we believe that teachers can make a profound difference in the motivational dispositions of their students. There are many ways that teachers can create an interest in reading among their students (Gambrell, 1996). One of the most effective ways to motivate students is to value reading in your classroom (Rasinski & Padak, 2000). One way to value reading is to become a reading role model. Teachers need to model for their students a genuine love of reading and a desire to read. They can model their love of reading in many ways. Teachers can discuss books and other printed materials they have read for personal enjoyment; they can discus their reading habits (e.g., reading before going to bed); and they can tell their students about authors they particularly enjoy. Teachers who exhibit a passion for reading are taking the first step in motivating their students to read.

For students to become effective, lifelong readers, they must have both the skill and the will to read. Therefore, an important role of the teacher is to provide activities and strategies that encourage students to read. This chapter focuses on ways teachers can help motivate their students to read so that reading becomes personally satisfying to them.

> Motivated readers are better readers.

> One way to value reading is to become a reading role model.

TECHNOLOGY RESOURCES

Education Place

www.eduplace.com/index.html
Contains a variety of activities including book talks

Books Every Child Should Read

http://homearts.com/depts/relat/bookintr.html
Provides interviews with well-known personalities who recommend books for children

Learning About the Author and Illustrator Pages

http://www.scils.rutgers.edu/special/kay/author.html
Includes more than 600 sites about authors and illustrators of children's literature

SECTION 1.1

Lack of Motivation

Behavior Observed	The student can read but chooses not to read.
Anticipated Outcome	The student will become more motivated to read and will begin to choose reading as an activity.

BACKGROUND

Students who can read but who do so infrequently may be called *reluctant* or *aliterate* readers. Such readers generally comprise two groups. One group is composed of students who are not particularly good readers. They can read but they are reading below grade level; moreover, they do not appear interested in improving their reading. Instead, they prefer to watch television and to participate in activities that do not involve reading.

The second group of reluctant readers is comprised of students who can read quite well but who choose not to read. These students are reading at or above grade level; however, they are not apt to read in their spare time. Reading does not provide the same satisfaction as nonreading activities. Such students frequently appear to their teachers as bored or apathetic.

To encourage reluctant readers, it may be helpful to consider two types of motivation: internal (intrinsic) and external (extrinsic). Reluctant readers, by definition, possess little intrinsic motivation to interact with books and other reading materials. Whatever the causes, these students have

> **Reluctant Readers**
> - Students who are not good readers.
> - Students who read well but choose not to read.

become indifferent or antagonistic toward reading. Because many reluctant readers possess little or no intrinsic motivation for reading, one of the central tasks of teachers is to use techniques to bring students and books together.

Extrinsic motivation may be needed because reluctant readers, on their own, have not found much satisfaction in reading. Teachers therefore must develop strategies that move these students toward books and other types of printed materials in order for students to gain a tangible reward. As reading becomes a more pleasant and satisfying experience, it is hoped that extrinsic motivation will be replaced with intrinsic motivation to read. The teacher who seeks to motivate the reluctant reader is consciously trying to change the student's behavior and attitude toward reading from one of apathy to one of self-satisfaction and involvement. The teacher should also use techniques that will encourage the student to view reading as an activity that merits his or her time and energy. The following strategies and activities should be useful.

STRATEGY 1 READING ROLE MODELS

1. Tell students that many people love to read and that you will be bringing in special speakers who will tell them about the kinds of books they read. Explain to students that you will be bringing in two Reading Role Models a month. Ask students to help make scheduling decisions about when the Reading Role Models will speak to the class.

2. Prepare a speakers' schedule and begin asking people if they would be interested in telling your class about their reading habits. To find special speakers contact your local police officers or fire fighters, city council members, newspaper writers, radio or TV personalities, sports stars, and even your local football team (Cunningham & Allington, 1999). As you contact potential speakers, tell them something like the following:

 I'm making a concerted effort this year to motivate my students to read. I know that my students look up to you, and they would be mightily impressed if you could come to school and tell them about the reading you do in your life.

 You will find so many individuals interested in helping you motivate your students that you will probably have a waiting list.

3. Tell your speakers that you want them to talk about all of the different types of reading that they do. Stress the variety of reading people do throughout the day, not just book reading. You might tell your speakers about your reading preferences and habits as an example of the kind of thing you want them to tell your students. For example, you might say:

 I read every chance I get. I read the newspaper during breakfast in the morning. When I get to school, I get a cup of coffee and spend some time reviewing my teaching lessons. If I have time, I then reread the literature selection of the day. When the students come into the classroom, I read the notes they bring me, the announcements, and the lunch menu. Throughout the day I read students' papers. After school, I read professional journals and news magazines. I might also read a cookbook if I'm making something new for dinner. In the evening I grade my students' papers for an hour or so; then I read to my children. After the children are in bed, I snuggle up with the latest New York Times *best seller until I go to bed.*

4. After you have scheduled your speakers, print T-shirts with a catchy slogan such as "Real Men Read Books" or "Real Women Love to Read." Give the special speakers a T-shirt to wear as they tell your class about their reading habits.

STRATEGY 2

MOTIVATION TO READ PROFILE: READING SURVEY*

1. Tell students you are interested in their views about reading. Explain to students that you will be giving them a survey to take that will help you understand how they feel.

2. Reproduce and distribute copies of the Motivation to Read Profile (MRP).

3. Ask students to write their names in the space provided and tell them the following:

 I am going to read some sentences to you. I want to know how you feel about your reading. There are no right or wrong answers, so tell me honestly what you think. I will read each sentence twice. Do not mark your answer until I tell you to. After I read the sentence the first time, I want you to think about the best answer for you. Then after I read the sentence the second time, I want you to fill in the space beside your best answer. Mark only one answer.

4. Have students complete the survey and collect them. Score them by assigning a numerical value for each item: 1 point for the first answer, 2 points for the second answer, 3 points for the third answer, and 4 points for the fourth answer. For some of the questions the scoring is reversed. Recode the answers that have an asterisk next to them on the MRP Reading Survey scoring sheet.

5. Interpret your students' scores on the Motivation to Read Profile by calculating the students' scores about their self-concept as a reader and the value they place on reading. Use the results of the surveys to tailor your motivational plans for individual students as well as for your class.

Students are happy to share their reading interests.

*Gambrell, Palmer, Codling, & Mazzoni, 1996.

Name _____ Date _____

Motivation to Read Profile: Reading Survey

Sample 1: I am in _____.

❑ Second grade ❑ Fifth grade
❑ Third grade ❑ Sixth grade
❑ Fourth grade

Sample 2: I am a _____.

❑ boy
❑ girl

1. My friends think I am _____.
 ❑ a very good reader
 ❑ a good reader
 ❑ an OK reader
 ❑ a poor reader

2. Reading a book is something I like to do.
 ❑ Never
 ❑ Not very often
 ❑ Sometimes
 ❑ Often

3. I read _____.
 ❑ not as well as my friends
 ❑ about the same as my friends
 ❑ a little better than my friends
 ❑ a lot better than my friends

4. My best friends think reading is _____.
 ❑ really fun
 ❑ fun
 ❑ OK to do
 ❑ no fun at all

5. When I come to a word I don't know, I can _____.
 ❑ almost always figure it out
 ❑ sometimes figure it out
 ❑ almost never figure it out
 ❑ never figure it out

6. I tell my friends about good books I read.
 ❑ I never do this.
 ❑ I almost never do this.
 ❑ I do this some of the time.
 ❑ I do this a lot.

Gambrell, L.B., Palmer, B.M., Codling, R.M., & Mazzoni, S.A. (1996). Assessing reading motivation. *The Reading Teacher, 49,* 518–533.

7. When I am reading by myself, I understand _____.
 - ❏ almost everything I read
 - ❏ some of what I read
 - ❏ almost none of what I read
 - ❏ none of what I read

8. People who read a lot are _____.
 - ❏ very interesting
 - ❏ interesting
 - ❏ not very interesting
 - ❏ boring

9. I am _____.
 - ❏ a poor reader
 - ❏ an OK reader
 - ❏ a good reader
 - ❏ a very good reader

10. I think libraries are _____.
 - ❏ a great place to spend time
 - ❏ an interesting place to spend time
 - ❏ an OK place to spend time
 - ❏ a boring place to spend time

11. I worry about what other kids think about my reading _____.
 - ❏ every day
 - ❏ almost every day
 - ❏ once in a while
 - ❏ never

12. Knowing how to read well is _____.
 - ❏ not very important
 - ❏ sort of important
 - ❏ important
 - ❏ very important

13. When my teacher asks me a question about what I have read, I _____.
 - ❏ can never think of an answer
 - ❏ have trouble thinking of an answer
 - ❏ sometimes think of an answer
 - ❏ always think of an answer

Gambrell, L.B., Palmer, B.M., Codling, R.M., & Mazzoni, S.A. (1996). Assessing reading motivation. *The Reading Teacher, 49,* 518–533.

14. I think reading is _____.
 ❏ a boring way to spend time
 ❏ an OK way to spend time
 ❏ an interesting way to spend time
 ❏ a great way to spend time

15. Reading is _____.
 ❏ very easy for me
 ❏ kind of easy for me
 ❏ kind of hard for me
 ❏ very hard for me

16. When I grow up I will spend _____.
 ❏ none of my time reading
 ❏ very little of my time reading
 ❏ some of my time reading
 ❏ a lot of my time reading

17. When I am in a group talking about stories, I _____.
 ❏ almost never talk about my ideas
 ❏ sometimes talk about my ideas
 ❏ almost always talk about my ideas
 ❏ always talk about my ideas

18. I would like for my teacher to read books out loud to the class _____.
 ❏ every day
 ❏ almost every day
 ❏ once in a while
 ❏ never

19. When I read out loud I am a _____.
 ❏ poor reader
 ❏ fair reader
 ❏ good reader
 ❏ very good reader

20. When someone gives me a book for a present, I feel _____.
 ❏ very happy
 ❏ sort of happy
 ❏ sort of unhappy
 ❏ unhappy

Gambrell, L.B., Palmer, B.M., Codling, R.M., & Mazzoni, S.A. (1996). Assessing reading motivation. *The Reading Teacher, 49,* 518–533.

MRP Reading Survey Scoring Sheet

Student Name _____

Grade _____ Teacher _____

Administration Date _____

Recoding Scale
1 = 4
2 = 3
3 = 2
4 = 1

Self-Concept as a Reader		**Value of Reading**	
*recode	1. _____		2. _____
	3. _____	*recode	4. _____
*recode	5. _____		6. _____
*recode	7. _____	*recode	8. _____
	9. _____	*recode	10. _____
*recode	11. _____		12. _____
	13. _____		14. _____
*recode	15. _____		16. _____
	17. _____	*recode	18. _____
	19. _____	*recode	20. _____

SC raw score: _____ /40 **V raw score:** _____ /40

Full survey raw score (Self-Concept & Value): _____ /80

Percentage scores Self-Concept []
Value []
Full Survey []

Comments: _____

Gambrell, L.B., Palmer, B.M., Codling, R.M., & Mazzoni, S.A. (1996). Assessing reading motivation. *The Reading Teacher, 49,* 518–533.

STRATEGY 3 THUMBS-UP OR THUMBS-DOWN

1. Tell students that their opinions about the books they read are important and that you will be providing them with an opportunity to share their views with their class members.

2. Duplicate and distribute the Thumbs-Up (Good) and Thumbs-Down (Not So Good) sheets that follow this strategy. Have students cut out the picture of the hand that best represents their view of a book they have recently read.

3. Ask students to write the title of the book, the name of the author, a one-sentence plot summary, and the reason for their rating on the hand picture. Tell students that all of their reasons will be considered valid as long as they can justify their opinions.

4. Display the Thumbs-Up and Thumbs-Down pictures in your room at the students' eye level. Encourage students frequently to read their class members' opinions about books. From time to time, highlight a particularly good book that students have enjoyed.

5. Have additional copies of the Thumbs-Up and Thumbs-Down pictures available for students to use on an ongoing basis.

Practice and Reinforcement Activities

1. Have students bring in a photograph of themselves, family members, or pets. Tell students that they will be cutting the photograph and it will not be returned. Give students copies of precut bookmarks made out of plain construction paper. Have students cut a picture from the photograph that will fit on the bookmark and glue the picture in place. Then have students decorate their bookmarks.

2. Provide a wide variety of reading materials. Paperback books, magazines, newspapers, and high-interest, low-vocabulary materials often help motivate students to read.

3. Design attractive book displays and bulletin boards with information about books and authors. Students may find something of interest on them.

4. Read orally to students. Such reading may pique students' interests and encourage them to read independently. Introduce a new book periodically and read only the beginning to students or highlight interesting chapters. This procedure may entice a reluctant reader to borrow the featured book.

5. Provide reading corners with comfortable cushions, a rug, bean-bag chairs, or a couch. Students can plan and decorate the area. Use cardboard boxes of various sizes or boards and bricks as bookshelves.

6. Bring in thought-provoking objects that will stimulate questions and prompt students' desire to read books about specific topics. Many such objects can be found in closets and other storage areas.

7. Use appropriate popular music to inspire interest in reading by having students write down and examine the lyrics. Use the lyrics for discussions and lessons.

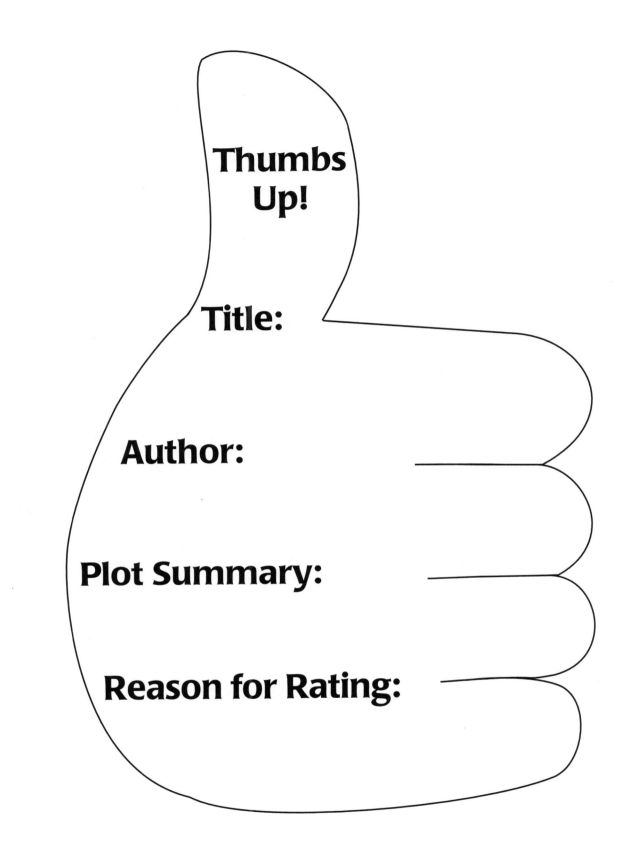

Thumbs Up!

Title:

Author:

Plot Summary:

Reason for Rating:

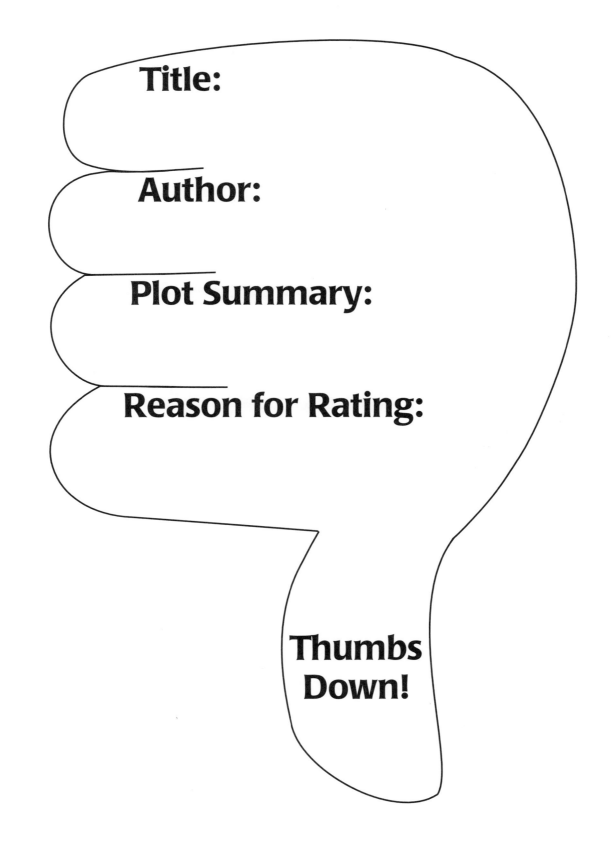

Title:

Author:

Plot Summary:

Reason for Rating:

Thumbs Down!

13

8. Provide periods of time for independent silent reading so students can interact directly with printed material of their own choice. Silent reading has been introduced to students using acronyms. Numerous examples follow.

SSR	Sustained Silent Reading
RIP	Read in Peace
DEAR	Drop Everything and Read
SQUIRT	Sustained Quiet Uninterrupted Independent Reading Time
RABBIT	Read a Book Because It's There
WALTER	We All Like the Extra Reading
SURE	Sustained Uninterrupted Reading Enjoyment
GRAB	Go Read a Book
FRED	Free Reading Every Day
WAR	We All Read
RINGO	Reading Is Now Going On
RIOT	Reading Is Our Thing
OSCAR	Our School Cares About Reading
GRINCH	Good Reading Is Now Coming Here
RIBET	Reading Is Bringing Everyone Together
SUPER	Silent Undisturbed Private Entertainment Reading
FRISBEE	Free Reading in School by Everyone Everywhere
SAFARI	Students and Faculty All Read Independently
ZYLAR	Zip Your Lips and Read

9. Encourage parents to set aside a few minutes each day when everyone in the family reads self-selected materials. The program could be called FRED: Family Reading Every Day.

10. A student may be motivated to read materials designed to help him or her accomplish a task of interest (for instance, model building or cooking).

11. Emphasize the practical nature of reading. For example, an older student may be motivated to read a driver's manual if he or she hopes to obtain a driver's license. Younger students can be encouraged to read environmental print.

12. Show enthusiasm for reading. Perhaps the most important ingredient in motivating the reluctant reader is your own attitude toward books and reading. Your enthusiasm for reading may naturally be passed on to your students.

13. For a set period of time (six to eight weeks), hold a weekly reading challenge. Brainstorm with your students about ideas for topics of reading that are interesting to the students. Topics that work well are sports, animals, fantasy stories, and so on. Have students read books about the class topics. On a bulletin board, keep track of the books the students have read for each topic.

14. Have a reading riot. In the center of the room, place many books that are easy to read. Have two or three students come to the pile of books and, in 30 seconds, choose one book to read. After each student has a book, give them time to read.

15. Stress the idea that reading is a fun activity.

16. Sprinkle your teaching with comments that are intrinsically motivating by including comments of anticipation, novelty, security, completion, identification, and feedback (Rinne, 1998). For example, a comment that includes the idea of novelty, or something out of the ordinary, would be "I've never read *Holes* to a fifth-grade class before, but I think you will really enjoy it." The resource chart on the following pages has additional suggestions of motivational comments.

Suggested Motivational Comments

Possible Intrinsic Appeals in Subject Matter	Description	Examples of Cue Words
Novelty	The opposite of routine	• Here's something different . . . • For the very first time this year, we are going to . . . • I'll bet you have never met anybody like the characters you'll meet in this book . . .
Surprise	An unexpected turn of events	• You will not believe your eyes . . . • You will be delighted . . . • Just wait until you see this . . .
Anticipation	Prompts curiosity and suspense	• Today we are going to . . . • See if . . . • Can you figure out how to . . . • Be sure to watch for . . .
Security	The reassurance of familiarity, safety, and efficacy	• You already know . . . • If you have difficulty, I will be here to help you . . . • This is just like we did . . .
Challenge	A problem that begs to be solved, a question that resists an answer, an obstacle that needs to be overcome, a goal that might be reached	• Can you do it like the experts? • I wonder how that could be done. • Can you . . . • You can only use . . . • What makes it behave that way? • What do you think?
Completion	One part of the lesson is used in another part of the same lesson	• You're wondering why we are doing this now? Because later . . . • After you finish this task, use it as you . . . • Complete this job so you will be ready to . . .
Application	Using the skills somewhere outside the lesson	• You can use this some day when . . . • People often find this useful when . . . • As you do this, you are doing what (engineers, scientists, librarians, authors) do . . .
Feedback	Sees the immediate results of engagement with the content	• You will know immediately whether you were correct . . . • If everything goes as planned, you should be able to see/hear . . . • Yes, that is exactly what we are looking for . . .

(continued)

Possible Intrinsic Appeals in Subject Matter	Description	Examples of Cue Words
Identification a. Possession b. Belonging c. Achievement d. Projection	The personal tie between content and the self-image of the student a. Ownership b. A place, status, sense of self c. Mega-cognition of achieving mastery d. Identification with a role model, a hero/heroine, an adventure	• Show/demonstrate your (possession) to the class . . . • Your team . . . • You will be a member of . . . • You are all in this together . . . • See if you can beat your own record . . . • When you have finished, you will find you can . . . • Teach someone else . . . • Pretend you are . . . • If you were _____, what would you do?
Competition	"Winning"	• The way to win is . . . • Whoever comes in first . . . • Whoever does the best . . .

From Rinne, C. (1998). Motivating students is a percentage game. *Phi Delta Kappan, 79,* 620–627.

Negative Attitude Toward Reading

Behavior Observed	The student does not like to read or exhibits a negative attitude toward reading.
Anticipated Outcome	The student will gain a more positive attitude toward reading.

BACKGROUND

A student who does not like to read or who exhibits a negative attitude toward reading is not necessarily unmotivated to read. Motivation is different from attitude toward reading (McKenna, Kear, & Ellsworth, 1995). Think about students who are motivated to do well in school. They keep trying even though they may not like what they are doing. Those students are motivated but have a negative attitude. On the other hand, there are students who may not be motivated but who have a positive attitude. It might be useful to think about yourself for this example. Perhaps you like to exercise and you know you should exercise, but you just don't. You probably aren't very motivated even though you have a positive attitude. This example illustrates the distinction between motivation and attitude.

A student who has a negative attitude toward reading is often—but not always—having difficulty with reading. Some students have a positive attitude toward reading regardless of their reading ability.

> Motivation is different from attitude.

However, many students may have a negative attitude toward reading because reading is difficult for them. When something is difficult, there seems to be a natural tendency to avoid or shy away from it. Other students may not have had enough positive experiences with reading to know what a wonderful activity reading is. These students may have a negative attitude simply because they were not read to in their early years.

Whatever the reasons why students have negative attitudes toward reading, you can listen actively and observe to find out why they don't like to read. These clues may provide a means of working with students to explore ways of helping them. Most teachers can tell when a student has a negative attitude toward reading, and there are surveys to help teachers assess students' attitudes toward reading. Teachers can use the results of surveys as a basis for experiences or materials to help their students develop more positive attitudes toward reading.

STRATEGY 1

ATTITUDE SURVEYS

1. Look at the two surveys following this teaching strategy and determine which one is more appropriate for your students. The Elementary Reading Attitude Survey is typically popular with young students, and the Rhody Secondary Reading Attitude Assessment is more appropriate for upper elementary, middle, and older students. Duplicate the survey that you have chosen.

2. Tell students that you would like to find out how they feel about reading. Emphasize that this is not a test and that there are no "right" or "wrong" answers. Encourage honesty.

3. If you have chosen the Elementary Reading Attitude Survey, distribute the survey forms and, if you wish to monitor the attitudes of specific students, ask them to write their names in the space at the top. Hold up a copy of the survey so that students can see the first page. Point to the picture of Garfield at the far left of the first item. Ask students to look at this same picture on their own survey form. Discuss with them the mood Garfield seems to be in (very happy). Then move to the next picture and again discuss Garfield's mood (this time, a little happy). In the same way, move to the third and fourth pictures and talk about Garfield's moods—a little upset and very upset. It is helpful to point out the position of Garfield's mouth, especially in the middle two figures.

4. Have students complete the survey independently as you read the statements to them. Ask students to respond with the answer that best describes how they feel.

5. If you have chosen the Rhody Secondary Reading Attitude Assessment, have students follow the directions on the survey.

6. Score the surveys using the scoring instructions that follow each of the surveys.

7. Use the information from the surveys to determine students' attitudes toward reading. Then take steps to help students build more positive attitudes toward reading.

Elementary Reading Attitude Survey

1. How do you feel when you read a book on a rainy Saturday?

2. How do you feel when you read a book in a school during free time?

3. How do you feel about reading for fun at home?

4. How do you feel about getting a book for a present?

GARFIELD: © 1978 United Feature Syndicate, Inc.

5. How do you feel about spending free time reading?

6. How do you feel about starting a new book?

7. How do you feel about reading during summer?

8. How do you feel about reading instead of playing?

GARFIELD: © 1978 United Feature Syndicate, Inc.

9. How do you feel about going to a bookstore?

10. How do you feel about reading different kinds of books?

11. How do you feel when the teacher asks you questions about what you read?

12. How do you feel about doing reading workbook pages and worksheets?

GARFIELD: © 1978 United Feature Syndicate, Inc.

4

5

17. How do you feel about the stories you read in reading class?

18. How do you feel when you read out loud in class?

19. How do you feel about using a dictionary?

20. How do you feel about taking a reading test?

GARFIELD: © 1978 United Feature Syndicate, Inc.

Elementary Reading Attitude Survey

Michael C. McKenna and Dennis J. Kear

Scoring and Interpretation

1. To score the survey, count four points for each leftmost (happiest) Garfield circled, three for each slightly smiling Garfield, two for each mildly upset Garfield, and one point for each very upset (rightmost) Garfield. Three scores for each student can be obtained: the total for the first 10 items, the total for the second 10, and a composite total. The first half of the survey relates to attitude toward recreational reading; the second half relates to attitude toward academic aspects of reading.

2. You can interpret scores in two ways. One is to note informally where the score falls in regard to the four points on the scale. A total score of 50, for example, would fall about midway on the scale, between the slightly happy and slightly upset figures, therefore indicating a relatively indifferent overall attitude toward reading. The other approach is more formal. It involves converting the raw scores into percentile ranks by means of Table 1. Be sure to use the norms for the right grade level and to note the column headings (Rec = recreational reading, Aca = academic reading, Tot = total score). If you wish to determine the average percentile rank for your class, average the raw scores first; then use the table to locate the percentile rank corresponding to the raw score mean. Percentile ranks cannot be averaged directly.

Norms for the Elementary Reading Attitude Survey

To create norms for the interpretation of the Elementary Reading Attitude Survey scores, a large-scale study was conducted in late January 1989, at which time the survey was administered to 18,138 students in Grades 1–6. Several steps were taken to achieve a sample that was sufficiently stratified (that is, reflective of the American population) to allow confident generalizations. Children were drawn from 95 school districts in 38 states. The number of girls exceeded by only 5 the number of boys. Ethnic distribution of the sample was also close to that of the U.S. population in 1989. The proportion of Blacks (9.5%) was within 3% of the national proportion, whereas the proportion of Hispanics (6.2%) was within 2%.

Percentile ranks at each grade for both subscales and the full scale are presented in Table 1. These data can be used to compare individual students' scores with the national sample and they can be interpreted like achievement-test percentile ranks.

McKenna, M.C., & Kear, D.J. (1990). Measuring attitude toward reading: A new tool for teachers. *The Reading Teacher, 43,* 626–639. Reprinted with permission of Michael C. McKenna and the International Reading Association.

Elementary Reading Attitude Survey Scoring Sheet

Student Name _____

Teacher _____

Grade _____ Administration Date _____

Scoring Guide

4 points	Happiest Garfield
3 points	Slightly smiling Garfield
2 points	Mildly upset Garfield
1 point	Very upset Garfield

Recreational reading	Academic reading
1. _____	11. _____
2. _____	12. _____
3. _____	13. _____
4. _____	14. _____
5. _____	15. _____
6. _____	16. _____
7. _____	17. _____
8. _____	18. _____
9. _____	19. _____
10. _____	20. _____
Raw score: _____	Raw score: _____

Total raw score (Recreational + Academic): _____

Percentile Ranks

Recreational	
Academic	
Full scale	

From Jerry L. Johns and Susan Davis Lenski, *Improving Reading: Strategies and Resources* (3rd ed.). Copyright © 2001 Kendall/Hunt Publishing Company (1-800-247-3458, ext. 5). May be reproduced for noncommercial educational purposes.

Table 1. Mid-Year Percentile Ranks by Grade and Scale

Raw Score	Grade 1			Grade 2			Grade 3			Grade 4			Grade 5			Grade 6		
	Rec	Aca	Tot	Rec	Aca	Tot	Rec	Ac	Tot	Rec	Aca	Tot	Rec	Aca	Tot	Rec	Aca	Tot
80			99			99			99			99			99			99
79			95			96			98			99			99			99
78			93			95			97			98			99			99
77			92			94			97			98			99			99
76			90			93			96			97			98			99
75			88			92			95			96			98			99
74			86			90			94			95			97			99
73			84			88			92			94			97			98
72			82			86			91			93			96			98
71			80			84			89			91			95			97
70			78			82			86			89			94			96
69			75			79			84			88			92			95
68			72			77			81			86			91			93
67			69			74			79			83			89			92
66			66			71			76			50			87			90
65			62			69			73			78			84			88
64			59			66			70			75			82			86
63			55			63			67			72			79			84
62			52			60			64			69			76			82
61			49			57			61			66			73			79
60			46			54			58			62			70			76
59			43			51			55			59			67			73
58			40			47			51			56			64			69
57			37			45			48			53			61			68
56			34			41			44			48			57			62
55			31			38			41			45			53			58
54			28			35			38			41			50			55
53			25			32			34			38			46			52
52			22			29			31			35			42			48
51			20			26			28			32			39			44
50			18			23			25			28			36			40
49			15			20			23			26			33			37
48			13			18			20			23			29			33
47			12			15			17			20			26			30
46			10			13			15			18			23			27
45			8			11			13			16			20			25
44			7			9			11			13			17			22
43			6			8			9			12			15			20
42			5			7			9			10			13			17
41			5			6			7			9			12			15
40	99	99	4	99	99	5	99	99	6	99	99	7	99	99	10	99	99	13
39	92	91	3	94	94	4	96	97	5	97	98	6	98	99	9	99	99	12
38	89	88	3	92	92	2	94	95	4	95	97	5	96	98	8	97	99	10
37	86	85	2	88	89	2	90	93	3	92	95	4	94	98	7	95	99	8
36	81	79	2	84	85	2	87	91	2	88	93	3	91	96	6	92	98	7
35	77	75	1	79	81	1	81	88	2	84	90	3	87	95	4	88	97	6
34	72	69	1	74	78	1	75	83	2	78	87	2	82	93	4	83	95	5
33	65	63	1	68	73	1	69	79	1	72	83	2	77	90	3	79	93	4
32	58	58	1	62	67	1	63	74	1	66	79	1	71	86	3	74	91	3
31	52	53	1	56	62	1	57	69	0	60	75	1	65	82	2	69	87	2
30	44	49	1	50	57	0	51	63	0	54	70	1	59	77	1	63	82	2
29	38	44	0	44	51	0	45	58	0	47	64	1	53	71	1	58	78	1
28	32	39	0	37	46	0	38	52	0	41	58	1	48	66	1	51	73	1
27	26	34	0	31	41	0	33	47	0	35	52	1	42	60	1	46	67	1
26	21	30	0	25	37	0	26	41	0	29	46	0	36	54	0	39	60	1
25	17	25	0	20	32	0	21	36	0	23	40	0	30	49	0	34	54	0
24	12	21	0	15	27	0	17	31	0	19	35	0	25	42	0	29	49	0
23	9	18	0	11	23	0	13	26	0	14	29	0	20	37	0	24	42	0
22	7	14	0	8	18	0	9	22	0	11	25	0	16	31	0	19	36	0
21	5	11	0	6	15	0	6	18	0	9	20	0	13	26	0	15	30	0
20	4	9	0	4	11	0	5	14	0	6	16	0	10	21	0	12	24	0
19	2	7		2	8		3	11		5	13		7	17		10	20	
18	2	5		2	6		2	8		3	9		6	13		8	15	
17	1	4		1	5		1	5		2	7		4	9		6	11	
16	1	3		1	3		1	4		2	5		3	6		4	8	
15	0	2		0	2		0	3		1	3		2	4		3	6	
14	0	2		0	1		0	1		1	2		1	2		1	3	
13	0	1		0	1		0	1		0	1		1	2		1	2	
12	0	1		0	0		0	0		0	1		0	1		0	1	
11	0	0		0	0		0	0		0	0		0	0		0	0	
10	0	0		0	0		0	0		0	0		0	0		0	0	

Rhody Secondary Reading Attitude Assessment

Regina Tullock-Rhody and J. Estill Alexander

Purpose

To acquire a quantitative idea of students' attitudes toward reading. The assessment can be used with students in grades seven through twelve.

Administration

1. Reproduce the sheet titled "Rhody Secondary Reading Attitude Assessment."

2. Assure students that the score will not affect their grades in any way.

3. Explain how the students should mark their answers. See directions on students' copy.

4. Read each of the statements aloud as students read them silently and give students ample time to mark their responses.

Scoring and Interpretation

1. Assign numerical values to each of the 25 items as follows:

Type and Number of Item		*Numerical Values*				
		SD	D	U	A	SA
Positive:	4, 5, 6, 7, 8, 10, 15, 17, 20, 22, 23, 24, 25	1	2	3	4	5
Negative:	1, 2, 3, 9, 11, 12, 13, 14, 16, 18, 19, 21	5	4	3	2	1

2. Add the numerical scores for all the statements. The student's score is a quantitative reflection of his or her attitude toward reading. The possible range of scores is 25 to 125. Interpret the score informally.

3. Items on the scale have been grouped into clusters to help teachers understand students' feelings toward areas of the reading environment. Use the cluster data informally.

Cluster	*Item Number*
Reading in the library	9, 20
Reading in the home	4, 10
Other recreational reading items	5, 17, 22, 24, 25
General reading	1, 2, 3, 6, 7, 8, 12, 13, 14, 15, 16, 19, 21, 23

4. Consult the original article for further information on the development of the attitude assessment.

Tullock-Rhody, R., & Alexander, J.E. (1980). A scale for assessing attitudes toward reading in secondary schools. *Journal of Reading, 23,* 609–614. Reprinted with permission of Regina Tullock and the International Reading Association.

Rhody Secondary Reading Attitude Assessment

Directions: This is a test to tell how you feel about reading. The score will not affect your grade in any way. You read the statements silently as I read them aloud. Then put an ☒ on the box under the letter or letters that represent how you feel about the statement.

SD = Strongly Disagree	A = Agree
D = Disagree	SA = Strongly Agree
U = Undecided	

		SD	D	U	A	SA
1.	You feel you have better things to do than read.	❏	❏	❏	❏	❏
2.	You seldom buy a book.	❏	❏	❏	❏	❏
3.	You are willing to tell people that you do not like to read.	❏	❏	❏	❏	❏
4.	You have a lot of books in your room at home.	❏	❏	❏	❏	❏
5.	You like to read a book whenever you have free time.	❏	❏	❏	❏	❏
6.	You get really excited about books you have read.	❏	❏	❏	❏	❏
7.	You love to read.	❏	❏	❏	❏	❏
8.	You like to read books by well-known authors.	❏	❏	❏	❏	❏
9.	You never check out a book from the library.	❏	❏	❏	❏	❏
10.	You like to stay at home and read.	❏	❏	❏	❏	❏
11.	You seldom read except when you have to do a book report.	❏	❏	❏	❏	❏
12.	You think reading is a waste of time.	❏	❏	❏	❏	❏
13.	You think reading is boring.	❏	❏	❏	❏	❏
14.	You think people are strange when they read a lot.	❏	❏	❏	❏	❏
15.	You like to read to escape from problems.	❏	❏	❏	❏	❏
16.	You make fun of people who read a lot.	❏	❏	❏	❏	❏
17.	You like to share books with your friends.	❏	❏	❏	❏	❏
18.	You would rather someone just tell you information so that you won't have to read to get it.	❏	❏	❏	❏	❏
19.	You hate reading.	❏	❏	❏	❏	❏
20.	You generally check out a book when you go to the library.	❏	❏	❏	❏	❏
21.	It takes you a long time to read a book.	❏	❏	❏	❏	❏
22.	You like to broaden your interests through reading.	❏	❏	❏	❏	❏
23.	You read a lot.	❏	❏	❏	❏	❏
24.	You like to improve your vocabulary so you can use more words.	❏	❏	❏	❏	❏
25.	You like to get books for gifts.	❏	❏	❏	❏	❏

STRATEGY 2 PICTURE BOOK SONGS*

1. Explain to students that many popular songs have been made into picture books. Show students examples of songs made into picture books such as *The Ants Go Marching* or *This Old Man*. (A list of additional picture books made from songs follows this strategy.) Play or sing the songs for the students.

2. Identify a picture book song that students would enjoy singing. Write the words of the song on a chart, an overhead transparency, or on sentence strips.

3. Teach students the words of the song by reading the written words.

4. Teach the tune of the song using a tape, CD, or a keyboard.

5. Listen to the music as you show the illustrations of the book. Track each line of the song as the students look at the words and listen to the music.

6. Ask students to sing along with the music. Practice a few lines at a time; then sing the entire song.

7. Make the book and tape available at the classroom listening center for students to use independently.

STRATEGY 3 USING HUMOR**

1. Set up a humorous literature center in your classroom. You might use a countertop, a desk, or even the chalkboard ledge. Tell students that this area will be devoted to fun reading.

2. Stock the humorous literature center with joke books, riddles, humorous poetry, and books of word play. Include books with a variety of reading levels. (Examples of humorous literature follow on page 31.)

3. Introduce students to the types of books in the humorous literature center. For example, read a riddle from one of the riddle books.

4. Invite students to read books from the humorous literature center during independent reading time. Tell students that they don't have to read any of the books from the first page to the last page but that they can read selectively in these types of books.

5. Provide students with the opportunity to share some of the fun from these with other class members. You might give students five minutes at the end of independent reading time to share a joke, riddle, or poem.

6. Change the selection of books in the humorous literature center every few weeks. Invite students to submit books to the center as well.

*Towell, 1999/2000.
**Klesius, Laframboise, & Gaier, 1998.

Picture Books Made From Songs

B-52s. *Wig!* New York: Hyperion, 1995. (available on tape)

Bates, Katharine Lee. *O Beautiful for Spacious Skies.* San Francisco: Chronicle, 1994.

Carpenter, Mary Chapin. *Halley Came to Jackson.* New York: HarperCollins, 1998. (with tape)

Collins, Judy. *My Father.* Boston: Little, Brown, 1968. (available on CD)

Garcia, Jerry, & Grisman, David. *The Teddy Bears' Picnic.* New York: HarperCollins, 1996. (with tape)

Judd, Naomi. *Love Can Build a Bridge.* New York: HarperCollins, 1999. (with tape)

Messenger, Jannat illustrations. *Twinkle, Twinkle, Little Star.* New York: Piggy Toes, 1997. (with music)

Parton, Dolly. *A Coat of Many Colors.* New York: HarperCollins, 1994. (music available on CD)

Raffi. *Down by the Bay.* New York: Crown, 1990. (tape is available)

Rounds, Glen (illustration). *Old MacDonald Had a Farm.* New York: Holiday House, 1989.

Trapani, Iza. *The Itsy Bitsy Spider.* Dallas: Whispering Coyote, 1993.

Weeks, Sarah. *Follow the Moon.* New York: Laura Geringer, 1995. (with tape)

Weiss, George David, & Thick, Bob. *What a Wonderful World.* New York: Atheneum, 1996.

Westcott, Nadine. *The Lady With the Alligator Purse.* Boston: Little, Brown, 1998.

Wood, Don and Audrey. *Piggies.* San Diego: Voyager, 1991. (with tape)

Books for Mood Music

de Paola, Tomie. *Fin M'Coul—the Giant of Knockmany Hill.* New York: Holiday House, 1982. (Irish music)

Downing, Julie. *Mozart Tonight.* New York: Bradbury, 1991. (classical music)

Gatti, Anne. *The Magic Flute.* San Francisco: Chronicle, 1997. (music by Mozart, comes with CD)

London, Jonathan. *Hip Cat.* San Francisco: Chronicle, 1993. (jazz)

Nichol, Barbara. *Beethoven Lives Upstairs.* New York: Orchard Books, 1993. (classical music)

Pinkney, Andrea Davis. *Duke Ellington.* New York: Hyperion, 1998. (swing, ragtime music)

Pratt, Kristin Joy. *A Walk in the Rainforest.* Nevada City: Dawn, 1992. (rainforest music)

Sheldon, Dyan. *The Whale's Song.* New York: Dial, 1990. (ocean music)

Yolen, Jane. *Owl Moon.* New York: Philomel, 1987. (classical music)

Towell, J.H. (2000). Motivating students through music and literature. *The Reading Teacher, 53,* 284–287.

Recommended Humorous Literature

Allard, Harry, & James Marshall. *Miss Nelson has a Field Day.* Boston: Houghton Mifflin, 1981.

Barrett, Judi. *Animals Should Definitely Not Wear Clothes.* New York: Macmillan, 1970.

Berenstein, Stan & Jan. *The Bike Lesson.* New York: Random House, 1964.

Berger, Melvin. *101 Wacky State Jokes.* New York: Scholastic, 1991.

Birdseye, Tom. *A Regular Flood of Mishaps.* New York: Holiday House, 1994.

Bridwell, Norman. *Clifford, the Big Red Dog.* New York: Scholastic, 1963.

Coville, Bruce. *My Teacher Is an Alien.* New York: Pocket Books, 1989.

Day, Alexandra. *Carl Goes to Daycare.* New York: Farrar, Straus & Giroux, 1993.

Gelman, Rita. *More Spaghetti, I Say.* New York: Scholastic, 1987.

Gwynne, Fred. *A Chocolate Moose for Dinner.* New York: Prentice-Hall, 1976.

Hepworth, Cathi. *Antics: An Alphabetical Anthology.* New York: G. P. Putnam's Sons, 1991.

Hirsch, Phil. *101 Dinosaur Jokes.* New York: Scholastic, 1988.

Lyon, George. *The Outside Inn.* New York: Orchard, 1991.

Macauley, David. *Why the Chicken Crossed the Road.* Boston: Houghton Mifflin, 1987.

Mayer, Mercer. *Little Critter's Joke Book.* New York: Golden Book, 1993.

Meddaugh, Susan. *Martha Speaks.* Boston: Houghton Mifflin, 1992.

Monsell, Mary. *Underwear.* Morton Grove, IL: Albert Whitman, 1988.

Most, Bernard. *The Cow That Went Oink.* New York: Harcourt Brace Jovanovich, 1990.

Noble, Trinka Hakes. *Jimmy's Boa and the Big Splash Birthday Bath.* New York: Trumpet, 1989.

Pinkwater, Daniel. *The Wugglie Norple Story.* New York: Trumpet, 1980.

Sachaar, Louis. *Sideways Stories from Wayside School.* New York: Avon, 1978.

Sachaar, Louis. *There's a Boy in the Girls' Bathroom.* New York: Alfred A. Knopf, 1978.

Schwartz, Amy. *Bea and Mr. Jones.* Scarsdale, NY: Bradbury, 1982.

Shaw, Nancy. *Sheep in a Jeep.* Boston: Houghton Mifflin, 1986.

Terban, Marvin. *Hey, Hay! A Wagonload of Funny Homonym Riddles.* New York: Clarion, 1991.

Thaler, Mike. *The Teacher from the Black Lagoon.* New York: Scholastic, 1989.

Van Laan, Nancy. *Possum Come A-knockin'.* New York: Trumpet, 1990.

Weisner, David. *Tuesday.* New York: Clarion Books, 1991.

Willis, Jeanne. *Earth Weather as Explained by Professor Xargle.* New York: Dutton, 1991.

Wood, Audrey. *King Bridgood's in the Bathtub.* New York: Harcourt, 1985.

Klesius, J., Laframboise, K.L., & Gaier, M. (1998). Humorous literature: Motivation for reluctant readers. *Reading Research and Instruction, 37,* 253–261.

Practice and Reinforcement Activities

1. Have students write, illustrate, and bind their own books. Good titles for books might be *All About Me* or *An Experience I Had.* Write the stories on paper or use a computer. Let students illustrate their stories and share them with one another. Some students may prefer to illustrate their stories before they write or dictate them to help maintain the story line. Also, remember that some students may write more easily when topics are general and abstract. Provide this option.

2. Have a book scavenger hunt. Divide the class into teams and give each team a copy of the same book. Give students 15 minutes to find the page numbers of particular objects, events, or people in the book. After the time is over, have students share their results.

3. Give positive reinforcement when the students read. Encourage your students to share what was read.

4. Create a book nook where students can display their favorite books. Encourage students to make murals, pictures, or original book jackets to promote their books. Big pillows and bean-bag chairs can help make the book nook inviting. These displays may help reluctant readers realize that many of their peers enjoy reading.

5. Choose a picture book with a small amount of text to read to your students. Read the picture book to your students without telling them the title or showing them the cover. After reading the book, divide the class into groups of three or four students and have students brainstorm a title for the book. Share the titles that the students created and then show students the title and cover of the book.

6. Invite guest speakers to tell students how they use reading in jobs or every day situations. (See Section 1.1 in this chapter.)

7. Model your love of reading to your students. Bring copies of books you read for pleasure and read aloud appropriate short passages from the books. Share other types of printed materials that you read.

8. Invite a storyteller to your classroom. Explain to students that before books were available people shared stories by telling them to others. Discuss ways books have made stories accessible to more people.

9. Arrange students' chairs back to back in a semicircle. Place a book under each chair. Have students sit on the chairs without looking at the books. Play some music that students like. Tell students to walk around the chairs while the music is playing and to stop and sit in the nearest chair when the music stops. Have students preview the book that is under the chair by reading the title and the first page and paging through the rest of the book. Repeat this procedure more than once. Place the books on the chalkboard ledge or at another accessible place for students to read during independent reading time.

Limited Reading Interests

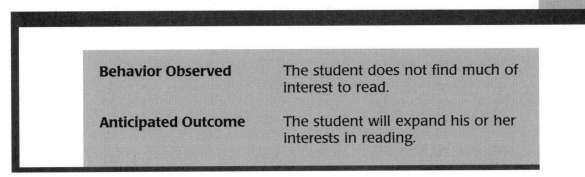

Behavior Observed	The student does not find much of interest to read.
Anticipated Outcome	The student will expand his or her interests in reading.

BACKGROUND

What contributes to a student's interests? It's hard to say why one student might be fascinated with rocks while another can't stand the topic. Certainly, familiarity may be a contributing factor to the formation of interests. Students who have spent hours with an adult collecting different kinds of rocks may have a natural interest in them. However, that doesn't always work. Sometimes spending time experiencing or learning about a topic doesn't increase one's interest.

Interest is not only hard to define; it's also changeable. What interests a student in fourth grade may not be interesting in fifth grade. Indeed, many students go through phases in reading and learning.

> Capturing a student's interest isn't easy.

There are trends and fads in literature just as there are in other social events. Capturing a student's interest isn't easy.

Although it may be difficult to identify students' interests, learning about what interests students is important. Students who read texts that are interesting to them tend to spend more time reading (McLoyd, 1979). Furthermore, students tend to have higher achievement in a topic that interests them (McPhail et al., 2000). Therefore, teachers should take the time to tailor students' reading to their interests. This section provides teaching strategies and activities to help in this undertaking.

STRATEGY 1 INTEREST INVENTORY

1. Choose an Interest Inventory to administer to your students. News About Me is typically popular with elementary students and the Inventory of Experiences is more appropriate for upper elementary and middle school students.

2. Duplicate and distribute the appropriate Interest Inventory.

3. Explain to students that you would like them to complete either the News About Me or the Inventory of Experiences. Say something like the following:

 I would like to know more about you and what interests you. I want to know so I can find books that fit your interests and study the topics you want to learn. Please complete the inventories and include as many details as possible.

4. Allow adequate time for students to complete the Interest Inventory. (You may need to read it to some students.)

5. After the students have completed the inventory, have them discuss their interests with class members. Divide the class into groups of three or four students. Tell students to share their responses with their group members. Ask one of the group members to list the interests shared in discussion.

6. Have students share their interest lists with the entire class. After each entry, ask the class if others are interested in the topic. For example, if one student states that ice hockey is interesting, ask how many other students are interested in ice hockey. Encourage students with similar interests to share their knowledge about the topic.

7. Find books about many of the topics of interest. A librarian may help you. Place the books in a visible place in the classroom and allow students time to read books about topics that interest them.

8. Administer the interest inventories every few months. Interests change and you will find it useful to assess your students' current interests throughout the year.

News About Me

A News Story About _____

(write your name here)

News About My Family

I have _____ brothers and sisters.

They are _____ years old.

I like to play with _____.

My mother and I like to _____.

My father and I like to _____.

I (like/do not like) to play alone.

I help at home by_____.

The thing I like to do at home is _____

_____.

News About My Pets

I have a pet _____.

I (do/do not) take care of my pet.

I do not have a pet because_____

_____.

I would like to have a pet _____.

News About My Books and My Reading

I like to read about _____

The best book I ever read was_____

_____.

I (do get/do not get) books from the library.

I have_____ books of my own at home.

I read aloud to_____.

My_____ reads to me.

News About My Friends

My best friend is_____.

I like (him/her) because_____

_____.

We play_____.

I would rather play (at my house/at my
friend's house) because _____

_____.

News About Things I Like and Dislike

I do not like_____.

I like_____.

I am afraid of_____.

I am not afraid of_____.

News About My Wishes

When I grow up, I want to be_____

_____.

If I could have three wishes I would wish

(1) _____

_____.

(2) _____

_____.

(3) _____

_____.

page 1

News About My Travels and Adventures

I have traveled by:

____ bus ____ car

____ airplane ____ truck

____ boat ____ train

____ bicycle ____ van

I have visited these interesting places:

____ circus ____ zoo

____ farm ____ park

____ hotel ____ museum

____ bakery ____ library

____ airport ____ fire station

____ factory, and _____.

The best adventure I ever had was _____
_____.

News About My School Subjects

My favorite subject is _____.

The subject I dislike most is _____.

I am best at _____.

I wish I was better in _____.

Write any other news about yourself below.

News About My Hobbies and Collections

One of my best hobbies is _____
_____.

I collect _____.

I want to collect _____.

My other hobbies are _____
_____.

Movie, Radio, and Television Favorites

I see _____ movies each week.

I like to listen to _____ on the radio.

I see _____ television programs a day.

My favorite programs are _____
_____.

page 2

Inventory of Experiences

Special Interests

1. Which outdoor sports do you like?
2. Which indoor games do you like?
3. What types of collections or hobbies do you have?
4. Have you had classes or lessons in music, dancing, or art?
 Describe _____
5. Do you belong to any clubs or groups like 4-H or Scouts?
 Describe _____
6. Do you have any pets?
7. What are your favorite TV programs? Movies?
8. What is your favorite subject at school?
9. What do you do with your free time?
10. Who are some of your best friends, and what do you enjoy doing with them?

Your Family

1. What are the names and ages of your brothers and sisters?
2. What are some things you do together?
3. Do you ever go places or play games with your *entire* family?
4. What trips have you taken?
5. Do you receive an allowance or spending money from your parents?
6. Do you have some regular duties or chores to do at home?

You and Books

1. What books and magazines do you have at home?
2. Do you have a library card?
3. What kinds of books or stories do you like?
4. Do you like to have someone read to you?
5. Do you like to read to others?

STRATEGY 2 BOOK TALKS

1. One good way to interest students in books is by giving a book talk. A book talk is a brief talk about a book with the purpose of enticing others to read it. There are several formats for sharing books through book talks:

 - Schedule a regular book talk every few days during which you can share one book you have read.
 - Read books about a theme and share them with the class before you begin the unit.
 - Share several books from the same author.
 - Share different versions of the same story (e.g., Cinderella).

2. Read the book and prepare a short talk that will motivate your students to read the book. As you prepare a book talk, remember that you do not want to give away the end of the story. If you tell the end of the story, you will destroy the students' suspense as they read it. Second, try to get the attention of the students during the first sentence. Third, try to make the book talk as appealing to your students as possible. A book talk is not a report on a book, but a motivational technique to encourage students to read the book. Finally, make the book talk short. Three to five minutes are best.

3. There are several ways you can organize your book talk. Different books require different methods. Use whichever organizational pattern fits you and the book.

 - **Relate the book to a personal experience.**

 Ruckman, Ivy. (1984). *Night of the Twisters.* New York: HarperCollins.

 I've always been afraid of tornadoes. Whenever the siren rings out, I run to the basement with my radio, a bottle of water, and a hammer. My fear stems from a tornado that hit without warning in a nearby town. As I read *Night of the Twisters,* I felt what it would really be like to be caught in a tornado and what I would hear and see. Now I run to the basement whenever there's a tornado watch!

 - **Use quotations or excerpts from the book.**

 Paulsen, Gary. (1987). *Hatchet.* New York: Puffin Books.

 Imagine flying in a small airplane over the vast north woods of Canada. You are on your way to visit your father when suddenly something happens to the pilot, and he slumps over in his seat. *[Read pp. 9–12 where the pilot has a heart attack.]* You are the only one aboard to land the airplane, and when you land, you are all alone far away from civilization trying to survive with only a hatchet and your own wits.

 - **Use props whenever appropriate.**

 Hesse, Karen. (1992). *Letters from Rifka.* New York: Henry Holt.

 [Wear a scarf, apron, and/or shawl.]

 Have you ever been to a new school? Remember how you felt: new, different, lonely? Rifka left Russia during the height of the Russian Revolution in 1919. She arrived in America sick and not knowing English. This diary shows how she felt and how she coped with the newness of America.

- **Dramatize the book talk by telling the book in the first person, using the main character's speech and dialect when appropriate.**

 Gardiner, John Reynolds. (1980). *Stone Fox.* New York: Thomas Y. Crowell.

 If only I had enough money to save my granpappy's farm. It's only $500, that's all I need. But $500 is a heap of money, more than I could git in a lifetime. Thar's only one way I can be fixin' to git the money, and that's not goin' to be easy. My dog, Searchlight, is the onliest chance I got. If he kin jist beat that ole Stone Fox, my granpappy's farm might be saved.

- **Prepare a short interview with the main character or the author.**

 Paterson, Katherine. (1978). *The Great Gilly Hopkins.* New York: Thomas Y. Crowell.

 > *Interviewer:* Gilly, how did it feel to be put in a foster home again?
 > *Gilly:* Man, I get sick of all these new places. Here I'm with this crazy lady, name of Maime Trotter, and William Ernest.
 > *Interviewer:* Why are you here?
 > *Gilly:* Well, my mom has had some trouble and couldn't take care of me.
 > *Interviewer:* What will you do?
 > *Gilly:* I'm going to find my mom and get out of here.

- **Prepare a script for a scene from the book. Ask students to read it, practice it, then perform it for the class.**

 Lowry, Lois. (1989). *Number the Stars.* New York: Bantam Doubleday, Dell.

 Annemarie walks outside where Uncle Henry is milking the cow.

 > *Annemarie:* Uncle Henry, you're lying to me.
 > *Uncle Henry:* You're angry.
 > *Annemarie:* Yes. Mama has never lied to me before. Never. Why now?
 > *Uncle Henry:* How brave are you, Annemarie? Are you brave enough to know the truth?

 They return to the house together. Several people are gathered around a casket.

 > *Mama:* Remember, Annemarie, this is Great-aunt Birte. If anyone asks you, you must convince them. It could mean the safety of our family and our friends!

 Pounding on the door, boots stomping in.

 > *Officer:* Why are all of you gathered here?
 > *Annemarie:* (trembling) My Great-aunt Birte has just died.

Section 1.3

STRATEGY 3 USING POPULAR CULTURE*

1. Tell students that you will be asking them for ideas that are of interest to them to use as reading topics. Explain to students that their interests are valued in your class.

2. Ask students to list their three favorite types of media. For example, you might say something like the following:

 I'd like you to list your three favorite media. If I were to list my favorite media, I'd list the radio, movies, and the Internet. What are your favorite media?

*Alvermann, Moon, & Hagood, 1999.

3. After students have listed their favorite media, probe deeper by asking them to list their favorite shows, web sites, or stations. For example you might say,

> *I like listening to* Prairie Home Companion *and* Car Talk *on National Public Radio. I also like to watch movies that are set in Ireland.*

4. Have students continue making lists of their popular culture by asking them to list favorite movie stars, sports heroes, television characters, and/or radio personalities.

5. Ask students to share their lists with class members. Divide the class into groups of three or four students and have students tell their classmates about their media interests. Allow enough time for all students to share.

6. Ask students to volunteer to share their interests with the entire class. As students discuss their media interests, create a list of the things that interest them. Post the list in a visible place in your classroom.

Do you think the teacher knows what interests these boys out of school?

7. Collect books and magazine articles about the media interests of the students. Place the materials in an accessible place in the classroom. Tell students that they can also bring in reading material. Allow students time to browse the materials and suggest that they select this reading material for independent reading.

Practice and Reinforcement Activities

1. Do your best to help students find books of interest. Sooner or later, interests will be directed toward related areas or completely new areas. When this occurs, be ready to help students find books that will satisfy the emerging interest areas.

2. To help expand interests, invite community members to share their special interests, hobbies, or experiences. Try to link their sharing to books available in the school or classroom library.

3. Provide plenty of reading material that varies in difficulty, content, and genre.

4. Poll students to determine their major interests and create numerous reading experiences in these areas.

5. Read to students daily. Select a wide variety of material from various genres. Assist students who would like other books similar in nature to the ones you have read to them. Perhaps they would like a different book by the same author. Encourage book-sharing ideas among classmates. Introduce a "book of the week" or an "author of the week" (or month).

6. Use movies, filmstrips, photographs, videotapes, and concrete objects to help stimulate an interest in different subjects. Secure books or other reading materials that relate to these subjects and have the material available for the students to read.

7. If available, local authors can be invited to talk about books they have written. Parents can also be invited into the classroom to share the kinds of materials they like to read.

8. Develop a paperback book exchange in the classroom.

9. Encourage students to follow up on their natural curiosity by brainstorming a list of interests that students have. Then conduct a search of books at the students' grade level that would support the students' interests. Staple the lists inside the students' reading folders and invite students to read at least two books from each list.

10. Have students from other classes or schools at your grade level develop a list of their top 20 books. Share each class's list with other participating classes. Post the lists in a prominent place and encourage your students to read books from each list.

11. Decorate a box to place in your room that you can use as a Suggestion Box. Invite students to think about topics that interest them and have them list the ideas on an index card. Then have them drop the card in the Suggestion Box. Explain that any time students have ideas about books they would like to read, they should write the ideas on a card and drop it in the box. Use the suggestions students submit to guide your choices of read alouds and book talks.

12. When students self-select books, encourage them to ask themselves why they have chosen the book. Ask them occasionally to write about their book selections in their journals. You might ask some students to keep track of their reasons for choosing their books on a book choice chart.

13. In literature circles have students discuss self-selected readings and why they chose each book.

14. Encourage students to present their own book talks. Videotape them to play back when students are inside during recess or when you want to reinforce the idea of varying book selections.

15. Ask students to prepare a poster advertising a genre of books.

16. Ask the librarian to highlight new books in the library that would be appropriate for your grade level.

17. Prepare individual bingo sheets with the different genres printed in each block. As a motivational tool, ask students to keep track of their self-selected reading. When they get four down or across, award them with additional free reading time.

Book Genre Bingo			
historical fiction	fantasy	"how-to"	folktales
realistic fiction	plays	biographies	science fiction
realistic fiction	picture books	folktales	historical fiction
picture books	realistic fiction	fantasy	informational books

Low Confidence in Reading Ability

Behavior Observed	The student has a low level of confidence in his or her reading ability.
Anticipated Outcome	The student will gain greater confidence in reading.

BACKGROUND

Confidence, or the belief that you can succeed, is an important factor in motivation (Ryan & Deci, 2000). Younger students may lack confidence in reading because there are many unknown words in their books. Older students, especially those who have experienced difficulty with reading, may have a fear of repeated failure. In both cases, students need to experience success with reading. The following strategies and activities may prove useful for students with low confidence in their reading ability.

Section 1.4

STRATEGY 1 READER SELF-PERCEPTION SCALE*

1. Tell students that you will be giving them a survey to determine how they feel about reading. Explain to students that you are interested in their honest responses and that their responses on the survey will not affect their grade.

2. Duplicate and distribute the Reader Self-Perception Scale. Have students write their name on the top of the survey.

3. Read the directions on the survey form with the students. If students are able to read the survey, have them complete it independently. Allow ample time for students to complete the surveys. For students experiencing difficulty with reading, read the statements aloud.

4. Collect the surveys and use the scoring sheet following the surveys to determine each student's reading self-perception.

5. For students who have a low level of confidence in their reading ability, try several strategies and activities and make a concerted effort to help them gain confidence in reading.

*Henk & Melnick, 1995.

The Reader Self-Perception Scale

Purpose

The Reader Self-Perception Scale (RSPS) is intended to provide an assessment of how children feel about themselves as readers. The scale consists of 33 items that assess self-perceptions along four dimensions of self-efficacy (Progress, Observational Comparison, Social Feedback, and Physiological States). Children are asked to indicate how strongly they agree or disagree with each statement on a 5-point scale (5 = Strongly Agree, 1 = Strongly Disagree). The information gained from this scale can be used to devise ways to enhance children's self-esteem in reading and, ideally, to increase their motivation to read. The following directions explain specifically what you are to do.

Administration

1. For the results to be of any use, the children must understand exactly what they are to do, have sufficient time to complete all items, and respond honestly and thoughtfully.

2. Briefly explain to the children that they are being asked to complete a questionnaire about reading. Emphasize that this is not a *test* and that there are no *right* answers. Tell them that they should be as honest as possible because their responses will be confidential.

3. Ask the children to fill in their names, grade levels, and classrooms as appropriate.

4. Read the directions aloud and work through the example with the students as a group. Before moving on, discuss the response options and make sure that all children understand the rating scale. It is important that children know that they may raise their hands to ask questions about any words or ideas they do not understand.

5. The children should then read each item and circle their response for the item. They should work at their own pace. Remind the children that they should be sure to respond to all items.

6. When all items are completed, the children should stop, put their pencils down, and wait for further instructions.

7. Care should be taken that children who work more slowly are not disturbed by children who have already finished.

Scoring and Interpretation

1. To score the RSPS, enter the following point values for each response on the RSPS scoring sheet (Strongly Agree = 5, Agree = 4, Undecided = 3, Disagree = 2, Strongly Disagree = 1) for each item number under the appropriate scale. Add each column to obtain a raw score for each of the four specific scales.

Henk, W. A., & Melnick, S. A. (1995). The Reader Self-Perception Scale (RSPS): A new tool for measuring how children feel about themselves as readers. *The Reading Teacher, 48,* 470–482. Reprinted with permission.

2. Each scale is interpreted in relation to its total possible score. For example, because the RSPS uses a 5-point scale and the Progress scale consists of 9 items, the highest score for Progress is 45 ($9 \times 5 = 45$). Therefore, a score that would fall approximately in the middle of the range (22–23) would indicate a child's somewhat indifferent perception of herself or himself as a reader with respect to Progress. Note that each scale has a different possible total raw score (Progress = 45, Observational Comparison = 30, Social Feedback, = 45, and Physiological States = 40) and should be interpreted accordingly.

Henk, W. A., & Melnick, S. A. (1995). The Reader Self-Perception Scale (RSPS): A new tool for measuring how children feel about themselves as readers. *The Reading Teacher, 48,* 470–482. Reprinted with permission.

The Reader Self-Perception Scale

Listed below are statements about reading. Please read each statement carefully. Then circle the letters that show how much you agree or disagree with the statement. Use the following scale.

SA = Strongly Agree
A = Agree
U = Undecided
D = Disagree
SD = Strongly Disagree

Example: **I think pizza with pepperoni is best.** SA A U D SD

If you are *really positive* that pepperoni pizza is best, circle SA (Strongly Agree).
If you *think* that it is good but maybe not great, circle A (Agree).
If you *can't decide* whether or not it is best, circle U (Undecided).
If you *think* that pepperoni pizza is not all that good, circle D (Disagree).
If you are *really positive* that pepperoni pizza is not very good, circle SD (Strongly Disagree).

1. I think I am a good reader. SA A U D SD

2. I can tell that my teacher likes to listen to me read. SA A U D SD

3. My teacher thinks that my reading is fine. SA A U D SD

4. I read faster than other kids. SA A U D SD

5. I like to read aloud. SA A U D SD

6. When I read, I can figure out words better than other kids. SA A U D SD

7. My classmates like to listen to me read. SA A U D SD

8. I feel good inside when I read. SA A U D SD

9. My classmates think that I read pretty well. SA A U D SD

10. When I read, I don't have to try as hard as I used to. SA A U D SD

11. I seem to know more words than other kids when I read. SA A U D SD

12. People in my family think I am a good reader. SA A U D SD

Henk, W.A., & Melnick, S. A. (1995). The Reader Self-Perception Scale (RSPS): A new tool for measuring how children feel about themselves as readers. *The Reading Teacher, 48*, 470–482. Reprinted with permission.

13. I am getting better at reading. SA A U D SD

14. I understand what I read as well as other kids do. SA A U D SD

15. When I read, I need less help than I used to. SA A U D SD

16. Reading makes me feel happy inside. SA A U D SD

17. My teacher thinks I am a good reader. SA A U D SD

18. Reading is easier for me than it used to be. SA A U D SD

19. I read faster than I could before. SA A U D SD

20. I read better than other kids in my class. SA A U D SD

21. I feel calm when I read. SA A U D SD

22. I read more than other kids. SA A U D SD

23. I understand what I read better than I could before. SA A U D SD

24. I can figure out words better than I could before. SA A U D SD

25. I feel comfortable when I read. SA A U D SD

26. I think reading is relaxing. SA A U D SD

27. I read better now than I could before. SA A U D SD

28. When I read, I recognize more words than I used to. SA A U D SD

29. Reading makes me feel good. SA A U D SD

30. Other kids think I'm a good reader. SA A U D SD

31. People in my family think I read pretty well. SA A U D SD

32. I enjoy reading. SA A U D SD

33. People in my family like to listen to me read. SA A U D SD

Henk, W.A., & Melnick, S. A. (1995). The Reader Self-Perception Scale (RSPS): A new tool for measuring how children feel about themselves as readers. *The Reading Teacher, 48*, 470–482. Reprinted with permission.

The Reader Self-Perception Scale Scoring Sheet

Student Name _____

Teacher _____

Grade _____ Date _____

Scoring key: 5 = Strongly Agree (SA)
4 = Agree (A)
3 = Undecided (U)
2 = Disagree (D)
1 = Strongly Disagree (SD)

Scales				
General Perception	Progress	Observational Comparison	Social Feedback	Physiological States
1._____	10._____	4._____	2._____	5._____
	13._____	6._____	3._____	8._____
	15._____	11._____	7._____	16._____
	18._____	14._____	9._____	21._____
	19._____	20._____	12._____	25._____
	23._____	22._____	17._____	26._____
	24._____		30._____	29._____
	27._____		31._____	32._____
	28._____		33._____	
Raw score	_____ of 45	_____ of 30	_____ of 45	_____ of 40
Score interpretation				
High	44+	26+	38+	37+
Average	39	21	33	31
Low	34	16	27	25

STRATEGY 2 WE-CAN CHARTS*

1. Determine specific reading skills and strategies to teach students over a three- or four-week period and list them on the We-Can Chart.

2. Read the list of reading skills and strategies with students. Have students contribute additional things they want to learn.

3. Make a copy of the We-Can Chart for each student. Have students place the chart in their reading folders.

4. Tell students that you will be working with them on the skills and strategies listed on the chart. Explain to students that they will learn each of these skills and strategies in the next few weeks. You might say something like the following:

 For the next few weeks we will be learning how to identify the setting of a story, how to decode compound words, and how to make predictions while reading. As we work on these skills and strategies, you will find that you are able to do them well. After a few weeks, we'll add them to the We-Can column of the chart and add more items to our list.

5. After you have taught a skill or strategy, have students write the sentence "We can _____ (name of skill or strategy)." Express your delight that the students are learning so well.

6. Remind students frequently of the many things they have learned how to do.

STRATEGY 3 CUSHIONING**

1. Tell students that no one can do everything, learn everything, and be the best at everything. Explain to students that people often *cushion* themselves when they are facing a difficult task.

2. Describe the word *cushion* by having students visualize the bumper of a car. For example say:

 Cars have front and rear bumpers to prevent damage if they are hit. The bumper absorbs the impact before it gets to the main car. When you cushion, you are putting a barrier like a car bumper in front of you.

3. Give students examples of statements that are meant to cushion their egos. For example, if you are introducing a difficult skill like syllabication, say something like the following:

 We are going to learn how to divide two-syllable words today. The rules are kind of difficult to learn, but if you try really hard, you'll learn the rules in time.

4. Provide students with examples of your own cushioning attempts. For example you might say:

 I know I need to exercise, but I can't do it every day. I try to exercise three times a week.

*Cleland, 1999.
**Harmin, 1995.

We-Can Chart

Name:	Date:
Skill or Strategy	We-Can Sentence

5. Introduce a difficult skill and have students practice cushioning statements. Have them write their statements on an overhead transparency or on the chalkboard. Then have the class read the statements together.

6. Explain to students that cushioning is an important skill to learn in school and that they need to be in charge of building their own confidence by expecting just the right amount from themselves.

Practice and Reinforcement Activities

1. The best way to instill confidence in the student is to ensure that reading material is at the student's independent level. At this level the student should have no difficulty pronouncing words (1% error rate) or understanding the passage. In short, the independent level is that level at which the student can read fluently without teacher assistance.

2. Praise the student. Use positive reinforcement as much as possible. Encourage the student whenever he or she is reading.

3. Provide opportunities for the student to read and reread materials several times. Rereading materials often provides the practice needed to make reading more fluent. Resources for Chapter 3 contain a description of Structured Repeated Readings.

4. If the student appears to be overwhelmed by books, provide phrases, sentences, or short paragraphs that the student can read prior to attempting full-length passages or books. In addition, some teachers have found that converting basal readers, anthologies, or longer stories into small "books" can help build a student's confidence.

5. Use progress charts or visuals that show the student's gains in areas such as words known, strategies mastered, passages read, or books completed. Construct the charts or visuals in such a way that small gains reveal progress. This approach can be especially motivating if the student is invited to select a theme or format for the activity. For example, a student can draw a jar shape on construction paper and then cut out jelly bean shapes from construction paper. When a new word is learned, the student can write it on a jelly bean and paste it to the jar. You can also use student-decorated boxes for words learned.

6. Have the student prepare a story or book to be shared with a younger student or a small group of students. Allow time for previewing and practicing the selection to be read.

7. Have the student prepare a story or book to be read to another teacher, the school secretary, volunteers, or the principal. Encourage rereading of stories or books by having the student gather signatures from students, parents, or other adults (the principal, secretary, and so on) who have listened to the book being read.

8. Use pattern books to motivate students to write their own stories. A repeated phrase or theme can help students create stories. For example, a repeated pattern or sentence might be "Little dog, little dog, why do you dig?" Students write the question and create a response. Students should try to think of several different responses to the questions. Appendix C contains a list of pattern books that may be useful for developing students' stories.

9. Encourage parents to reinforce any reading that is done at home.

10. Use a taped version of a book or story and have students listen and follow along.

11. Employ choral reading activities to help students gain confidence in sharing a poem with the rest of the class.

12. Permit students to choose what they will read without coercion or encouragement from anyone.

13. Have a small microphone available for students to use to read a book to the class. Have students practice reading a book several times and then give them the opportunity to go "on stage."

14. Remember the positive influence of the student's friends. "My friends were really the push I had for reading. My best friend read the encyclopedias for fun! She introduced me to many high-brow books and poetry. I imagine we were some of the few seventh graders that had read *Candide* twice" (Carlsen & Sherrill, 1988, p. 72).

15. Decorate a cardboard box as a book box. Put classroom-made books into the book box. Invite students to read these books to a selected audience such as the principal, the students' friends, or their families.

16. Try book stacking with students who have low confidence in their reading ability. Place a stack of five or six books that are very easy to read on each student's desk. When students come into the classroom, ask them to begin reading the stack of books in order. Allow time for students to read all of the books.

Reluctant to Set Goals

Behavior Observed	The student does not set reading goals.
Anticipated Outcome	The student will learn how to set goals to improve reading.

BACKGROUND

An important component of motivation is the ability to set goals (Ames, 1992). When students set achievement goals, they make a determination to learn, feel a sense of accomplishment, and take control over their own learning. Students who are motivated to set learning goals have a better self-concept; the act of setting goals and completing a task gives students the belief that they can learn. As a result, students who set learning goals have a better self-concept about their abilities as students (Ames, 1992).

Students who set achievement goals

- are determined to learn.
- feel a sense of accomplishment.
- take control over their own learning.

Learning goals are different from extrinsic rewards for learning. Students who set learning goals are internalizing and organizing their learning tasks; they are not merely receiving rewards for their accomplishments. The distinction between having students set learning goals and giving them rewards is in the outcome of the activity. Students who are setting learning goals are keeping track of their achievements, not for a reward but for their own advancement. Teachers can help their students become more goal oriented by using the strategies and activities that follow.

Section 1.5

STRATEGY 1 DAILY READING RECORD

1. Explain to students that good readers often keep track of the number of pages that they read. Emphasize that readers keep track of their reading to accomplish learning goals, not for rewards.

2. Tell students that they can keep track of their reading with a Daily Reading Record. Explain to students that a Daily Reading Record is a system to record how many pages, chapters, stories, or books they have read each day.

3. Duplicate and distribute the copy of Juanita's Daily Reading Record that follows or make a transparency and place it on the overhead projector. Explain how the graph was made by saying something like the following:

This is a graph that shows Juanita's Daily Reading Record. On the left-hand side of the graph you will find the numbers 1 through 10+. The number 1 is at the bottom of the graph and the numbers ascend through 10+. These numbers indicate how many pages Juanita read. On the bottom of the page are the days of the week. For each day the bar is at the height of the number of pages Juanita read.

4. Ask students to practice reading the graph by choosing a day and then ask students how many pages Juanita read. Repeat this process until the students are comfortable reading the graph.

5. Duplicate and distribute to students the blank copy of the Daily Reading Record. Ask students to put their names in the blank at the top of the graph. Tell students that this copy will be their way of recording the number of pages they have read.

6. Ask students to record the number of pages they have read each day. Keep copies of the graphs in a folder for future reference. Tell students to try in increase the number of pages they read with each graph.

7. After students have completed several weeks of Daily Reading Records, have them reflect on any improvements they have shown.

8. An alternative to charting the number of pages read is charting the amount of time students have read.

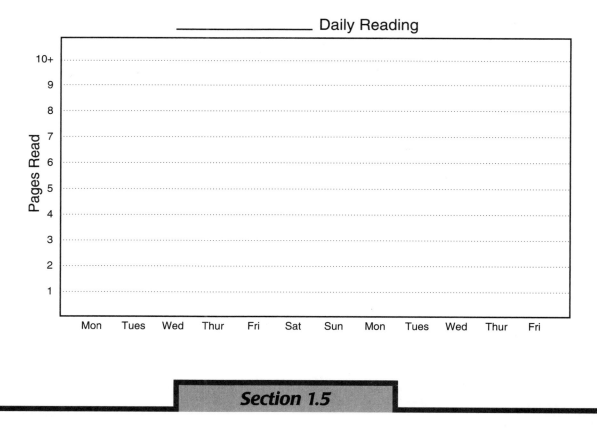

_____ Daily Reading

Pages Read

10+
9
8
7
6
5
4
3
2
1

Mon Tues Wed Thur Fri Sat Sun Mon Tues Wed Thur Fri

Section 1.5

STRATEGY 2 GENRE CHARTS

1. Tell students that good readers often keep track of the kinds of books they read in order to challenge themselves to read a variety of books. Say something like the following:

 Sometimes readers get in a rut. They keep reading the same type of books. It's not wrong to read the same kind of book week after week, but good readers know that they need variety to improve their reading skills. I usually read mysteries at home, but I try to read a different kind of book every two weeks. Last week I read a science fiction book, and I really liked it.

2. Duplicate and distribute copies of the Book Record Chart. Tell students that you want them to record the types of books they read during the next several weeks. Show students how to use the chart by making an overhead transparency of the sample Book Record Chart and putting it on an overhead projector. Show students where to place their names, the titles of the books, the authors, the dates, and the genres.

3. Keep track of your own independent reading in the same way.

4. Tell students that if they are unsure of the genre of the book that they should look on the spine of the book or ask a friend, a librarian, or you. Explain to students that books are classified by genre but that sometimes people can disagree about the name of the genre.

5. After several weeks of students keeping track of the books they have read, have them record their reading choices on the Reading Genre Chart.

6. Duplicate and distribute copies of the Reading Genre Chart. To explain how to use the chart, make an overhead transparency of a blank copy of the chart (or use the sample) and put it on the overhead projector. Use your own Book Record Chart to fill in your reading choices. To complete the Reading Genre Chart, color one grid per book next to the genre of each book read. For example, if you read two informational books, color two boxes next to the term informational books.

7. Have students complete their own Reading Genre Chart. Then have students reflect on their book choices and set personal goals for adding more variety to their reading.

Reading Genre Chart

	Number of Completed Books											
	1	2	3	4	5	6	7	8	9	10	11	12
Informational books												
Picture books												
Historical fiction												
Science fiction												
Biographies												
Fantasy												
Realistic fiction												
Folktales												
Plays												
"How-to" books												

STRATEGY 3 CHALLENGING BOOK CALENDAR

1. Explain to students that good readers try to challenge themselves by reading challenging books. Say something like the following:

 I like to read mysteries and informational books, but sometimes I read poetry to challenge myself. I try to read at least one challenging book every month. Last month I read a book called War and Peace. *It's an extremely long book set in Russia. It was difficult for me because of the Russian names, but I kept with it and finished it. I felt really good about myself because I know that I am becoming a better reader by reading challenging books.*

2. Ask students to take out their independent reading books. Have students scan through the pages thinking about how challenging the books are for them. Tell students to decide whether the books are pretty easy, medium, or difficult. Have students who are reading books that are difficult raise their hands and tell the class why the book is challenging.

3. Discuss what makes a book challenging for students at your grade level. Probably the length of the book, the size of the print, the difficulty of the sentences, and the content will be some reasons why a book is easy or difficult.

4. Help students identify books that are challenging for them. Have students write a list of books that they could read but that would not be easy.

5. Explain to students that good readers don't always read challenging books but that they make a point to read them occasionally. Duplicate and distribute the calendar that follows. Have students write their names and the date on the calendar.

6. Ask students to place one or more stars on the calendar for the days when they predict they will finish a challenging book. Say something like the following:

 I'm going to read two challenging books this month so I will place two stars on the calendar two weeks apart. My goal is to have a challenging book read on the date by the star.

7. Remind students every few weeks to update their Challenging Book Calendar. Praise students for reading challenging books and encourage them to feel good about accomplishing a learning goal.

Name _____ Date _____

Challenging Book Calendar

Sunday	Monday	Tuesday	Wednesday	Thursday	Friday	Saturday

Practice and Reinforcement Activities

1. Remind students that all sorts of people set goals. For example, sports figures often set goals such as improving a batting average, decreasing the amount of time to run a marathon, or climbing a higher mountain. Have students collect other examples of goal setting. Encourage students to ask their friends and parents to help them. Suggest that students use information from television and magazines. After students have collected a number of examples of goal setting, remind them that they should set goals for learning as well. Explain to students that learning is an activity similar to sports activities and that they need to continue to have learning goals throughout their lives.

2. Tell students that when people set goals they engage in self-talk. Provide an example for students such as the following:

> *I am reading a very challenging book right now. It's a book about the formation of mountains. I don't know much about this subject, but I'm eager to learn, so I'll struggle through this book. I'm about halfway through the book, and I'm really enjoying the feeling of accomplishing something difficult.*

Remind students to talk to themselves about their goals during difficult learning tasks.

3. Explain to students that when they are working toward their goal they may enter what is called the "flow" state (Csikszentmihalyi, 1991). Tell students that when they are truly absorbed in what they are doing, they may forget about the task and just enjoy themselves. Tell students about a time when you felt that "flow" as in the following example:

> *I was sitting at the computer last night looking up sites on the Internet about travel in Alaska. I was fascinated with all of the wonderful things to see and do in Alaska, and I was entranced with the pictures of the wildlife. Before I knew it, it was already an hour past bedtime. I shut down the computer, but I knew that I had really become involved with what I was doing.*

Have students share examples of similar situations. Then tell students that they should also become aware of the "flow state" when they are learning. Explain to students that, as they work toward their learning goals, they also need to learn to become totally involved in learning.

4. Have students create daily learning goals on an index card for each day of the week. Take a few minutes at the end of the day to encourage students to reflect on ways they met that goal.

5. At the beginning of the school year or at the beginning of a unit of study, ask the students what they would like to learn. Encourage students to discuss the process of learning rather than topics. For example, in a unit on penguins, the students may want to learn *how* to memorize the types of penguins and their habitats. Write the phrase *memorization of names and places* on a sheet of colored paper and post it on a bulletin board. From these ideas, create a bulletin board titled Class Learning Goals.

6. Have your students interview students in the next higher grade to determine what these students have been learning. For example, if you teach second grade, have your students interview third graders. Have students ask questions such as "What are you learning in reading? What have you learned about learning vocabulary words? and What have you learned about becoming a better reader?" Have your students create a list of next-grade learning goals. Post the list. Then explain to your students that they can work on next-grade goals any time they want. Encourage students to use next-grade goals as part of their own learning goals.

7. Praise students who have set learning goals and have achieved them. Without giving external rewards, let students know that you are aware of their hard work and their accomplishments. When a student has accomplished a learning goal say something like the following:

> *You've really worked hard on finishing that goal. You must feel very proud of yourself. I'm glad to see that you're becoming such a good learner.*

Encourage students to praise themselves for finishing their learning goals as well.

8. Write the word *contract* on the chalkboard or on an overhead transparency. Ask how many students know the definition of the word *contract*. Have students provide their definitions and write them below the word. Explain that one definition for contract is "agreement." Tell students that as they set learning goals they should form contracts with a friend. Tell students that these "friendly contracts" can help them achieve their learning goals. Begin with an example using yourself as in the following:

> *I'm going to enter into a friendly contract with my best friend, Pam. Pam knows that I want to improve my reading vocabulary in science so that I can read books about geology. I've been writing down words that I've come across in my reading that I want to learn. However, I sometimes forget to look them up in a dictionary. I'm going to use the idea of a 'friendly contract' to have Pam periodically check in with me to see how I'm doing on my learning goal.*

After you have given students an example, have them think of examples of friendly contracts into which they could enter. Give students several minutes to think. Then divide the class into groups of three or four students and have students share their ideas. Encourage students to actually make these contracts. See the following page for an example.

Name _____ Date _____

Friendly Contract

My friend _____ will check

with me from time to time to see how well I'm doing on _____

Date My Friend's Comments

_____ _____

_____ _____

_____ _____

_____ _____

CHAPTER 2

Fostering Emergent Literacy and Beginning Reading

with
Regina Slattery

OVERVIEW

Many children gain knowledge about print from literacy experiences prior to entering school. Beginning readers may also be helped to unlock print by direct teaching. This chapter offers activities and strategies to teachers for helping students acquire or refine abilities related to the nature and purpose of reading, concepts about print and words, oral language, phonological awareness, story schema, auditory and visual discrimination, and rhyming. It is important to connect these activities and strategies to experiences with texts.

Beginning readers often have vague or limited concepts about the purpose and nature of reading. They also may not understand the terms used by teachers such as letters, words, sounds, context, and beginning. In addition, they may not know that reading is a process of constructing meaning from print.

In addition to vague concepts about reading, students frequently exhibit confusion regarding the terms teachers use in instruction. Younger students, for example, often confuse letters with words, or vice versa. They may also show confusion with terms such as beginning, middle, and end. Teachers often assume that students understand these basic, instructional terms. Unfortunately, when this assumption is made, students may be at a great disadvantage for learning. In the box are some basic

Phonemic Awareness

• is the ability to hear and manipulate individual sounds in words

concepts that students should understand. Teachers may choose to assess which concepts students know and which they do not yet understand.

Consider these concepts and the language you use during instruction. Be alert for other terms or concepts that your students may not understand. By looking at your instruction through the eyes of your students, you may discover that you take too much for granted when you teach. Plan appropriate instruction to help students develop concepts about print and the specialized terms used in instruction.

One of the most important areas related to emergent literacy and later success in reading is the ability to hear and manipulate phonemes (individual sounds) in words (Gillet & Temple, 1990) and understand how these sounds are connected to print (International Reading Association, 1999, 2000). This ability is called phonemic awareness (PA). PA and letter recognition are the two best predictors, upon school entry, of reading acquisition during the first two years of instruction (National Reading Panel, 2000). Letter recognition often results in an interest in letter sounds and spelling. It also plays an important role in helping students store printed words into memory, focusing on the ordered sequence of letters rather than a holistic pattern (Adams, 1990b). Moreover, letter recognition facilitates reading and spelling acquisition

Basic Reading Concepts

- Reading is making sense of print.
- Reading is essentially making sense of language that has been written down.
- Most words are made up of more than one letter (*I* and *a* are the exceptions).
- Words can be different lengths. The number of letters determines whether a word is short, medium, or long.
- There are white spaces between words.
- Words can be organized into sentences.
- With the exception of long vowels, letter names and the sounds associated with words are usually different.
- Reading can be done for different reasons or purposes.
- There is usually a relationship between the words on a page and pictures or illustrations.
- Words are arranged in sentences, sentences into paragraphs, and paragraphs into stories or books.

when letters are used during PA instruction (National Reading Panel, 2000).

Making connections between letters, PA, and print is important for reading and spelling acquisition. In fact, PA instruction is most effective when it involves an explicit connection to print and when letters are used to help students make connections to reading and spelling (National Reading Panel, 2000). PA enables students to use letter-sound relationships in spelling and reading. Students attend to the phonemes in words as they segment the individual sounds in words during invented spelling (Adams, 1990b), attend to phonetic (letter-sound) cues during early attempts to read, and later blend the individual sounds in words as they develop cipher reading (decoding skills) (Ehri & Wilce, 1985).

PA is part of a broad range of skills, called phonological awareness, that work together to help emergent readers hear phonemes in words (Treiman & Zukowski, 1996). Phonological awareness is the ability to hear and manipulate larger units of sound in spoken language, such as syllables, onsets, and rimes. It appears that phonological awareness progresses from whole to part. First, students are able to hear words in sentences and then progress to hear syllables in words, onsets in words, rimes in words, and phonemes in words (Treiman & Zukowski, 1991). Furthermore, evidence suggests that phonological awareness tasks have a hierarchical degree of difficulty (Yopp, 1988). Rhyming tasks appear to be the easiest, followed by blending and segmenting; the most difficult are phoneme deletion tasks. Sections 2.4 through 2.10 in this chapter relate directly or indirectly to the area of phonological awareness. We urge you to give careful attention to these sections as you teach emergent or struggling readers.

TECHNOLOGY RESOURCES

Beginning Reading Instruction

http://www.just4kids.org/html/bri/html
Provides information about teaching young readers

Preventing Reading Difficulties in Young Children

http://www.nap.edu/readingroom/books/prdyc/
Research synthesis on early reading development

Reading Recovery

http://indiana.edu/~eric_rec/ieo/digests/d106.html
Describes Reading Recovery program

Oral Language

Behavior Observed	The student has limited oral expression.
Anticipated Outcome	The student will orally communicate in an effective and appropriate manner.

PERSPECTIVE AND STRATEGIES

Successful readers draw upon what they know about language to interpret fine shades of meaning or to simply understand print. Students who do not have a rich, diverse language background may have difficulty understanding and interpreting text. Oral language, then, may be regarded as the basis for reading. Fostering oral expression provides students with the opportunity to learn language and its structures and to build vocabulary.

The following suggestions are helpful for increasing the quantity and quality of oral communication among students. Although these activities may be adapted for work with one student, language learning may be more successful in small groups because it increases interaction and provides more opportunity for oral expression.

1. Be open to what students want to talk about. Make encouraging comments to promote their language use. Listen carefully to what students say and try to spend 80% of your time listening.

2. Provide a concrete experience and have students discuss the event. Opportunities for expression and interaction should be encouraged. During the discussion, list some key terms on the chalkboard. Next, write an experience story incorporating the key terms. Read chorally and take turns so that each student gets a chance to read alone or with a group.

3. Echo reading gives students an opportunity to repeat sentences that use appropriate syntax. Read a line of a story or poem aloud. Students repeat exactly what has been said. Repeat and allow students to echo read line by line. Using the sentence patterns, students may more readily communicate their own material.

4. Provide students with pictures and encourage sharing. Ask questions where appropriate. Invite students to bring in interesting photographs for discussion.

5. Bring in objects and have students discuss what they know about them.

6. Provide care for an animal to help foster a lively interchange of ideas.

7. Read a variety of books to students and discuss them.

8. Encourage students to make up a story that goes along with wordless picture books. A listing of books without words can be found in Appendix A.

9. Use puppets to promote communication among students. Puppets often encourage the shy students to participate in discussions.

10. Plan and take interesting field trips around the school and the community.

11. Introduce concept words such as *same-different, in-out,* and *over-under.*

12. Have students speak into a tape recorder one at a time. For the first experience, students may say their name, age, and something that they like to do. Play the tape back after each student has had an opportunity to speak. Exercise caution with students who are hesitant to participate in this activity; do not force the activity upon them. The teacher may also participate in this activity and serve as a role model. Later, students can tape-record a story that they have made up or one to accompany a wordless picture book. Students will sometimes tell more elaborate stories when they speak into a tape recorder. The teacher or classroom volunteer may then make a copy of the individual story and have students illustrate it.

13. Expand the student's utterances. For example, if the student says, "The cat is black," the teacher may comment, "Yes, the cat is black except for the white markings on its paws."

14. Provide parents or caregivers with a list of suggestions for promoting rich oral language in the home. Some suggestions are in the box below.

 Chapter 8 contains additional suggestions for working with families.

15. Encourage conversation by asking questions that require more than a "yes-or-no" answer.

16. Classify objects in various ways: by color, by shape, or by purpose. For example, have students list things that are green. Also, discuss an object in as much detail as possible.

17. Invite adults or older students into the classroom to listen to small groups of students share. Topics could include favorite play activities, television, or animals.

18. Create a picture file so students can take a picture and talk about it with a partner or small group of classmates.

19. Provide play or real telephones so students can have conversations with each other.

20. Encourage small-group and one-on-one discussions. Some of the best conversations may be the natural, language-rich activities that are part of daily classroom routines.

21. Provide props, possibly in a drama center, for students to act out their favorite stories and books. Label a bag or box with the title of the story and include the book with one or more of the following props: character felt pieces and a felt board, puppets, articles of clothing, or artifacts from the story. For example, for the book *If You Give a Mouse a Cookie* (Numeroff, 1996), include items from the story such as a napkin, straw, and scissors for students to use when acting out the sequence of the story.

Suggestions for Promoting Rich Oral Language

- Read stories and books. Ask questions about the content, talk about the illustrations, and discuss points of interest.
- Listen to your students. Provide many opportunities to use language. Don't become frustrated or impatient if they have difficulty expressing themselves clearly.
- Take walks or excursions in the neighborhood or community. Talk about what you see. Point out things that students might miss. Give labels to these things and explain them in words appropriate for the student's level of maturity.
- Talk to your students. Encourage them to talk about friends, interests, and special events at school.
- Play card and board games that provide an opportunity for conversations about the game and other topics.
- Help students expand their statements.

22. Create new verses to songs. After students have learned a song, invite them to write additional verses. Choose a song with a predictable, repetitive pattern. Write the pattern that repeats in black on chart paper, leaving blank lines for the words that change. For example, in Ella Jenkins' (1997) song titled "You'll Sing a Song and I'll Sing a Song," a line from the second verse, similar to the title, replaces *sing* and *song* with *play* and *tune* respectively. Prepare chart paper with a template verse, beginning with the line

You'll ____ a ____ and I'll ____ a ____.

Sing the phrase together placing the words sing/ song and then play/tune into the blanks. Record these word pairs on the chart below the template verse or on a separate piece of chart paper. Have students think of their own word pairs to create new verses. Record the new word pairs. Sing your new song together. To extend this activity, create a class book with each child filling in his or her own word pairs and illustrating the new verse.

You'll ____ a ____ and I'll ____ a ____.

sing	song		sing	song
play	tune		play	tune
jump	rope		jump	rope
read	book		read	book

Concepts About the Nature and Purpose of Reading

Behavior Observed	The student is unaware of the basic functions of print.
Anticipated Outcome	The student will understand that print conveys meaning.

PERSPECTIVE AND STRATEGIES

Students at all ages must realize that reading is the process of making sense from print. They must learn that spoken language—their own and that of others—is made up of words that can also be written down. Later, they will understand that these words can be broken down into parts, or syllables, and further into sound units, or phonemes.

1. Introduce a picture book by reading it to an individual or a group of students more than once. Have students join in with the reading as they become more familiar with the story. Give the book to a student and encourage "reading" of the book. Provide all students opportunities for storybook reading on a daily basis. Some useful pattern books can be found in Appendix C.

2. Place a big book (two to three feet high) on a chart stand where it can readily be seen by a group of students. Read a familiar story and have the students read along. Point out features of print: where the text begins on a page, the left-to-right progression of reading, the return sweep, the white spaces between words, and punctuation.

3. Write together about classroom experiences or stories that have been read aloud together. For stories, choose a favorite part, retell the story, or provide a new ending. Draw a picture to provide focus for the writing. Ask students to tell

Even very young children need to understand that reading is the process of making sense from print.

you what to write, providing guiding questions as needed to elicit their responses. After writing each new sentence, invite the students to read the text from the beginning to make sure it makes sense, making any necessary changes. As you write, model and describe features of print during initial writings. When you feel your students are able, have them tell you what they know by asking the following questions as you write.

? Where should we begin to write our first word?

What do we need to do after this word?

We wrote a great sentence. What do we need to put at the end of the sentence?

Should we write a capital letter or lower-case letter when we start our new sentence?

We are out of space on this line. Where should we write next?

We are out of space on this paper. Where do we write next?

4. Help students create their own books, using their chosen vocabulary. Each page of these short books is student dictated and has one word, phrase, or sentence on it. The student reads the text for a page and then illustrates it. These books can be used to practice the vocabulary associated with directions such as *up, down, in,* and *out.* Repeated readings to classmates and family members should be encouraged. Building a collection of these books to share within the classroom will help improve sight vocabulary and develop print awareness.

5. Use familiar poems, songs, and text that have been committed to memory. Show the printed form, line by line. Read aloud, pointing to each word. The students then read aloud, pointing to each word, modeling the teacher's behavior. When the student appears to be familiar with the short text and points word by word while reading, the teacher may point to a single word and ask the student to say it. This technique may also be used with short, dictated experience stories as the text.

6. Write *kingcup* on the chalkboard. Ask a student to pronounce the word. Ask other students if they agree. Continue the process until the class agrees that the word is *kingcup*. Ask students whether they can *read* the word. Most students will respond that they can read the word because they view reading as a process of decoding. When this point is reached, ask the students, "How do you know that you can *read* the

word?" Many students will respond by saying, "I can read the word because I can pronounce it." Sooner or later, a student is likely to ask what the word means. Lead students to the conclusion that reading involves understanding. Distinguish between being able to say a word and knowing what a word means. Invite students to suggest ways they might be able to find out what the word *kingcup* means. A common response is to have someone look it up in a dictionary. Have students look up the word and discuss its meaning (a plant with yellow flowers; the marsh marigold). Have students use the word in a sentence. Point out to students that they can now read the word *kingcup*. Tell them that readers are always concerned with meaning. Follow this activity with other words that students can probably pronounce even though the meaning is unknown. Some possible words include yegg, tutu, dingo, truffle, and eyelet.

7. The following example is designed to help students realize that (1) reading is a form of communication, (2) reading can be talk written down, and (3) reading is constructing meaning from print.

> *Teacher:* If you wanted to tell Eric a secret, how would you do it?
>
> *Beth:* I would just tell him.
>
> *Teacher:* You mean you would talk to him or whisper to him?
>
> *Beth:* Yes, that's what I'd do.
>
> *Teacher:* What would you do if Eric weren't here and you still wanted him to know?
>
> *Beth:* I might write him a note.
>
> *Teacher:* OK, and when Eric gets here, what should he do?
>
> *Beth:* He should read what I wrote down.
>
> *Teacher:* Good. Have you communicated with Eric?
>
> *Beth:* Yes.

In this example, Eric has received a note that a student has written. But what did Beth write down? She wrote down what she would have said to Eric if he were here. In other words, her talk has been written down. Each printed word

represents only one spoken word, and we can now say that a word is a verbal symbol. The following example demonstrates this concept.

Teacher: Suppose that you were going to tell Eric that you have some new baseball cards. Because you had to write it down, it probably looked like this: I have some new baseball cards. Eric took this note and began to say what you had written. He said to himself: I-have-some-new-base-ball-cards. If he were to say that out loud, would that sound like what you were going to say?

Beth: Yes, that's what I would have said.

Teacher: But Eric still has not read what you have written down. He has said the words out loud, but he has not read them. In order to be really reading, Eric must understand what you have said. He must make some meaning from those symbols called words. If he comes to you later and asks to see your hat you wrote about, he has not read anything. You told him about some new baseball cards, not a hat, so he did not read that note. He had not gotten meaning; therefore, no reading has taken place. Reading involves meaning, and if you do not know what something means, you have not read it! Now, what are some of the things in daily life that you read—some things you get meaning from?

Beth: We read road signs on the highways like SLOW and STOP. We read cereal boxes that say FREE TOY INSIDE.

8. Use *Hey! I'm Reading!* (Miles, 1995) as a fun and engaging way to help students learn about reading. This book would also be good for parents to share with their children.

Knowledge of the Alphabet

Behavior Observed	The student does not know the letters of the alphabet.
Anticipated Outcome	The student will learn the alphabet.

PERSPECTIVE AND STRATEGIES

Letter knowledge can help students learn how the alphabetic system works. Such knowledge can also help with spelling and associating certain sounds with certain letters. To help assess alphabet knowledge, an easy-to-use Assessment of Alphabet Knowledge is included in this section. For students who could benefit from increasing their alphabet knowledge, the following strategies may be useful.

1. Try your best to use meaningful activities within the context of your classroom. As students begin to write their names, their attention is being directed to specific letters. Be direct and tell students that their names are made up of letters. Using students' names is a powerful way to focus on meaningful instruction. Teach students the names of the letters that comprise their names. Make name cards for each student and invite students to learn or generalize their knowledge by asking questions such as the following ones.

? Does anyone have a name that begins with the same letter as Rosanna's name? Invite students to share and discuss their ideas. Compare the first letters of the names and comment appropriately.

Does anyone have a letter **in** their name that is the same as the first letter in Rosanna's name? Invite

students to hold up their name cards and point to the letter in their name that is the same. Use the opportunity to discuss upper-case letters and lower-case letters.

Working with alphabet blocks can help a child learn letters.

Who has a name that begins with *N*?

Does your name have a lower-case letter that has the same name as the upper-case letter *O* that I'm writing on the chalkboard? If so, hold up your name card and point to the letter. Does anyone have two *Os*?

2. Make individual, laminated name puzzles (see sample) that are kept in separate envelopes with the name printed on the envelope. You can help students see the letters as tall (A), small (m), and fall (y) letters by writing the names on grids three squares high, with each being one inch square. Cut each letter on the vertical line separating each letter. To make the puzzles a multi-level learning manipulative, print the vowels and consonants in two different colors (Slattery, 2000b).

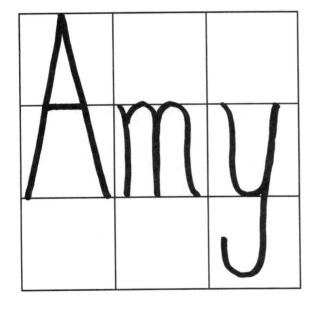

3. Because students learn letters by their distinctive features (open or closed, curved or slanted, above or below the line), introduce at least two different letters at a time. Talk about the letters and what makes them similar and/or different. Although you will probably begin with letters that have dissimilar features such as *i* and *b*, you will want to eventually contrast similar letters such as *b* and *d* and verbalize the reasons they are different. It is through such experiences that students will learn what makes the letters differ-

ent. Dunn-Rankin (1968) noted the following groups of letters that tend to confuse students.

- b, d, p, and o, g, h
- f, l, t, k, i, and h when combined
- e, a, s, c, o
- n, m, u, and h and r

4. Refer to print on signs and posters in the room and talk about the letters that make up the words.

5. Invite students to bring in objects such as cereal boxes, toothpaste boxes, paper bags, and newspapers. Discuss the words and the letters that make up the words on these items.

6. Be sure a model alphabet is displayed in the room so students can see how the letters are formed. They should also be able to see the corresponding upper-case and lower-case letters.

7. Use a variety of hands-on activities to help students learn the names of the letters and to practice how they are written: alphabet cereal, finger painting, sandpaper letters, Play Doh letters, and so on.

8. Help students create their personalized alphabet books. Invite students to share them with one another.

9. Make a big book that contains the alphabet song. Have different students point to the letters and words as the students sing along. Take time to discuss the difference between letters and words. Invite students to ask each other questions about the letters and words.

10. Sing or play recordings of songs that spell out words or that use letters as part of the song (for example, "Bingo," "Old MacDonald Had a Farm"). Chart and display these songs.

11. Use the newspaper and invite students to find and circle as many examples (upper-case and lower-case) of a particular letter as they can within a specific time limit. Use the exercise to also encourage identification of known words.

12. Develop cards for alphabet bingo or dominoes. For bingo, have a student assist in calling the letters. Game cards can include upper-case letters, lower-case letters, or a combination of both.

13. Secure a keyboard and invite students to type and explore the alphabet. If a computer is avail-

Young students refer often to the alphabet poster in their classroom.

able with speech capability, there are computer programs that will say the name of the letter when the key is depressed. Other programs have activities that will help students learn the letters.

14. Supply students with magnetic letters and stamp printing sets to stimulate involvement with the alphabet and making words.

15. Take time to point out the differences between the manuscript *a* and the typeset *a*. Do the same for the letter *g*.

16. Provide a print-rich environment in which students are encouraged to explore and talk about their literacy experiences. Encourage students to "read the room" at center or free choice time.

17. Develop a writing center where students can compose and draw. Remember that writing is developmental and students may be making letter-like forms as they progress to conventional printing. Include pencils, colored pencils, markers, letter stamps, and various shapes and colors of paper.

18. Have students learn and sing the alphabet song. Point to the letters as they sing. After modeling this process, invite a student to point. Once students are able to sing the song, invite them to be the "alphabet" as they line up to go somewhere (Cunningham, 1995). Laminate a set of alphabet cards and mix them up. Pass them out randomly so each student has one. The teacher keeps any extras. Then have the class sing the alphabet song slowly as each student gets into line.

19. Read alphabet books (see Appendix B) as well as other books that students enjoy. Engage in natural and meaningful sharing about letters, words, and meaning. Some of the books listed in Resources for Chapter 2 will be especially appropriate.

20. Play Go Fish with alphabet letters written on index cards. Make two of each upper-case letter, lower-case letter, or upper-case and lower-case pairs. Play with two to four students.

21. Create letter-sequencing activities with several letters at a time. Write the letter pairs to be sequenced in boxes in mixed-up order. Provide each student with a strip of mixed-up letter pairs and a strip of construction paper on which to glue the letter pairs after cutting them apart.

| Bb | Ee | Aa | Dd | Cc |

22. Make upper-case and lower-case letter-pair puzzles by purchasing and laminating an alphabet chart. These charts usually have pairs of letters and a picture of an object beginning with each letter. Cut out each letter pair and picture into a box and cut between the upper-case and lower-case letters. Have students match the upper-case and lower-case letters of the puzzle. These puzzles are self-correcting, with each half only matching its corresponding part.

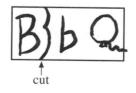
cut

STRATEGY 1 DETERMINING ALPHABET KNOWLEDGE

1. Duplicate the Alphabet Knowledge Record sheet on the next page and get two 3" x 5" cards.

2. Place the Alphabet Knowledge Student Sheet before the student and ask him or her to identify any known letters. Say,

 Here are some letters. I want to see how many you know.

 Have the student say "pass" or "skip it" if a particular letter is unknown.

3. Use the 3" x 5" cards to block off everything but the lines being read. If necessary, point to each letter with a finger.

4. As the student responds, use the Record Sheet to note correct (+) and incorrect responses. When responses are incorrect, record the actual response or D.K. (student doesn't know) above the stimulus letter. If the student self-corrects, write ok; self-corrections can be made at any time.

Letter	*Meaning of Recording*
+ O	Identified correctly
D.K. H	Don't Know
C S	Said C for S
B ok E	Said B for E but self-corrected

5. Count the correct number of responses for the upper-case letters. Based on the number of correct responses, make a judgment of the student's alphabet knowledge. Unknown letters or incorrect responses may help form the basis for instructional interventions.

6. Refer to the strategies on pages 72–74 for instructional interventions.

Alphabet Knowledge Record Sheet

Directions: Present the alphabet sheet. Use 3" x 5" cards to block off everything but the lines being read. If necessary, point to each letter with a finger. Then say, "Here are some letters. I want to see how many you know." Place + above correctly identified letters. Record the student's responses for incorrect letters. Total correct responses and record the score in the box.

O	H	S	E	G	P	
X	V	I	M	J	D	K
B	T	R	Z	F	N	
Y	Q	W	C	U	A	L

Scores

☐

b	x	e	c	j	m	g
l	u	r	t	q	h	y
s	d	o	a	k	w	g
i	p	v	f	n	z	a

+ ☐

Total Score ☐

Alphabet Knowledge Student Sheet

```
O   H   S   E   G   P
X   V   I   M   J   D   K
B   T   R   Z   F   N
Y   Q   W   C   U   A   L

b   x   e   c   j   m   g
l   u   r   t   q   h   y
s   d   o   a   k   w   g
i   p   v   f   n   z   a
```

SECTION 2.4

Auditory Discrimination

Behavior Observed	The student has difficulty distinguishing fine differences in the sounds of spoken words.
Anticipated Outcome	The student will distinguish fine differences in the sounds of spoken words.

PERSPECTIVE AND STRATEGIES

Auditory discrimination is the ability to distinguish between fine sound differences in language. Discriminatory ability is developmental and may not be fully achieved until a student is eight years old. Students who have problems with auditory discrimination may have trouble in beginning reading, especially if intensive phonics instruction is used.

An informal hierarchy of auditory discrimination abilities consists of four levels.

Level 1 Environmental sounds that are grossly different, such as a dog barking and a telephone ringing.
Level 2 Words that are grossly different, like *the* and *banana.*
Level 3 Words that are somewhat different, like *father* and *mother.*
Level 4 Words that differ in only one phoneme, such as *big* and *pig.*

An Assessment of Auditory Discrimination can be found in this section. If an auditory discrimination problem is apparent, be sure to investigate possible physical causes through a hearing screening. The school nurse can often conduct the screening. Another physical aspect to check is whether the stu-

> Auditory discrimination ability may not be fully achieved until a student is eight years old.

dent has a cold or allergy. Students with allergies, as well as those who swim regularly, may experience temporary hearing difficulties.

Although a physical problem may be present, a more common finding is that the student has not been taught to recognize the fine differences between sounds and words. Also important to remember is that speech sounds may vary from one dialect to another. For example, the difference between standard English and students' everyday language may be great.

Before auditory discrimination instruction can actually begin, the student must be aware of the concepts of same and different. It is best to use actual concrete objects to develop these concepts. Next, progress to sounds. Commercial or teacher-made recordings can be used to practice environmental sounds. A piano can be used to help students differentiate sounds.

It is difficult to isolate auditory discrimination teaching from practice. The following ideas should be useful.

1. If students do not understand the concepts of same and different, begin with environmental sounds and move to words that are obviously different (such as *big–truck*). Some students

find it easier to use the words *yes* for *same* and *no* for *different*.

2. Begin with word pairs whose initial sounds differ. Include words that are also the same. Pronounce the two words and have students indicate whether they are the same or different. Progress to words that differ in ending sounds and then to words that differ in medial sounds. Possible words for practice are listed here. Additional practice endings can be found in the Resources for Chapter 3.

Beginnings	Middles	Endings
take–make	cat–cut	cat–cap
car–far	sit–sat	fan–fat
dark–bark	log–leg	lad–lap
sod–rod	luck–lick	mom–mop
lit–mitt	pot–pit	rap–rat
dead–bed	Tim–Tom	lip–lit
rock–sock	pet–pat	hot–hop

3. Have students tell whether word pairs are different in the beginning, middle, or end. Be sure the students understand concepts of beginning, middle, and end. Students will also profit from a visual representation of the word pair. They may then develop the concept that words sounding differently usually contain at least one different letter. Homonyms are, of course, the exception.

4. Encourage students to discuss the meanings of words so that they can begin to understand that words that sound different usually do not mean the same thing. Synonyms are the exception.

5. Remember that speech sounds vary from dialect to dialect. For example, *pin* and *pen* may be pronounced the same by some speakers, whereas other speakers use different sounds for the *i* and *e*. See Oral Reading as Performance in Chapter 4 for helpful information on students' dialects.

6. Consult the section on rhyming in this chapter for additional ideas.

Games

Yes-No. Each student has two cards that contain the words *same* and *different* (or *yes* and *no*). The teacher pronounces two words and the students hold up a card that indicates whether the words are the same or different. Points may be given for correct answers.

Picture Pairs. Develop a series of picture pairs whose names differ in only one sound, as shown here.

Name both pairs and have students take turns pointing to the picture that was named a second time. A variation is to number the picture pairs and have students hold up cards or fingers to indicate the picture that was named a second time. The following words may make good picture pairs.

chair–hair	mail–snail	cap–map
train–rain	cake–lake	grape–cape
nail–pail	snake–rake	car–star
ball–wall	man–pan	farm–arm
ham–lamb	plane–mane	gate–skate

Additional word pairs can be found in Resources for Chapter 4.

Funny Questions. Ask students questions where the correct answer is one of two words that differ in only one sound. Take turns or allow students to volunteer. Several possible questions are given here.

Would you put your feet in fox or socks?
Would you open a door with a bee or a key?
Would you hit a ball with a bat or a cat?
Would you sit on a mat or a map?

A variation of the game is to have students make up similar questions that could be posed to others in the group.

Pronounce a Word. Have students pronounce the same word after you. Using individual chalkboards or wipe-off cards divided into fourths, have students write each word you pronounce. After all four words are written, ask students to erase words one by one. Observe whether they erase each word as it is pronounced.

Section 2.4

STRATEGY 1

DETERMINING AUDITORY DISCRIMINATION ABILITY

1. Practice the words on the Auditory Discrimination Record Sheet: Forms A and B. You should say the words in a clear, normal voice.

2. Do not rush the student during the testing. Darken the Same or Different box if the student responds correctly. Draw a line through the square if the student makes an incorrect response.

3. If the student asks for a pair of words to be repeated, return to them at the conclusion of the test.

4. Facing the student, say:

 Listen to the two words I am about to say: FAIR–FAR.

 Do they sound exactly the same or are they different?

 Yes, they are different.

 Listen to these two words: CAP–CAP.

 Are they the same or different?

*Now I am going to read you pairs of words. I want you to tell me if they are the same
or different. Do you understand what you are to do? Please turn your back to me and
listen very carefully.*

5. Say all the words distinctly but in a normal voice.

6. When finished, add up the incorrect Same and Different responses and enter the number in the
 error score boxes. The following error score indicates inadequate auditory ability.

 > 5-year-olds—errors in Different box greater than 6
 > 6-year-olds—errors in Different box greater than 5
 > 7-year-olds—errors in Different box greater than 4
 > 8-year-olds—errors in Different box greater than 3

7. More than three errors in the Same box indicates an invalid test. The alternate form of the test
 should be used.

8. Refer to the strategies on the previous pages in Section 2.4 for instructional interventions.

Auditory Discrimination Record Sheet: Forms A and B

Form A		Same	Different	Form B		Same	Different
1. though	– show		❏	1. breathe	– brief		❏
2. bad	– dad		❏	2. grove	– growth		❏
3. sit	– sick		❏	3. fuss	– thus		❏
4. jump	– jump	❏		4. mall	– mall	❏	
5. buff	– bus		❏	5. fame	– feign		❏
6. mat	– gnat		❏	6. mast	– mask		❏
7. dub	– dug		❏	7. thing	– thing	❏	
8. oath	– oaf		❏	8. disk	– desk		❏
9. lag	– lad		❏	9. duck	– dock		❏
10. judge	– judge	❏		10. suit	– soup		❏
11. set	– sit		❏	11. crab	– crag		❏
12. watch	– watch	❏		12. zig	– zig	❏	
13. ball	– bowl		❏	13. brash	– brass		❏
14. sink	– think		❏	14. sad	– said		❏
15. luck	– lock		❏	15. van	– than		❏
16. tot	– top		❏	16. thin	– shin		❏
17. duck	– duck	❏		17. mud	– mug		❏
18. foam	– phone		❏	18. save	– shave		❏
19. mauve	– moth		❏	19. bask	– bath		❏
20. seek	– sheik		❏	20. age	– age	❏	
21. fought	– thought		❏	21. froze	– froze	❏	
22. done	– gun		❏	22. sew	– saw		❏
23. chop	– chop	❏		23. bib	– bid		❏
24. can	– tan		❏	24. came	– tame		❏
25. boat	– goat		❏	25. cat	– pat		❏
26. lab	– lad		❏	26. busy	– dizzy		❏
27. light	– sight		❏	27. debt	– get		❏

Form A		Same	Different	Form B		Same	Different
28. zinc	– zinc	❑		28. tank	– thank		❑
29. sing	– sing	❑		29. fought	– sought		❑
30. bed	– bad		❑	30. guessed	– best		❑
31. moss	– moth		❑	31. touch	– touch	❑	
32. till	– pill		❑	32. tick	– tip		❑
33. fall	– fall	❑		33. tail	– pail		❑
34. mass	– mash		❑	34. jury	– jury	❑	
35. vine	– thine		❑	35. champ	– champ	❑	
36. rode	– rode	❑		36. lass	– laugh		❑
37. cot	– pot		❑	37. maze	– maze	❑	
38. rap	– rack		❑	38. math	– mass		❑
39. mash	– math		❑	39. star	– star	❑	
40. mar	– mar	❑		40. nice	– mice		❑

	Same	Different			Same	Different
Error Score:	▢	▢		Error Score:	▢	▢

Inadequate auditory discrimination is indicated by more than:

6 errors in Different box for 5-year-olds 4 errors in Different box for 7-year-olds
5 errors in Different box for 6-year-olds 3 errors in Different box for 8-year-olds

An invalid test is indicated by more than 3 errors in Same box.

SECTION 2.5

Concept of a Word

Behavior Observed	The student does not seem to understand what words are.
Anticipated Outcome	The student will develop the concept of a word.

PERSPECTIVE AND STRATEGIES

Words are critical in reading, yet many emergent and struggling readers have difficulty understanding what is meant by a "word." Johns (1980), for example, found that below-average first graders had significantly greater difficulty in locating one or two words than did average and above-average first graders. Even some struggling readers in third grade had difficulty consistently identifying one word or one letter (Johns, 1977). McGee and Richgels (1996) note that emergent readers and writers may use various ways to show words in their writing. One student used a dot between words, another wrote each word in a different color, and a third student circled each word.

Because a concept of word is often a basis for instruction in rhyming, phonological awareness, and phonics, the following concepts may need to be taught explicitly to students.

- Most words are made up of more than one letter (*I* and *a* are the exceptions).
- Words can be different lengths. The number of phonemes determines whether a word is short, medium, or long.
- There are spaces between words.
- Words can be organized into sentences.

Consider the following strategies and activities to help students develop the concept for a word and word boundaries. Remember, too, that an awareness of words develops over time with language use and can be enhanced by reading and writing (Roberts, 1992).

1. A student's name is extremely meaningful. Print it on a card and show it to the student. Point to the student's first name, say it, and then point to the student's last name and say it. Show the student the space that separates the first and last name by pointing to it. Tell the student there are two words on the card, framing each with your hands. In subsequent interactions, you may wish to talk about letters that make the name.

2. Refer to words in the room and ask students how many words are shown. Have them explain their answer. Provide explanations or clarifications as needed. Help students understand that words (except *I* and *a*) are made up of more than one letter.

3. Encourage students to show you words they can write or read. Have them frame a word with their hands. They can also name and talk about the number of letters that make up the word.

4. Provide ample opportunities for students to talk with each other, write, and read. Although their reading and writing may be in an emergent stage, promoting a risk-taking and supportive environment in the classroom will pay rich dividends in literacy acquisition.

5. Practice counting words (adapted from Cunningham, 2000). Give students 10 counters (plastic disks, paper squares, raisins, or anything manipulable) in a paper cup. Start by counting some familiar objects in the room (bulletin boards, doors, plants, pillows, etc.). Have students place one of their counters on their desks as each object is pointed to. Be sure students return their counters to their cup at the end of each count. Then tell students you can also count words by putting down a counter for each word said. Model the process with the sentence "I am your teacher." First, say the sentence naturally. Then say the sentence slowly, pausing after each word, so students can put down a marker for each word said. Ask students how many words you said. Proceed to other sentences capitalizing on your student's experiences (Vinnie is wearing blue today. I saw Clay at the store. Carlos will be seven years old tomorrow). As students begin to understand the concept of sentences, invite them to offer sentences. They should say the sentence twice, once in the normal way and then one word at a time. Familiar nursery rhymes may also be used. Later, provide written sentence strips and invite students to count words by placing a counter beneath each. Provide instruction and support as needed (e.g., cutting the sentence strip into individual words). Variations of this activity could include clapping or moving a block forward for each spoken word.

6. Have students point to words as they read experience stories, big books, wall charts, poems, and books. Pointing helps students practice the match between printed words and spoken words.

7. Prepare a cloze sentence on a one-inch strip of paper, based on a simple, predictable book. For example, write

My dad is _____.

Have students fill in the blank. Write the complete sentence on an envelope. With the sentence on the envelope as a guide, have students cut their sentence into words. Ask students to use their words to remake the sentence. Send these envelopes home for students to practice using words to build a sentence. This activity works best with a small group.

8. Write sentences from a familiar book on sentence strips. Make two sets. Choose a story, or part of a story, with short sentences. Cut one set of sentences apart into words. Place the other set in sequential order in a pocket chart, one sentence per pocket. Pass out the words to students, telling them the word if necessary. Read the first sentence as a group. Have students with the words from the sentence bring up their words, placing them on top of the word from the sentence. Continue the activity with the remaining sentences. Place the words, folded sentences, and book in a bag to use as a center for independent practice. This center activity works well with partners.

Rhyming

Behavior Observed	The student does not understand the concept of rhyming.
Anticipated Outcome	The student will demonstrate the concept of rhyming by supplying words that rhyme.

PERSPECTIVE AND STRATEGIES

Rhyming is a valuable tool in the early stages of reading. Fox (2000) notes that rhyming activities will benefit reading ability regardless of the age or intelligence of the student. Rhymes help students develop an understanding that phonograms (letter clusters or families) can represent the same sound in different words. Phonograms that can be used to develop the concept of rhyming are given in Resources for Chapter 3.

Rhyming activities are also important for emergent readers because they provide an entry to phonological awareness. Phonological awareness is the ability to hear and manipulate the different sound units in spoken language. Rhyming ability is necessary before more developmentally complex phonological tasks can be attempted without frustration. The purpose of these rhyming activities is to provide opportunities for students to begin to develop their ability to attend to sounds in language.

The activities and strategies are organized in the following developmental sequence: listening, reciting, discriminating, and producing strategies. Students who are unable to identify rhymes need daily experiences hearing and reciting rhymes before they

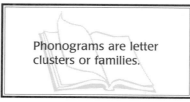

Phonograms are letter clusters or families.

will be able to identify or produce rhymes. They will enjoy hearing the playful language and will need to have the rhyming words pointed out to them at this beginning stage.

Listening Strategies and Activities

1. Use nursery rhymes as a natural starting point for helping students develop an understanding of words as units of sound that can be manipulated independently of meaning. Students often enjoy nonsense words, catchy rhymes, and rhythms. Encourage students to experiment with familiar rhymes and words.

2. Read to students daily from books with rhyming elements.

3. Listen to rhyming books on tape to help solidify the concept of rhyme.

4. Listen to rhyming poetry. Reread poems, placing additional stress on the rhyming words. Point out words that rhyme.

Children have fun with rhyming activities.

5. Create rhyming names for students. Use rhyming names only for those who enjoy theirs. This is an excellent way to provide second language students, who may have minimal rhyming patterns in their first language, with rhyming background knowledge. Some examples include Bravo Gustavo, Okay Jose, and Carolina Ballerina. Be extremely careful not to create a negative name.

Reciting Strategies and Activities

6. Recite poems, finger plays, and chants. Write the poems, finger plays, or chants on chart paper, using rebus picture clues such as a 5 and a duck over the respective words in the finger play "Five Little Ducks." First, read the entire text. Then, recite the first line, inviting all the students to echo back the line. Continue to add one more line as you start again from the beginning; each time you recite, they echo read until all lines are learned.

7. Sing rhyming songs. Chart these, following the steps described in strategy 6. Examples include "Five Little Pumpkins," "I'm a Little Teapot," "Mitten Song," "Teddy Bear," and "Going to the Zoo."

Discriminating Strategies and Activities

8. Read or recite a nursery rhyme that has been written on chart paper. Chose several rhyming word pairs from the rhyme and draw pictures on index cards to represent the words. Have students match the rhyming pictures. For example, for the rhyme "One, Two, Buckle My Shoe," prepare these rhyming pair illustrations: 2 and shoe, 4 and door, 6 and sticks, 8 and straight (a straight line will do), and 10 and hen. This activity is also a good assessment to determine whether students are able to hear rhyming patterns. Those unable to hear the rhymes need additional experiences hearing and reciting rhymes.

9. Draw or cut out pictures of word pairs that rhyme. Mix the word pairs and have students take turns selecting word pairs that rhyme. Ask students to say the words aloud. Possible word pairs are listed below.

nest	box	ten	hat	car	can
chest	fox	hen	cat	jar	fan
green	top	log	pan	late	mice
queen	mop	dog	man	gate	rice
tree	duck	boat	bug	toad	bone
bee	truck	coat	rug	road	cone
book	corn	growl			
hook	horn	owl			

10. Present students with four cards containing illustrations. Three of the cards should rhyme; one of the cards should not rhyme with the other three. Invite students to sort the cards and explain their reasoning. Three sets of sample cards follow.

Set 1

Set 2

Set 3

11. Create a rhyming bulletin board. Put blank sheets of paper on the bulletin board where they can be readily reached by students. Invite students to search newspapers or magazines for pictures that rhyme and fasten them to the appropriate piece of paper. Pictures might also be drawn by students.

Producing Strategies and Activities

12. Begin with part of a familiar poem (perhaps "Jack and Jill") that contains a rhyming element. Say the line and print it on the chalkboard.

Jack and Jill
Went up the hill

Tell students that two words rhyme: *Jill* and *hill.* Say, "Rhymes are words that sound alike at the ends." Have students inspect the words to find the common element (-ill). Tell them that *Jill* rhymes with *ill* and begins with *jjj.* Ask them what word rhymes with *ill* and begins

with *hhh.* Practice other words that fit the same pattern (*pill, mill, bill, dill, kill, till, will*). Use the following format: What word rhymes with *ill* and begins with *ppp?* Model when necessary and give students ample opportunities to respond individually. Have students use the words in sentences. Extend the preceding strategy to nursery rhymes or Dr. Seuss books. Have students listen for and locate rhyming words. They could also underline or circle the rhyming words.

13. Sing songs that have one or more rhyming words. Invite students to identify the rhyming words.

14. Use poetry that contains rhyming words. Help students to identify the words that rhyme. Then read the poem aloud and leave out selected words. Have students supply the rhyming word that was left out.

15. Do riddles with body parts. Fox (1996) offers the following riddles in which all the answers rhyme with *head.*

 What can you toast? (bread)

What do you call something that's not living anymore? (dead)

What is the color of blood? (red)

What do you use to ride down snowy hills? (sled)

Where do you sleep? (bed)

Encourage students to make up riddles and questions that rhyme with certain words.

16. Use magnetic letters or letter cards to help the students see how changing the initial letter can make a new word that rhymes with the original word. Help students understand that rhyming words have the same endings. An example follows.

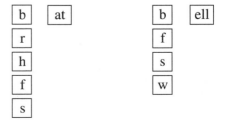

17. Encourage students to determine a rhyming word when you say: "What word rhymes with (use a phonogram) and begins with (use an initial sound)?" A few examples follow.

> oy: boy, joy, toy, Roy
> um: drum, thumb, gum
> op: crop, drop, pop, shop, stop, mop

Rhymes are very generalizable. Nearly 500 primary grade words can be derived from the following set of only 37 phonograms (Whylie & Durrell, 1970, as cited in Adams, 1990b, pp. 321–322).

-ack	-ail	-ain	-ake	-ale	-ame
-an	-ank	-ap	-ash	-at	-ate
-aw	-ay	-eat	-ell	-est	-ice
-ick	-ide	-ight	-ill	-in	-ine
-ing	-ink	-ip	-ir	-ock	-oke
-op	-or	-ore	-uck	-ug	-ump
-unk					

18. Tell students, "I'm thinking of a word that begins with *b* and rhymes with *cat*." Have students make up other "I'm thinking of" riddles.

19. Encourage students to write rhyming words and explain how they are able to create the words.

20. Use poems, songs, and chants as ways to encourage students to create their own rhymes.

21. Make class-rhyming books. Read a poem together. Create a sentence, based on the topic of the poem, with two blanks that students will fill in with rhyming pairs. For example,

In my house I have a _____ and a _____.

This sentence could be used after reading "My House" by Jane W. Krows (1993). Have each student fill in a sentence and illustrate the page. These books make wonderful independent reading materials for emergent readers. They enjoy reading their own books and become more familiar with the spelling features of rhymes.

22. Have students brainstorm as many rhyming words as they can in 30 seconds. Repeat this activity often to reinforce rhyming skills.

23. Have students create their own poem using words that rhyme.

Games

Find a Rhyme. Make a pair of rhyming words for each two students. Put each word on a note card. Each student gets a card. The object of the game is to find the other person who has the word that rhymes. This game can be repeated several times by mixing the cards.

Remember and Rhyme. For oral practice with rhyming words, students can form small groups and play a game. One student in the group begins with a simple one-syllable word (for example, *nice*, *best*, or *stop*) and says the word aloud. The next player in the group has to say the first student's rhyming word and then add one of his or her own. This process continues until no other rhyming word can be given. Begin again and play with a new word.

Find These Rhyming Words. Try a rhyming word scavenger hunt with a small group of students. Begin with one word that has many others that rhyme with it (for instance, *cake*, *bug*, or *top*). Give the students 10 minutes to look for items that rhyme with the given word. Pictures from magazines can be included along with symbols that represent the word. For example, a twig may represent the word *nest*. Following the 10-minute word-hunting period, form a group and share items found. Write the rhyming words on the chalkboard.

Group Me. Use a deck of cards containing groups of rhyming words. Shuffle the cards and encourage the students to categorize the rhyming words into their appropriate groups after saying each word out loud.

SECTION
2.7

Syllabic Awareness

Behavior Observed	The student is unable to segment words into syllables and blend syllables into words.
Anticipated Outcome	The student will successfully segment words into syllables and blend syllables into words.

BACKGROUND

Once students have developed the concept of a word, they will be ready to learn that words are made up of strings of smaller units of speech called syllables. Research (Adams, 1990b) suggests that syllabic awareness is an essential link between the ability to rhyme and the developmentally harder-to-acquire ability to hear and manipulate phonemes, the individual sounds in spoken language. Developing students' ability to reflect on syllables as smaller units of sound in words is a useful step in preparing them to later develop phonemic awareness, found to be causally related to reading acquisition (Bradley & Bryant, 1983; Lundberg, Frost, & Petersen, 1988).

Syllabic awareness links rhyme with the ability to hear and manipulate phonemes.

We encourage you to use the following teaching strategies to develop students' syllabic awareness. Be careful to enunciate words clearly and to use only familiar words with your students.

Section 2.7

STRATEGY 1 SEGMENTING SYLLABLES*

1. Begin teaching separation of words into syllables after students are proficient at separating an oral phrase or sentence into words. If students have difficulty with this task, refer to the appropriate section of Chapter 2 for some useful strategies.

2. Use the names of your students for initial activities. Say the first name of one student; then say the name again and clap the syllables. Clap as you say each syllable.

*Cunningham, 1995.

3. Say the first names of other students and clap the syllables as you say them the second time. Encourage students to clap with you.

4. Continue with other names. As students become proficient, use some of their middle and/or last names. The word *beat* may be a more easily understood term than syllables for young students. By clapping, students should realize that *Bob* is a one-beat word, *Giti* is a two-beat word, *Natalie* is a three-beat word, and so on.

5. When students can clap beats easily, help them see that the length of the word is usually related to the number of claps it gets. Start with student names that begin with the same letter. Then print the names on different strips of paper so that the short words have short strips and the long words have long strips, as in the following example.

Before showing the words, say *Bob* and *Barbara* and have students decide that *Bob* is a one-beat word and *Barbara* takes more claps and is a three-beat word. Ask them to predict which word is probably longer and has more letters. Then show them the words and develop the understanding that, because longer words (like *Barbara*) take several claps, they probably have more letters than shorter words. Use some of the other names of your students to further develop and practice this basic understanding.

6. Extend this activity by having students sort pictures of classmates or their names written on index cards according to the number of syllables in their names. Provide number cards as header cards to sort under. Make the activity self-correcting by writing the number of syllables on the back of the pictures or names. Use this activity to assess an individual student's syllabic segmentation ability and as an independent center activity.

7. Then use a similar procedure with word pairs (or triplets). Possible categories and words to use are shown below.

States		Animals	
Maine	Ohio	canary	bobcat
Michigan	Oklahoma	cat	bear
Alabama	Tennessee	chimpanzee	beaver
Alaska	Texas	camel	bear
Maine	Massachusetts	hippopotamus	giraffe
Maryland	Missouri	horse	goat

8. A variation is to show students two words they probably can't read and ask, "Who can figure out which of the two words I'm holding is canary and which is cat?" The goal is to have students recognize that words requiring more claps probably contain more letters.

9. Moving blocks to represent each syllable or tapping a pencil or other object could be used instead of clapping syllables. Such variations may help sustain students' attention.

STRATEGY 2 BLENDING SYLLABLES*

1. Begin this strategy by reading *The Three Billy Goats Gruff* to help students gain an understanding of what a troll is. When the troll talks in the story, say the words syllable by syllable.

2. Then pretend to be a troll. Tell students you will say words and students must figure out the words being named. Provide and discuss several examples.

3. Use words like *paper, pencil, candy, marker, erasers, notebook, automobile, airplane, buggy, hamburger,* and *chalkboard.* If possible, have the actual objects so that students can make a visual association **after** they have identified the word.

4. Extend the lesson by having students use tokens (see Strategy 1 in Section 2.10) for each syllable heard or hold up a finger for each syllable.

5. Invite students to volunteer for the troll's role. Provide guidance and support as needed.

6. Create an audiotape of the troll words used in the lesson. Record each troll word and its normally spoken equivalent. Provide these directions.

 * Listen to the troll word.
 * Push the pause button after you hear the troll word.
 * Say the word normally.
 * Push the pause button again to listen to the word spoken normally.

*Lundberg, Frost, & Peterson, 1988.

Practice and Reinforcement Activities

1. Have students categorize the names of pictures according to the number of syllables. Some possible pictures to use follow.

2. Clap or tap to the beat (syllables) of songs.
3. Write a cloze sentence on the board, placing dashes to represent the number of syllables in the missing word. For example write

I like _____ _____ _____ chip cookies.

Read the sentence aloud, clapping three times to represent the three syllables in the word choc-o-late. Have students think of possible word choices that make sense and have the correct number of syllables. Accept any reasonable response.

4. Practice blending action word syllables. Perform an action, segmenting the spoken word into syllables while simultaneously segmenting the action to represent the number of syllables. For example, say *walk* taking one step and *ing* taking a second step. Have students blend the syllables into the action word *walking*. Other action words to say and act out in segmented syllables include *breathing, snapping, singing, batting, throwing, coloring,* and *following.*

Alphabetic Principle

Behavior Observed	The student lacks knowledge of sounds associated with letters of the alphabet.
Anticipated Outcome	The student will become aware of associating letters with their sounds.

PERSPECTIVE AND STRATEGIES

Once beginning readers understand the language and concepts of printed materials, further progress is made by developing the alphabetic principle. The following activities focus on introducing the student to associate selected letters of the alphabet with their sounds.

1. See Chapter 3 for an expanded explanation of letter-sound correspondences.

2. Introduce the concept of beginning sounds by reading aloud alphabet books (see Appendix B) or pattern books (see Appendix C). Draw attention to words that begin with the same sound. *The Little Book of Big Tongue Twisters* by Foley Curtis (New York: Harvey House, 1977) contains alliterative pieces that could be used to introduce most of the beginning sounds.

3. Use graphic displays that combine the letter form with a picture of something that begins with that letter. Draw letters within the picture rather than next to the picture, as demonstrated below.

Give students lots of practice with the pictures, perhaps drawn on cards, until the letter drawn and its associated object become familiar. Large cards displayed around the classroom are a helpful reminder. Read alphabet books to your class and request that parents do the same at home. Immersion in the alphabetic principle will facilitate sound-symbol association. Appendix B lists some titles of alphabet books.

4. Make alphabet books with your students. At first, simply paste or draw pictures of objects beginning with a given letter on its letter page. For example, the *Ss* page might have a silly smile, a snake, scissors, and spinach. Upon completion of the first step, subsequent alphabet books might carry a theme, such as animals. In this case, the *Ss* page might have pictures of a squirrel, a snake, and a squid. Taken one step further, the alphabet book might include a combination of pictures and written words that begin with *s*.

5. Say a word and have students indicate whether their names begin with the same sound. Remember to stress sounds so names like *Cecil* and *Sam* begin with the same sound as *circus*. Clarify students' responses as necessary.

6. Play the game "I Spy." Tell students that you see or spy something in the room that begins with the same sound as *paper*. As students say words, note words with incorrect sounds ("I'm sorry, *box* does not begin like *paper*") or note that "The word *pen* begins like *paper* but it isn't the word I was thinking." A more advanced version of the game could involve an ending sound.

7. Model the use of picture sorts of various types. One type (a closed sort) is to sort by pictures those names that have a particular beginning sound. A second type (an open sort) has a num- ber of pictures, and students sort them into dif- ferent beginning sounds. Have students explain their sorts. Choose pictures with initial letter sounds that cannot be confused. Do not com- bine pictures that begin with *c* and *s*, *c* and *k*, or *g* and *j*.

8. Establish mailboxes for each student (hanging file folders in a plastic crate work well) and en- courage students to write to each other.

9. Provide plenty of opportunities for students to engage in writing and be supportive of their efforts.

SECTION 2.9

Onsets and Rimes*

Behavior Observed	The student is unable to segment, blend, and manipulate onsets and rimes.
Anticipated Outcome	The student will be able to segment, blend, and manipulate onsets and rimes.

BACKGROUND

A rime is the vowel and the letters that follow in a syllable. In the one-syllable word *sing,* the rime is *ing.* The onset is the letter or letters that precede the rime. In the word sing, the onset is *s.* In the word *swing,* the onset is *sw.* Teaching students onsets and rimes helps them to understand that phonograms (letter clusters or word families) can represent the same sound in different words. This knowledge enables students to decode words by analogy (National Reading Panel, 2000). Knowing how to read *cat* provides a basis for students to read *bat, fat, hat, mat, pat, rat, sat,* and *flat.*

A rime is the vowel and the letters that follow in a syllable.

Begin teaching segmenting and blending of onsets and rimes after students are able to separate words into syllables. After students are able to hear syllables in words, the next unit of sound they are able to hear is onset followed by rime (Treiman & Zukowski, 1991). Separating syllables into onsets and rimes is easier than separating them into other sound units. *Ran* is more easily divided into *r-an* than *ra-n* or *r-a-n* (Cunningham, 2000).

*Slattery, 2000a.

STRATEGY 1 SEGMENTING ONSETS AND RIMES

1. Select or make illustrations of familiar *c* and *r* rhyming words to make the rhyming pairs. Choose rhyming pairs that share the same initial letters. For example you can use *cake* and *rake* and *cat* and *rat*. See Word Patterns in Resources for Chapter 3 for possible choices.

2. Mix up the pictures and have students sort the pictures by the onsets. If you would like to do this activity with blends, have students sort by the blends (onsets) before the rimes.

3. After students have sorted the pictures into two columns, one with c words and the other with r words, ask the students

 *What **sound** do you hear at the beginning of these words (pointing to those beginning with c)? Similarly, ask the same question for those beginning with r.*

4. Ask what **letter** makes the /c/ and /r/ sound respectively at the beginning of each group of sorted pictures. As the students tell you the letters, write a c and an r in black on index cards, placing the corresponding letter over the group of rhyming pictures.

5. Gather the picture cards. Have students sort them according to their rimes. Explain that this time you are going to listen to the part of the word that comes after the first sound. Hold up a picture, modeling the process saying "*Cat* starts with /c/ and ends with /at/ c-at." Pick up the next picture asking: "What sound do you hear at the beginning of *rake*?" and "What comes after the /r/ sound?" "Does /ake/ sound like /at/?" When pictures have the same rime, group them together.

6. After all the rime pairs have been grouped together, place index cards with the rimes written in red above each set.

7. Say each rime pair segmenting the onset from the rime. Model this process saying "c-at, r-at." This activity works best with small groups. You may want to use the illustrations from this activity to assess whether students are able to segment onsets and rimes.

8. Extend the activity by having students take turns blending the correct onset card with the rime header card to form the word for the picture.

9. Extend the activity further by mixing the red rime cards and having students make rhyming words by blending the onsets and rimes.

STRATEGY 2 BLENDING ONSETS AND RIMES

1. Create and read rhyming words from a word students can read. Choose a word they can already read and write it on an index card. The word *fish* will be used for this example. Prepare individual consonants cut out from index cards.

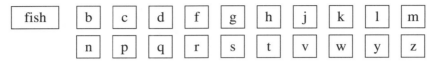

2. Tell students "We are going to make words that rhyme with a word we already know by using consonants."

3. Place the word *fish* in a pocket chart, asking the students to read the word.

4. Using the consonant letters in *consecutive* order, place one consonant at a time over the onset (f) in *fish*, asking the students to read the new 'word' and asking whether you have made a real word. Write all the real words on the chalkboard.

5. Read all the words together that are written on the chalkboard.

6. Help students understand that all the words have the same rime by asking,

 Do you notice any letters that are the same in all the words I wrote on the chalkboard?

 If students are unable to identify the entire *ish* phonogram (word family or letter clusters) and are only able to find one or two of the letters, ask,

 Are there any more letters that are the same in all the words?

7. Point out that knowing how to read and spell a rime like *ish* in *fish* helps students to read and spell other words with the same rime. In Strategy 3 (Show and Tell a Word) students will be taught to make this reading and spelling connection.

STRATEGY 3 SHOW AND TELL A WORD

1. Read a book or poem with rhyme patterns. After students are familiar with the rhyme patterns, prepare for the activity by choosing a word family or rime pattern from the text. This activity is based on the *at* word pattern found in Dr. Seuss' *Hop on Pop* (1965). Consider the following in making your choice: rimes that begin with a short /a/ appear most frequently in children's books, those beginning with a short /u/ rarely occur, and short /e/ is difficult for children to hear (Johnson & Kaufman, 1999).

2. Make the student onset and rime manipulatives, teacher manipulatives, and rhyming word cards. Write the rime *at* on a strip of two connected one-inch squares, placing an *a* and *t* in each square, and duplicate enough copies for students (see example below). Also, make a four-inch high version in red. Prepare individual one-inch squares with the onsets *b, c, h, P,* and *s* (see example) and make four-inch versions of these same onsets. (Blends and diagraphs can be used after

students are confident with single-letter onsets.) Write *at, bat, cat, hat, Pat,* and *sat* on index cards, writing the onset in black and the rime in red. Make two additional rhyming words, *mat* and *fat,* to be used in steps 12 and 13.

Rime
(Do not cut apart.)

a	t

Onset
(Cut apart.)

b	c	h	P	s

3. Place the four-inch high version of the rime in red in a pocket chart, with the onset letters in white above the rime. (Letter squares the same size as the students' letters can be used for small groups without a pocket chart.)

4. Provide each student with a set of onsets (*b, c, h, P,* and *s*) and the rime *at* on connected squares. These can be easily passed out as a strip of onsets that the students cut apart and a rime strip that the students are instructed to color red. Until they get used to this step, pass out the rime first and have them color it red like yours and then pass out the onset to be cut apart like yours. They quickly learn to look at the pocket chart for what needs to be colored and what needs to be cut apart.

5. Tell students:

 The letters in red are called the rime. You will notice that all rimes begin with a vowel.
 The letter before the rime is called the onset.

6. After several readings of *Hop on Pop* (Seuss, 1965), model the activity by placing the onset *c* in front of the rime *at* to show a word that they know from the book. Tell them what the rime and onset are. Place the rhyming word card *cat* in the pocket chart.

7. Invite a student to volunteer to show a word that can be made with the same rime and to tell the word and its onset and rime.

8. Have other students show the new word using their *at* rime strip and matching letter square.

 Ask them to tell the new word and its parts by pointing to each word part, stating: "The onset is _____, and the rime is _____." Place the new rhyming word card next to the word *cat* in the pocket chart.

9. Continue the activity repeating steps 7 and 8 until all of the rhyming words but two have been made, saving *mat* and *fat* for steps 12 and 13.

10. Read all the rhyming cards together and ask students to tell what they notice about the words. Some possible responses are provided below.

 • All the words have an *a*.
 • All the words have a *t*.
 • All the words have an *a* and *t*.

- All the words look the same except the first letter.
- I hear /at/ in all the words.

Encourage responses by asking if there is anything else that students notice.

11. Ask the following question.

 How do you think these words can help us?

 Try to elicit that knowing the rime pattern will help students pronounce and spell words.

12. Ask a student to **pronounce** *mat,* one of the remaining rhyming words in your hand, and ask the student how he or she was able to read the new word.

13. Invite another student to help you **spell** *fat,* the last rhyming word. Show the correctly spelled word, asking how the student knew how to spell the word.

 Making the connection to reading and spelling in steps 12 and 13 is extremely important. Without this explicit connection, many students will not be able to apply what is being taught in this activity to their own reading and spelling.

Practice and Reinforcement Activities

1. Read a rhyming poem or book. Copy the poem or section of the book on chart paper or a transparency. Cover the rime of corresponding rhyming words. Have students use the onsets to help figure out the word. Uncover the rime and read it aloud. Following are examples of poems to use.

- Charao, K. *Jumpety-Bumpety Hop: A Parade of Animal Poems.* New York: Dutton, 1997.
- Graham, J. "Steam." In *Splish Splash.* New York: Scholastic, 1994.
- McCord, D. "Notice." In *One at a Time.* Boston: Little, Brown, 1952.
- Rogers, S. *Earthsongs.* New York: Dutton, 1998.
- Silverstein, S. "Ickle Me, Pickle Me, Tickle Me Too." In *Where the Sidewalk Ends.* New York: HarperCollins, 1974.

Following are examples of books to use. Other titles can be found in Opitz (2000).

- Aylesworth, J. *Old Black Fly.* New York: Scholastic, 1992.
- Bunting, E. *Flower Garden.* New York: Harcourt Brace, 1994.
- Deming, A. *Who Is Tapping At My Window?* New York: Penguin, 1994.
- Lear, E. *A Was Once an Apple Pie.* Cambridge, MA: Candlewick, 1997.
- Westcott, N. *The Lady with the Alligator Purse.* Boston: Little, Brown, 1988.
- Wood, A. *Silly Sally.* San Diego: Harcourt Brace, 1992.

2. Write a sentence using several words from a word family, leaving the rime off of one of the words. Tell students that the missing rime has the same rime pattern as the underlined rhyming words in the sentence. Have students use the rime clues and onset clue to figure out the missing word. For example write the following sentence:

 The <u>big pig</u> danced a j __ __.

3. Sort two sets of word families, adding one or two additional word families as students show readiness. Begin with short vowel word families in the following order: *a, i, o, e*. Short /a/ word families are most commonly found in children's books, short /e/ is harder for children to hear than short /i/ and /o/, and short /u/ word families are not commonly used in children's books (Johnson & Kaufman, 1999). See Word Patterns in Resources for Chapter 3 for possible word families.

4. After students practice word sorts with a teacher, have students cut out and glue words, sorting them on paper.

5. Write rime patterns several times in large letters, providing a blank for students to fill in the onset. Duplicate these patterns for independent practice or laminate and use rime patterns for practice at a center.

6. After students have learned the word family, develop word wheels, sliders, or flip books where the various words can be made by turning a wheel, sliding a strip of paper, or flipping pages in a book. Possible words for this activity can be found in Word Patterns in Resources for Chapter 3.

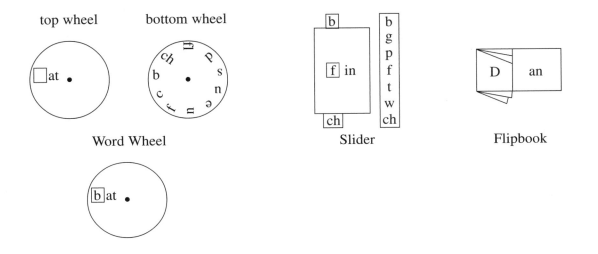

7. See rhyming section for additional activities.

Phonemic Awareness

Behavior Observed	The student is unable to segment, blend, and manipulate phonemes.
Anticipated Outcome	The student will successfully segment, blend, and manipulate phonemes.

BACKGROUND

Phonemic awareness is the ability to segment and manipulate individual sounds in words. It is strongly related to success in reading and spelling acquisition and is a powerful predictor of reading achievement (Yopp, 1995). In order to benefit from phonics instruction, students seem to require at least some basic level of phonemic awareness. Research reported by Bentin and Leshem (1993) and Tumner, Herriman, and Nesdale (1988) has led some to view phonemic awareness as a necessary prerequisite for success in learning to read. "No matter how they are taught, all students must grasp the abstract concepts that words are composed of separate sounds and that individual letters and combinations are used to represent those sounds" (Gunning, 1996).

> Phonemic awareness is a powerful predictor of reading achievement.

For a number of students, the ability to segment and manipulate sounds in words does not come naturally; nevertheless, explicit instruction in phonological awareness can be given before and during reading instruction. Some examples (Stanovich, 1993/1994) of questions related to phonological awareness tasks follow.

 Phoneme Deletion: What would be left if the /h/ sound were taken away from *hat*?

Word-to-Word Matching: Do *pen* and *paper* begin with the same sound?

Blending: What word would we have if you put these sounds together: /m/, /a/, /t/?

Phoneme Segmentation: What sounds do you hear in the word *hot*?

Phoneme Counting: How many sounds do you hear in the word *kite*?

Deleted Phoneme: What sound do you hear in *seat* that is missing in *eat*?

Odd Word Out: Which word starts with a different sound: *bag, nine, beach, bike*?

Sound to Word Matching: Is there a /k/ in *Mike*?

The National Reading Panel (2000) conducted a meta-analysis of the body of research on phonemic awareness and found that training students to segment and blend phonemes has a greater effect on students' reading than training them in multiple phonemic awareness skills. Segmenting phonemes helps students gain an awareness that speech consists of a series of sounds or phonemes (for ex-

ample, *mat* is made up of three segments). The ability to blend phonemes helps students to sound out words, blending the sounds associated with letters into a meaningful whole. Although the ultimate goal for the reader is to construct meaning from print, knowledge of phonemic segmentation is an excellent predictor of success in reading (Gillet & Temple, 1990). Providing instruction in blending skills concurrently with segmentation training enhances phonological awareness skills in general. Assuming that a student knows the sounds associated with letters, the task then becomes one of blending the sounds into a word that is already in the student's listening or meaning vocabulary.

Instructional and practice activities are offered here and in other sections of this chapter. See the sections on auditory discrimination (2.4), concept of a word (2.5), rhyming (2.6), syllabic awareness (2.7), and onsets and rimes (2.9). The following strategies are most effective when used in small groups (National Reading Panel, 2000) and when students have developed a concept for words, a concept for rhyme, the ability to rhyme words, the ability to segment syllables, and the ability to hear onsets and rimes (Treiman & Zukowski, 1991). Then proceed to separating words into phonemes and blending phonemes into words.

Section 2.10

STRATEGY 1 SEGMENTING PHONEMES*

1. Prepare cards with a simple illustration along with a matrix that contains a box for each sound (phoneme) in the word. Note that the boxes represent each sound, not necessarily each letter. The words selected should be familiar to students. Secure sufficient tokens (plastic, pennies, cardboard squares) for each of your students. Additional cards appear in the Resources for Chapter 2. They can be copied on heavy paper and cut out for use. An example of a sound box is shown below. Use empty boxes until letter recognition and letter/sound correspondence begin to develop (Ball & Blachman, 1991; Hohn & Ehri, 1983). After letter recognition and letter/sound correspondence begin to develop, place letters in the boxes (see duck and kite), making sure to leave enough space in the boxes so tokens do not cover the letters.

2. Instruct a small group so you can provide assistance as needed. Guide students through the task. Slowly say the word while pushing tokens into the boxes sound by sound. Model the process a second time. Then invite the students to say the word, perhaps stretching the sounds, so they can hear the separate sounds while you move the tokens. Invite students to push the tokens into the boxes while you say the word slowly.

3. Then provide another example and begin to transfer the responsibility to the students. Encourage a student to identify the picture and then pronounce the word very carefully and deliberately. The goal is to emphasize each sound without distorting the word and to put a token in each box while saying each sound.

*Elkonin, 1973.

4. Use other examples to help students catch on to the concept of segmenting. Some examples of sound boxes can be found in the Resources for Chapter 2.

5. The following are useful variations that will solidify and expand students' abilities.

- Eliminate the boxes below the pictures and have students just move their tokens to the bottom of the picture.
- Say a word aloud and have students repeat it and count the number of sounds on their fingers. Ask, "How many sounds are in the word?" In the beginning, it may be beneficial to stretch out the sounds and repeat the process for each word two or three times.
- Have students simply tell you how many sounds are in the word shown in the picture after they have pronounced it. The pictures used should contain no boxes.
- Record a word's letters in boxes and have students put tokens in the box that represents the segmented sounds. Make sure there is enough space in the boxes so that the tokens do not cover the letters.
- After students are quite proficient at counting the number of sounds in a word, ask questions about the order of sounds, such as the following ones.

 What is the first sound you hear in *duck*?

What sounds do you hear after /u/ in duck?

- Invite students to pronounce the word in the picture and then write letters or place plastic letters in the boxes instead of using tokens. See the example below.

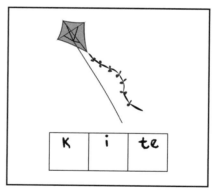

STRATEGY 2

WORD GAME ASSESSMENT FOR SEGMENTING PHONEMES*

1. Duplicate the Phoneme Segmentation Record Sheet.

2. With the student, say,

 Today we're going to play a word game. I'm going to say a word and I want you to break the word apart. You are going to tell me each sound in the word in order. For example, if I say 'old,' you should say '/o/-/l/-/d/.'

 Be sure to say the sounds, not the letters, in the word.

3. Then say, "Let's try a few together." The practice items are *ride, go,* and *man.* If necessary, segment the word for the student. Encourage the student to repeat the segmented sounds.

4. During the test, feedback is provided to the student. You could nod or say "Right" or "That's right." If the student is incorrect, correct him or her. You should also provide the appropriate response.

5. Proceed through all 22 items. Circle those items that the student correctly segments. Incorrect responses may be recorded on the blank line following the item.

6. The student's score is the number of items he or she correctly segments into all constituent phonemes. No partial credit is given. For example, *she* (item 5) contains two phonemes /sh/-/e/; *grew* (item 7) contains three phonemes /g/-/r/-/ew/; and *three* (item 15) contains three phonemes /th/-/r/-/ee/. If the student notes letter names instead of sounds, the response is coded as incorrect, and the type of error is noted in the record sheet. Such notes are helpful in understanding the student. Some students may partially segment, simply repeat the stimulus item, provide nonsense responses, or give letter names. A wide range of scores is likely. Yopp (1995) reported that the two samples of kindergartners achieved mean scores of 11.78 and 11.39.

7. Refer to the strategies in this section for instructional interventions.

STRATEGY 3

BLENDING PHONEMES

1. Begin with a picture that has been cut into several pieces and show how the pieces, when put together properly, make a picture. Simple puzzles can be used. Tell the students that sometimes words can be identified by putting together the sounds associated with the letters or letter combinations.

2. Write several words on the chalkboard that the students may or may not know by sight (such as *sat, sit,* or *map*). Students should know, at an automatic level, the letter-sound relationships used in the blending exercises.

*Yopp, 1995.

Phoneme Segmentation Record Sheet

Directions:	Today we're going to play a word game. I'm going to say a word and I want you to break the word apart. You are going to tell me each sound in the word in order. For example, if I say "old," you should say "/o/-/l/-/d/." (**Be sure to say the sounds, not the letters, in the word.**) Let's try a few together.

Practice items: (*Assist the child in segmenting these items as necessary.*) ride, go, man

Test items: (*Circle those items that the student correctly segments; incorrect responses may be recorded on the blank line following the item.*) The correct number of phonemes is indicated in parentheses.

1. dog (3) _____

2. keep (3) _____

3. fine (3) _____

4. no (2) _____

5. she (2) _____

6. wave (3) _____

7. grew (3) _____

8. that (3) _____

9. red (3) _____

10. me (2) _____

11. sat (3) _____

12. lay (2) _____

13. race (3) _____

14. zoo (2) _____

15. three (3) _____

16. job (3) _____

17. in (2) _____

18. ice (2) _____

19. at (2) _____

20. top (3) _____

21. by (2) _____

22. do (2) _____

Total Correct ☐

The author, Hallie Kay Yopp, California State University, Fullerton, grants permission for this test to be reproduced. The author acknowledges the contribution of the late Harry Singer to the development of this test. Adapted from Yopp, H.K. (1995). A test for assessing phonemic awareness in young children. *The Reading Teacher, 49,* 20–29.

3. Have the students watch while you blend the sounds associated with each letter into a whole word. Tell them that you will point to the next letter. Initially, sound the letters in *sat* for about a second (except for the final letter). When done with the sounding procedure, say the word as you would in normal pronunciation.

4. Next, have students sound out the word with you. Touch the letters and sound out the word with the students (for example, *sssaaat*). Repeat the process until students respond correctly. At the end of the sounding, always ask the students to say the word. Because of the limitations in short-term memory, the longer the pause between sounding and saying the word, the greater the possibility that students will have difficulty saying the word.

5. After students gain confidence with the process, have them sound out words together and individually. Gradually reduce the time during which they sound the individual letter.

6. Note that all vowels and some consonants can be given a continuous sound in blending. Other consonants rely on the following vowel (for example, *ham, cat*). To teach blending with such words, have students initially make the sound for the vowel, because they will need to move quickly from the sound associated with the consonant to the sound associated with the vowel.

7. Point out to students that this strategy is not usually the first method of word recognition they will try and that it does not always work. Blending is a useful skill; however, some students tend to have difficulty using it or overuse it even after careful teaching.

8. After numerous blending exercises, help students understand that the goal of blending is to be able to pronounce or say a word that they have already heard.

9. Once parts of a word have been blended into a whole, focus on meaning. For example, if the blended word is *map,* ask students, "What is a map?" or "How could you use map in a sentence?" Keep the focus on meaning, not merely pronunciation.

Section 2.10

STRATEGY 4 BLENDING PATHWAYS*

1. The basic procedure is for students to imagine the sounds of a word lined up on their shoulder to their hand. This is the blending pathway.

2. Demonstrate the procedure with a word like *kite.* Say the first sound as you place your right hand on your left shoulder, the second sound as you place your hand in the crook of your arm, and the third sound as you place your hand near your wrist. Then slide your right hand down your left arm from your shoulder to your wrist blending the sounds as your arm moves. For left-handed students, use your left hand on your right shoulder.

3. Model the process several times and have students join you.

4. Say the individual sounds in another word, have students place their hands on their arms at the shoulder, and have students blend the sounds together as they slide their hands down their arms. Then ask students what the word is. Repeat the process with other words.

5. When students are comfortable with the technique, have them blend silently. Then ask a student to say the entire word.

*Fox, 2000.

6. One variation is to enlarge the drawing of a slide and place it on the chalkboard tray. Tape or print letters on the slide so they go from the top to the bottom. Pronounce each sound as you slide your hand under each letter. Then ask a student to say the word, and write it at the bottom of the slide. Invite students to do the activity themselves, and provide guidance as necessary.

Practice and Reinforcement Activities

1. Use children's literature that playfully deals with sounds in language. In addition to the Dr. Seuss books, other books are listed below. Many additional titles have been compiled by Opitz (2000) and Griffith and Olson (1992).

- Degan, B. *Jamberry.* New York: Harper and Row, 1983.
- Hutchins, P. *Don't Forget the Bacon!* New York: Morrow, 1976.
- Leedy, L. *Pingo the Plaid Panda.* New York: Holiday House, 1989.
- Most, B. *Cock-A-Doodle-Moo.* New York: Harcourt Brace, 1996.
- Pomerantz, C. *How Many Trucks Can a Tow Truck Tow?* New York: Random House, 1987.
- Shaw, N. *Sheep on a Ship.* Boston: Houghton Mifflin, 1989.
- Van Laan, N. *Possum Come-A-Knockin'.* New York: Knopf, 1990.

2. Use a variation of the troll activity presented in Strategy 2 in Section 2.7. In this case, the troll pronounces individual phonemes of a word instead of syllables, and students must combine the sounds to identify the word.

3. Say a sound and let students whose names include that sound line up. Be sure students respond to the **sound.** For example, if you say *"kkk,"* Ken, Cathy, and Nikki could all respond.

4. Place three or four familiar pictures on the chalkboard tray and invite a student to say each word, one sound at a time. Another student is asked to identify the picture. Gradually increase the number of pictures and possibly use some pictures whose sounds are similar.

5. Provide time daily for writing using invented spelling, even if students are only writing single words or short phrases to accompany illustrations. The process students go through listening to the sounds in words as they write using invented spelling helps them to attend to the individual sounds in words. Invented spellings provide information about students' development of letter-sound relationships. Writing also helps develop phonemic awareness (McCormick, 1995).

Principles for Encouraging Spelling

1. Some students lack confidence to attempt their own spellings, because they are afraid to make a mistake. Help them feel comfortable by modeling the use of invented spelling and by stressing that it is okay to make a mistake. For example, when writing a class story together, ask, "What sound do you hear at the beginning of *play*?" After they respond "/p/," intentionally make a mistake by writing /g/ saying "Oops! I made a mistake, but that's okay. I'll try again." Have a student show you what a /p/ looks like (Slattery, 2000b).

2. Some students will feel it necessary to ask the teacher to spell each word for them. Ask the students what sound the word begins with, what sound is heard next, and so on, until the word is spelled. With encouragement and practice, students should become willing to attempt spelling on their own and may need only an occasional sound spelled for them.

3. Spelling provides a clue as to the progress of phonemic segmentation. For example, *gowe* eventually becomes *going* in a student's writing development. The ability to write increasingly conventional spellings is a key to improved reading ability and should be encouraged through writing.

Provide individual assistance, as you observe students writing, based on their developmental spellings. Some examples (Slattery, 2000b) of scaffolding strategies follow.

- **Prephonemic Spellings:** Create a shared background of letter knowledge with students' names. Make a Picture Wall with pictures of students in the class. Label the pictures with their names. Use other familiar pictures to represent the letters that do not start students' names. Take time to study each student's name and discuss the letters and their sounds. Refer to the Picture Wall when students are unable to identify an initial or ending letter sound. If a student is trying to spell *boat* and you have spent time learning that Bobby's name starts with /B/ ask "What **sound** do you hear in the beginning of *boat*?" After the student responds "/b/," focus on the letter sound asking "Is there anyone in our class whose name begins with the same sound?" When the student answers "Bobby's name begins with /b/. But I don't know what that letter is," go over to the Picture Wall and point to the letter at the beginning of Bobby's name.

- **Phonemic Spellings:** Students' spellings at the phonemic stage represent beginning, middle, and ending letter sounds. Short vowels are represented by a vowel whose letter name sounds closest to the letter sound. Provide help identifying the short vowel by connecting the sound to something with which the student is familiar. For example, if the student is struggling with short *i*, bring him or her to a chart displaying the familiar finger play, "Itsy, Bitsy Spider." After reading and tracking the title together, ask, "Can you find a letter with the same sound as /i/?" Have the student track the words of the title again as you remind him or her that you are listening for the short *i* sound.

- **Transitional Spellings:** Students' spellings at this stage creatively represent long vowel sounds. Complement these students for the way they use what they know about long vowels. Also, provide small group time for these students to sort words with long vowel patterns. When they sort words like *team, read, meal, knee, feed,* and *feel,* have them practice picturing the word in the mind, since the /ea/ and /ee/ patterns both have the long e sound.

4. The following chart illustrates aspects of the developmental stages of students' spellings (Morris & Perney, 1984). The stages may be thought of as a continuum and, in most cases, are not hard and fast. As students gain knowledge of the English phonological system, they gain control of conventional spelling.

Developmental Spelling Stages							
Prephonemic		Phonemic	Transitional	Correct			
B	BC	BAC	BACK (c)	back			
S	SK	SEK	SINC	sink			
M	ML	MAL	MALLE	mail			
J	JS	JRAS	DRES	dress			
C	CD	SID	SIED	side			
F	FT	FET	FEAT	feet			
B	BK	BIK	BICKE	bike			
S	SK	SEK	STIK	stick			

1. Prephonemic spellers perceive and represent initial and final consonants in one-syllable words, often using letter names to represent phonemes (*j, js,* or *jc* for *dress*).
2. Phonemic (letter name) spellers produce spellings that have short vowels produced as phonologically appropriate substitutions (*sek* for *sink*).
3. Transitional spellers begin to represent short vowels correctly, although the vowel markers are often incorrectly placed (*sied* for *side*).
4. Correct spelling is evidenced by spellers who nearly always spell words conventionally.

Visual Discrimination

Behavior Observed	The student has trouble visually discriminating differences among letters and words.
Anticipated Outcome	The student will visually discriminate differences among letters and words.

BACKGROUND

Reading is more than a visual process; nevertheless, being able to discriminate letters and words accurately is crucial for efficient reading. A hierarchy of five levels for visual discrimination is shown below.

VISUAL DISCRIMINATION

Level 1	Concrete objects
Level 2	Pictures
Level 3	Geometric shapes
Level 4	Letters
Level 5	Words and phrases

A student experiencing difficulty in the visual discrimination of letters or words may need to begin by differentiating similarities and differences in concrete objects, pictures, or geometric shapes. The emphasis should then move to exercises related to letters, words, and phrases, because these areas have the closest relationship to reading.

Prior to visual discrimination training, ensure that any visual problems are checked through visual screening or testing. Sometimes, especially in the early stages of reading instruction, there may be a visual cause that is responsible for discrimination problems. Once the visual problem has been corrected by lenses or treatment, specific teaching and practice strategies may be undertaken.

Before beginning instruction in visual discrimination, be sure the student understands the concepts of same and different. Beginning readers, and some older students experiencing difficulty in reading, fail to understand the "same-different" concepts. Usually, with the aid of concrete objects, these concepts can be established.

STRATEGY 1 LETTERS

1. For students who are having difficulty discriminating between letters, begin with unlike pairs that are grossly different (for example, *x–o, n–p*) and move to pairs that require finer discrimination (such as *c–o, r–n, m–n, p–q, b–d*).

2. Provide various tactile activities for students to draw, write, or form letter pairs. For example, use cornmeal, sand, shaving cream, chalk, clay, finger paint, or paint. Students also enjoy using a large brush with water on the sidewalk.

3. Encourage students to verbalize reasons why the letter pairs are different. Let the students know that some letter pairs are particularly difficult to tell apart and model appropriate types of comments (for example, the *m* and the *n* are different because one letter has two humps and the other has one hump).

STRATEGY 2 WORDS

1. If students demonstrate the ability to discriminate between concrete objects, pictures, and geometric forms, proceed with words. On the chalkboard, write words that have gross structural or physical differences (such as *house, elephant*) and also words that are the same (for example, *run, run*). Discuss the similarities and differences in the word pairs.

2. Encourage students to express their thoughts on why the words are the same or different. Use questions such as the following.

Are these words the same or different?

How do you know?

Are you sure that the different words have a different number of letters? Count them.

Are you sure that the two words have exactly the same number of letters and kinds of letters?

Are the letters in exactly the same position?

3. As these and other questions are asked, it is often useful to place one word of a pair under the other to aid discussion and promote a clearer grasp of the concept. For example, the first word pair is different because the first letter in each word is different; the other word pair is the same because all the letters are identical and occur in the same position.

h o u s e r u n
 ↕ ↕ ↕
e l e p h a n t r u n

4. Use a similar procedure when a certain part of the word is different from that of another word. Some examples follow.

h o p e p e n h o t
r o p e p i n h o p

5. Use a variety of words and encourage students to discuss why the words are the same or different. Some possible word pairs are provided below.

| grandfather | bang | boy | went |
| grandmother | banging | boys | want |

6. Prepare a short passage, display a particular word (such as *cat*), and have students circle the word each time it occurs in the passage.

Practice and Reinforcement Activities

1. Most practice activities are variations of matching games. A common activity is to ask students to draw a circle around a letter or word that is the same as the example. The choices vary in difficulty. A variation of this activity is to have students put a line through the letter or word that does not match the sample.

2. Use two columns of words (or letters) and have students draw lines from words in the left column to the same words (or letters) in the right column.

3. Give students a set of cards containing words (or letters) and have them hold up the word (or letter) that matches your sample.

4. Prepare a page with a letter or word at the top of the page and have students circle the letter or word each time it appears.

5. Cut out a set of large upper-case and lower-case letters from construction paper. Have students find the same upper-case and lower-case letters in magazines or copies of duplicated text. Then glue the found letters to the appropriate construction paper letters. Hang these letters in the classroom, referring, for example, to the pink Pp letters.

Games

Wordo. Word Name or Letter Bingo. Prepare cards containing words, students' names, or letters. Hold up a stimulus card and have students place a marker on the square that is the same as the stimulus. The first student who gets Wordo wins.

W	O	R	D	O
big	if	was	it	on
no	get	to	then	when
saw	where	got	too	there

W	O	R	D	O
no	where	to	too	there
saw	get	was	then	on
big	if	got	it	when

Match. Prepare two cards for each letter or word that tends to cause confusion. Students take turns matching the letters or words. The student who gets the most pairs wins. One variation of the game involves the use of a stopwatch or timer. Each student attempts to better his or her previous time.

Letters and Names. Prepare a large set of cards containing the letters of the alphabet (capital and lower-case letters). Give students their names on individual letter cards. Hold up one large card at a time. Students who have the same letter(s) turn over the appropriate card(s) in their names. Play the game until the students designated have turned over all the letters in their names. The games can be played with first names, last names, or entire names. One variation is to have students exchange names with a friend. Favorite words can also be used.

Go Fish. Prepare two sets of letter or word cards. Pass out four cards to each student. Students take turns asking another student if he or she has a match to a letter or word they have in their hand. If the other student does not have the matching card, he or she tells the other student "Go fish." The student then fishes for a card in the draw pile. When students get a match, they place the match in front of them and take another turn. The student with the most matches wins.

Letter and Word Reversals

Behavior Observed	The student reverses letters or words.
Anticipated Outcome	The student will reduce the number of reversals.

PERSPECTIVE AND STRATEGIES

It is not unusual for some beginning readers and for older students experiencing difficulty in reading to reverse letters or words. To succeed in reading, students must learn that reading is a left-to-right activity.

> Students must learn that reading is a left-to-right activity.

Researchers have hypothesized many causes to explain reversals. Among them are visual problems and mixed dominance as well as an unfamiliarity with directionality as it relates to letter and word discrimination. The recommended procedure is to provide direct instruction with letters or words that are causing the student difficulty. If the student is a beginning reader, some reversals may be developmental in nature; however, if they persist, referral for more intensive study may be warranted. The following strategies may be helpful.

1. Teach students the concepts of left and right by showing them the difference between their left hand and right hand. Give oral directions where students must use their left hand or right hand to touch a book, pick up a pencil, open the door, and so on. Other body parts may also be used.

2. Transfer the concepts of left and right to reading by demonstrating how names are read from left to right.

3. Develop brief stories that can be placed on the chalkboard. Choose one student to point to the words as they are read to the class. Stress that reading goes from left to right. The hand or pointer indicates the required direction in reading. A sample is shown here.

Today is December 17.
The weather is cold and snowy.
Winter vacation begins after school today.
Winter will soon be here.

4. Provide exercises where students draw lines to connect dots horizontally and obliquely and relate the activity to lines of print. An example follows.

5. Have students draw an arrow, pointing to the right, under the first letter of a word or sentence.

6. Provide exercises to help eliminate common reversals (such as *was* and *saw, no* and *on*) by practicing on paper where the student is directed to trace over a word whenever it appears. An example follows.

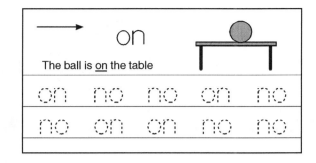

The ball is <u>on</u> the table

on no no on no
no on on no no

7. Provide sentences in which a reversal will result in a sentence that doesn't make sense. When students read each sentence ask, "Does it make sense?" Ask this question, even when sentences are read correctly, to promote thinking while reading. Several sample sentences follow.

Was–Saw Confusion
I *saw* my dad.
She *was* eating an apple.
We *saw* the book.
It *was* in the box.

There–Three confusion
We have *three* cats.
There is his dog.
Put the book over *there*.
The *three* boys are playing.

8. Place commonly reversed words so they can be closely compared. Discuss similarities and differences. An example follows.

was Both have three letters.
 Both have the same three letters but in different positions.
saw Both have an *a* in the middle.

9. Use a sentence that the student can read (or a word he or she can spell); make an elongated picture (snake, dragon, alligator); and write the sentence over the picture. Cut out the sentence and ask the student to put the sentence back together from left to right. Then have the student write the sentence. Words or stories can be substituted for sentences in this activity.

10. Provide lots of practice using a multisensory approach that involves forming the letter or word in sand, finger paint, or shaving cream. Pipe cleaners, Play Doh, or sandpaper can also be used to make letters or words.

11. Use the word *bed* to help the student learn *b* and *d*. Teach the student to spell *bed* and draw attention to the two "posts" on the bed to help with letter formation. Find and share a good illustration of a poster bed with the student or use the following illustration.

12. Use the word *pig* to help the student learn *p* and *g*. Teach the spelling and use the following graphic to help the student see that the *p* and *g* can help form the lines of a circle.

13. Provide letter or word activities where the student is asked to circle a particular letter or word. For example, circle every *n*.

n x o m n u m u n
w h n n v m n v h

Games

Fish. On paper fish write words that students frequently confuse. Attach a paper clip to each fish. Using a fishing pole made of a yardstick, string, and magnet, have the student fish for words. If the word can be pronounced correctly, the student keeps it; if not, he or she throws it back. Students having difficulty should play this game with students who already recognize the words. The words can also be used in sentences.

Tricky Words. Students who have some reading ability should be encouraged to read troublesome words or phrases in short sentences. Prepare a game board with phrases or sentences containing frequently confused words (for example, I saw the bear. He was here.). Students roll dice and proceed to the appropriate space. If the student can read the phrase, he or she can stay there. If the phrase or word is not read correctly, the student returns to his or her previous position. The student who first crosses the finish line wins.

Sense of Story

Behavior Observed	The student does not understand the parts of a story and may be unable to retell story events successfully.
Anticipated Outcome	The student will understand the parts of a story and will retell story events accurately.

BACKGROUND

Good readers possess background for text structure that allows them to anticipate and understand how the details relate to the main theme of a written piece of discourse. For beginning readers, this sense of story must be developed sufficiently for comprehension to occur.

Simple stories include characters, a sequence of events, conflict, and resolution. In reading, a sense of what composes stories influences the student's prediction, comprehension, and recall of stories. In writing, students often create stories around their internal concept or understanding of those elements that compose a story.

Texts contain a variety of elements, or story structures, that relate characters and occur in a certain sequence. Most story structures include the following elements.

STORY STRUCTURE

setting

initiating event

internal response

attempt

outcome

consequence

reaction

These elements make up episodes. There may be one or more per story.

STRATEGY 1

STORY STRUCTURE FOR YOUNGER STUDENTS

1. Secure a copy of *Aunt Isabel Tells a Good One* by Kate Duke (1992). This book is about a mouse called Penelope who wants her Aunt Isabel to tell a story. Aunt Isabel asks Penelope to help with the story by asking questions such as "When does this story begin?" and "Who shall be in this story?" The book can help provide students with a literature-based introduction to story structure.

2. Preread the story and decide the best way to introduce it to your students. For example, say:

 I'm going to read you a story about a little mouse that helps her aunt make up a story. Listen to the story. Then we'll talk about it and make up a story.

3. Read the story to students and share the colorful illustrations. Encourage students to react to the story and make predictions. For example, Penelope asks, "What are they going to do?" Invite students to predict what might be done.

4. Discuss the story with students. Then guide students to share some of the things that make up a good story. Some of the elements from the story include when, where, who, problem, solution. Refer, if necessary, to specific parts in the story to help students understand and write the story elements on the chalkboard.

5. Decide where it would be best to create a class story using some of the elements that students learned about in *Aunt Isabel Tells a Good One*. A new story could be created immediately following the discussion or at a later time, depending on your students' interest and engagement. When a story is being created, refer to the book and model some of the questions used by Aunt Isabel. A list of the questions could be written on the chalkboard to guide the development of the story.

6. Consider writing a draft of the story on large chart paper to model the writing, revising, and editing processes. When completed, the story could then be read and enjoyed by students.

7. Encourage students who are interested in writing their own stories to do so. See Lenski and Johns (2000) for five teaching strategies for writing fictional stories that use writing frames, graphic organizers, and character webs.

8. Remember that helping students understand story structure has several important benefits. First, it helps students understand that stories are made up of certain elements. Second, these elements appear in the stories students read and write. Third, knowing the elements should help students remember and retell stories. Take time to explicitly explain these fundamental benefits of story structure to students. Use vocabulary that students will understand.

STRATEGY 2 PREDICTING STORY STRUCTURE

1. Encourage students to predict what the material or story will be about using clues such as title and cover illustrations. Read a little of the text, perhaps one or two pages. Discuss the accuracy of the predictions. Predict what will happen next by asking open-ended questions. Check out that prediction by asking students to defend their answers from material specific to the story or text. Continue the prediction-confirmation pattern until the passage has been completed. Daily practice with predictions will enhance knowledge of story structure and improve comprehension.

2. Begin with a well-known story such as *Goldilocks and the Three Bears* or *Little Red Riding Hood.* Encourage students to share what they remember about the story. Write their responses on the chalkboard. See the example that follows.

 There was a little girl named Goldilocks.
 There were three bears.
 Goldilocks went into the bears' house when they were gone.

3. After students have shared their responses, ask them to name some of the parts of a story. Responses might include where it takes place, people, animals, and things happening. Use words offered by the students and begin to develop the concept that stories are made up of places (settings), people and/or animals (characters), and things happening (actions or episodes). Also, tell students that stories have a beginning, middle, and end.

4. Write three major story elements on the chalkboard and have students that have previously shared information classify their responses under the proper elements, as in the following example.

Goldilocks and the Three Bears

Places	People and Animals	Things That Happen
in the woods	Goldilocks	She went into the
house	Papa Bear	bears' house.

5. Then read the story to the class and encourage students to listen carefully so they can confirm or enlarge upon their earlier contributions. After the story has been read, have students share story elements. Write them on the chalkboard. Encourage a discussion that emphasizes and expands major story elements.

Goldilocks and the Three Bears

Places	People and Animals	Things That Happen
a house in the woods	Goldilocks	The bears went for a walk in the woods.
kitchen	three bears	Goldilocks went into their house while they were away.
living room	Papa Bear	She found three bowls of porridge.
bedroom	Mama Bear	She ate Baby Bear's porridge.
	Baby Bear	She sat in the three bears' chairs.
		She broke Baby Bear's chair.
		She went into the bedroom and tried out the beds.
		She fell asleep in Baby Bear's bed.
		The three bears returned.

6. Repeat this basic procedure with other stories. Emphasize how students can use their knowledge of story structure to better understand or remember a story. Knowledge of story structure may also aid in predicting what might happen next in new stories.

Section 2.13

STRATEGY 3 STORY STRUCTURE

1. It is possible to develop the elements of story structure in greater depth through character analysis, details of the setting, and a discussion of theme and plot. Also, some variations of well-known stories can be analyzed. For example, five versions of Cinderella are provided below.

 - Climo, S. *The Egyptian Cinderella.* New York: HarperCollins, 1989.
 - Huck, C. *Princess Furball.* New York: Greenwillow, 1989.
 - Martin, R. *The Rough-Face Girl.* New York: Putnam, 1992.
 - Steel, F.A. *Tattercoats,* New York: Bradbury, 1976.
 - Steptoe, J. *Mufaro's Beautiful Daughters.* New York: Lathrop, Lee & Shepárdi, 1993.

2. Use a visual representation of story structure to help students understand major story elements. Discuss them. Students should understand that the setting is the place or location of the story and the time (present, past, or future) when the story takes place. The characters are the people or animals that the story focuses on. There can be major or minor characters. The plot is the general plan of the story, which is composed of actions or episodes. The episodes lead to a climax, which is the high point of the story.

3. After the story elements have been presented and discussed, read a well-known story (for example, *The City Mouse and the Country Mouse* or *The Three Billy Goats Gruff*) and have students form small groups to construct a visual representation of the story. Have the various groups discuss their representations. Encourage the use of proper terminology (setting, character, episodes) presented earlier. Repeat this basic procedure with other stories. The use of key questions can be used to help students uncover the major story elements. See the following example.

?

Setting	Where does the story take place?
	When does the story take place?
	Does the action of this story occur in different places? If so, where?
Characters	Who are the people or animals in this story?
	Are some people more important than others? If so, which ones?
	What words does the author use to describe the characters or animals?
	What other words can also be used to describe the characters?
Plot	What happens in this story?
	What problems or difficulties are there?
	How are the problems or difficulties solved?
	In what order do the major events happen?
	Who or what started the events in the story?

Practice and Reinforcement Activities

1. Encourage parents to read to their children. Reading aloud often helps the listener to internalize the story structure. Discussions with the child can also help in developing a sense of story structure.

2. Provide many opportunities for students to hear and read many different kinds of literature. Discuss the major story elements with them. Storytelling can also be used.

3. When appropriate, have students role play or dramatize stories. If an entire story does not lend itself to dramatization, select one or more episodes and have several groups of students present scenes to the class.

4. Have students make drawings or illustrations of the major events in a story. These drawings can serve as a basis for retelling the story.

5. Retell a familiar story by changing certain key elements (settings, characters, and events). Then, have students correct the retelling. Depending on the students involved, you may want to change "obvious" characters, events, or settings. Later, brief written summaries of stories can be used. After students read the summaries, they correct the erroneous information. An excellent story of this type is *The True Story of the 3 Pigs by A. Wolf* (Scieszka, 1989).

6. Help students learn to use semantic webbing. According to Freeman and Reynolds (1980), semantic webbing contains the following elements:

- a core question—focus of the web, which is initially chosen by the teacher;
- web strands—answers that students give to the core questions;
- strand supports—facts, inferences, and generalizations that students give to differentiate one strand from another; and
- strand ties—the relationships that strands have with one another. As students become more comfortable with semantic webbing, they can show relationships among characters and events (adapted from Freeman & Reynolds, 1980) as is shown here.

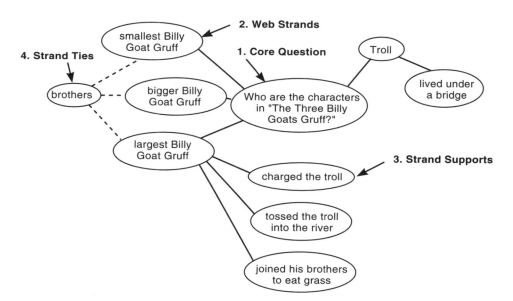

7. Semantic webbing is especially useful for helping students to identify story elements related to characters and events. Possible core questions of a generic nature are listed below.

Who are the characters?

What words describe the characters?

What are the major events?

What happens in each major event?

8. The example below, based on "Little Miss Muffet," may be used to help students visualize the major elements in the story. The terminology can be changed to match the words used in lessons. Acting out nursery rhymes with logical sequences can help students identify story elements. Change the order of events so students will see how the new order destroys the story line.

9. Have older students begin a story by writing the setting. Then have students exchange papers and write about characters. Repeat the process with problem/conflict and solution/resolution. Then return the story to the student who began it. After giving time for independent reading, invite students to share in small groups.

10. Write or dictate stories based on wordless picture books. A list of such books can be found in Appendix A.

Identifying Words

OVERVIEW

The ability to identify words is a foundation of the reading process (Stanovich, 1991). Although we realize that the meaning of text is much larger than the sum of the definitions of each word, it is important for students to have strategies to identify words.

There are several strategies readers use as they encounter words. One strategy is to read words by sight. That means that you see the word and pronounce it correctly. There are many words you read by sight—probably all of the words in this paragraph, in fact. You don't need to try to figure out the words because they belong to your lexicon of *sight words*. All proficient readers have a large number of words they can read by sight.

No reader knows all words by sight. As far as we know, no one knows all 600,000 words in the English language. When readers come to words they don't know by sight, they can figure out the words by one or more of these ways: by decoding, by analogy to known spelling patterns, by using context clues, by using structural analysis, and by using a dictionary.

When you come to a word you can't pronounce, you could try to figure it out initially by using the sounds symbolized by the letters or letter combinations and then blending those sounds together. For example, if you don't know the word *enigmatic,* you can give each letter one or more sounds from the variety of sounds the letters symbolize to decode the word, trying various pronunciations in an effort to have the word sound like one you have heard before.

Because English is not a highly phonetic language, not all words can be read using their letter sounds. The word *tough,* for example, cannot be read by its letter sounds. Many words that do not have phonetic spelling have syllables that can be read by analogy to a known spelling pattern. For example, students who have never seen the word *tough* can use what they know about the word part *ough* sound in the known word *rough* to figure out the word. Many words in text have at least one part that can be read by analogy.

Phonological recoding and analogy can give readers a good sense of an unfamiliar word; however, students need to test the words within the context of the text to see whether they make sense. If students use what they know about letter sounds and spelling patterns and the word makes sense in the context of the text, it is probably correct. Context can help students test words and it is also useful to assist students in identifying unknown words. Context clues, therefore, can be an additional way for students to identify words.

As you know, identifying words is only part of reading. We all have encountered students who can identify words without understanding them. That's because words are actually symbols for concepts. Words don't have a single meaning. They have a range of meanings that are unique to each individual. All of us, for example, have had experience with the word *picnic.* When you see that word, you may have a different picture in your mind than we do. You may picture an idyllic scene by a lake; someone else may picture eating fried chicken on a stoop of an apartment building. No one has the exact same concept of any word because all people's experiences are different.

This chapter is about identifying words using phonics, word patterns, structural analysis, sight, context, and the dictionary. Many sections in Chapter 2 contain ideas that will also be helpful in developing or strengthening students' word identification (see 2.5, 2.8, 2.9, and 2.10).

> Identifying words is only part of reading.

TECHNOLOGY RESOURCES

Blue Web'n: Blue Ribbon Learning Sites on the Web

http://www.kn.pacbell.com/wired/bluewebn/index.html
Contains Internet sites that link to lessons, resources, and activities

Teachers.Net Reading

http://www.teachers.net/cgi-bin/lessons/sort.cgi?searchterm=Reading
Contains reading lesson plans for a variety of reading skills and strategies

Stony Brook Reading and Language Project

http://www.read+lang.sbs.sunysb.edu/
Contains a project description, papers, and publications of the Stony Brook Reading and
Language Project

The Reading Wars

http://www.theatlantic.com/issues/97nov/read.html
Discusses the differences between the whole language approach and phonics approaches to
teaching reading

Phonics: Consonants

Behavior Observed	The student has difficulty associating the sounds that consonants symbolize.
Anticipated Outcome	The student will be able to use the sounds of consonants to phonologically recode unknown words.

BACKGROUND

The whole idea of phonics is to give students a means to associate sounds with letters and letter combinations so students can pronounce a word that is not known at sight. If the pronounciation can be related to a word in the student's experience, there is a connection with meaning. Phonics only helps students read (understand) words for which they already have meaning. For example, if the student sounds *yyy-eeeg* and says *yegg,* but has no meaning for the word, phonics is of little value. Fortunately, however, students have meanings for many words, and if they can decode a word, they are often able to associate meaning with the word, especially in the first few years of school.

Using phonics, or the sounds people assign to letters and letter combinations, is one way students can pronounce unfamiliar words. The value of phonics should not be underestimated. Phonics is one of the cueing systems readers use for words that are not in their sight vocabulary. Unfortunately, the teaching of phonics has been the topic of controversy for decades. An examination of the research literature concerning phonics instruction by the National Reading Panel (2000) led to the finding that "systematic phonics instruction enhances children's suc-

> The value of phonics should not be underestimated.

cess in learning to read and . . . is significantly more effective than instruction that teaches little or no phonics" (p. 9). It is our belief that phonics should be an important foundation of a quality reading program, and it should be taught as one of the strategies readers can use when they want to identify an unfamiliar word. In short, phonics is a vital component (along with context and structural analysis) of balanced word identification.

Although there are 26 letters (graphemes) in the English alphabet, there are (depending on the dialect) forty or more sounds (phonemes). Because the consonants are more regular than the vowels, they are often introduced first. For the 25 consonant sounds listed in the box (adapted from Gunning, 2000), begin teaching sounds that occur with the highest frequency and that are quite easy for students to say (e.g., sounds for *m, r,* and *s*).

The basic teaching strategies and practice and reinforcement activities used for initial consonants can be used with final consonants, consonant diagraphs (e.g., *ch, gh, kn, ph, sc, si, th, ti, wh, wr*), consonant blends in the initial position (e.g., *bl, cl, fl, gl, pl, sl, br, cr, dr, fr, sch, sm, sl*), and blends in the final position (e.g., *ld, lf, lk, nce, nk, nt*).

Letter-Sound Correspondences for Consonants

Sound (Phoneme)	Letter (Grapheme)	Initial	Final	Key Words
/b/	b, bb	barn	ebb, cab, robe	bell, ball
/d/	d, dd, ed	deer	bad	dog
/f/	f, ff, ph, lf	fun, photo	laugh	fish
/g/	g, gg, gh	gate, ghost, guide	rag	goat
/h/	h, wh	house, who		horse, hat
/hw/	wh	whale		whale
/j/	g, j, dg	jug, gym, soldier	age, judge	jar
/k/	k, lk, ck, q	can, kite, quick, chaos	back, ache	cat, key
/l/	l, ll	lion	mail	leaf
/m/	m, mm	me	him, comb, autumn	monkey, man
/n/	n, nn, kn, gn	now, know, gnu, pneumonia	pan	nest, nail
/p/	p, pp	pot	top	pencil, pen
/r/	r, rr, wr	ride, write		rabbit, ring
/s/	s, c, ss	sight, city	bus, miss, face	sun, Santa
/t/	t, tt, ed	time	rat, watt, jumped	table
/v/	v [f in of]	vase	love	valentine, vest
/w/	w	we, wheel		wagon
/y/	y, i	yacht, onion		yo-yo
/z/	z, zz	zipper	has, buzz	zebra
/ch/	ch	chip, cello, question	match	chair
/zh/	z, si	azure, version	beige, garage	garage
/th/	th	thin	breath	thumb
/th/	th	this	breathe	the
/sh/	sh, ti, ssi, s, si, sci	ship, sure, chef, action	push, special, mission	sheep
/ŋ/	n, ng		sing	ring

Section 3.1

STRATEGY 1 DIRECT PHONICS

1. Younger students may need to be told directly that letters have a name and that a sound can also be associated with the letter. Sometimes teachers say that letters make sounds, but that is not correct. Letters do not say anything; however, sounds can be associated with the letters. Begin by teaching letter-sound correspondences in the initial position of the word.

2. Print an uppercase and a lowercase *d* on the chalkboard and name words that begin with a *d*. Encourage students to think of names of children in the class or friends whose names begin with a *d*. Pictures and concrete objects can also be used.

3. Record the responses on the chalkboard as in this example:

D	d
Don	dad
Dave	duck
Donna	dog
Debbi	door
Dan	down
Dion	deer

4. Ask the students to examine each list and note similarities and differences between the words. As the discussion continues, develop the concept that the *d* represents the same sound at the beginning of each word listed on the chalkboard. Be direct in connecting a sound with the letter.

5. Say each word on the list while you move your hand under the word. Emphasize the *d* sound distinctly so the students can hear it. Have students pronounce each word after you. Help students see that all the words begin with the same letter and that the letter *d* stands for the sound *ddd* heard at the beginning of each word.

6. Ask the students to think of other words that begin with the sound associated with *d*. Add these words to the list.

7. Conclude the lesson by asking students to listen while you say some words. If a word begins with the sound associated with *d*, have them raise their hand. If the word begins with a different sound, they should not raise their hand. Use words from the list on the chalkboard as well as new words (for instance, *Dave, Tom, door, Marie, zoo, down*).

8. Refer to the Practice and Reinforcement Activities for additional ideas.

Section 3.1

STRATEGY 2 EAR TO EYE PHONICS

1. Say five or six words and have students listen carefully to hear how each word begins. When you say the sounds, elongate but do not separate the sound associated with the initial consonant, for example, *bbball, bbbat,* and *bbboy.*

2. Ask the students what they noticed about the beginning sounds of all the words that you pronounced. The expected response is that they all begin with the same sound.

3. Encourage students to give other words with the same sound that is heard at the beginning of *ball, bat,* and *boy.*

4. To provide auditory training, say three words (two that have the same beginning sound and one that is different) and have students say the words that begin alike. Elongate the initial consonant sound in each word. Repeat this procedure several times. Pictures and concrete objects can also be used (box, bear, badge, banana, balloon, beaver). The purpose of this activity is to provide ear training.

5. Place the letter *b* on the chalkboard and make a list of words that begin with *b*. Encourage students to suggest additional words. Explore what all the words have in common. Guide students to realize that words all begin alike when you see them and sound alike at the beginning when you hear them.

6. Use a picture or concrete object to help students associate the sound with the letter. Sometimes the pictures can be put together or arranged to make the shape of the letter that is associated with a particular sound being learned, as shown below.

Section 3.1

STRATEGY 3 USING ALPHABET BOOKS

1. Secure an alphabet book. Various publishers have colorful, small books for each letter of the alphabet. Appendix B contains a listing of alphabet books that may be useful. Choose the page dealing with the consonant being taught (for example, *t*).

2. Read the *T* page aloud: "Tiny Tom told Tim to take a toy." Tell students that many of the words begin the same way. Then read the page again pointing to each word that begins with *t*.

3. Help students realize that *t* spells the sound heard at the beginning of almost all the words.

4. Secure another alphabet book and read the sentence. Invite students to help identify the *t* words. Relate the words in the two books by writing them on the chalkboard or a poster. Then show students that the words begin with *t* and have the *ttt* sound.

5. Invite students to practice by providing cards with words from the alphabet books as well as new words (for example *tag*). Show the word, cover the *t*, point to the remaining part of the word, and say, "This part of the word says *ag*. Now I'll uncover the *t*. What is the word? Guide students as needed and provide additional practice using words such as those below.

tail	tall	take	talk
tape	tank	team	ten
tent	tooth	tongue	toot

Refer to the pictures in the alphabet books whenever possible to keep the focus on the word's meaning. In addition, use students' names to help practice the letter-sound relationship.

STRATEGY 4 USING WHOLE TEXT

1. Read a story to the class that has words with the consonant sound you wish to emphasize.

2. Write several sentences from the story on sentence strips.

3. Read the sentences to the class and have students echo read each sentence after you.

4. Point to the target words and ask the students to read them after you.

5. Ask students to identify the letters in the target words. Then ask them which sound is the same in each word. Have the students make the sound with you.

6. Reread the sentences emphasizing the targeted sound.

7. Encourage the students to read the sentences and to use the letter sound in their writing.

Practice and Reinforcement Activities

The following activities are exemplified with the letter *d* but can be adapted to other consonants.

1. Have students look through magazines and stories to find pictures that can be associated with the sound *d*. The pictures can be arranged on a bulletin board or on individual letter sheets. Include the capital and lowercase letters on the display.

2. Use oral sentences where the missing word begins with the letter-sound association being learned. After students share responses that might make sense, have them choose the words that make sense and begin with the correct sound. For *d,* possible sentences might include

My _____ loves me. (dad)

I gave my _____ a bone. (dog)

I saw a _____ at the farm. (duck, dog)

The toy cost me a _____. (dime, dollar)

3. Provide a group of pictures and have students take turns sorting those whose names begin with the sound being studied. Pictures can also be sorted according to whether the sound at the beginning, middle, or end of the words is different or the same.

4. Have students bring in objects whose names begin with the sound being studied.

5. Place pictures and/or objects in a box. Some of the items should begin with the sound being studied; a few should not. Have a student reach into the box, take out an item, name it, and indicate whether the initial sound of the object is the same as or different from the sound being studied. Then have the student use the word in a sentence.

6. List words on the chalkboard that begin with consonants not being studied which can be erased and replaced with the consonant that is being practiced. Have a student pronounce the word. Then erase the first letter of the word and put a *d* in its place to make a new word. Have students use their knowledge of the letter-sound association for *d* to pronounce the new word. Repeat this procedure with each

of the other words listed here. Have students use the new words in sentences. Resources for Chapter 3 include a list of pattern words that should be helpful for this activity.

hot	dot
tip	dip
tog	dog
sent	dent
pig	dig
kid	did
him	dim

7. When students are reading and come across an unfamiliar word that contains the letter being studied, encourage them to use the context along with their knowledge of the letter sound to pronounce the word.

8. Orally read sentences where students give a word beginning with the sound being learned. The word must make sense in the sentence. Some examples follow.

Jim's pet is a _____. (dog)

Another name for a plate is a _____. (dish)

At night it is _____. (dark)

It's about time to eat _____. (dinner)

9. Have students name objects in the classroom that begin with the sound associated with the letter being learned. A variation is to have students find objects in the classroom with the same beginning sounds as their names.

10. Read words that begin with different sounds on a tape recorder. Play the tape for the students asking them to stand up if they hear a word that begins with the letter *d*.

11. Place 10 or more word cards in a pocket chart each beginning with a different sound. Ask a student to think of another word that begins with one of the beginning sounds of the words. For example, if one of the word cards contained *little,* the student might say the word *like.* Play until all 10 sounds are used. The meanings of the words in the pocket chart should be known to students.

12. Use the sounds of consonants during your regular school routine. For example, when the class is dismissed for the day, ask students whose last names begin with *D* to leave first.

13. Have teams of students create tongue twisters with the letter *d*. For example, a sample sentence might be: Dan drove to the downtown Dairy Dream for diet drinks.

14. Have students think of words beginning with the letter *d*. Students take turns saying a new word without repeating any words. When a student is unable to add a new word, ask another student to suggest one.

15. Place pictures in an envelope and have students sort the pictures according to initial, medial, or final sound.

16. Prepare a list of sentences that have a missing word. Sketch or cut out pictures that complete each sentence. Put them on cards and ask students to select the appropriate card or cards to complete each sentence that begins with a particular sound.

I saw a _____.

17. Connect an action with each consonant sound. For example, when you teach the sound *d,* ask the students to dance. You can make a game of this activity after you have taught several of the letter sounds. Make a card with each letter. Show one letter to the class and call on a student to show the class the action you learned for that letter. Examples of actions for consonants, digraphs, and blends follow (Cunningham, 1993).

b	bounce	t	talk	fl	fly
c	catch	v	vacuum	fr	frown
d	dance	w	wiggle	gr	grab
f	fall	y	yawn	pl	plant
g	gallop	z	zip	sw	swim
h	hop	ch	cheer	sk	skip
j	jump	sh	shiver	sl	sleep
k	kick	th	think	sm	smile
l	laugh	wh	whistle	sp	spin
m	march	br	breathe	st	stand
n	nod	bl	blink	tr	track
p	paint	cr	crawl	tw	twist
r	run	cl	climb		
s	sit	dr	drive		

18. When students have learned several consonant sounds, provide sentences or stories with a word missing and invite students to use the context and their knowledge of certain sounds to predict the word. For example, We ran ____ the stairs. Remind students that the word begins with the sound that begins like *dog.* If a word is given that makes sense but does not begin with *d* (for example, up) discuss why it is not the right answer. Invite students to share their thinking about particular responses and guide them as necessary.

Games

Pick Up. Give the student 10 cards with a different consonant on each card. Lay out 10 cards on the table. As you read a list of words, ask the student to pick up the card corresponding to the initial, medial, or final sound of the word.

Consonant Rummy. Use a deck of cards with a consonant on each one. Each player is dealt eight cards. The first player asks another player for the consonant that begins a certain word. For example, "I'd like Jen to give me a letter that begins the word down." If the player does not have the letter d, the caller picks a card from the deck and the next student takes a turn. The first student to have four cards of the same letter is the winner.

Phonics: Vowels

SECTION
3.2

Behavior Observed	The student has difficulty associating the sounds that vowels symbolize.
Anticipated Outcome	The student will be able to use the sounds of vowels to help decode unknown words.

BACKGROUND

Vowels are much more difficult for students to learn than consonants. Unlike most consonants, vowels can represent more than one sound. Most vowels have two or three common sounds, but there are also many exceptions for certain vowels. For example, the long *e* sound can be spelled 16 different ways: *see, team, equal, he, key, Caesar, deceive, receipt, people, demesne, machine, field, debris, amoeba, quay,* and *pity* (May, 1990). Although it is not necessary to teach students rules for each of these vowel sounds, there are some vowel generalizations that can help students as they learn to decode words.

Beginning readers need to begin to learn the sounds for long and short vowels, and as students progress in reading, they can also learn about some of the less frequently occurring vowel sounds in the English language. As you teach your students vowel sounds, however, you need to remember that having students learn the sounds of vowels is not useful in itself. The purpose of teaching vowel sounds is for students to be able to make better predictions about unfamiliar words. If you find that you are spending more time teaching the sounds associated with the letters than your students spend reading text, you should probably balance the proportion of time you are spending teaching phonics with opportunities for students to read printed materials.

Teaching the various sounds of the vowels will probably span at least two grade levels. Generally, "short" vowels are taught first because they have fewer spellings. Some "long" vowels, however, are quite easy to learn, especially when they are the final letter in two-letter words (e.g., *me, he, we*). Even though vowels can be taught in a manner similar to consonants (see 3.1), we have provided teaching strategies for two different vowels.

Teachers need to balance time spent teaching letter sounds with the time students spend reading.

The following are some of the sounds associated with vowels.

		Vowel Digraphs	
a as in *age*	*oi* as in *oil*	*ee, ea*	*e* as in *ease*
a as in *an*	*ou* as in *out*	*ai, ay*	*a* as in *age*
e as in *ease*	*oo* as in *too*	*oa, ow*	*o* as in *old*
e as in *end*	*oo* as in *good*	*oo*	*oo* as in *too*
i as in *ice*	*a* as in *dare*	*oo*	*oo* as in *good*
i as in *inch*	*u* as in *her*	*ou, ow*	*ou* as in *out*
o as in *old*	*a* as in *about*	*oi*	*oi* as in *oil*
o as in *odd*	*a* as in *father*	*au*	*o* as in *off*
u as in *use*	*o* as in *off*		
u as in *up*			

Section 3.2

STRATEGY 1 SHORT i

1. Students may need to be reminded that there are vowels and consonants and that sounds can be associated with both vowels and consonants.

2. Write the vowels on the chalkboard and circle the vowel that will be the focus of the lesson. Tell the students that there are two common sounds (long and short) associated with *i* and that they will be taught to associate the short sound with *i*.

3. If possible, select some objects and pictures whose names exemplify the short sound associated with *i* (for example, baseball *mitt,* fish's *fin,* jar *lid*). Appropriate names of class members may also be used (for example, *Bill, Jill*). Say the words and have students listen for the sound of the vowel.

4. Place the words on the chalkboard in a single column. Point to each word and pronounce it, emphasizing the sound associated with *i.* Have the students say each word as you move your hand from left to right under the word.

5. Ask the students to inspect the words and note their similarities and differences. When students note that all the words have an *i,* emphasize that the sound associated with this letter is called the short sound of *i.*

6. Then pronounce pairs of words orally (one containing the short sound of *i*) and have students identify the word containing the short *i.* By using some words with the long sound of *i,* students should be able to note how this sound differs from the short sound of *i.* An alternative is to pronounce a word and have students show a card with a short *i* if the word contains that sound. Some possible words follow.

fit–fat	ham–him
line–lit	dig–dog
rid–ride	mitt–met
rim–ram	jam–Jim

7. Encourage students to think of additional words with the short *i* vowel sound. List those words on the chalkboard. Have students use the words in sentences.

8. If desired, help students understand the generalization that the vowel *i* in the middle of a word and surrounded by consonants usually has a short sound. This generalization can also be applied to other vowels in a similar position.

9. After the students have learned the vowel sounds, develop word wheels where the various words can be made by turning the wheel. Possible words for this activity can be found in Resources for Chapter 4.

| Top | Bottom | Pieces Together | Another Example |

STRATEGY 2 LONG e

1. Tell students that you will help them learn the long sound for *e*. Print *e* on the chalkboard and ask students to tell you the name of the letter.

2. Help students realize that the name of the letter and the long sound are the same. You might say,

 Notice that the name of the letter and the long sound of the vowel are the same.

 Have the students say the sound together.

3. Then say, "Watch as I put a letter in front of the e and make a word." Print an *m* and say, "I know the sound *mmm* and when I put it with the *e* it makes *me*." Have the students repeat the sounds and make the word by blending the sounds.

4. Guide students in creating other words that end with *e* (*be, he, we*).

Practice and Reinforcement Activities

1. Provide cards with the vowel, a key word for that vowel, and a picture for that word. For example, you may want to remember the sound for *i* with the word *twins*. The card should have a picture of twins with the word and the letter.

2. Place on the chalkboard a column of words that contain the short vowel sounds. Show students that adding a final *e* to the words often changes the vowel sound from short to long. Begin a second column where an *e* is added to each word. Have a student pronounce these words and use each of them in a sentence. Emphasize the change in vowel sound when the final *e* is added. Sample words are shown below.

can	cane	bit	bite
man	mane	hop	hope
tub	tube	cut	cute
hid	hide	not	note
rid	ride	mad	made
rob	robe	kit	kite

3. Have students read a short passage and circle words with long vowel sounds. Then copy the words on a separate sheet of paper in an attempt to categorize them. Each category should then be labeled with a description of what the long-vowel words have in common.

4. Create cards that have long vowel sounds, short vowel sounds, and r-controlled vowel sounds. Have students sort each card into the categories by vowel sounds.

5. Teach students the importance of vowels by placing the cards with the consonants on a table. Ask a volunteer to make a word with the letter cards. The students should quickly see that it is impossible to write words without vowels. Then include vowel cards and ask the students to make words (DeGenaro, 1993).

6. Write basic sight words using two colors of crayons—one color for vowels and another color for consonants.

7. Provide students with letter tiles and have them engage in word-building activities. Fox (1996) provides many helpful suggestions for word building.

8. Use Venn diagrams, such as those below, to help students explore letters that represent more than one sound in words.

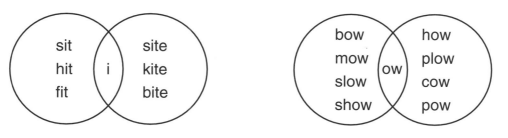

9. Help students experience printed materials that contain specific phonic elements or rhymes. If some of the books are too difficult for independent reading, they can be shared aloud and discussed. Some books that contain phonic elements or rhymes follow.

Oppenheim, J. (1990). *Wake, Up Baby!* New York: Bantam. (long *a*)

Ziefert, H. (1990). *Follow Me!* New York: Puffin. (long *e*)

Hoff, S. (1988). *Mrs. Brice's Mice.* New York: Harper. (long *i*)

Schade, S. (1992). *Toad on the Road.* New York: Random House. (long *o*)

Demarest, C. (1998). *Farmer Nat.* San Diego: Red Wagon/Harcourt. (rhyme)

Hague, K. (1999). *Ten Little Bears: A Counting Rhyme.* New York: Morrow. (rhyme)

10. Provide letter tiles and encourage students to build words with onsets and rimes. Letters can be written on bathroom tiles (1") with a permanent marker. Velcro can be attached to a small plywood board. After using the letter tiles, they can be secured on the plywood board for easy storage.

11. Encourage students to write sentences with rhymes being learned.

12. Use books that contain patterns being studied. In addition, some of the older linguistic readers (The cat sat on a mat, etc.) could be used for practice with certain onsets and rimes.

13. Use pocket charts so students can manipulate various letters to create words.

Game

Tic-Tac-Toe. Prepare cards that have the vowel sounds you have taught. For example, perhaps you have taught long *i*, long *a*, long *e*, and short *i*. Each student should select a card. On the tic-tac-toe board, students should write a word with the vowel on the card that was selected.

SECTION

3.3 Word Patterns and Word Building

Behavior Observed	The student is unable to use knowledge about word patterns to identify unfamiliar words.
Anticipated Outcome	The student will be able to identify unfamiliar words by using common word patterns.

BACKGROUND

Proficient readers rarely sound out words letter by letter. Instead, they use what they know about common spelling patterns to figure out the word. This means that readers will make the association between spelling patterns they know and unfamiliar words. For example, if students encounter the word *hobbit* in reading, they may know that the word pattern *ob* may sound like *rob* or *mob* and that the pattern *it* may sound like *mit* or *bit*. Using what they know about consonant sounds, then, students can figure out a word that they do not know by sight.

Using word patterns is another strategy that students should use as they read. Like phonics and context clues, using word patterns is not a panacea; not all unfamiliar words will have familiar word patterns in them. For instructional purposes, however, you should help your students use this strategy as one more way to read unfamiliar words.

A word pattern has two components: an onset and a rime (Adams, 1990a).

- The onset is the initial part of a word that precedes a vowel (for example, the *h* in *hat* or the *sh* in *ship*).
- The rime is the part of the word that rhymes (for example, the *at* in *hat* or the *ip* in *ship*).

Rimes are also known as word families or phonograms. A list of word patterns is included in the Resources for Chapter 3. The list will be helpful for teaching.

An innovative developmental approach that helps students explore letter patterns, letter-sound correspondences, and words has been developed by Cunningham and Cunningham (1992). The approach involves students in making words, and over 300 lessons have been developed for students in the elementary school (Cunningham & Hall, 1994a, 1994b, 1997). The steps for making word lessons are shown on the next page (adapted from Cunningham and Cunningham, 1992).

Planning Lessons to Make Words

1. Choose the word that will be made last in the lesson (for example, *stand*). Consider your students' interests and word knowledge when selecting words.
2. Make a list of other words that can be made from *stand* (*at, sat, as, Stan, Dan, tan, Tad, an, and, sand*). From these words, arrange the words in order from the shortest to the longest.
3. Decide on the words you will use based on patterns, words of various sizes, words that can be made by rearranging the letters (for example, *and, Dan*), and proper names to show the use of capital letters. When making your final selections, keep in mind that most students should have *heard* the words and know what they mean.
4. Make big letter cards to use in a pocket chart or on the ledge of the chalkboard. Then prepare an envelope that contains the order of the words and the patterns that will be stressed. Finally, print the words on cards.

Section 3.3

STRATEGY 1 MAKING WORDS

1. Use the above box to plan the lesson or consult Cunningham and Hall (1994a, 1994b, 1997) for ready-made lessons. Distribute the necessary letters to each student. Keep the letters in reclosable bags and have individual students pass out the different letters. Each card should contain an uppercase letter on one side and a lowercase letter on the other. At the end of the lesson, the same students pick up the letters they originally distributed. Finally, you should have large letter cards that you can use with a pocket chart or on the chalkboard ledge to model as necessary. Below is a sample lesson.

2. Have the letters (a, d, n, s, t) distributed. If necessary, hold up the large letter cards and have students hold up their small letter cards that match your card.

3. Say, "Use two letters to make *at*." Use the word in a sentence.

4. Invite a student to assemble the correct response using the large letter cards in the pocket chart or on the chalkboard ledge. Have the student read the word and have students correct their individual responses as necessary. Students should be able to fix their word by comparing their word to the large letter cards.

5. Continue steps 3 and 4 with other word-making directions such as those shown below.

 - Add a letter to make *sat*.
 - Remove a letter to make *at*.
 - Change a letter to make *an*.
 - Add a letter to make *tan*.
 - Add a letter to make *Stan*.
 - See what word you can make with all the letters (*stand*).

6. When all the words have been made, take words you previously printed on index cards and put them in the pocket chart or on the ledge of the chalkboard. Keep these guidelines in mind.

 - Do one word at a time.
 - Present the words in the order they were made.
 - Have students say and spell the words with you.

- Use the words for sorting and pointing out patterns (for example, find the word that has the same pattern as *tan*). Align the words so students can see the patterns.
- Transfer word learning to writing by asking students to spell a few of the words you say.

7. Remember that word building can be used with upper-grade students and students of all ages who are struggling with reading (Cunningham & Hall, 1994a).

8. Consider using the following book to introduce making words. Falwell, C. (1998). *Word Wizard*. New York: Clarion.

Section 3.3

STRATEGY 2 PHONOGRAM -ay

1. Write the word *day* on the chalkboard or on a sentence strip.

2. Read the word to the students drawing attention to the *-ay* sound.

3. Substitute a different initial consonant such as *m* for *may*. Say, if d-a-y spells *day*, what do you think m-a-y spells? Repeat this activity with three or four different consonants. Write each word on the chalkboard or a sentence strip.

4. Ask the students to say each of the words. Although this may seem like an easy activity, many young students have difficulty reading rhyming words.

5. Write a sentence for each word or have students write sentences for the words. Ask students to read the sentences aloud paying close attention to the word pattern that is being studied.

6. For students who are able to progress to the next step, write an unfamiliar word on the chalkboard that contains the word pattern. An example for *-ay* may be to*day* or *may*be.

Section 3.3

STRATEGY 3 PHONOGRAM -ill

1. Write *-ill* on the chalkboard and ask students what letter would need to be added to *ill* to make the word *hill*.

2. Add the *h* to *ill*, pronounce the sounds, and then blend the sounds as you say the whole word. Have students repeat the blending.

3. Then write *ill* underneath *hill* and ask students what letter should be added to *ill* to make the word *Bill*. Ask a student to blend the sounds to form the word.

4. Invite students to examine the two words and note how they are the same and how they are different. Guide students to understand that the words end with the letters *i, l, l* which make the sounds heard in *ill*; the words are different in the initial sounds and that accounts for the two different words.

5. Continue with other examples and model words like *Jill* and *fill*. Invite students to suggest other onsets that could be used to make a new word.

6. Use the words in oral sentences and written sentences and possibly create stories. Some examples follow.

Jill climbed a hill. She looked for Bill. She saw Bill fill a bucket.

Structural Analysis

Behavior Observed	The student is unable to use word structure to help decode unfamiliar words.
Anticipated Outcome	The student will use word structure to help decode unfamiliar words.

BACKGROUND

When students come to an unknown word that is made up of more than one syllable, they can use structural analysis skills to divide that word into pronounceable units. Structural analysis skills can allow students to focus on the larger units of letter patterns within words. Such skills typically include inflectional endings, prefixes, suffixes, contractions, compound words, and syllabication. You can teach students how to figure out longer words by using background knowledge students have about words and word parts, focusing on that knowledge, applying what students know to a new reading situation, and extending what students already know by imparting additional knowledge about words.

Section 3.4

STRATEGY 1 INFLECTIONAL ENDINGS FOR YOUNGER STUDENTS

1. For younger students, draw one of the four figures on the chalkboard without the tail. Print the word inside the figure and have students pronounce it. Then ask students to look at the figure and tell you what is missing (the tail).

2. Tell students the missing tail contains an ending that can be put on the word. Draw the tail and put one of the endings in it. Have a student pronounce the new word. Ask another student to use the word in a sentence. Then write the word on the chalkboard.

3. Repeat the process with the other endings. Be sure to write the new words under one another as in the example below.

jumps

jumping

jumped

4. Draw students' attention to what is the same (*jump*) and different (the ending) in the words. Help students realize that some words have endings. Have students apply this knowledge to a known word with different endings in sentences. Provide some sentences and invite students to locate the common root word in the sentences. See the following examples.

I want some food.	They were playing ball.
She wants to play.	He played a board game.
He wanted to go home.	She plays with her friend.

5. Use some of the other illustrations for additional practice or independent activities. Encourage students to try some different endings or common words to build new words. Use words that do not involve spelling changes. Some examples follow.

look	walk	bark	work
play	talk	laugh	record
pack	fill	help	end

6. Conclude the lesson by reminding students that some words have endings. By covering the ending, they may recognize the root word. Then they can add the ending and pronounce the word.

Section 3.4

STRATEGY 2 INFLECTIONAL ENDINGS

1. Tell students that inflectional endings are the endings that can form a plural noun (dogs, quizzes), show the present tense of a verb (barks, wishes), are the present participle of a verb (walking), show past tense (talked), show possession (Jerry's), and show comparisons in adjectives and adverbs (bigger, biggest).

2. Present a root word that your students know from previous lessons. Write the word on a sentence strip or on the chalkboard. Have the students pronounce the word and use it in a sentence.

3. Then have the students watch carefully while you add an ending to the word. Have different students pronounce each derived word. If a student makes an error, cover the ending and have the student pronounce the root word. Then have the student try the changed word again.

4. Once the words are pronounced correctly, have students use each new word in a sentence. Discuss the change in meaning that occurred when the ending was added. Students should understand that adding an ending to words may change the way the word is used in a sentence.

5. Conclude the lesson by helping students realize that some long words are really root words with inflected endings added. Encourage them to look for such endings when they are unable to pronounce a word at sight.

STRATEGY 3

THE NIFTY THRIFTY FIFTY*

1. The Nifty Thrifty Fifty (Cunningham, 2000, p. 165) is a list of 50 words containing "all the most useful prefixes, suffixes, and spelling changes" that should be understood by most fourth graders. Helping students learn to spell and build words using the affixes and spelling changes will require sustained instruction throughout the school year. Your efforts will be rewarded by students who gain confidence in decoding longer words. The 50 words can be found on pages 564–565.

2. Teach students to spell the words gradually over time and look for ways in daily instruction to share how the words can help students decode other words. Begin by explaining that many big words are smaller words with prefixes and suffixes added to them. Choose 5 or 6 words from The Nifty Thrifty Fifty to teach. Write them on the chalkboard or an overhead transparency.

3. Chant each word several times. Then help students analyze the words by noting prefixes, suffixes, and any spelling changes. Word meanings should also be discussed. For example, you might model by saying the following:

 > Dishonest *means not honest. The root word is* honest *and the prefix is* dis. *In many words, the prefix* dis *changes the word to an opposite. An example of another word using* dis *is* disobey.

4. Invite students to suggest other words with the same prefix. Some possible words are presented below.

discourage	disappear	disjointed
disengage	disadvantage	disagree
disappoint	disapprove	disarm
disarmament	disarray	disassemble
disband	disbelief	disclaim
disclose	discolor	discomfort
discompose	disconnect	discontinue
discredit	disappear	

5. Use a similar procedure for the other words in the lesson and then have students write each of the 5 or 6 words you have presented. Give clues to the word to be written. Several examples are provided below using words from The Nifty Thrifty Fifty.

dishonest	For number 1, write the word that is the opposite of honest.
employee	Number 2 could be used to describe someone who works for a business owner.
swimming	Number 3 is an activity that takes place in a lake.

6. Have students check their work by "once more chanting the letters aloud, underlining each as they say it" (Cunningham, 2000, p. 169).

7. Teach another 5 or 6 words the next week and then show students how parts of the words can be combined to spell other words. In addition, because the same word parts can be found in different words, the parts can be used to help pronounce many long words. You might use a think aloud like the following:

*Cunningham, 2000.

I know the word dishonest. *If I see the word* displease *(write it on the chalkboard) in my reading, I can remove the* dis *and then see the word* please. *I can then put the two parts together to pronounce the word. If I look for patterns or chunks in the big words in my reading, I can probably use what I know to help pronounce words.*

8. The Nifty Thrifty Fifty list can be found in the Resources for Chapter 3. Lessons based on this list can be found in Cunningham and Hall (1998).

Section 3.4

STRATEGY 4 AFFIXES

1. Affixes are prefixes and suffixes that are attached to a base word. Resources for Chapter 5 contain prefixes and suffixes that can be used for teaching and practice.

2. Explain to students that prefixes and suffixes form syllables because they are a pronunciation unit. They can be added to root words to change their meanings or part of speech. Provide examples.

 reread *re* is a prefix; *read* is a root word
 painless *pain* is a root word; *less* is a suffix

3. Have students supply some words that contain affixes. Write them on the chalkboard. Then ask students how they think knowing prefixes and suffixes can help them in reading. Through discussion, lead students to the following conclusions about prefixes and suffixes:

 - Knowing them can help me recognize words more rapidly; I don't have to sound out an unknown word letter by letter.
 - They can help me figure out some of the longer words in reading.
 - Sometimes I can use affixes to help determine the meaning of the word.

4. Model how to figure out unfamiliar words with prefixes and suffixes. Think aloud as you read. For example, if the word is *unicycle*, the following might be shared.

 I can't recognize the word immediately, so I look for the root word. It is cycle, *and I know what a cycle is. I can see that the prefix is* uni-. *I know that the word is* unicycle, *but what does it mean? Because I know that* uni- *often means one, I have a pretty good idea that unicycle means a one-wheeled cycle. I may need to look up the word in a dictionary to be sure of its meaning, but I now have an idea of the word and can ask myself whether the meaning makes sense in the sentence.*

Section 3.4

STRATEGY 5 CONTRACTIONS

1. Tell students that some words in our language, called contractions, are really two words joined together so that not all of the sounds are heard. Give students an example of a contraction such as *didn't*. Explain that *didn't* is a contraction for *did not*.

2. Show students how to write the contraction *didn't* by writing both *did* and *not* on the chalkboard. Explain that when forming a contraction the letters that are not written are replaced by an apostrophe. Show the students how to write an apostrophe in the word *didn't*.

3. Have the students write a sentence that uses *did not*. Then ask them to replace *did not* with the contraction *didn't*.

4. Repeat these steps with other contractions that are found in the Resources for Chapter 3.

STRATEGY 6 COMPOUND WORDS

1. Explain to students that two words are sometimes put together to make a longer word. These words are called *compound words*.

2. Write several compound words on sentence strips. Ask students to pronounce the words and to use each one in a sentence. Write the sentences on strips and find the two words that make up each compound word.

3. Stress that looking for compound words in longer words may help students pronounce such words. Make it clear that some seemingly difficult words are actually compound words.

4. Provide sentences and help students identify the compound word and the two words that compose it. Sample sentences follow.

 I saw a footprint in the snow.
 There was an earthquake in California.
 Please put the dishes in the dishwasher.

5. Conclude the lesson by helping students realize that they can sometimes recognize a longer word by identifying the two words that comprise it.

6. Repeat these steps with other compound words that are found in the Resources for Chapter 3.

STRATEGY 7 DECODING POLYSYLLABIC WORDS

1. Help students realize how you might go about decoding polysyllabic words by modeling: show and talk about what you do.

2. Select a word and write it on the chalkboard or an overhead transparency. Be sure that the word is presented in a sentence. An example follows.

 Her *unexpected* arrival caused a change in our plans.

3. Model by saying something like the following:

 I'm going to tell you how I might say or decode the word in italics. I will think aloud to help you understand what's going on in my brain. If you already know the word, please don't say anything. In a few minutes, I'll give you a chance to model what you do when you come across a polysyllabic word that you can't pronounce.

4. Read the sentence aloud, skipping over the unknown word. Then say

 I've read the entire sentence and skipped the word I don't know. I think I'll look for parts I know. The first part is the prefix un. *The next part is the word* expect *and there is an* ed *at the end. The word has three parts:* un-expect-ed. *The* un *is like the begin-*

ning of uncover *and the* ed *is like the end of* wanted. *I can put the parts together and get* un-expect-ed. *I have heard that word before. In the sentence it makes sense. Her arrival was not expected and plans were changed.*

5. Present sentences to students that contain one or more polysyllabic words. Ask students to select a partner and think aloud while trying to pronounce the italicized words. Stress that it is best to think aloud only for words that cannot already be pronounced. Develop sentences based on what you know about your students. Several of the following sentences might be used or adapted.

> The *seaport* is now *unimportant*, and it is used for *recreational purposes*.
> Can you name some *important* products that are *exported* from the *shipyard?*
> The *manager* of the *convenience* store *expressed* his *appreciation* for my *assistance*.
> I *corrected* the *subtraction problem* in *mathematics*.
> The *unfriendly canine barked loudly* at the *mail carrier*.

6. Have students volunteer to share some of their think alouds. For any words that students are unable to decode, model the process for them.

7. Gather additional polysyllabic words and devote a few minutes to modeling think alouds from time to time. Invite students to share polysyllabic words from their reading and explain how they were able to pronounce them.

Section 3.4

STRATEGY 8 SYLLABICATION

1. Tell students that long words can be divided into smaller sections or syllables. By knowing how to divide words into syllables, students can have another strategy to figure out words as they read.

2. Say a multisyllabic word such as *bicycle*. Have the students say *bicycle* several times.

3. Tell students that you will clap your hands one time for each syllable in the word *bicycle*. As you say the word, clapping for each syllable, stretch out the word such as *bi—cy—cle*.

4. Say several more words that have more than one syllable, clapping one time for each syllable. Have students clap with you.

5. Explain that there are generalizations for the ways words are divided into syllables. Spend time teaching the syllables in words that follow the syllable generalizations in the box below.

Syllable Generalizations*

1. When there are two like consonants, divide between them as in *pup/py*.
2. When there are two unlike consonants, divide between them as in *wal/rus*.
3. When a consonant is between two vowels, divide after the first vowel as in *si/lent*.
4. Prefixes, suffixes, and inflectional endings are their own syllables as in *pre/heat*.
5. When a syllable ends in a vowel, the vowel is long as in *o/pen*.
6. When a syllable ends in a consonant, the vowel is short as in *cab/in*.

*McCormick, 1999.

Practice and Reinforcement Activities

1. Provide sentences containing root words that have the inflected ending omitted. Students read each sentence and add the appropriate ending. Consider the following examples.

Bill was look _____ for his mother.

The cat jump _____ over the branch.

I miss _____ the school bus.

2. Prepare one set of cards that has root words and another set that contains different inflected endings (such as *s, ed, ing, er, est*). The root words for this activity should be the type that remains unchanged when an inflected ending is added. Students draw a card from each set and try to match the root-word card with an inflected-ending card to make a new word. Have students write the new words formed and use them in a sentence. Possible root words for this activity are listed below.

ask	play	warm
call	thank	deep
help	new	hard
jump	small	

3. Ask the students to circle the inflected endings in one of their pieces of writing. After finding endings in their own writing, they may want to read a story written by a classmate and find endings in a classmate's writing.

4. Write two columns of root words on the chalkboard, one that requires no change in spelling before adding an *ed*, and the other that requires doubling the final consonant before the *ed* is added. Try to use words that are in the students' sight vocabularies. Pronounce the words in the first group, add *ed* to the words, and have the students pronounce the new words. If students have difficulty, cover the ending, have them pronounce the root word, and then try the word with the *ed*. Ask students to use the words in sentences before and after adding *ed*.

5. Invite students to bring personal possessions to the front of the classroom. Tell students that they will be learning different ways of saying the same thing. For example, take Annette's barrette and say the following sentences.

This is the barrette of Annette.

The barrette belongs to Annette.

This is Annette's barrette.

Emphasize that each of the sentences means the same thing. Then write the sentences on sentence strips and direct the attention of the students to the last sentence. Identify the apostrophe and say that the *'s* on the end of the word Annette shows that the noun following her name belongs to her. Encourage the class to suggest phrases or sentences in which *'s* is used to show possession. Write the sentences on sentence strips.

6. Print prefixes and suffixes on tagboard or file cards. Pass out the cards to students. Write root words on sentence strips. Hold one root word card in front of the class. A student who has a prefix or suffix that would make a new word comes up to the front of the class and places the card in front of or behind the root word card. The student pronounces the word, and, if correct, the student may take the root word. Invite students to use the word in a sentence and, if necessary, have them discuss the meaning of the word.

7. As you introduce a new suffix, prepare several flip strips. To create a flip strip, print root words on the front left-hand side of colored strips of construction paper. On the back, print suffixes so that when the paper is folded a new word appears. Give the flip strips to students to practice making words with suffixes.

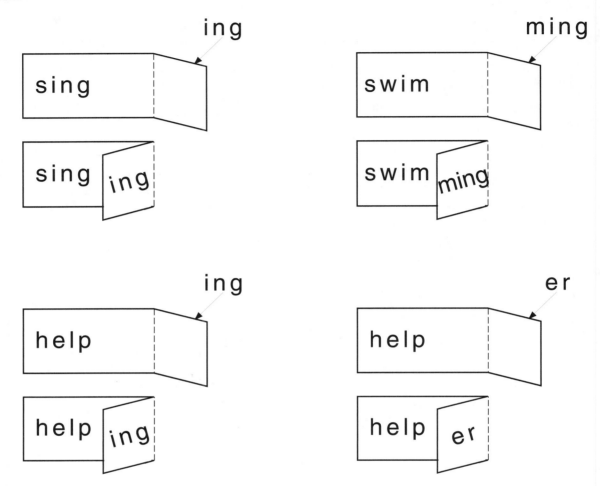

8. For compound words, make two lists. Write half of the compound words in List A and the other half of the compound words in List B. The words should not be in the correct order. Have students draw a line from a word in List A to a word in List B to form a complete compound word. Invite students to use the compound word in an oral or written sentence.

List A	List B
break	out
day	day
birth	fast
sell	light

9. Place several headings on the chalkboard (for example, places, people, rides, things, times). Have students write compound words that will fit under each heading.

10. Provide a series of words and invite students to write the antonym of each word and then combine the words to make a compound word. A completed example is given below.

rest + in

work + out = workout

Other words to use include the following.

night + dark	adult + stand
empty + front	death + night
tall + go	over + sky
by + in	laugh + adult
mend + slow	

11. Make sentence strips containing compound words. The sentences should be constructed so they can be illustrated easily. Each student chooses a sentence strip. Have the student copy the sentence on the bottom of a sheet of paper and illustrate the sentence. The picture of the compound word should be circled in red. Display the papers so that students can read each other's sentences, look at the circled pictures of the compound words, and then find the compound words in the sentences. See the following sample sentences.

The goldfish was swimming in a tank with a red fish and a green fish.

There was a hammer, a box of nails, and a piece of wood on the workbench.

The blue and red airplane flew above the trees and houses.

The typewriter is on the desk next to the lamp and a picture of a family.

The big, brown bear climbed the hill to get closer to the beehive.

Three boats were sailing near the shore by the lighthouse.

The golden dog sat between the doghouse and a big, tall tree.

I have a sandwich, popcorn, an apple, and carrots for lunch.

12. Prepare a list of sentences with a blank space for a compound word. Invite students to read the sentence to themselves and have a volunteer suggest a compound word that makes sense. Have the student explain how the word was selected, and, if it is correct, write it in the blank space. Some possible sentences are given here.

At my *(birthday)* party we had cake and ice cream.

There was not a cloud in the sky and the *(sunshine)* streamed in through the windows.

We did not go to school in the morning, but we did go in the *(afternoon)*.

The jets and planes flew in and out of the *(airport)*.

At the movies we had buttered *(popcorn)*.

The man's boots left deep *(footprints)* in the snow.

My sister's chore is to put the dishes into the *(dishwasher)*.

My dad told me to walk on the *(sidewalk)* and not on the grass.

The dog ran into the *(doghouse)*.

The football player threw the *(football)*.

I put stamps on the letters and dropped them into the *(mailbox)*.

At recess, the boys and girls played on the *(playground)*.

Because it was raining, I wore my *(raincoat)*.

When the lights went out, my father got a *(flashlight)* so we could see.

When Tom was sick, he had to stay *(inside)* the house.

Frosty is a famous *(snowman)*.

The train moves on the *(railroad)* track.

I squeezed toothpaste on my *(toothbrush)*.

Games

Group Ball Toss. Draw a target on a piece of felt with a marker and write in root words. Glue a strip of velcro around a lightweight ball. Mount the target on the chalkboard and beside the target write word endings. Divide students into teams and let them take turns throwing the ball at the target. When the ball hits the target, the student reads the word closest to the ball and then writes the word on the chalkboard with one of the inflectional endings. If the word is correct, the team scores one point. The students can play until one team gets 20 points (McCormick, 1995).

Compound Word Dominoes. Write two compound words on tagboard or index cards cut in half. Write the words facing the short sides and draw a line down the center. Distribute the cards to four students. Have students take turns making compound words by matching the words with two different cards. The Resources for Chapter 3 have a list of compound words that might be useful.

```
+--------+
|  bull  |
+--------+
|  dog   |
+--------+--------+
|  dog   |houae   |
+--------+--------+
         |house   |
         +--------+--------+
         | boat   | boat | man  |
                  +------+------+
                         | man  |
                         +------+
                         | kind |
                         +------+
```

Twister. Draw 20 large circles on a 6' x 4' oilcloth and attach words written on cards in the center of these circles. Using two teams, have students from team 1 put a hand on one word and a foot on a second word of a compound word. Then the student places a second hand on a word and a second foot on another word that would make sense as a compound word. If the words are correct, a student from team 2 tries the same activity. The team 2 student, however, needs to manipulate around the student from team 1. Then another student from team 1 joins the two students on the Twister board and so on until no more words can be formed.

The Affix Stopped Me. Make a set of 50 game cards. (Resources for Chapter 3 contain a list of compound words.) On 40 of the cards, write compound words. On the remaining 10 cards, write words with affixes. Shuffle the cards and place the deck on the table. Each student takes a turn flipping the cards over one at a time. As each card is turned, the student reads the card and determines if it is a compound word or a word with affixes. If the student correctly identifies the word as a compound word, the student pronounces the word and, if correct, keeps the card and turns the next card over. The turn continues until the student incorrectly identifies a card or when a word with an affix is uncovered. Continue until the cards are gone. The winner is the student with the most cards. This game is intended for a small group of four or five students. If more students want to play, the number of cards must be increased. Variations of the game include pronouncing the word correctly and using it in a sentence.

One, Two, or Three. Make a deck of 20 cards with each card containing 3 sentences. One sentence will contain a compound word. Two sentences will not have compound words. Number the sentences 1, 2, and 3. Vary the cards so that the compound word sentences appear in all three locations. To play the game, shuffle the cards and place the deck on the table. The first student takes the top card, reads the sentences, and decides which sentence contains a compound word. If the student correctly identifies the first sentence as containing the compound word, the student receives one marker, a button, or a bean. If the second sentence contains the compound word, the student receives two markers for correctly identifying it. If it is in the third sentence, the student receives three markers, and the turn ends. If the student is incorrect, no markers are earned and the turn is over. The winner is the student with the most markers when all the cards have been used. Variations of the game could include sentences with affixes.

Four in a Row. Choose 20 compound words and write them on the chalkboard. Each student divides a piece of paper into 16 squares. Then have students choose 16 of the 20 words and write them in the boxes. A box of markers will be needed. To play the game, say one of the words in a sentence. Have students listen for the compound word in the sentence and look for it on their paper. If they find it, they should cover the space with a marker. Continue creating sentences for the compound words until a student has four marked squares in a row. A variation of the game could involve a student creating the sentences.

Wheel Spin. Construct two circles of tagboard, one smaller than the other, and fasten them in the center with a brad. Print a verb on the smaller circle and print the endings s, er, ed, and ing on the larger circle. Several examples are illustrated below.

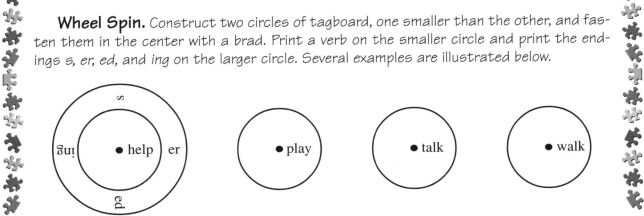

Two students can play. One student spins the top circle and pronounces the word that is made. The other student uses the word in a sentence. Students can change the top wheel to gain practice with other words.

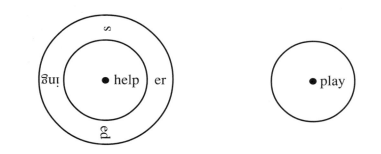

Basic Sight Words

Behavior Observed	The student cannot identify basic sight words automatically.
Anticipated Outcome	The student will be able to identify basic sight words without hesitation.

BACKGROUND

There are certain words in the English language that occur regularly in text. Look at the thirteen words below.

a and for he in is it of that
the to was you

These words account for approximately 25% of all of the words in school texts. Because they occur so frequently, they are called *basic sight words* or *high-frequency words.* You probably noticed that the words are difficult to define or describe. That's because they are *function words,* or words that are used to connect other words. They have little meaning themselves. Obviously, students who can read basic sight words automatically will have a much easier time reading text, but because basic sight words are abstract, they are difficult to teach.

The 13 words listed above are not the only high-frequency words in the English language. In fact, 109 words make up over 50% of the words used in school texts, and only 5,000 words make up 90% of the words in texts (Adams, 1990b). Although that may seem like a lot of words, remember that a typical high school senior will have a vocabulary of approximately 40,000 words and that students generally learn 3,000 words per year. Knowing how quickly students learn words makes the task of teaching sight words much more man-

Thirteen words make up approximately 25% of all words used in school texts.

ageable. You may be wondering what words make up the high frequency list of words. There are five word lists in the Resources for Chapter 3 for you to use in selecting sight words to teach.

Because more and more teachers fuse instruction in reading and writing, we thought you might also be interested in the most frequent words children use in their writing. Look at these 10 words.

I and the a to was in it of my

According to a research study conducted by Hillerich (1978), these 10 words account for over 25% of the words used by approximately 3,000 students in grades one through six. These words have great overlap with the 13 most frequently occurring words in the English language. Students should be taught to recognize and spell these words in the beginning stages of the instructional program. In addition, the words in the Revised Dolch List and the Alphabetized List of the 100 Words Used Most Frequently by Students in Their Writing (see Resources for Chapter 3) comprise over half the words students read and write. These lists may be useful for instruction. It is important that students learn to read and spell these words as soon as possible. The reason is clear: these high-frequency words are a critical, though not sufficient, component for efficient and effective literacy.

STRATEGY 1 WORD WALL*

1. Decide which words to include on your word wall. Your word wall should include about 100 to 120 words by the end of the school year that students use frequently in their reading and writing. A word wall begins with five words, and you should add about five words each week. Consider words from two lists included in the Resources for Chapter 3: Revised Dolch List and Alphabetized List of the 100 Words Used Most Frequently by Students in Their Writing. Teachers in the primary grades often begin with students' names and then add common words students need for reading and writing.

2. Write the words in big, black letters on different colored paper. Be sure to use a variety of colors for words that are frequently confused (*then, when*) or words that are pronounced the same (*to, two, too*). Some teachers cut around the shape of the word to provide another clue for students. Place the words in alphabetical order where all students can see them easily.

3. Begin the activity by having students number a sheet of paper from one to five. Pronounce each word, use it in a sentence, and have a student locate and point to the word on the word wall. Then have students clap and chant the spelling of the word before they write the word. Repeat this basic process for each of the remaining four words.

4. Lead students in checking the accuracy of the words they have written and make corrections as needed. The charting, writing, and checking can take about 10 minutes. As the school year progresses, students become more proficient in this basic activity, and a few minutes can be spent on an activity using the back of the paper on which the five words were written.

5. Consider some of these activities that Cunningham identifies as the "most popular and productive" (p. 64).

 - **Easy Rhyming:** Teach students how word-wall words that rhyme help them pronounce and spell words (for example, *be, he, she, we*). Use the words in context and have students write the words.
 - **Easy Ending Activity:** Help students add an ending to five word-wall words (for example, *s* to *boy, car, girl, school, tree; ed* to *ask, want, need, play, walk*). Other related activities include *ing* or *er*.
 - **Harder Ending Activity:** Work on how to spell five word-wall words when different endings are needed. Provide a sentence and have students find the word on the word wall, identify the end, decide how the word is spelled, and write it on their papers *(wanted, playing, walks)*.
 - **Combine Rhyme and Endings:** Say a sentence containing a word that rhymes with a word-wall word (for example, My bicycle *brakes* are broken). Model how you can find *make* on the word wall, change the beginning to make *brake*, and add an *s* to make *brakes*. Have students spell the word aloud before writing it.
 - **Mind Reader:** Think of a word on the word wall, write it on a piece of paper without students seeing it, and give students five clues to the word. Have students write a word after each clue. By the fifth clue, all students should have read your mind. An example follows.

 1. It's one of the words on our word wall.
 2. It has five letters.

*Cunningham, 2000.

3. It begins with *n*.
4. Both vowels are *e*.
5. It makes sense in this sentence: I _____ walked on the moon.

Then show students the word (*never*) and find out which students read your mind and wrote *never* next to numeral 4, 3, 2, or 1.

6. Refer to Cunningham's (2000) book for many additional ideas. Remember that the real power in a word wall comes from **using it**—not just having it. That means using word-wall activities on a daily basis for about 10 minutes.

Section 3.5

STRATEGY 2 EXPLICIT INSTRUCTION

1. Select a word that the students want to learn to read by sight. The word may be one that is in a story the class is reading, or it may be one that students need for writing.

2. Write the word on the chalkboard and ask the students to write the word on a card. If a student is unable to copy the word correctly, you may want to write it for him or her. Chant the word.

3. Locate a story or create a language experience story that uses the word several times.

4. Read the story to the class. Each time you say the sight word, ask students to raise their cards.

5. Ask the students to read the word on their cards, saying the word and then each letter.

6. Cut the word into letters and ask the students to arrange them to make up the word. Place the letters in envelopes so that the students can practice arranging the letters at other times during the day.

7. Write several sentences on the chalkboard with a blank space for the word. Ask the students to write the word in the blank and then read the sentences out loud.

8. Give the students text in which the word under study occurs frequently. Ask the students to carefully notice the word while reading.

Section 3.5

STRATEGY 3 PATTERN BOOKS

1. Select a pattern book that emphasizes the word you want the students to learn. A list of pattern books can be found in Appendix C.

2. Read the book aloud to the students. If possible, secure a big book version so students can follow along.

3. Read the book again, asking the students to join in whenever they can. Point to each word as it is being read.

4. Ask the students to take turns reading the book with you and to each other.

5. Write the text of the book on sentence strips or ask the students to write it for you. Then ask the students to read the text from sentence strips.

6. Write the word being studied on word cards. Ask students to match the word to the sentence strips.

7. Cut the sentence strips into words. Mix up the words and ask the students to arrange them in order.

8. Take out the word being studied from the sentence and ask students to write the word from memory.

9. Ask the students to create a sentence using the targeted word.

10. Create a rebus story using the word under study. Draw pictures for the nouns so that the students must read the high frequency words.

Practice and Reinforcement Activities

Even though students have had many exposures to a particular sight word during the previous teaching strategies, the words need to be practiced many more times before they become automatic. The following activities are designed to reinforce sight words.

1. Place the sight words on a word wall as explained in Strategy 1 in Section 3.5.

2. Have the students put selected sight word cards in alphabetical order.

3. Have students sort the words by categories. They may make up imaginative categories for the words, because most of them have little concrete meaning. Sample categories for some of the words on the Revised Dolch List (see Resources for Chapter 3) are shown in the box.

Category	Examples
Numbers	one, two, three
Other People	he, her, him, she, them
Talk Words	call, say, tell, ask
Action Words	run, leave, put, walk
Question Words	who, what, when, would
Size Words	big, little, long, round
Color Words	black, blue, white, red
Temperature Words	cold, hot, warm

4. Ask the students to find the words in texts around the room. For example, the word *and* may be on a "Friends and Neighbors" bulletin board.

5. Use word games such as Bingo, Hangman, Word Dominoes, Word Checkers, or Go Fish.

6. Have students use the buddy system to practice word cards.

7. Place word cards in a file box to use as a word bank of known words for writing.

8. Prepare cards that contain an illustrated sentence with the basic sight word underlined. Cards containing words and phrases may also be used.

9. Develop line searches. Be sure that the words only go from left to right. Ask students to circle the hidden word among each line of letters. Students can also be asked to use the word in an oral or a written sentence. Following are examples of line searches.

m f d ⟨b i g⟩ k d d s a ⟨b l u e⟩ d s d e ⟨t h a t⟩ d s d e s d ⟨w h e n⟩ d s

10. Use familiar rhymes to help students learn basic sight words in a meaningful context. Write a rhyme on the chalkboard or on sentence strips. Write the basic sight words in a color that is different from the color of the rest of the rhyme. In the following example, the basic sight words are in italics.

> Humpty Dumpty
> Sat *on a* wall.
> Humpty Dumpty
> *Had a* great fall.

11. Chant the spelling of words.

12. Have students write words. Writing provides a kinesthetic mode to help students learn and remember words.

13. Have students unscramble words they are learning as in the following example.

tge	flul	mrfo	egno	tgo	og	dogo
get	*full*	_____	_____	_____	_____	_____

14. Use a tachistoscope (a quick-exposure device) or cards to briefly expose a word, phrase, or sentence. Give students repeated practice over several days.

15. Provide sentences where the student writes the correct word in the blank. Provide choices for the answer.

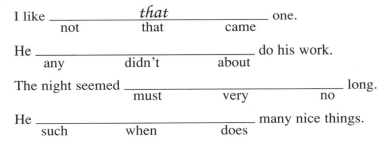

I like _____ *that* _____ one.
 not that came

He _____ do his work.
 any didn't about

The night seemed _____ long.
 must very no

He _____ many nice things.
 such when does

16. Have students locate the most common basic sight words (*a, and, for, he, in, is, it, of, that, the, to, was, you*) in newspapers or magazines. This activity will help students realize how frequently such words occur. Use a selection about one hundred words in length.

17. Create "flexible" sentences using words from the Revised Dolch List and the list of high frequency nouns. Students can read the many different sentences with a partner.

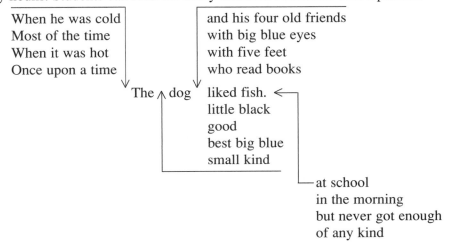

When he was cold and his four old friends
Most of the time with big blue eyes
When it was hot with five feet
Once upon a time who read books

 The ∧ dog liked fish. ←
 little black
 good
 best big blue
 small kind

 at school
 in the morning
 but never got enough
 of any kind

two	ways
many	things
four	cars
both	books

The little boy found six short tables at school.

big	new
small	white
fast	other
first	round

18. To aid in the practice of words such as *in, on, under, over, behind,* get a cup and straw. Place the straw in various positions and ask students to use a word that answers the question "Where is the straw?" Alternative ideas include a stuffed animal and a cardboard box.

19. Provide lots of easy reading materials.

Sight Vocabulary

Behavior Observed	The student's sight vocabulary is so limited that it interferes with reading fluency.
Anticipated Outcome	The student will increase his or her sight vocabulary.

BACKGROUND

Students who know words by sight are able to pronounce them automatically. A large sight vocabulary enables students to read fluently and to focus their attention on making sense of the passage. It also helps students use other reading strategies, such as context clues, more effectively.

A student's sight vocabulary, then, is composed of all of the words recognized in an instant. Some words recognized on sight occur very frequently in printed materials and are often referred to as basic sight words (for example, *when, then, the*). Basic sight words are a vital part of the student's sight vocabulary but are a subset of the total number of sight words a student may recognize. The following list shows the basic sight vocabulary in relation to the student's entire sight vocabulary.

Basic sight words tend to be abstract words. The other words that comprise sight vocabulary usually refer to real things. This difference generally permits greater variety in teaching and practicing words that are not basic sight words.

When selecting words to teach as sight words, remember that many repetitions of the word may be necessary before the word becomes part of the student's sight vocabulary. The crucial variable is often the meaningfulness of the word to the student. The word *sled,* for example, might become a sight word quickly for a student who uses a sled frequently. A student who has never used a sled may have greater difficulty learning the word.

Total Sight Vocabulary

when*	elephant	Kmart
big	Illinois	Bryan
there	Ms. Grant	grandma
so	Garfield	library
was	baseball	chocolate

*Basic sight vocabulary is in bold print.

STRATEGY 1 SIGHT WORDS

1. When possible, use the actual object or a picture of the word being taught. Have a student identify the object. If you have no access to a visual representation of the word, begin with the next step.

2. Pronounce the word and write it on the chalkboard. Have students pronounce it. If necessary, discuss the meaning of the word with the students. Have students try to think of synonyms for the word. Students should also be encouraged to relate the word to their experiences.

3. Encourage students to use the word in different sentences. Write some of these sentences on the chalkboard and underline the word being taught. If a word has more than one meaning, be sure sentences are provided that exemplify these meanings.

4. If students are confusing two or more words (for example, *chair* and *chew*), compare the words by having students point out similarities and differences between the words. Students might also close their eyes and picture the word that is being taught.

Practice and Reinforcement Activities

1. See Section 3.5 for additional activities.

2. Students should read many books that are easy for them. There are many books appropriate for students who have limited sight vocabularies. See Appendix C for a list of pattern books.

3. For words that can be represented by a picture, print the word on the front of a card under the picture. The back of the card should contain the printed word. You can use logos from stores and businesses for some sight words.

A list of leveled books for students in the early stages of reading has been provided by Brooks (1996) and Gunning (1998). Several titles recommended for emerging to beginning readers are listed below.

> Avery, M. W., & Avery, D.M. (1995). *What is Beautiful?* Berkeley, CA: Tricycle.
> Cocca-Leffler, M. (1994). *What a Pest!* New York: Grosset and Dunlap.
> dePaola, T. (1994). *Kit and Kat*. New York: Grosset and Dunlap.
> Farjeon, E. (1996). *Cats Sleep Anywhere*. Scranton, PA: HarperCollins.
> Ziefert, H. (1995). *Nicky, 1-2-3*. New York: Puffin.

4. Provide many varied opportunities for students to interact with print. Use some of the following techniques.

- sustained silent reading
- read-along stories and books
- repeated readings
- shared reading
- poems, songs, and rhymes

Games

How Many? Have students write the words on cards. Each word should have at least four cards. The students can then play the card game "How Many?" The word cards are shuffled and the deck is placed face down. Students take turns rolling a die to determine how many words are drawn from the deck. Each word is pronounced, placed on the table, and used in a sentence. Any words pronounced incorrectly are returned to the bottom of the deck. The student with the most words wins.

Word Sort. Prepare 10 word cards relating to each of the categories appropriate for the words. Shuffle the cards and deal them to each of the players. Players take turns rolling a die and placing one or two words under the correct category.

Around the World. Using sight word flash cards, show a card to a pair of students. The student who responds correctly first can move on to another student. The object is for a student to make it around the class, or around the world. The winning student can then hold the cards for you while the class resumes play.

Word Hunt. Place several sight word cards around the room. Ask the students to hunt for the cards, reading them aloud when they find one. The student with the most cards wins.

Concentration. Place several pairs of sight word cards face down on a table. Have students take turns uncovering and pronouncing two cards, looking for pairs. When a student finds a pair, he or she pronounces the word and takes the cards. The student with the most pairs of cards wins the game.

SECTION 3.7 Using Context to Predict Known Words

Behavior Observed	The student has difficulty using context clues to anticipate a familiar word.
Anticipated Outcome	The student will use context as one reading strategy to anticipate known words.

BACKGROUND

The context of a word is the words surrounding it. One of the ways to identify words is to use the other words in the sentence and to make a prediction about what word would make sense. Using context clues to anticipate known words can make reading a more efficient process.

To make a good prediction about a word, the student's knowledge and experiences play an important role. For example, consider these sentences.

The dog was chewing on a _____.

Peaches grow on _____.

The baby began to _____.

Students with prior knowledge about dogs, peaches, and babies should have little difficulty supplying a word that would make sense in the sentences. The students are able to draw upon their ex-

isting knowledge to make a prediction about the missing words.

Unfortunately, some students' reading comes to an abrupt halt when they come across a word they don't recognize on sight, even if only one word would make sense in the sentence. For example, peaches only grow on trees. No other response would make sense in the sentence. For the other sentences, however, the student would also need to consider at least the initial sound in the unknown word. For example, the baby began to *sm-* or the baby began to *cr-* would elicit two different responses, each correct in the context. Context clues, therefore, are helpful but should not be considered the only strategy to use when students try to read unfamiliar words.

STRATEGY 1 WORD PREDICTION

1. Before students arrive in the classroom, write several words on the chalkboard and cover them. Develop a sentence containing each word that should be helpful in predicting the covered word. These sentences will be part of the lesson. Some examples are listed below.

Covered Words	Sample Sentence
bark	I heard the dog _____.
book	I was reading chapter 2 of the _____.
tree	The squirrel climbed a _____.
rings	School begins when the bell _____.
laughed	The joke was funny and I _____.

2. Tell students that they can sometimes use the other words in a sentence to predict or guess a word they have heard before. Stress that the sentence may contain helpful clues.

3. Point to the card covering the word *bark* and ask students if they know the word behind the card. They may have many ideas, but they are only guessing. Tell students that if that word were in a sentence, they might be able to use sentence clues to make a better guess or prediction. Ask students to be word detectives and focus on the clues that may be in a sentence you are going to write on the chalkboard.

4. Place a line for each word in the sentence and begin to write the sentence as shown below.

 _____I_____ ____heard____ _____ _____ _____ .

 After writing *heard,* invite students to predict things they might hear. Write these words on the chalkboard and stress that the words are things that can be heard. Suggest a few additional words (*thunder, smoke, light*) and have students evaluate whether they would be good choices. Model as needed. For example: "*Smoke* would probably not be a good choice, because I don't hear *smoke*. I see *smoke*."

5. Continue writing the sentence on the lines but do not include the last word.

 _____I_____ ____heard____ ____the____ ____dog____ _____ .

 Most students will say the word *bark* after you have written *dog*. Take a moment to have a student explain why the word makes sense. Then uncover the word to confirm the word. Invite students to suggest other words that would also make sense (*cry, run, growl*). Confirm such words as good choices. Note that authors can sometimes use several words, but the author decides which words to use.

6. Use some of the other examples as needed. Invite a student to assist you and model as necessary. Be sure to help students realize that they may not always predict the exact word, but they should at least predict words that make sense.

7. Take time to have students create oral or written sentences and omit a specific word in each sentence. Give students an opportunity to share sentences with a partner and make predictions about the missing word.

8. Conclude the lesson by telling students that they can sometimes predict a word in their reading by using the other words in the sentence. Then share a few preselected sentences from books in your classroom and have students listen carefully and try to predict the missing word. An example from *A Prairie Year* (Bannatyne-Cugnet, 1994, p. 4) follows.

"For Matthew, January means no sleeping in and no Saturday morning cartoons on _____."

Section 3.7

STRATEGY 2 ADVANCED WORD PREDICTION

1. Consider adapting the approach used with younger students by using specific examples from instructional materials. Extend the lesson by including initial letter clues to help students refine their predictions.

2. Be sure students understand that context refers to words around a particular word. Help them realize that sometimes they can use their background knowledge and sense of language to predict a word—even before seeing it in print.

3. Provide an example and guide the process for students. A sample sentence from *The Giver* (Lowry, 1993, p. 78) that might be used follows.

"The man paused, seeming to search his mind for the right words of _____." (description)

4. Write the sentence on the chalkboard or an overhead transparency, replacing the last word with a line. Have students read the sentence silently and think of words that might make sense in the blank. Students should write their ideas on a piece of paper.

5. Ask students to form small groups and share their words. Encourage each group to decide on its best word choices. Take time for students to share their words and reasons for their choices. Write these words on the chalkboard or an overhead transparency.

6. Compliment students on their predictions and then say something like the following.

 You have suggested some good possibilities that fit the context of the sentence. I'm now going to provide a further clue to help you eliminate some of your words and help you refine your predictions. The first letter of the word is d. Which words can we eliminate? Which words are still possible? Are there any new words you want to suggest?

7. Continue providing additional letters in *description* until students identify the word. Invite students to share their thinking. Guide the process as necessary.

8. Tell students that the sense of the sentence and letter clues sometimes can be used to help pronounce a word that they have heard before. Repeat the core lesson using other sentences. Include at least one sentence where the context will probably not help predict the word because it is not a known word in students' listening vocabularies. For example, I took a walk near the *quay*. Other sentences for possible use include the following.

 The job was very *dangerous*.
 I ran so far that I was *exhausted*.
 The camper needed to *filter* the liquid.
 Fingerprints can be used to identify a specific person.
 The sun helped the water *evaporate*.
 Flippers help seals and whales swim.

Practice and Reinforcement Activities

1. Daily routine activities will help students use oral context skills to predict words. Some examples follow.

> Today is _____.
> The two students absent are _____ and _____.

2. Read familiar pattern books to the students, pausing at appropriate places so students can predict the missing word. A list of pattern books can be found in Appendix C.

3. Make tape recordings of books and omit several words. Give the students a copy of the text to underline the words omitted on the tape.

4. Use a book at the students' independent level and mask selected words with tape. (Post-it Notes also work well.) Have the students make predictions for the words before the tape is removed. Then remove the tape to see what the author has written. Discuss different responses to determine overall appropriateness.

5. Provide a passage from a text in which selected words have been replaced with lines. Instruct students to read the passage and write in their choices of words. Stress that their words should make sense. Later, discuss their choices in conjunction with the words used by the author.

6. Using a text the students will be reading, read several sentences while omitting several words and have students predict the words that have been omitted. Then tell students the words used by the author and develop the idea that it is sometimes possible to predict a word the author will use.

7. Select a text that the students will need to read. Preview the text and determine which words might give the students difficulty. Model how you would use the context to help figure out the words. Think aloud so the students can hear your strategies.

8. List some common topics that students might be asked to read about and encourage them to list words that are likely to appear in the stories. Develop the notion that certain words might be expected to be associated with a particular topic.

9. Present incomplete sentences orally and have students suggest words that would make sense. Begin with sentences in which a large number of meaningful responses are possible and conclude with a sentence in which only a few choices make sense. Help students understand that if they listen to a sentence they can usually think of a word that makes sense. Some possible sentences follow.

> I like to eat _____.
>
> One day of the week is _____.
>
> There is no school on _____.

10. Write sentences with a missing word on the chalkboard and have students suggest words that make sense. Supply additional words, including some that do not make sense, and ask students why a particular word is or is not appropriate. Discuss clues within the sentence that may help students make decisions. Underline such clues. For example, in "I like to eat _____," the words *like* and *eat* are important clues; *eat* is probably the most important clue.

Dictionary: Word Pronunciation

Behavior Observed	The student is unable to use the dictionary to help pronounce unknown words.
Anticipated Outcome	The student will be able to use the dictionary as one strategy to help pronounce unknown words.

BACKGROUND

We know that using the dictionary to help pronounce unknown words is a difficult undertaking for many students. There are numerous skills that the students must possess: knowledge of the alphabet and alphabetical sequence, how to use guide words and the pronunciation key, and how to actually apply these skills to arrive at the pronunciation of an unknown word.

The focus of dictionary use in this section is to help students pronounce unknown words. Section 5.4 offers strategies for using the dictionary to help determine the meanings of an unknown word. Sections 3.8 and 5.4 may be taught together.

Dictionary use should be purposeful and meaningful to students. It is seldom the strategy of choice when a word is unknown in either pronunciation or meaning. Other strategies (context, phonics, structural analysis, morphemic analysis) that were taught are the logical and efficient places to begin. When the word is still unknown, a dictionary should be a viable resource. Using a dictionary for pronunciation can be difficult, even for adults. The pronun-

ciation key seems to work well when we can already pronounce the word. When the word is unknown, the pronunciation key often becomes more challenging. The goal in using the pronunciation key is to enable students to associate the appropriate sounds with letters and letter combinations in an effort to say the word and hopefully recognize the word because it has been heard before. If the word is unfamiliar, students will be unable to decide whether it was pronounced correctly. An expert source (you or another student) would be needed to confirm the correct pronunciation.

The use of a pronunciation key, pronunciation symbols, or phonetic respellings to help pronounce unknown words is a complex skill that requires good instruction, guided practice opportunities, and plenty of encouragement to students as they apply what was taught. The teaching strategies in this section represent some useful beginnings. Be sure to adapt and extend the strategies so they are meaningful and useful to your students.

STRATEGY 1

ARRANGEMENT OF ALPHABET IN DICTIONARIES

1. Be sure students know the alphabet in sequence. If the alphabet is above the chalkboard, use it to visually demonstrate what alphabetical sequence means. Then tell students that the words in a dictionary are arranged in alphabetical sequence or order. Have students survey their dictionaries to confirm this arrangement.

2. Take time to develop the understanding that not all letters encompass the same number of words. For example, help students locate the number of pages devoted to words beginning with *s* and *x*. They will see that there are more *s* words. Use other examples as needed. Tell students that approximately one fourth of all the words are covered by the letters a through d; the remaining three fourths of the words are covered by the following groups of letters: e through l, m through r, and s through z. Present this information in a chart like that shown below.

a-d	e-l	m-r	s-z
a b c d	e f g h i j k l	m n o p q r	s t u v w x y z

3. Model how this information can be used to find where a word is located. You might say:

 If I want to look up the word language, *I can see that* l *words are near the middle of the dictionary* (point to the l in the chart). *I can then open my dictionary to about the middle to find the* l *words.*

4. Invite students to use their dictionaries and try to open them to the middle to see if *l* words are there. Show students what to do if they open to a different set of words. Model as needed. For example, you might say:

 When I opened my dictionary to find the l *words for* language, *I was in the* n *section, because I see words beginning with* n *at the top of the page. By looking at the chart, I see I need to go a little more toward the front of the dictionary.* (Turn more to the front.) *Yes, now I've found the* l *section.*

5. Use numerous examples with students to practice finding the general place in a dictionary where specific words could be found. The goal is to locate the general area, not the specific word. Invite students to suggest words and locate the general area of the dictionary where the words can be found. Some possible words to use are listed below.

ball	run	noon	infest	pot
energy	contest	unicorn	solar	fortify

6. Conclude the lesson by asking students where their names could be found if they were listed in a dictionary. Refer to the chart and have students gather in one of four groups (a-d, e-l, m-r, or s-z). Students could group themselves in three different ways for practice: first names, last names, and middle names.

STRATEGY 2 ALPHABETICAL ORDER

1. Tell students that words in a dictionary are arranged in alphabetical order (*a* to *z*) by first letter and then second letter, and so on. Then tell students that you are going to help them learn how to find words in a dictionary.

2. Use the names of two students whose names begin with the same first letter and write their names on the chalkboard. For example, use the following names.

 Jerry

 Jana

3. Explain that because both names begin with the same letter, you go to the second letter and ask, "Which letter comes first in the alphabet—*e* or *a*?" Point to the two letters on an alphabet wall chart so students can see which letter comes first. Because *a* comes before *e* in the alphabet, *Jana* would come before *Jerry* if the words were to be placed in alphabetical order. Place these two words in alphabetical order on the chalkboard.

4. Ask for volunteers whose names begin with the same letter to come forward and print their names on the chalkboard. Repeat the above process and, if needed, show how you would go to the third or fourth letter of the names. Several examples follow.

 Jane

 Jana

 Jamall

 Have students make a name card and practice with classmates whose names begin with the same first letter. Name cards for both first and last names can be used.

5. Then have about one half of the students arrange themselves in alphabetical order by first name. Invite classmates at their seats to help verify the order and ask questions when needed. Repeat the activity with the remaining group of students using last names.

6. Transfer this knowledge to the dictionary by supplying several words on cards and having students put the words in alphabetical order. Once correct alphabetical order is achieved, tell students the page numbers in their dictionaries where each word can be found and have students check the page to find the word to confirm alphabetical order. Consider using only guide words from students' dictionaries in the initial practice exercises. Two sets of examples are shown below, but you should select words from your students' dictionaries.

 crown, p. 173 dachshund, p. 179
 crutch, p. 174 dahlia, p. 180
 cyclist, p. 179 dapper, p. 181

7. Provide students with more practice but increase the difficulty as appropriate. Include three or four words that appear on the same page of the students' dictionaries and have them put them in alphabetical order. When they are finished, tell students the page numbers where the words are found so they can check whether the words were alphabetized correctly.

 daisy daffodil daddy-longlegs (p. 180)
 example exact excellent (p. 246)
 fossil foul forty (p. 281)

Keep the focus on understanding alphabetical order, not actually looking up words. The next lesson will help students use guide words in a dictionary to help locate words.

8. To provide practice in using guide words, give students the actual guide words and page numbers from several pages of their dictionary. In a second column, provide words and have students indicate on what page the word would be found. After completing the exercise, students can self-check their work by consulting dictionaries and noting whether they were correct. A sample is shown below.

Guide Words and Page	Word	Page	Were You Correct?
close-club, 134	collect	_____	_____ yes _____ no
collar-colon, 139	compass	_____	_____ yes _____ no
compare-complain, 145	cloth	_____	_____ yes _____ no
compost-concern, 147	concept	_____	_____ yes _____ no
	complain	_____	_____ yes _____ no
	collier	_____	_____ yes _____ no
	cloud	_____	_____ yes _____ no
	compete	_____	_____ yes _____ no
	cologne	_____	_____ yes _____ no
	compress	_____	_____ yes _____ no
	clover	_____	_____ yes _____ no

Practice and Reinforcement Activities

1. Use daily opportunities in the classroom, such as the following activities, to help students to practice alphabetical order.

- Have students put three spelling words beginning with the same letter in alphabetical order.
- Ask students who are wearing a particular color of clothing to line up in alphabetical order.
- Invite students to offer short lists of words (states, birds, games) that classmates could put in alphabetical order.

2. Make a chart like the following example.

a-d	e-l	m-r	s-z
a b c d	e f g h i j k l	m n o p q r	s t u v w x y z

Have students tab (using Post-it Notes) these areas in their dictionaries: the beginning of the *e, m,* and *s* words. Tell them the page numbers where to place the tabs. Then have them use the chart along with their dictionary tabs to locate the general area of the dictionary where words could be found. Begin with areas in the dictionary that are easier to find and remind students to use their tabs. Some possible words to use are listed below.

accordion	mailbox	reel
zebra	scooter	dimple
equator	bicycle	quill

Game

Envelope Alphabet. Prepare a group of envelopes, each with 10 to 15 index cards to be arranged in alphabetical order. Have the students take an envelope, remove the cards, and place them in correct alphabetical order. The game can be made self-checking by numbering the cards on the back or putting an answer sheet inside the envelope. Number the envelopes and make the higher numbers increasingly difficult to arrange. Three increasingly difficult lists are given below in alphabetical order.

List 1	List 5	List 10
1. almost	1. about	1. hinge
2. for	2. after	2. hint
3. happy	3. back	3. hip
4. just	4. because	4. hippopotamus
5. pretty	5. day	5. hire
6. red	6. did	6. his
7. street	7. do	7. hiss
8. then	8. we	8. history
9. where	9. will	9. hit
10. yellow	10. would	10. hive

Section 3.8

STRATEGY 3 GUIDE WORDS

1. Ask students to open their dictionaries to a predetermined page. Direct their attention to the top of the page where the two guide words are found (for example, *cook* and *copra*).

2. Tell students that guide words will help them determine whether a particular word can be found on that page just by using the guide words. Show students that *cook* is the first word or entry on that page and *copra* is the last word or entry. Have students turn to other pages in their dictionaries to confirm this basic information about guide words.

3. Then tell students that you will help them learn to use guide words. Use the example provided or preselect several students' names that begin with the same letter and choose two names as guide words. Add additional names if needed. Then write the two names on the chalkboard or an overhead transparency as guide words (Hayes and Hull, for example).

Hayes	Hull

4. Model for students how you would determine if Hernandez would be found on this page. For example, say the following:

 I begin with the first letter (h) and know I'm in the right area of the dictionary. Then I look at the second letter in Hernandez (e) and the second letter in Hayes (a). Because the e comes after the a, I know Hernandez comes in the alphabet after Hayes. Next, I look at the second letter in Hull (u) and ask myself whether the second letter in Hernandez (e) comes before or after u. *Because* e *comes before* u *in the alphabet, I know that Hernandez comes before Hull. Because Hernandez comes after Hayes and before Hull, I know that word will be found on the page with those guide words.*

5. Model several additional examples to help students see how some words would be found on earlier pages or later pages. Then invite students to share their thought processes with additional words. Some possible names to use are listed below.

Earlier Page	**On Page**	**Later Page**
Harris	Henry	Humphry
Harty	Hill	Hurley
Hanson	Holt	Hynd
Hall	Hoover	Hynes

6. Invite students to play detective by deducing whether a list of words would be found on a particular page of their dictionaries. Choose a page from their dictionaries and develop a list of words. Use examples that reflect students' general level of understanding. Some words can be very easy to assign to one of the three categories below. Write the list of words on the chalkboard or an overhead transparency and have students work in pairs to assign the words to the appropriate category. A completed example is shown below for the guide words *cook* and *copra*.

Earlier Page	**On Page**	**Later Page**
brain	cool	copse
archer	coop	corn
convey	coot	cork
control	copilot	delta
continue	copper	fawn

7. Discuss the completed chart and clarify as needed. Encourage students to share their thinking and reinforce students who were able to explain and show why their answers were correct or incorrect.

8. Challenge students to apply their learning by completing a sheet where you present two guide words from their dictionaries and a small group of words. Have students complete the sheet before looking in their dictionaries. Check their work. For further practice, students could actually write the page numbers for those words on an "earlier" or "later" page. A sample sheet is included on the next page.

Name _____ Date _____

Dictionary Detective

Words: _____

Where would the above words be found in your dictionary? Use your detective skills, knowledge of guide words, and alphabetical order to put the words where they belong. For the words that come before and after the guide words, look up the words in your dictionary and write the page numbers where they are found.

	Guide Words	
Earlier Page	_____ _____	Later Page

page _____ page _____

page _____ page _____

page _____ page _____

page _____ page _____

From Jerry L. Johns and Susan Davis Lenski, *Improving Reading: Strategies and Resources* (3rd ed.). Copyright © 2001 Kendall/Hunt Publishing Company (1-800-247-3458, ext. 5). May be reproduced for noncommercial educational purposes.

STRATEGY 4 PRONUNCIATION SYMBOLS

1. Be sensitive to your students' dialects and the region of the country in which you live. Dictionaries show how words are pronounced by people who speak what is called General American. Canadian dictionaries will have a number of pronunciation differences when compared to dictionaries published for the United States. Keep this information in mind when you teach the pronunciation symbols—they may not be entirely appropriate for the area where you live. Remember also that this lesson is an introduction. Students will need numerous opportunities to learn and use pronunciation symbols in their dictionaries.

2. Introduce pronunciation symbols by having students find them at the bottom of one of their dictionary pages. Tell students that the special symbols in parentheses after the entry word, when used with the pronunciation key at the bottom of the page, are intended to help with word pronunciation. Take time to teach or review the long mark (macron) for the vowels (ā, ē, ī, ō, ū), no marks for the short sounds of the vowels, and perhaps some of the special marks shown below. Refer to the pronunciation key as needed.

Some Special Pronunciation Symbols					
Name	*Symbol*	*Example*	*Name*	*Symbol*	*Example*
Two-dot a	ä	cär	Tilde u	ũ	fũr
Circumflex o	ô	hôrn	Schwa	ə	a in ago

3. Give students an opportunity to look at the special symbols in parenthesis in their dictionaries, especially for words they can pronounce. Then have them look up a word they can pronounce (for example, *be*). Write the pronunciation symbols for *be* on the chalkboard or an overhead transparency (bē). Help students see how this information, while easy to use with a word they know, can be used with a word that might be unknown. You could use a think aloud:

 The word be *is easy for me to pronounce, but I can remember that the long mark over the vowel means that I say the name of the vowel when trying to pronounce a vowel. I can use that sound along with other sounds in the word and try different pronunciations. If I say a word I've heard before, I've probably pronounced the word correctly.*

4. Present only the pronunciation symbols for *bias* (bī´əs). Cover everything but the *bi* and ask for a volunteer to pronounce that part of the word. Then present the remaining pronunciation symbols and point out the accent mark and the spacing that indicates that the word has two syllables. Invite students to refer to the pronunciation key to try to pronounce the word. Encourage different pronunciations and stress to students that they are probably right if they say a word with those sounds that they have heard before. Confirm the pronunciation and take time to find the word and examine the meanings for *bias*.

5. Write (kē) on the chalkboard or an overhead transparency. Ask students what word it represents. Most students should say *key*. Have them confirm the word by locating it in their dictionaries and looking at the pronunciation symbols. You might also take time to explore the meanings that can be associated with *key*.

6. Use similar activities with the pronunciation symbols for other words. Invite students to try to pronounce the words. Confirm the correct pronunciation and, if necessary, refer to the dictionary for meanings. Be sure to try to build on the students' existing knowledge. Some possible words to use are given below along with the pronunciation symbols from a dictionary. Be sure to use symbols that are in your students' dictionaries.

Pronunciation Symbols	Words
(kik)	kick
(kil or kiln)	kiln
(kid´ni)	kidney
(kip´ər)	kipper
(kin)	kin
(joor´i)	jury
(jo͞o lī)	July
(sit´i)	city
(sũr´ kəs)	circus

7. Conclude the lesson by stressing that pronunciation symbols can be useful aids to help pronounce unknown words. Remind students that they need to be willing to try different pronunciations until they say a word they have heard before.

Section 3.8

STRATEGY 5 PRONOUNCING UNKNOWN WORDS

1. Begin by helping students realize that pronouncing words is not the same as reading words. When a word is read, one or more meanings are associated with the word. Remind students that a dictionary can be a resource for both meanings and pronunciations.

2. Select a few words from upcoming lessons that students may be unable to pronounce. Adapt the procedure used with the word *quay*. Remember, however, that the real power of such lessons comes from using words students have encountered or will encounter in their reading.

3. Tell students you will show them how to use a dictionary to help pronounce an unknown word. Write the word *quay* on the chalkboard or an overhead transparency. Then write the following sentence:

The dog was near the quay.

Have students read the sentence to themselves and then offer possible pronunciations for *quay*. It is possible that most students will agree that the word is pronounced (kwā) to rhyme with *way*.

4. Explore students' ideas about the meaning of the word. List their ideas on the chalkboard or an overhead transparency. Then ask students how they could find out the pronunciation and meaning. Common responses include asking someone and using a dictionary.

5. Place the following information on the chalkboard or overhead transparency or have students use their dictionaries.

 quay (kē, kā) a wharf for loading or unloading ships, usually made of stone or concrete

6. Have students use the pronunciation symbols to pronounce the word and compare it with their initial ideas. Help students realize there are two pronunciations given in this dictionary entry. You might model word pronunciation, using the following think aloud:

 When I saw the word in the sentence, I thought it was pronounced (kwā). Now that I've looked at the pronunciation symbols, I see I was wrong. The word is pronounced as key *(kē) or* kay *(kā). I can see that some words can be pronounced more than one way. I also see that the meaning of quay is a wharf. That means that the dog was near a wharf which is near a body of water. The dictionary helped me with both pronunciation and meaning.*

7. Present several additional words that are difficult for most students to pronounce. Give them the dictionary pages on which the words are found and have small groups work together using the pronunciation symbols to say the words. Any student who already knows how to pronounce any of the words should not participate for that particular word. Instead, the student can be the expert source when the correct pronunciation is needed. Spend time with the meanings of the words and encourage students to relate the words to their experiences.

8. For additional practice, use words that are pronounced in different ways. Have groups of students use their dictionaries to find or confirm the different pronunciations. Help students realize that some of these differences are due to the part of speech. Other pronunciations are due to regional differences. Some possible words to use for this activity are given below.

either	duty	object	read
route	creek	wind	bow
tear	house	minute	lead
dove	wound	live	idea

9. Conclude the lesson by telling students that a dictionary is a source to use to help pronounce unknown words. Have students offer other strategies that can also be used (context, phonics, structural analysis). Remind students that they should be flexible in their approach and remember that a dictionary should be used if the other strategies have not been helpful and the pronunciation or meaning of the word is needed.

Practice and Reinforcement Activities

1. Invite students to use the pronunciation symbols from their dictionaries and answer the following questions.

> Which is part of a building?
> (ruf) (flou´ər) (sē´ling)

> Which is an insect?
> (flī) (bēd) (spē´dar)

> Which one crawls?
> (snak) (wôm) (kat´ər pil´ər)

2. Provide pronunciation symbols for some words and have students use these symbols and try to pronounce the words. Then provide a helpful context where the pronunciation is likely to be confirmed. Remember that different publishers use different pronunciation symbols. Some examples of words and sentences are presented below.

(kwit)	I *quit* playing the game.
(māt)	Where is the *mate* to my sock?
(sit´i)	Do you live in a large *city*?
(sūr kəs)	I saw a clown at the *circus*.
(rēd)	I will *read* the exciting story.

3. Use electronic dictionaries for students who have not yet learned how to use pronunciation symbols. Such dictionaries can also be useful for readers who struggle because these dictionaries pronounce the word and read the definition. Remember, however, that the definition read may not fit the context of the sentence being read.

4. Choose some particularly interesting words in terms of spelling and pronunciation and have students look up the words and use the pronunciation symbols to try to pronounce the words. Some possible words are listed below.

aviary	axis	calyx	czar	depot

Lack of Flexible Word-Identification Strategies

Behavior Observed	The student does not use a variety of word-identification strategies.
Anticipated Outcome	The student will use various strategies for identifying unknown words.

BACKGROUND

Students with difficulty in reading often do not apply all of the word-identification strategies they have learned. They may, for example, use decoding, but they rarely use the context of the sentence when they encounter an unknown word. Good readers, however, recognize that the most efficient method of figuring out unknown words varies with the reading situation. Therefore, teachers need to emphasize that students use reading strategies most appropriate for the situation.

The following ideas are meant to help teachers begin to refine the process of teaching students to develop a set of flexible word-identification strategies.

Students need a variety of word-identification strategies that they can use independently.

STRATEGY 1

CSSR: CONTEXT, STRUCTURE, SOUND, REFERENCE*

1. **C** **Context.** Tell students that when they come to a word they don't know, they should read to the end of the sentence to see whether the rest of the sentence defines the word. Students needing practice in figuring out unfamiliar words from context should be taught the strategies in Sections 3.7 and 5.2.

2. **S** **Structure.** If the word cannot be identified by the context, students should look at the parts of the words. They should look for any familiar word parts that can help them understand the new word. For teaching strategies using the structure of words, see Sections 3.4, 3.5, and 5.3.

3. **S** **Sound.** If the word has familiar word parts, students should try to pronounce the word using their knowledge of the sounds of consonants and vowels. After trying to give some of the letters the sounds they represent, students should reread the sentence, thinking about the way the word is used. Often students will be able to read the word using these three steps. For teaching strategies using the sounds associated with letters, see Sections 3.1 and 3.2.

4. **R** **Reference.** If students are unable to identify the word, they may use reference materials such as a glossary or a dictionary. After finding a word in the dictionary, however, students still need to determine how it is used in the context of the sentence. For teaching strategies using a dictionary, see Sections 3.8 and 5.4.

5. You may want to model the CSSR with your students. For example, consider the unknown word *amicable* in the sentence "The family came to an amicable agreement about vacation plans." You might say:

> *I don't know the word a-m-i-c-a-b-l-e, so I would first read to the end of the sentence. I know that the word describes agreement, but nothing in the sentence tells me what kind of agreement they had. It might have been friendly, but it might not have been. After reading to the end of the sentence, I look for word parts that I know. The word has parts I can pronounce, but it doesn't have a base word or affixes that will help me understand the word. Next, I try to read the word by giving the letters the sounds that I know (sound out word). I know the sounds in the word, so I can pronounce it. After pronouncing* amicable, *I reread the sentence. Yes, I've heard the word before, and it makes sense in the sentence. Just to be sure, however, I check the dictionary and find that* amicable *means 'friendly or peaceable.' I think I'll remember the word the next time I see it.*

*Ruddell, 1993.

Ineffective Use of Word-Identification Strategies

Behavior Observed	The student knows word-identification strategies but does not use them effectively.
Anticipated Outcome	The student will become more effective in using word-identification strategies.

BACKGROUND

One student always seems to sound out unknown words. Another student substitutes a word that makes sense but changes the author's meaning. A third student stops reading completely when confronted with an unfamiliar word. These and other reading behaviors, when observed consistently, can work against students becoming proficient readers.

The basic problem is that often the student has not learned why a particular strategy works and/or when to use it for figuring out unfamiliar words. It is also possible that the student does not know when to abandon one strategy and move to another. Usually, the student is overreliant on one word-identification strategy even though he or she may have learned other strategies. This situation usually occurs because the student has not been taught how to use a *combination* of strategies flexibly when confronted with an unknown word. Your primary responsibility in such a situation is to help the student use word-identification strategies in combination with one another to produce a word that makes sense in the sentence and has graphic characteristics similar to the word printed in the text. Students might be told that this is the "sound-sense strategy." If a specific strategy like context or phonics needs

to be taught, refer to the ideas presented in Chapter 3. The following strategy should help you begin to refine the process of teaching students to develop a set of flexible word-identification strategies.

Could this student be pondering which strategy will help her figure out a word?

STRATEGY 1 BE FLEXIBLE

1. Invite students to share some of the strategies they use when they come across an unknown word. Typical responses may include sounding it out (phonics), skipping it, trying to figure it out from the other words in the sentence (context), breaking it into parts (syllabication), looking it up in a dictionary, and asking someone. Acknowledge that all these strategies may be used at one time or another and encourage students to provide examples of times when they have used each of them. List all of them on the chalkboard.

2. Tell students that strategic readers are flexible in terms of how they try to recognize unfamiliar words. This means that they know several strategies and use the most efficient and/or effective one(s) to figure out unknown words. Provide several examples where context can be used to figure out the unknown word. Have them identify the strategy that is used.

 The man put a _____ on his head. (hat)

 The color of milk is _____. (white)

3. Help students recognize that there are times when context can be used; moreover, stress that skilled readers also rely on context clues. Guide students to realize that context clues are used to help answer the question "What word would make sense in the sentence?"

4. Provide another sentence for which context clues can be used to predict more than one word that may sound right or make sense in the sentence.

 Jake climbed a tree and picked a red _____. (for instance, apple, cherry)

 After the words have been given by students, list them on the chalkboard and ask, "Does *apple* make sense in this sentence? Why?" Repeat this question for each word listed on the chalkboard. Then use a word that does not make sense and have students explain why the word would not be a good choice.

5. Ask students whether the word the author used in step 4 can be correctly predicted from its context. Because it cannot, provide an initial letter clue.

 Jake climbed a tree and picked a red a_____.

 Students should now be able to determine that the word is *apple*. If additional clues are necessary, supply another letter or two. Once the correct word is supplied, help students realize that they used context and some letter clues to figure out the word. Stress that context and phonics were used in combination. Use other examples, such as those included below, and have students think aloud.

 I like _____.

 The game lasted more than _____ hours.

 In the first example, a student might say, "I like. . . . Let's see. There are many words that make sense here: *soccer, candy,* and *music.* From the context or words provided, I can't really know the word so I need some letters in the word (teacher writes in a *b*). The word could be *bears,* a girl's name like *Brenda* or *Barb,* or. . . . No, wait, it can't be *Brenda* or *Barb,* because a small *b* is there and people's names begin with capital letters. It must be *bears* or *beans* or something like that. I still need more information (teacher writes *ban*). Well, I guess it can't be *bears* or *beans* because they are not spelled that way. Perhaps the word is *bands.* I need more letters (teacher

writes *banan*). No, it isn't *bands*; *ban-na, ba-nan* (student tries different pronunciations). Oh, *banana* could be the word; I mean *bananas,* because it makes sense, and I think that's the way the word is spelled."

6. After several similar examples, remind students that in reading all the words are always there. It is easier to make predictions because both context and letter clues are readily available in natural text.

7. Provide another example in which the missing word is difficult for students to pronounce and have them try to predict the unknown word. With context clues, many words are possible.

The story was _____. (unbelievable)

Supply the initial letter and the student may still not know the word. Sometimes it is possible to find prefixes, suffixes, endings, and a root word. Write the word in the sentence and encourage students to use this knowledge. Draw lines between the major word parts and have students try to pronounce the word. Encourage discussion about how affixes can be used to determine the word's meaning. Then ask whether it sounds like a word they know and whether it makes sense in the sentence.

8. When numerous activities such as the foregoing have been completed, help students develop a flexible approach to use when figuring out unknown words. Two charts that might be adapted follow.

Strategies to Figure Out Unknown Words

1. Use the words around the unknown word to help think of a word that makes sense in the sentence.
2. Use the letters, the sounds associated with the letters, and the words around the unknown word to say a word that makes sense in the sentence.
3. Look for root words, prefixes, suffixes, and endings. Try to pronounce the various word parts to see whether you have heard it before. Try various pronunciations, especially for the vowels.
4. Continue reading. Later sentences may help you figure out the unfamiliar word.
5. As a last resort, use the dictionary, ask someone, or skip the unknown word.

Questions for Figuring Out Unknown Words

1. What makes sense here?
2. What sound does it start with?
3. Are there root words, prefixes, suffixes, or endings that I know?
4. Should I skip the word and keep reading?
5. Can a dictionary help me?
6. Should I ask someone?

9. Help students realize that *flexibility* is essential to identifying unknown words. Good readers don't keep trying something that doesn't work; they move to another strategy. Strategy 3 in Section 7.5, where the notion of a critter was developed, may be useful in helping students monitor the effectiveness of the strategies they use to identify unknown words.

Practice and Reinforcement Activities

1. Have students share a word they are unable to figure out, along with the context in which it is found. If the student is unable to share his or her strategies, model how a combination of strategies might be used to figure out the unknown word. Help students refine the effectiveness of their strategies.

2. Encourage students to record and share their successful attempts at figuring out unknown words by verbalizing the various strategies they used.

3. Develop exercises where a modified cloze procedure is used to refine students' ability to use context and letter clues. Discuss the word choices with the students, as in the following example.

> She left a _____ on the table.
>
> She left a p _____ on the table.
>
> She left a p ___ ___ on the table.
>
> She left a p ___ n on the table.

Students may request another letter to determine whether the word is *pin*, *pen*, or *pan*.

4. Younger students may profit from picture clues in cloze exercises, as illustrated below.

> There is a _____.

5. Have students write sentences with space for a word that is missing. Students can exchange papers with one another and attempt to fill in the missing word. Papers are returned to the authors for verification. If students have difficulty, the authors can supply the first letter or two of the missing word. This activity may also lead students to an understanding of synonyms.

6. Have students keep a log in which they record unfamiliar, unknown words, the context (a phrase or sentence), and the strategies used to pronounce the words and determine their meanings. Provide opportunities for small group sharing. Be sure especially useful efforts are shared with the entire class.

Date	Book/Page	Underlined Word in Sentence	What Was Done
3-12-01	*Sitting Bull, p. 1*	*But inside the cone-shaped, buffalo-hide <u>tipi</u> on the south bank of the river . . .*	*From the words buffalo hide and cone-shaped, I decided it was a tepee. When I looked up the word tipi, I was correct.*

7. Apply strategies for identifying unknown words within the ongoing instructional program.

CHAPTER 4

Developing Fluency and Successful Oral Reading Behaviors

OVERVIEW

Reading fluency is the ability to read text in a normal speaking voice with appropriate intonation and inflection. Students who read fluently have developed automaticity (Samuels, 1994). Automaticity means that students do not have to devote their attention to the task of decoding words; they can focus on constructing the meaning of what they are reading. Suppose Maria is able to read each of the words in a passage correctly, but pauses after each word. She may have difficulty understanding the passage because of her lack of fluency. Good readers read fluently without much thought about how they are reading. On the other hand, readers who struggle may read word by word in a monotone or spend so much time trying to pronounce words that they have little or no attention focused on constructing meaning.

> Good teachers understand that both silent reading and oral reading are valuable tools for instructional decisions.

Related to fluency are various oral reading behaviors. Although oral reading has traditionally been misused, good teachers understand that both silent reading and oral reading are valuable tools for instructional decisions. Just as silent reading tends to be a better method for assessing reading comprehension, oral reading provides important information about the reader's proficiency in applying reading strategies.

Oral reading can serve two primary purposes: assessment and performance. When used as assessment, oral reading should be private. Teachers should listen to students individually to assess reading miscues or to identify problems with reading fluency. On the other hand, oral reading can be an end in itself, a public performance. If students are reading aloud for the purpose of performing, they should read for an appropriate audience.

This chapter is divided into two parts. The first part examines oral reading as assessment. It begins with a rationale for using oral reading as a diagnostic tool and then considers fluency and common difficulties students may have when reading aloud. The second part discusses reading as performance. Again, it begins with a rationale for oral reading as performance and then provides suggestions for using oral reading in the classroom.

Oral Reading as Assessment

Oral reading can provide teachers with useful diagnostic information about the strategies students employ as they read. Imagine a second-grade student, Maria, who has just silently read a grade-appropriate book. Maria is unable to retell any part of the story. Is Maria's comprehension problem the result of insufficient background knowledge, a weak understanding of story structure, or the result of too many miscues? Of course, the answer is impossible to determine without listening to Maria read aloud.

Suppose you ask Maria to read her favorite part of the story. Using picture clues, Maria turns to her chosen chapter, but, as she reads, you notice she makes several miscues per page. These miscues, or deviations from the text, signal to you that Maria's lack of comprehension may be attributed, at least in part, to oral reading difficulties. You can then pinpoint Maria's problems and use some of the recommendations in this chapter to create minilessons for Maria and other students with the same problem.

You may have students who read all of the words in a passage correctly but still do not understand what the words are saying because they are not reading them in natural phrases. Word-by-word reading can hinder comprehension. If you have students who are not fluent readers, refer to Sections 4.1 and 4.2 for strategies to help build reading fluency.

You should not use oral reading as a diagnostic tool in a public setting or in the traditional round-robin reading situation. Round-robin reading is asking one student to read aloud while a group of students listens. Think back to your own days in school. Most likely you had at least one teacher who used round-robin reading. Were you uncomfortable when it was your turn to read? Many students who are asked to read aloud in front of a group are acutely embarrassed. What did you do when other students were reading? Students often read ahead, lose their place, yell out corrections, or simply tune out. None of these behaviors promote good reading or a stimu-

Oral reading needs to be private when used as an assessment.

lating reading discussion, yet some teachers persist in round-robin reading in their classes. Round-robin reading is not a good use of class time. See Resources for Chapter 4 for Oral Reading Alternatives to Round-Robin Reading. Additional ideas can be found in Opitz and Rasinski (1998).

How, then, should you listen to students read aloud if you don't have them read in front of the class? Remember, listening to oral reading is a private performance between you and the student. Instead of wasting time with round-robin reading, make a commitment to listen to each student read every two or three weeks. That means you should listen to two or three students read aloud to you every day.

Reading with individual students should take only 10 minutes out of your daily schedule. While the class is completing reading-writing activities, simply ask one student at a time to read with you. Make this a personal time between you and the student. Don't sit at your desk, but move to the student's desk or to another table. During the session, alternate between choosing the selection for the student and letting the student make the decision about what to read. The passage you select may be from a reading book, trade book, or graded reading passage. When you select material for oral read-

ing, choose a passage the student has not yet read. Remember, your purpose is to listen for the reading strategies the student uses while reading rather than to hear a practiced piece of prose.

When the student reads to you, note the kinds of miscues he or she makes. You may jot down the miscues while you are tape-recording the student and record them on a chart (see Resources for Chapter 4). As the student reads, you can also assess the use of comprehension strategies by asking the student to retell the story.

At the end of two or three weeks, you should have information about the oral reading strategies of each student. You can group the students for instruction by their reading needs. For example, students who are word-by-word readers can meet with you for a lesson on reading fluency. Students who tend to omit words can be grouped together for that lesson. It's important to remember that one of the purposes of listening to your students read aloud is to make instructional decisions. Listening to oral reading can be the basis for much of what you teach.

Listening to oral reading can also be the basis for retrospective miscue analysis. Retrospective miscue analysis invites and engages students to reflect upon and evaluate the reading process by analyzing their oral reading miscues (Goodman & Marek, 1996). In essence, students can use retrospective miscue analysis to realize the predicting, confirming, and correcting behaviors that characterize good readers; moreover, such analysis "can help them come to revalue themselves as readers" (Goodman & Marek, 1996, p. ix). We urge you, when appropriate, to use students' reading miscues for instructional purposes in the various situations we describe. For each situation, the behaviors are listed with the outcome you should anticipate after you have designed appropriate intervention. Please remember that you need not use every strategy listed in each part. Use only the ones that best complement the needs of your students.

TECHNOLOGY RESOURCE

Activities for Developing Fluent Readers

http://gamma.sil.org/lingualinks/library/literacy/fre371
Contains lessons to build students' reading fluency

Lack of Fluency

Behavior Observed	The student's oral reading lacks fluency.
Anticipated Outcome	The student will read more fluently.

PERSPECTIVE AND STRATEGIES

Many emergent readers lack fluency as they begin reading. They may be *choppy readers,* reading with many stops, starts, and hesitations. They may be *monotonous readers* and read with little or no expression, or they may be inappropriately *hasty readers* and race through the passage ignoring phrasing and punctuation (Wilson, 1988). The cause of fluency problems for beginning readers is that they are processing many new things at the same time. They are just beginning to expand their sight vocabulary and are learning word-identification strategies. For beginning readers, fluency may be considered a developmental process. As they learn more reading strategies and read a variety of materials, they become more fluent. Such is the case for most beginning readers, whatever their age.

Older readers may also have difficulty reading fluently. These students probably lack a basic sight vocabulary and effective word-identification strategies. They may also be reading books that are too difficult for them.

Clay (1967) has noted that average readers typically move through the four stages of reading described. Teachers who see students *remaining* at the second or third stages have cause for concern and may need to use intervention strategies.

Stage	Characteristics/Behaviors
1	• Reading sounds fluent, but students make many miscues. • Students are unaware or unconcerned that their reading does not accurately represent the passage or text.
2	• Students are conscious of matching their speech to words in the passage or text. • Students may point to individual words. • Students may read in a staccato fashion.
3	• Students continue reading word by word, but finger-pointing disappears. • Students are still conscious of matching their oral responses to each word.
4	• Students no longer read word by word. • Meaningful phrase units characterize reading.

In addition to Clay's stages, the Resources for Chapter 4 contain, among other items, a Procedure for Determining Words Per Minute, Median Oral Reading Rates for Students in Grades Two Through Five, and a Five-Point Fluency Scale for Reading. These three resources will be especially helpful in determining and assessing fluency in reading.

Numerous strategies for developing sight vocabulary and word identification are presented in Chapter 3, and they should be considered in tandem with the following strategies. Note that there are two major classifications of strategies—one for younger, emergent readers and another for readers who are struggling.

For Younger Readers

1. Recognize that reading is a developmental process and fluency will develop as students increase their sight vocabularies and acquire a repertoire of word-identification strategies. A lack of fluency may be expected at this level.

2. Encourage the repeated readings of pattern books. See Appendix C for a listing of pattern books and related activities. Plenty of practice will help students learn sight words automatically and will build their confidence. Students can read to each other, to their favorite stuffed animal, to parents and relatives, and so on.

3. Use daily class experience stories and guide students in the reading. A story could be as simple as the following one.

 - Today is _____.
 - The date is _____, November _____.
 - The weather is _____.

 Begin by inviting volunteers to supply missing words. Then read the story to the class. Encourage students to join you. Point to words and phrases. Use your hand to indicate phrases and have individuals and the whole class read and reread the story. Comment positively on the smoothness of the reading.

4. Provide opportunities for students to listen to talking books on audiotapes or computer programs. Capitalize on their interests when a particularly popular audiotape or computer program is identified by staying out of the way while students enjoy the same experience over and over.

5. Fasten a sheet of paper in the front of books that students can read to others at home or school. The sheet is signed by the person who has listened to the book.

6. Use echo reading where you read a phrase or sentence and the student repeats it after you and tries to "echo" your phrasing and expression.

7. Identify songs and rhymes that are enjoyed by students. Print the words on chart paper, the overhead projector, or the chalkboard. Engage in repeated readings or singings.

8. Read a passage for students, explaining that you are reading with expression. Tell students to pay attention to *how* you read the passage. Then ask students to read the passage with you. Ask students to try to read with the same expression that you use. Reread the passage together until students seem comfortable with the text. Next, fade out of the reading by lowering your voice or stopping reading while students continue. Finally, ask a student to read the passage alone and give praise for appropriate expression.

9. Make a videotape of yourself reading an easy book. Send the book and videotape home with the student to practice reading at home.

10. Use the Fluency Development Lesson developed by Rasinski, Padak, and Sturtevant (1994). The lesson was designed for teachers of students in the primary grades who struggle to achieve even initial stages of fluency (see Five-Point Fluency Scale for Reading in Resources for Chapter 4).

 - Make copies of a 50 to 150 word passage for each student and distribute them. Choose passages that will be enjoyable for students.
 - Read the passage to students while they follow along silently on their copies. You may want to reread the passage several times.
 - Discuss the content of the passage and the quality of your reading with students.
 - Guide students in choral readings of the passage. Vary the readings by using echo reading and responsive reading.
 - Have students select a partner and then practice reading the passage three times to the partner. The partner follows the passage, provides help if needed, and gives

affirmations. Then the students reverse roles.

- Invite students to read the text to the class. Individuals, partners, and groups up to four can read to the class. Seek other opportunities for students to share the passage with others in the school and receive positive reinforcement.
- Have students take the passage home to share with as many family members as possible. Be sure students are praised for their efforts.
- Maintain a file of short, interesting passages used in the lessons and encourage students to read them on their own.

11. Use a big book in a shared book experience. After the book is introduced, read, and discussed, it can be reread several times. Encourage students to read along. Provide regular-sized versions of the big book that students can access for additional readings at school. Encourage the books to be taken home and shared.

12. Locate short, enjoyable selections of poetry and make them available to students.

13. Encourage the reading and rereading of a variety of books and other printed materials.

For Older Readers Who Struggle

1. Be sure students are not asked to read books that are too difficult. A student who makes 10 or more miscues in 100 words is probably being asked to read material that is too difficult. Seek easier materials where the student will make fewer than seven miscues in every 100 words. Remember that word recognition must be accurate before it can become automatic.

2. The method of structured repeated readings found in the Resources for Chapter 4 is an excellent strategy. It motivates struggling readers and provides a visible means for them to see their progress.

3. Encourage wide reading and rereading of easy books.

4. Invite students to prepare a story to read orally to younger readers. Have the students practice with a tape recorder and also share the story with you before it is shared with the group of younger students. Ensure that the experience will be a positive one.

5. Have students practice so-called "easy" books that can be enjoyed by younger students. The books can be recorded on video and/or audiotape and shared with younger students.

6. Try the neurological impress method. The basic procedure is listed in the box on the following page.

7. Remember that the lack of fluency may be a symptom of an inadequate sight vocabulary and/or word-identification strategies. Refer to Chapter 3 for strategies to strengthen these areas.

Procedure for the Neurological Impress Method (NIM)*

1. The student sits slightly in front of the teacher so that the teacher's voice is close to the student's ear.
2. The student is told not to think about reading; you are helping him or her to slide the eyes across the paper. Another explanation is that, just as we practice swimming in order to become good swimmers, we need to practice reading to become good readers.
3. The teacher and student read the same material out loud *together*; the teacher reads a *little* louder and faster than the student.
4. *Reread* the initial lines or paragraph several times together before going on to new material (that is, wait until you feel the student is confident in reading that section). Drop your voice back behind the student's if you think he or she is gaining fluency.
5. In the *initial* sessions, 2 to 3 minutes of reading lines is sufficient. The aim is to establish a fluent reading pattern in the reader; appropriate *intonation* and *expression* in reading the lines are vital.
6. At *no* time correct the student or test the student in any way. The major concern is with the style of reading rather than with reading accuracy.
7. The teacher runs his or her finger under the words *simultaneously* with the words being read. The student should take over this function when he or she is confident enough. The teacher can help the student by placing his or her hand over the student's and guiding it smoothly. *Make sure finger and voice* are operating together.
8. *Echoing* is used as a supplementary technique to NIM if a student has extreme difficulty with saying a phrase or word. The student must repeat the phrase *after* the teacher several times, and when he or she has satisfactorily repeated the phrase, the teacher then goes back to the *written* version.
9. Periodically, the pace *must* be speeded up just for a few minutes.
10. Start with reading material *lower* than the student is presently able to handle.
11. Do 15 minutes a day to a total period of time of 8 to 12 hours over several weeks.

*Heckelman, 1969.

Lack of Fluency: Incorrect Phrasing

Behavior Observed	The student ignores punctuation, adds punctuation, or uses inappropriate intonation.
Anticipated Outcome	The student will read text more fluently.

PERSPECTIVE AND STRATEGIES

Incorrect phrasing may be the result of poor reading habits, a lack of fluency, or an overreliance on phonics. It may also be related to the failure to follow the author's flow of ideas. You need to hypothesize why the student is using incorrect phrasing and then select an approach to the situation. The following strategies may help.

1. The student should be shown examples where punctuation is ignored or substituted. Discuss whether the student should have paid closer attention to the punctuation. Be sure to consider possible impact on meaning. Invite students to hypothesize the predicting behaviors that may help explain the miscue. The following examples may be useful.

 Sharon Kay is my best friend.
 Sharon, Kay is my best friend.

 Jake, my puppy is sick.
 Jake, my puppy, is sick.

 John Allen and Mark Wayne are friends.
 John, Allen, and Mark Wayne are friends.

2. Write experience stories with the student. Ask the student to read the story back to you and to pay close attention to the natural phrasing of the words.

3. Read pattern books with the student. (See Appendix C for a list of pattern books.) Each time the pattern is repeated, ask the student to read it. Stress that the pattern should sound like speech.

4. List common phrases on cards and place them in a pocket chart. Ask the student to read the phrases as they would sound naturally. Some possible phrases are listed below.

in the lake	on the road
out of sight	near the school
over the hill	on the table
before the bell	in my room
in the closet	by my house
on the playground	by the river

 Words for phrase building can be found in the Resources for Chapter 3 (Revised Dolch List and High-Frequency Nouns).

5. On a page of copied text, place slash marks at each natural break. Have the student try to read fluently to each slash mark before pausing. Model phrases as needed.

 My friend and I / decided to / ride our bikes / to school today.

 Tomorrow / our class / will go / on a field trip.

6. Give the student ample opportunities to read with correct phrasing and punctuation by reading along with him or her. First, read an easy

text to the student. Then, ask the student to read along with you. Finally, ask the student to read the text independently as you support the effort by softly reading in the background.

7. Use echo reading to encourage reading fluency. Choose an easy text, read one line, and ask the student to read the same line with the same intonation that you used.

8. Often, students experiencing difficulty with reading hear only other novice readers reading aloud. Model good reading fluency in front of the entire class by reading to the class each day. Also, model good reading with the students having difficulty with inappropriate phrasing. Alternate reading pages or paragraphs with the students.

9. Use repeated readings with partners as a technique to build fluency. Ask two students to choose short selections and read them until they know them well. Have each student read the selection to the other.

10. Have students mark or note places in their readings where they have ignored punctuation, added unnecessary punctuation, or used inappropriate intonation. Then invite students to talk about these instances with you. Later, small groups of students could share their notes with each other. The goal is for students to learn from their miscues. Some guiding questions follow.

Why did I read the sentence that way?

What was I thinking about as I read?

Did I decide something didn't make sense? Why?

If it didn't make sense, what did I do (if anything)?

Did I repeat to confirm or correct what I was reading?

What have I learned about my reading from these examples?

11. Model phrasing by first reading a sentence word for word and asking the student to comment. Then use different phrasing to help the student grasp the idea that certain words go together.

The/little/puppy/began/to/bark.

The little/puppy/began/to bark.

The little puppy/began to bark.

12. Use the Oral Reading Opportunities that follow Section 4.11 to select natural, meaningful ways for students to share their reading using appropriate phrasing.

Failure to Attempt Unknown Words

Behavior Observed	The student waits to be told unknown words and does not attempt them independently.
Anticipated Outcome	The student will use appropriate strategies to decode unknown words.

PERSPECTIVE AND STRATEGIES

The failure of some students to attempt unknown words may be due to several factors. First, students may not have been taught a functional strategy for word identification, and they do not have a variety of strategies to use when confronted with an unknown word in reading. Although students may have been taught phonics and the use of context, they do not realize that these strategies may be used during reading. Second, the teacher may tell students unknown words, thereby reducing their need to acquire internal strategies for word identification. Third, students who are usually struggling may be reluctant to take risks. Instead, they manipulate the teacher or other students to tell them words they don't know. The following strategies may be useful.

1. When the student hesitates at an unknown word, wait ten seconds before saying anything. If there is no response, ask the student to try the word using the known sounds. Praise the student for any attempt at the word.

2. Discuss what the student thinks should be done when confronted with an unknown word.

 For example, ask the student to think about a time when he or she was reading and came to an unknown word. Ask the student what strategies were used to figure out the word. If the student is unable to suggest any strategies, guide the student in expressing strategies that emphasize the sound-symbol correspondence of the word (see Sections 3.1 and 3.2 in Chapter 3), strategies that use the meaning of the sentence, and strategies that use knowledge about the English language (see Section 3.7 in Chapter 3).

What strategy can be used when this student hesitates to attempt an unknown word?

3. Have the student give the word some sounds and take a guess at the word. Then have the student read on to the end of the phrase or sentence and decide whether the word makes sense.

4. Ask the student to go back a line and see if the preceding sentence and the words around the unknown word suggest a possibility. Read the sentence aloud for the student, skipping the unknown word, and ask what word would make sense in the blank.

5. Ask the student to reread the sentence and try to guess a word that begins with the initial sound of the unknown word and makes sense in the sentence.

6. Provide oral examples where the student uses context to anticipate the missing word.

> I really like to watch _____.
>
> I would like to see the _____ game.
>
> It's time to go to _____.
>
> I found _____ in my backpack.

7. Use easy cloze exercises where students are asked to predict a word that makes sense. Discuss various choices offered by the students and invite them to share how and why they made their specific predictions. Gradually include graphic information about the exact word the author used. Use examples like the following ones.

> I like _____.
>
> I like to go to _____.
>
> I like to go to s _ _ _ _ l.

8. If the student encounters several unknown words in a line of print, the reading material is probably too difficult. Provide reading material that is easy for the student to read.

9. Invite other students to share their experiences with unknown words using a chart like the one below.

Page	Difficult Word/ Phrase	What I Did	How It Worked

Have students complete the chart during a reading assignment by filling in the various categories. Then have students share their strategies by focusing on predicting, confirming, and correcting strategies. Be sure to reinforce the strategies that are especially good—even if they did not result in success. Help students also realize that sometimes the strategies used will not result in the correct pronunciation of the word.

10. Be alert for instances in your reading where you encounter a difficult word. Bring in the passage and model for students what you did to deal with the word. Thinking aloud is especially helpful.

Meaning-Changing Substitutions

Behavior Observed	The student substitutes a word or words, and the text does not make sense.
Anticipated Outcome	The student will read the text with fewer substitutions.

PERSPECTIVE AND STRATEGIES

Remind the student that reading is a process of constructing meaning from print. When reading, the student should ask, "Does this make sense?" This question serves as one way for the student to monitor his or her comprehension. The student should be taught to use semantic (meaning) cues in reading. Try the following strategies.

1. Remind the student to think while reading and encourage the student to stop and reread the material if it does not make sense. The student may be viewing reading as "saying words" rather than reading to construct meaning.

2. Give the student oral exercises to identify words that do not make sense in the context of the sentence. Some examples follow.

 - The mail carrier delivered the groceries.
 - Helen set her calendar so it would ring at seven o'clock.
 - Bill went to the store to buy some candy for her sister.

 Have the student explain why a particular word does not make sense and invite a substitute word or phrase. For example, if the student identifies *groceries* in the first sentence, have the student explain why the word doesn't make sense and offer a word that would make sense. The student might say:

Mail carriers do not deliver groceries, but they do deliver mail, letters, and packages. Any of those words would make sense.

You might also ask the student what word or words wouldn't make sense if *groceries* was the correct word (i.e., *mail carrier*) and what word or words might be substituted for mail carrier (e.g., employee, store, woman, girl, man, boy).

3. Give the student oral and written exercises containing cloze tasks and instruct the student to anticipate omitted words that make sense. Develop the idea that language dictates that only certain types of words can be placed after certain language structures.

 - After playing, the children _____ inside.
 - I will see you after _____.
 - He was reading a _____.
 - "I lost my money," _____ Carlos.

 For example, in the sentence "I saw an _____ in the tree," the word *an* signals that a word beginning with a vowel (e.g., apple) would be required. Provide another example where the preceding part of the sentence may signal an adjective or noun (e.g., The _____ frog jumped in the pond; The little _____ began to bark).

4. Use small-group activities in which certain key words in a story are covered. Ask for responses from the group and have students evaluate each response. The ultimate criterion is "Does the word make sense?" Invite students to explain how the words in the story help the reader to predict other words. Then uncover the word letter by letter and encourage students to refine their predictions and ultimately confirm the word.

5. Keep track of substitutions to see whether certain words are habitually associated with other words. Write selections where the grammatical structures make it highly unlikely for the habitual associations to occur. Consider the following examples.

was and *saw*

Once upon a time there *was* a girl named Jennifer. Her hair *was* long and brown. Jennifer liked to wear headbands in her hair. One day, while she *was* walking downtown, she *saw* some headbands in a store window. She *saw* blue, yellow, and pink headbands. The blue headband *was* the prettiest, so she bought it.

in and *on*

Vanessa liked to collect insects. She kept the spiders *in* a jar *on* top of her dresser. One Friday, her mother invited some friends to come over for coffee. They were talking *in* the kitchen. Vanessa took her jar of spiders *in* the kitchen and set it *on* the table. When one lady reached for a cup *on* the table, she bumped the jar. It landed *on* the floor. What do you think happened next?

when and *then*

Adam and his mother had some errands to do. His mother said, "I will get my coat; *then* I will be ready to go. *When* you find your jacket, come out to the car. First, we will go to the supermarket; *then* we can go to the pet shop to find out *when* the puppy will be ready to come home. *When* we bring the puppy home, you will get the basket out of the closet. *Then* the puppy will have a nice place to sleep."

6. Provide sentences from students' reading that contain a substituted word written above the text. Have students discuss whether the substituted word makes sense. Use the examples provided below or construct your own.

they
They went to the zoo because there were many things to see.

hat
He hit the ball out of the park.

saw
She was the first one to finish the race.

7. Provide exercises that contain substitutions two different readers made in the same sentence. Discuss which substitution appears to be closer to the author's meaning. Be sure students understand why one particular substitution may be better than another substitution. See the following examples.

the
Michael decided to ride along a little road.

walk
Michael decided to ride along a little road.

8. Tape-record the student's reading. Give the student a copy of what was read and have the student listen to the reading and note the substitutions that occur. Ask the student which word would make sense in the sentence. Then check the letters in the word to determine which word the author had written.

9. If there are many substitutions that distort the author's intended meaning, the book may be too difficult. Choose materials that are easy for the student to read. Generally, materials are appropriate for instruction if the student misses less than 7 of 100 running words in text.

10. Have students keep track of their reading and report instances where a word that did not make sense was substituted for a word in the text. Invite students to share how they dealt with the substitution. Help them realize the predicting, confirming, and correcting behaviors that they may have used.

11. Use actual examples from students' reading to model how they can monitor their reading. Such examples could be used in minilessons.

Nonmeaning-Changing Substitutions

Behavior Observed	The student substitutes a word or words, and the phrase or sentence still makes sense.
Anticipated Outcome	The student will read the text with fewer substitutions.

PERSPECTIVE AND STRATEGIES

Substitutions in reading may occur for several reasons.

- First, the student may be ignoring graphophonic cues in reading.

- Second, the student may be relying too heavily on context clues to predict words that make sense in the sentence.

- Third, the student's oral language may be different from the author's written language, and the student produces a response that makes sense. For example, the student may say "can't" for "cannot."

Because the basic meaning of the text is not adversely affected, there may be no need for the teacher to take any action. A student who continues to substitute words that differ from the text, however, may not be willing to take the time to identify unknown words. For students who habitually make these kinds of substitutions, you may want to try some of the following strategies.

1. After the student has completed the passage, point out the words that differ from the text. Ask the student to reread the sentence paying close attention to these words. If the student rereads the word correctly, mention the change. Tell the student that, although the first attempt may not have changed the author's meaning,

misreading words often leads to difficulty understanding the text. If the student repeats the miscue, draw attention to the sounds in the word. Ask the student to think of another word that uses the sounds represented by the letters in the word.

2. Some students make substitutions in reading because they are not given enough time to decode unknown words. As the student is reading, encourage all attempts at identifying unfamiliar words. Be patient and use wait time.

3. For a student who makes many substitutions, tape-record the student reading an easy passage. Give the student a copy of the text and play back the audiotape. Ask the student to underline any words from the audiotape that do not match the printed text. Ask the student to use the sounds associated with a letter or letter combination to help figure out the underlined word. If the student is unable to correct the miscue, model an effective strategy by thinking aloud.

4. Students who make many miscues in reading may be reading from a passage that is too difficult. Give the students easier reading material and stress the point that reading means understanding the printed text.

Nonword Substitutions

Behavior Observed	The student produces a nonword instead of a real word.
Anticipated Outcome	The student will say words that make sense in the text.

PERSPECTIVE AND STRATEGIES

The student must be helped to realize that reading is a meaningful process and words pronounced should make sense. Use or adapt Section 2 in Chapter 2. Reading should sound like oral language.

1. Ask the student what the nonword means. It is possible that the student knows the meaning but has mispronounced the word.

2. Provide oral and written examples in which the student attempts to predict the appropriate word that has been omitted. Stress that some words can be predicted from context and have students use their background knowledge to make predictions. The goal should be to say a real word, not a nonword.

 - After school, we went to play _____.

 - I will mail the _____.

 - The horse _____ over the fence.

3. Provide examples that contain a nonword and ask the student to tell what real word could replace the nonword. Have the student explain why he or she was able to give a real word. Praise the student for saying that the other words in the sentence provided cues. Some examples follow.

 - He drank a glass of fex. (milk, water, juice, etc.)

 - The zop bought some candy. (girl, boy, woman, person, etc.)

4. Place removable opaque tape over certain words in the student's reading materials that can be easily predicted. Encourage the student to supply a real word that makes sense. Help the student to transfer this same strategy to identifying unknown words.

5. Five or more nonwords per 100 words probably means that the reading material is too difficult. Provide materials that are easy for the student to read aloud.

6. Tape-record the student reading. Play back the audiotape pausing at each nonword. Ask the student,

 Does this make sense? What word would make sense in that spot?

 To avoid the student forming a mental set, ask the same question from time to time when the student's reading does make sense.

7. Model how you can use context and phonic knowledge to pronounce a word. For example, you could read *mansion* as *mīnsīn* in the following sentence.

 The big old mansion in the neighborhood had several broken windows.

 Then you could model as follows:

I know mīnsīn *doesn't make sense. Let me take another look at the word and think of words that could have broken windows. A* house, garage, *and* car *can have broken windows, but none of those words begins with the same beginning sound as the word. Let me try the word again. I see the word* man *but* mansin *doesn't sound like a word I know. Perhaps it's* mānsin. *No, that doesn't make sense. Let me try again:* mānshun, mănshun. *I've heard of a mansion. Let me try that word in the sentence to see if it makes sense. Yes, the word* mansion *makes sense. It is another name for a house that is big. I think that's it.*

Be sure students realize the predicting, correcting, and confirming behaviors that characterized your reading.

Repetitions of Words or Phrases

Behavior Observed	The student repeats words, phrases, or sentences.
Anticipated Outcome	The student will be able to read the text with fewer repetitions.

PERSPECTIVE AND STRATEGIES

Repetition may help the student understand what he or she has read. The teacher must decide whether the student is analyzing the repeated word, anticipating a difficult word, making a legitimate effort to have the reading make sense, or merely repeating from habit. Consider the following.

1. If the student's repetitions are frequent, it is possible that the reading material is too difficult. If this is the case, provide the student with reading material at a level that is easy to read.

2. Repetitions that serve as "stalls" provide the student with extra time to try to figure out an unknown word. This may be a normal part of the reading process. Excessive use of the stall technique, however, may indicate that the reading material is too difficult and/or effective reading strategies are needed. It may also indicate a need to teach how language clues can be used to anticipate words.

3. Praise the student when a word, phrase, or sentence is repeated to preserve ongoing meaning.

Tell the student that this behavior is fully acceptable in order to make sense of what is read.

4. If repetitions are merely a habit, it may be helpful to have the student record a passage on audiotape and discuss it with you. The student should be guided to note which repetitions are habitual, resulting in less efficient reading. Encourage rereadings.

5. Sometimes a student repeatedly overcorrects to ensure word-for-word accuracy. The student should be encouraged not to break the meaning flow of the text when what is read makes sense.

6. Invite students to share and discuss instances when they repeated words, phrases, or sentences in their reading. Help them see how their repetitions may contribute to or detract from efficient reading. For example, repeating to confirm meaning would be an effective use. Many repetitions may make reading less efficient because they are not done to correct a miscue or to help make sense of the passage.

Meaning-Changing Omissions

SECTION
4.8

Behavior Observed	The student omits one or more words, and the text does not make sense or distorts the author's intended meaning.
Anticipated Outcome	The student will read text with fewer omissions.

PERSPECTIVE AND STRATEGIES

Because this type of omission changes the meaning or does not make sense of the text, the student needs to understand that reading is the process of constructing meaning from print (see Section 2.2 in Chapter 2). Suggested strategies follow.

1. Frequent omissions may mean that the reading material is too difficult. Supply reading material at a lower level.

2. Provide exercises that contain omissions made by a reader. In a pocket chart, make sentences from word cards that have a word that can be omitted without losing the grammatical sense of the sentence. Have students discuss whether the omission changes the author's intended meaning and how they arrived at that conclusion. Use sentences like the following ones.

 - The large horse ate lots of oats. (large)
 - Jeff walked to the toy store. (toy)
 - I have twenty-five dollars. (five)

3. Remind the student that reading is supposed to make sense and convey the author's meaning. Ask the student,

 Did that make sense?

 Use this same question from time to time when the omission also makes sense. Help students reflect on their reading so they come to realize that some miscues may change the meaning and not be corrected—especially if they make sense in the context of the passage. At other times, students will correct miscues that do not make sense. Encourage students to explain their various behaviors so they gain greater insight into their reading.

4. Ask the student to follow the line of print with his or her finger or a marker. Often students who omit text are reading too fast. Following text with a marker or finger may slow the reading down and increase concentration on the text.

5. Place the student in a group for choral reading. Choral reading is reading text aloud in a group. By reading in a group, the student may pay closer attention to the text.

6. Have the student tape-record his or her reading. Using a printed copy of the selection, help the student mark the omissions. Then discuss the omissions with the student, seeking the student's insights about the omissions and their impact on meaning. Help the student realize the importance of monitoring his or her reading to construct meaning. Reinforce important observations the student made.

SECTION 4.9

Nonmeaning-Changing Omissions

Behavior Observed	The student omits one or more words, and the text still makes sense.
Anticipated Outcome	The student will read text with fewer omissions.

PERSPECTIVE AND STRATEGIES

Omissions that result in little or no change in meaning should not require any direct action from the teacher unless the student habitually omits words. If the omissions occur frequently, try the following strategies.

1. Ask the student to slow down when reading aloud. Younger students may wish to follow the line of print with a marker or their finger to make sure they do not omit text. Even expert readers occasionally use this strategy with challenging text, so do not discourage its use with young children.

2. Give the student several opportunities to read along with a taped story. Make it a challenge for the student to keep up with the reader without omitting words.

3. Older students develop an eye-voice span where their eyes are "ahead" of their voice. Omissions may occur when the student's eyes are reading faster than his or her voice. When this type of behavior is observed, discuss it with the student to gain insight.

4. Tape-record the student's reading and have him or her listen to the tape while following with the selection, paying particular attention to omissions. Then ask the student to evaluate the quality of the omissions and offer reasons why they occurred. During the discussion, help the student realize that, although the overall meaning is retained, some omitted words probably would have provided greater detail or a richer meaning.

Excessive Use of Phonics

Behavior Observed	The student habitually tries to sound out words when confronted with an unknown word in text.
Anticipated Outcome	The student will use both phonics and context to determine unknown words.

PERSPECTIVE AND STRATEGIES

Some students may have been taught that the appropriate strategy to figure out unknown words is to sound them out. These students may not have been taught other strategies that can be used with unknown words. In either case, teachers must instruct students to use their knowledge of language (syntax) and context (meaning) cues. The following strategies may be useful.

1. Ask the student why he or she uses phonics frequently. Use the student's response to make instructional decisions. For example, if phonics is the student's basic or first word-identification strategy, see Sections 3.4, 3.5, 3.7, 3.9, and 3.10 in Chapter 3.

2. Show students that they can sometimes correctly predict a word in oral language before hearing it. Help them transfer this same knowledge in reading. See the examples provided below.

 • He gave the kitten some _____.
 • Put a stamp on the _____.
 • Ten dimes make a _____.

3. Provide examples where two readers made different miscues on the same unknown word. Discuss the responses of the two readers in an attempt to decide which reader has been most effective and the reasons for the effectiveness. Be sure students give reasons for their decisions. Model appropriate responses as needed.

 Text The car went down the old street.
 Reader 1 The car went down the old road.
 Reader 2 The car went down the old stream.

4. Provide words that students are unable to pronounce. The difficult words can then be placed in a context that builds meaning for the words. Through these exercises, the students should realize that they can understand without always sounding out words.

 guerdon
 After finding a purse, Jason returned it to the owner. The owner of the purse gave a *guerdon* to Jason, who bought a model with it.

 engrossed
 Dana was *engrossed* in an adventure story. Her mom and dad both had to call her for dinner. Finally, she put the book down and came to the table.

5. Help students build fluency by using Structured Repeated Readings in Resources for Chapter 4.

6. Consult Chapter 3 for ways to help develop a variety of word-identification strategies and how to use them.

SECTION 4.11

Excessive Use of Background

Behavior Observed	The student overrelies on context while reading.
Anticipated Outcome	The student will use phonic information and word chunks with context while reading.

PERSPECTIVE AND STRATEGIES

You may have some students who "read" quite fluently; however, a number of the words students read may not have been written by the author. The students seem to rely heavily on their background knowledge to the partial exclusion of graphophonic knowledge. The result is often an interesting story that is quite different from the one in print. Effective reading requires the use of context, language, and graphophonic cues. The following strategies may be useful.

1. Tell the student that background knowledge is important in reading to help predict words while reading, but other cues can also be used. Model how initial sounds along with context can be used to pronounce words.

2. Tape-record the student's reading, listen to it, and mark the miscues. Then review selected miscues with the student and discuss how meaning has been disrupted even though a particular miscue may make sense. Model how some graphic information can be used to arrive at the word used by the author. Consider these examples.

 cat
My pet dog is very friendly.

 pleasant
She was very pleased.

3. Present a few sentences where the student can make initial predictions of the word.

 Milk is perhaps a favorite drink of
 _____ throughout the world. (children, men, women, boys, girls, people).

Then present some graphic information and have the student explain why some words may or may not be good choices based on the available information. For example, help the student see that, while all the words make sense, the beginning letter of the word used by the author will narrow the choices to only one of the words. Add the initial letter and have the student predict a word beginning with that letter that makes sense. Add additional letters if necessary. Help the student realize that the context and graphic information provide cues to help pronounce the word the author wrote. Use some other examples and then supply graphic information for the beginning, middle, or end of the word. Use examples from the student's reading or adapt the examples below.

The northern deserts of Mexico have lizards, (*rattlesnakes*), and prairie dogs.

(Perhaps use *r* and *snakes* as graphic cues.)

The early Indians used (*seashells*) for music and dances.

(Perhaps use *sea* and then *sh* as graphic cues.)

Popular sports in Mexico include baseball, soccer, and (*volleyball*).

(Perhaps use *v* and *ball* as graphic cues.)

4. Acknowledge that all readers will make miscues but stress the importance of trying to pronounce the words written by the author. Relate the situation to a piece of writing that the student has written. When it is read by someone else, the expectation is that the student's words will be read. You might be able to model how you could change words from the student's piece of writing and still have it make sense even though the student had a different message in mind. Below is a partial sample from a student's writing (Lenski & Johns, 2000) with miscues that change the meaning although the sentences still make sense.

Sally
Hello, I'm Sammy the cell phone. My owner

eating
dropped me when he was getting chicken.

Oral Reading as Performance

Because of the importance of speaking to an audience, teachers should give their students a wide range of opportunities to practice oral language. Students who read aloud for an audience are subtly learning several things. They are learning how language is used in written text; they are learning how to communicate to an audience; and they are learning how to interpret text. Students reading aloud can also stimulate interest in stories and encourage other students to read. Oral reading, therefore, is a beneficial practice when students have adequately prepared and are sharing their reading with an appropriate audience.

Teachers can provide different kinds of experiences with reading aloud. Some may be time-consuming and rather formal, such as reader's theater and storytelling. Others may be more spontaneous, such as reading an exciting part of a story. With both types of reading, however, students should always have the opportunity to read the passage silently before performing and should rehearse their part before reading before their audience. The following are examples of ways to use oral reading as performance.

Reader's Theater

Ask students to:

1. Choose a piece of literature with a strong story line or a chapter from a content area book that could be read in parts.

2. Read the piece silently. Discuss the contents of the story and ask the students to read it again.

3. Develop a script from the literature. Students may use the entire story, or they may decide to create a scene from the story.

4. Assign parts and rehearse the play.

5. Present the play to an appropriate audience.

Storytelling

Ask students to:

1. Choose a favorite piece of literature.

2. Read the story several times, thinking about the sequence of action in the plot.

3. Think or write the entire story without the text. Include the story line and the main point of the story.

4. Retell the story to a friend, a group, or for a tape recording.

Functional Situations for Oral Reading

- Poetry and rhymes
- Student-written advertisements
- Announcements from the office
- Riddles and jokes
- Letters from pen pals

Oral Reading Opportunities

- Read what a certain character said.
- Read the most exciting part of the story.
- Read a funny part of the story.
- Read the part you like best.
- Read the part that tells you the most about a character.

- Read the part that makes you see the setting most clearly.
- Read the most surprising part of the story.
- Read the part that explains the goal or problem of the main character.
- Read the part that explains the outcome or solution of the story.
- Read the part that you think your best friend would like.
- Read the part that supports your answer.
- Read the part that tells you what to do next.
- Read the part that explains why _____.

Two Sources for Plays

- Gerke, P. (1996). *Multicultural Plays for Children, Volume 1: Grades 1–3*. Lyme, NH: Smith and Kraus.
- Gerke, P. (1996). *Multicultural Plays for Children, Volume 2: Grades 4–6*. Lyme, NH: Smith and Kraus.

Taking Account of Dialects

Changes of sounds and endings in some words may be a result of the student's dialect (adapted from Kress, 1993 and Rubin, 1993). A dialect of English is a variation of standard English, which is the language most widely used in print and by the media. When students read aloud, they may pronounce standard written English with their own dialect and may even change grammatical structures. Because reading in dialect rarely affects comprehension, you should not consider dialect differences to be significant miscues.

Spanish

A student with a Spanish-language background might exhibit the following dialect differences when he or she reads standard English.

- The vowel sounds in the following words may be difficult for the Spanish-speaking student to pronounce: *i* in *bit, a* in *bat,* schwa sound in *but,* and *u* in *full*.
- There are several sounds in English that are not found in Spanish: *v* in *vote, th* in *then, z* in *zoo, zh* in *measure,* and *j* in *jump*. The Spanish-speaking child will probably replace these

sounds with similar sounds from the Spanish language.

- English words that end in *r* plus the final consonants *d, t, l, p,* or *s* are usually pronounced without the consonant (*car* for *card, car* for *cart*).
- English has many words that blend an *s* with a consonant, which does not occur in Spanish. Spanish-speaking children may have difficulty with words that end with an *s*-consonant blend: *wasp, last, disk*.
- In Spanish, no words begin with an *s*-consonant blend; a vowel always precedes the consonant. Spanish-speaking students may have difficulty beginning a word with an *s* sound and may even pronounce a vowel before the *s* (*es-tar* for *star*).
- There are also several grammatical differences between Spanish and English. Spanish-speaking students may have the following difficulties with standard English.

 Subject-verb agreement: The cars runs.

 Verb tense: I need help yesterday.

 Use of negatives: He no go to school.

 Omission of noun determiners: He is farmer.

 Omission of pronouns: Is farmer?

 Word order of adjectives: The hat red is pretty.

 Comparative forms: My car is more big.

- Some problem English sounds for native speakers of Spanish are *b, d, dg, h, j, m, n, ng, r, sh, t, th, v, w, y, z, s*-clusters, and end clusters.

African-American English

African-American students who speak with a nonstandard English dialect may read aloud using their dialect. Unless the changes interfere with meaning, they should not be considered significant miscues. The following differences exist between the African-American dialect and standard English.

- In African-American English, the *r* sound becomes a schwa or is not pronounced before vowels or consonants: *pass* for *Paris, cat* for *carrot*.
- The *l* sound is also dropped and may be replaced by a *u* sound: *hep* for *help, too* for *tool, awe* for *all, fought* for *fault*.

- Consonant clusters at the ends of words are often simplified to single consonants: *pass* for *past, men* for *meant, wine* for *wind, hole* for *hold, sick* for *six.*

- Endings of words may be dropped or changed: *boo* for *boot, row* for *road, feet* for *feed, see* for *seed.*

- The possessive forms of words may be deleted: *John cousin* for *John's cousin, they book* for *their book, you* or *you-all* for *your.*

- Speakers of the African-American dialect may make changes in verb forms as they read: *I be happy* for *I am happy. He goin'* for *He is going.*

- In African-American English, there is no third person singular marker. Students may read: *He don't* for *He doesn't, He do* for *He does,* or *He have* for *He has.*

- The past tense for regular verbs may be dropped, such as *miss* for *missed, fine* for *fined, raise* for *raised.*

- In African-American English, the word *ain't* is used as a past negative as in *I ain't neither.*

- African-American speakers may also use negatives differently than do standard American speakers: *Nobody had no bloody nose. She didn't play with none of us. Nobody don't know about no club.*

Chinese

Among the many Chinese dialects, Mandarin is spoken by the majority of the people in China, but most of the Chinese students in schools speak the Cantonese dialect. There are several difficulties

speakers of Cantonese may have as they read standard English.

- English has many more vowel sounds than Chinese, so students may have difficulty with the vowel sounds in *buy, bough, bought, beat,* and *bait.*

- English also has consonant sounds not found in Chinese: *th* in *that, s* in *she, n* in *need,* and *r* in *rice.*

- In Chinese, many consonants are not used to end words as they are in English. Students may add an extra syllable to a final sound, such as *day offu* for *day off.*

- Because consonant clusters do not exist in Cantonese, students may have difficulty with words such as the following: *wished, dogs, laughed.*

- In Chinese, most grammatical relationships are indicated by word order rather than by changes in form as in English. The Chinese student may say *Yesterday he give I two book* for *Yesterday he gave me two books.*

- The Chinese-speaking student may not use the plural form of nouns, because plurality is indicated by the word preceding the noun in their language. The student may read *three book* for *three books.*

- The word order for questions is not inverted in Chinese as it is in English. The Chinese-speaking student may have difficulty reading questions because of that difference.

- Some problem English sounds for native speakers of Chinese are *b, ch, d, dg, f, g, j, l, m, n, ng, ō, sh, s, th, TH, v, z, l*-clusters, and *r*-clusters.

CHAPTER 5

Developing and Extending Vocabulary

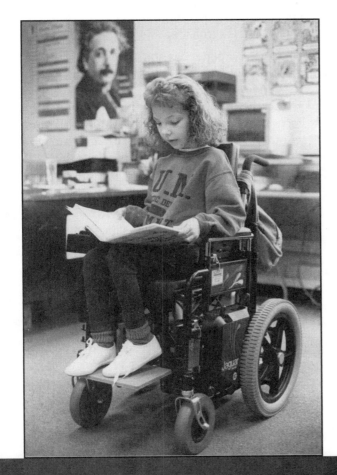

OVERVIEW

English has the largest vocabulary of all the languages in the world—600,000 to 1,000,000 words (Gillet & Temple, 2000). Although no reader knows all those words, Nagy and Anderson (1984) estimate that students must learn over 88,000 words by ninth grade in order to deal with the varied vocabulary in the books and other materials they are asked to read. It has been estimated that students learn 3,000 to 4,000 words each school year. That's a lot of words! And it is clear from this estimate that only a portion of these words is taught. You would need to teach 16 to 22 words every school day for students to learn 3,000 to 4,000 words a year. What all this means is that students acquire vocabulary on their own and through systematic instruction. You play an important role in creating a classroom environment that promotes an interest in words. You also need to provide systematic instruction to help students develop, extend, and refine their knowledge of words.

> Students must learn over 88,000 words by ninth grade.

Students have four vocabularies: listening, speaking, reading, and writing. The listening vocabulary is the first to develop, and Chall (1987) estimated that the average first grader knows 5,000 to 6,000 words (estimates vary from 2,500 to over 20,000 words). The student's listening vocabulary remains the student's largest vocabulary through the middle school years. Ultimately, the student's reading vocabulary may become the largest.

Learning words and expanding vocabulary knowledge have a strong influence on comprehension (Nagy & Scott, 2000). Developing and extending vocabulary is a complex process that requires multiple and varied encounters with words. We can tell you that *kingcup* is a flower, but that definition, while helpful, does not clarify the color of the flower, its size, or where you are likely to find it. "Knowing a word cannot be identified with knowing a definition" (Nagy & Scott, 2000, p. 273). When a word is known, the student can recognize it and use "knowledge of the word, in combination with other types of knowledge, to construct a meaning for a text" (Nagy & Scott, 2000, p. 273).

To help develop vocabulary within the context of a quality reading program, we suggest the following principles and practices. Use these basic ideas to provide a structure for students' learning.

1. Provide opportunities for students to read many types of materials that are of interest to them. Supply books and other types of printed materials at a range of reading levels.

2. Build students' experiential backgrounds. A rich variety of direct experiences in school, at home, and in the community can help build and expand what we like to call students' mental museums. Indirect experiences gained from listening to stories and informational books, watching films and videotapes, and viewing computer simulations can also build students' backgrounds.

3. Talk about experiences and relate vocabulary to students' backgrounds. Encourage students to be active learners. Word meanings have a greater likelihood of becoming working concepts through discussion and relating the word to other words. Numerous strategies are included in this chapter to assist students in establishing relationships between and among words.

4. Teach words to students and help them gain a depth of meaning. A common word like *run* has over 20 meanings in an elementary dictionary. Some of those meanings could be explored in a systematic manner through discussion, examples, and inviting students to relate particular meanings to their prior experiences. Other words may be important, specialized vocabulary particular to understanding a story or section in a content area text. Words such as *deceitful* and *treacherous* may lead to word study (e.g., the meaning of *ful*), dictionary use, and using examples with which students are familiar. Learning words generally requires numerous exposures in a variety of situations.

5. Create an interest in words and use a variety of means to help students develop and extend their vocabularies. Context clues, morphemic analysis, and effective dictionary use are some of the strategies that can be taught to students to help them engage in independent word learning while reading. Inviting students to share words of interest can help foster engagement in word study. Encouraging students' active sharing us-

ing materials they are reading will help promote vocabulary growth within a meaningful context.

Although several authorities have noted that vocabulary instruction and development "have not been a recent focus of professional writing and discussion" (Rupley, Logan, & Nichols, 1998/1999, p. 336), we believe a renewed interest is on the educa-tional horizon (Blachowicz & Fisher, 2000). With renewed interest, our hope is that teachers will use the ideas and strategies presented in this chapter in an authentic, meaningful, and integrated manner to engage students in expanding their vocabulary knowledge to better construct meaning from texts.

TECHNOLOGY RESOURCES

English Vocabulary Links

http://nanana.com/vocabulary.html
Contains a list of vocabulary activity links

Word Play

http://www.wolinshyweb.com/word.html
Contains more that 150 links to word puzzles and word play sites

Gateway to Educational Materials

http://www.thegateway.org
Contains over 300 lessons on reading skills and strategies

Extending Meaning Vocabulary

Behavior Observed	The student's knowledge of word meanings is limited.
Anticipated Outcome	The student will increase the number of known words and expand the range of meanings for words encountered in text.

BACKGROUND

Helping students expand and enrich their meaning vocabulary is not easily accomplished. You need to do far more than provide your students with a list of vocabulary words to study for a test on Friday. Students learn new vocabulary words in four ways (Manzo & Manzo, 1993).

- The first way is incidentally, through their own reading and conversation. Children come to school knowing approximately 5,000 words and acquire 2,700 to 3,000 words each year during elementary school, middle school, and high school (Snow, Burns, & Griffin, 1998). Many of these words are learned without teacher intervention; they are learned through students' exposure to language.

- The second way students learn new vocabulary is through direct instruction. Teachers can have an impact on students' learning vocabulary through well-thought-out vocabulary instruction. Giving students the definitions for new words, however, usually does not ensure that those words will become part of their vocabulary. That is because giving definitions for words merely provides students with the denotation, or general meaning, of a word. Each word, however, also has a connotation. The connotation of a word is the range of meanings it has and the specific context in which it occurs (Readence, Bean, & Baldwin, 1998).

- The third way students learn new vocabulary is through self-instruction. As students read, they can consciously try to learn new words. Teachers can help instill in students a desire to learn words, and they can provide students with strategies that help them make the new words part of their expressive vocabulary.

- Finally, students learn vocabulary through mental manipulation of words while thinking, speaking, and writing. Students are constantly exposed to new words in school, at home, and in books. As they use these new words, they begin to extend their knowledge of the words' meanings. Students learn new words to different degrees. With every word, students may be anywhere on a continuum from not knowing the word at all, having heard the word but being unsure about its meaning, having a general sense of the meaning of the word, to

How Students Learn New Words
- incidentally
- direct instruction
- self-instruction
- mental manipulation

Direct instruction is one way teachers help students learn new words.

Teaching the various meanings of a word, however, is not sufficient. Word knowledge should be constantly changing as new information is added to students' existing schemata (background knowledge) and as new schemata are developed. That means teachers need to encourage students to continue to expand their meanings of words on their own as well as to provide instruction on new words. Gunning (1996) suggests that, to assist students in enriching their meaning vocabulary, teachers need to provide students with experiences that will build their background knowledge, help them relate new words to that background, assist them in building relationships between words, help them develop depth of meaning of new words, present several exposures to each word to students, help students become interested in words, and help students transfer words to their own vocabulary. The following strategies will help students enrich their meaning vocabularies.

having the word in their expressive vocabulary (Beck & McKeown, 1991). Even if they know more meanings for a word, they often initially lack the understanding of a word's richness.

Section 5.1

STRATEGY 1 KNOWLEDGE RATING GUIDE*

A Knowledge Rating Guide can help students understand to what degree they initially know a specific word and can provide a vehicle for a class discussion that allows students to expand their background knowledge of the words. To prepare and use a Knowledge Rating Guide, use the following steps.

1. Prepare a list of words that you want the students to learn.

2. Next to each word, draw three columns similar to the example.

	Can define	**Have seen/heard**	**Unknown**
glacier	_____	_____	_____
avalanche	_____	_____	_____

3. Ask students to place a check in the column that best describes what they know about the new word. If they are unclear about the directions, model the procedure for them. For example, you could say the following.

> *The first word on this list is* glacier. *I know that a glacier is made of ice, and I have heard the word many times, but I'm not exactly sure if I could define the word. I think I'll place a check under the column* Have seen/heard. *On the other hand, I do know what an avalanche is. It's falling rock or snow. I'll check* Can define *for that word.*

*Blachowicz, 1986.

4. After students have filled out the Knowledge Rating Guide, discuss the words with them. Ask which words were difficult, which were easy, which most of the students knew, and which words few students knew. As you discuss the words, ask students to share their background knowledge and experience with the words.

5. From the class discussion, ask students to make predictions about further meanings of the words and how they would be used in a text.

Section 5.1

STRATEGY 2 POSSIBLE SENTENCES*

Possible Sentences is a vocabulary strategy where students predict the meanings of words in a passage to be read. This strategy helps students learn how to make predictions of unknown words as well as heightens motivation to read.

1. List 5 to 10 vocabulary words that are crucial to the meaning of the passage. Write these words on the chalkboard and read them to the class.

2. Ask students individually or in small groups to select at least two words from the list to write in one sentence that might occur in a reading passage. Ask the students to read their sentences aloud, write them on the chalkboard, and underline the vocabulary words. Continue writing sentences until all of the words have been used.

3. Ask the students to read the passage silently, looking for the vocabulary words and checking the accuracy of the "possible" sentences.

4. After all of the students have read the passage, lead a class discussion evaluating the sentences that the students created. Discuss to what extent the vocabulary was accurately used in the "possible" sentences.

5. Once students feel they know the meanings of the new words, ask them to create new sentences using the vocabulary words once more. These new sentences can be a check to determine whether or not the students have learned the meanings of the new words.

Section 5.1

STRATEGY 3 VOCABULARY SELF-COLLECTION**

Vocabulary Self-Collection (VSC) is a strategy that encourages students to find words from their environment to learn. VSC helps students understand that learning new words needs to be a consciously active process that should be part of their lives.

1. Ask students to look for unknown words in their reading, conversations, and their environment. As they find words, ask students to write them down on a note card.

2. Each day, up to five students who have found a new word should write the word on the chalkboard.

*Moore & Moore, 1986.
**Haggard, 1982.

3. At an appropriate time, ask the students who submitted the words to define them.

4. After each definition, ask the class to try to add to the word's definition or to further clarify its meaning.

5. All students should record the words with their meanings in a vocabulary notebook for reference as students read and write.

Section 5.1

STRATEGY 4 CONTEXTUAL REDEFINITION*

Contextual redefinition can give students a better understanding of how to learn words in the context of text as well as helping them discover the meanings of new words on their own.

1. Select unfamiliar words from the students' text that could be considered key to understanding the text.

2. Write sentences using words that give their meanings in context.

3. Then ask the students to define the new words aloud. Discuss how the context helped the students understand the meanings of the words.

4. Then ask students to verify their definitions by checking a dictionary. The dictionary can also help them learn other ways the words are used.

 For example, try to define the following words using your background knowledge.

 jejune _____

 convivial _____

 Now read the following sentences that contain the words *jejune* and *convivial.*

 The teacher was surprised by his *jejune,* immature answer to the problem.

 Her *convivial* personality was appealing to friends who enjoyed parties.

If you didn't know the words before, you probably know now that one of the definitions for *jejune* is immature and one of the definitions for *convivial* is sociable. Remember that words are symbols for concepts, so you can't understand the connotations for either word by reading one sentence. You do, however, get a sense of the meaning of each word, and if you would read either word in a text, you would probably know enough about the word to comprehend the phrase it was in.

Contextual redefinition is a useful strategy for a variety of reasons. First, the strategy illustrates how difficult it is to identify definitions of words in isolation. Second, students tap into their background knowledge by making a prediction about the word. Some students may have a tentative knowledge of the word before you teach its definition. This strategy helps them bring what they know to the teaching situation. Third, contextual redefinition helps students become engaged in the lesson rather than having them list sterile definitions, and, finally, the strategy encourages students to use the dictionary to confirm predictions rather than being the first strategy they use when they come to an unknown word.

*Readence, Bean, & Baldwin, 1998.

Strategy 5 Preview in Context*

Preview in Context is a strategy that has students look for words in the context of their text to give them a better understanding of which definition of the word will be used. Discussing key words before reading also helps students begin to develop schemata (background knowledge) for the topic of the text selection.

1. Select words from a text that you think will be unfamiliar to your students. Make sure you choose words that are key to the understanding of the text and don't make your list too long. It's better to have an effective lesson with four or five words than to have a lesson of 10 words that the students forget.

2. Show students where the words are in the text and read the context of the new word. You may read the passage aloud or have the students read it silently. If you are using a content area text, you might also want to spend some time explaining the concepts in the text.

3. Help students learn the word's meaning by discussing it in its context. You might want to ask the students questions leading them to the definition, as in the following example.

 > The protective coloring of the horned viper helps *camouflage* him by hiding him from his enemies and by helping him blend into his background.

Teacher:	What do you know about the word *camouflage* from this sentence?
Student:	The horned viper is hiding from his enemies.
Teacher:	How does being camouflaged help him?
Student:	He blends into his background.
Teacher:	What else does the sentence tell us about being camouflaged?
Student:	I think the part where it says *protective coloring* is another way of saying *camouflage*.

4. Expand word meanings. After students learn the initial meaning of the word, provide additional contexts for the same word. That way students who come across the word in different contexts will make predictions about what they know about the word's meaning to another situation.

Teacher:	How many of you have seen *camouflage* shirts or pants?
Student:	I have some on my GI Joe.
Teacher:	What are they like?
Student:	They're all different colors, but mostly brown and green.
Teacher:	Why do you think they are those particular colors?
Student:	So he can hide from the bad guys.
Teacher:	How are the GI Joe camouflage clothes similar to the snake's skin?
Student:	Both the clothes and the skin help them blend into the background.

*Readence, Bean, & Baldwin, 1998.

STRATEGY 6 LIST-GROUP-LABEL*

One of the ways students develop the concepts for words is to learn the relationship of that word to other words. Classification strategies such as list-group-label help students learn how words fit in relation to other words. These strategies also engage students in the content of the text they are reading.

1. Select one or more related topics about a passage the students have read. Make sure there are several subtopics for the topic you have chosen. For example, if the students read a chapter about animals, you might think of the subtopics farm animals, pets, wild animals, and characteristics of animals.

2. Write the name of the topic on the chalkboard. Ask students to think of all of the terms that are associated with the topic. List them on the chalkboard. The following list is an example of possible terms students might give for the topic animals.

dog	cat	lion	elephant
cow	hen	gerbil	warm-blooded
horse	hamster	giraffe	breathing
born alive	white mouse	cheetah	goat

3. Ask students to organize the list into groups and give each group a label. Students can work in small groups or alone. Be prepared for a variety of answers. Because the object of the lesson is for students to interact with the concepts, you can allow them to differ on some decisions about where an item would fit in a list. For example, white mouse in this list would probably be considered a pet, but some students may argue that the term would belong in a different category.

STRATEGY 7 FEATURE ANALYSIS**

Using a feature analysis helps students realize that several words may have certain features in common. It also helps them learn the distinguishing concepts behind different words.

1. Select a general category and list some words within the category. One example is the term *transportation*. Of that general category, car, bicycle, and airplane are all examples of modes of transportation.

2. List some features common to each word and one or more unique features for each word. For transportation, some of the features include two wheels, wings, uses fuel, has an engine, and carries passengers. You may suggest a feature or two and ask the students to think of other features. Students may not be able to think of features unless the teacher first provides some examples.

*Taba, 1967.
**Pittelman, Heimlich, Berglund, & French, 1991.

3. Ask students to determine which features fit with which words. Have them make an x for features that fit and a — if the features don't describe the word. The following is an example for the category *transportation*.

Transportation	two wheels	wings	uses fuel	engine	passengers
car	—	—	X	X	X
bicycle	X	—	—	—	X
airplane	—	X	X	X	X

4. Ask students to explain their rationale for each word. Then ask students how the terms are similar and how they are different.

5. Another way to introduce feature analysis is to ask students to use their own names as words to describe. For features, they might use such ideas as "has a brother," "owns a pet," or "has freckles." Students can have fun using feature analysis and can get to know each other as well. A blank form for the feature analysis follows.

Feature Chart

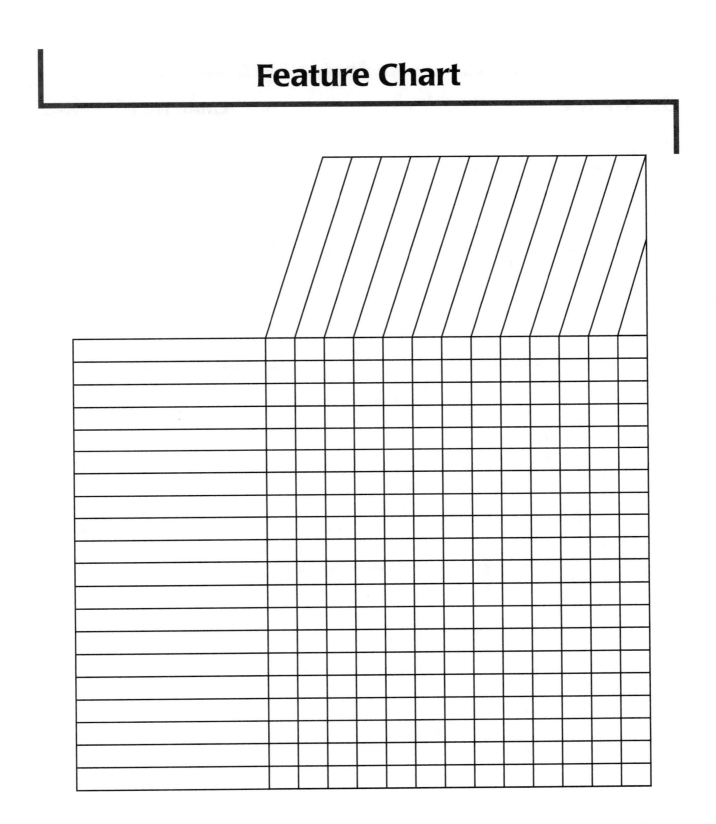

STRATEGY 8 SEMANTIC MAPPING*

A semantic map is a graphic representation of related concepts. Semantic mapping is another way students can learn the relationships among words.

1. Select a topic from the text you have been reading. For example, if students were reading text about band music, the key word might be musical instruments.

2. Write the word on the chalkboard.

3. Ask students to brainstorm as many related words as they can. Examples for musical instruments might be *cornet, clarinet, snare drum, cymbal, xylophone, oboe, flute, trumpet, French horn, saxophone*.

4. Organize the words into a diagram similar to the example.

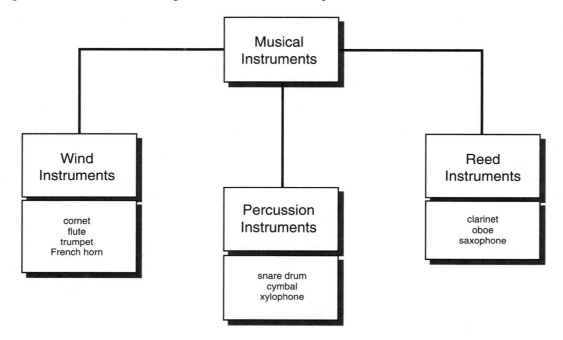

5. Students can add words to the diagram as they think of them.

6. Ask students to give names to the categories represented on the diagram. In this example, the category names are in larger type.

7. Discuss why the words fit into the categories. Ask the students to give the salient features that separate the categories.

*Heimlich & Pittelman, 1986.

STRATEGY 9 WORD MAP*

A word map helps students develop a framework for a word. A word map gives the category of the word, the ways it's different from other similar words, and examples.

1. Discuss the word map with the students, explaining how it helps students think about a variety of aspects of a concept.

2. Model an example such as the one that follows.

> *The term we have been studying is an emu. (Write emu in the middle box.) Let's think about what an emu is. We've learned that an emu is a bird, so that goes in the top box that represents the class or category of the term. On the right we will write properties or characteristics of the emu. We know that the emu is an Australian bird, that it is tall, and that it can't fly. At the bottom of the word map, we write examples or illustrations of the emu. In this case, we'll write that it is smaller than the ostrich and that it is like the rhea. That completes our word map.*

*Readence, Bean, & Baldwin, 1998.

3. After the students have listened to you complete a word map, give them a blank map and suggest a term to describe. You might suggest that students work in small groups.

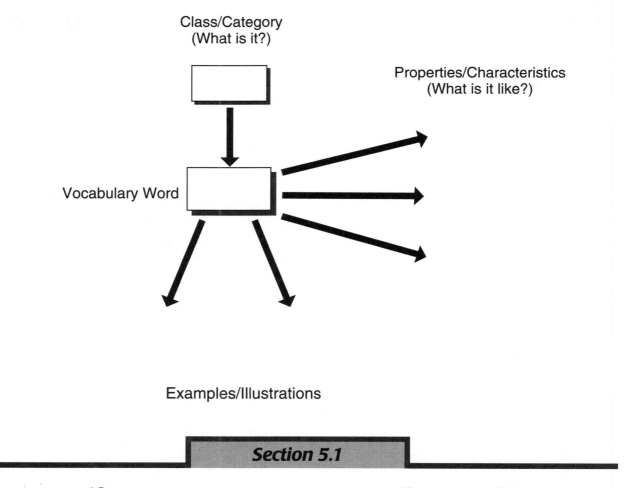

Class/Category
(What is it?)

Properties/Characteristics
(What is it like?)

Vocabulary Word

Examples/Illustrations

Section 5.1

STRATEGY 10 GRAPHIC ORGANIZERS

Graphic organizers are pictorial representations of how words are related. They can assist students in understanding the relationship between words and ideas.

1. To create a graphic organizer, first make a list of key terms from the text you are using.

2. Then cluster the terms by groups.

3. Finally, determine which kind of diagram fits the material best.

There are many types of graphic organizers, including the following ones.

Chain of Command

Continuum

Cycle

Venn Diagram

Hierarchy

Time Line

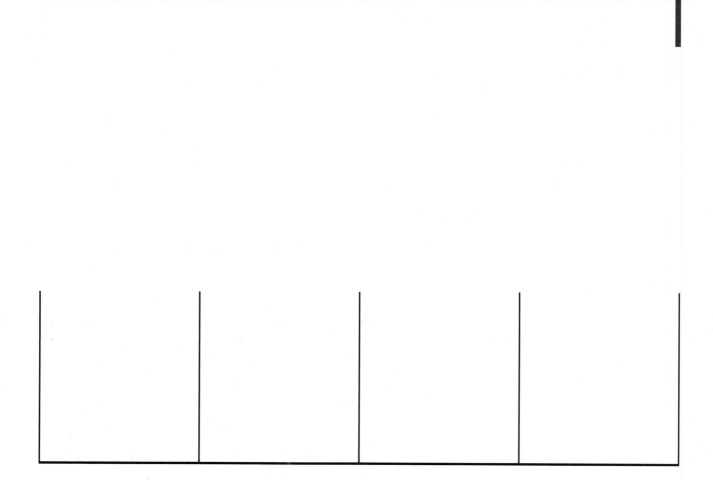

Overlapping Concepts

Cause-Effect

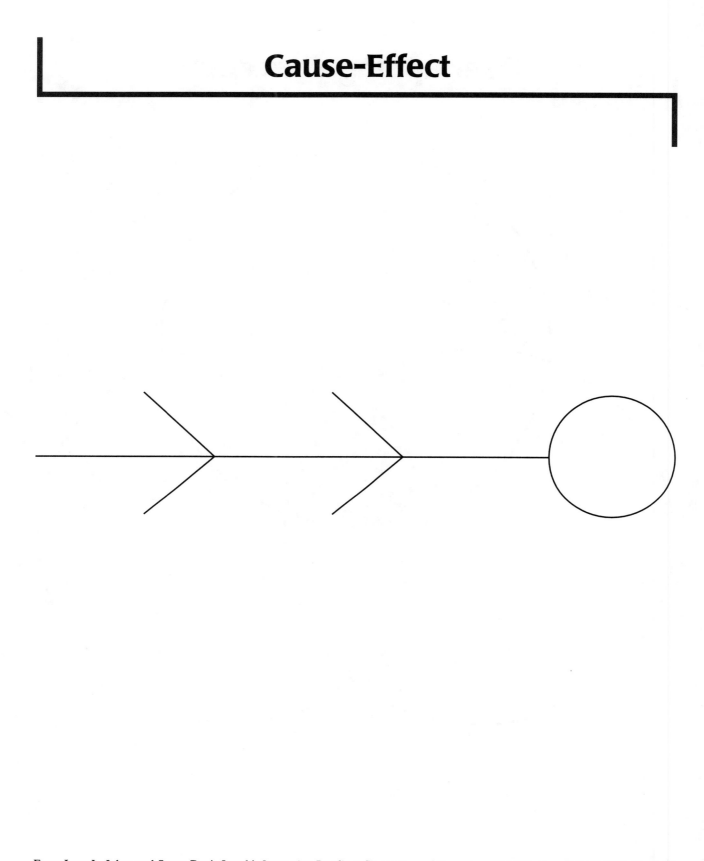

Parts of a Concept

Parts of a Whole

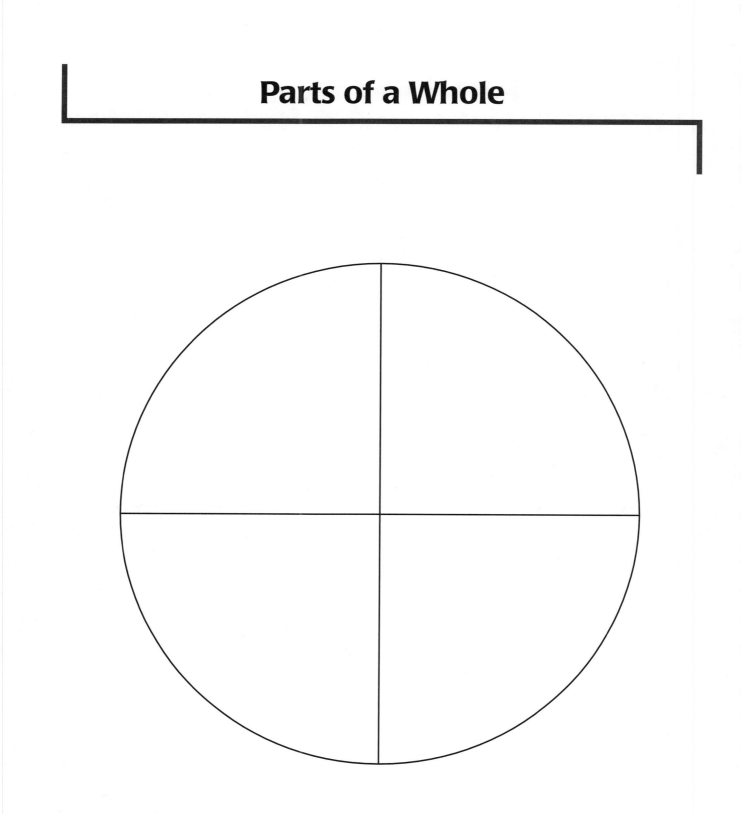

Priorities in Descending Order

Relationships

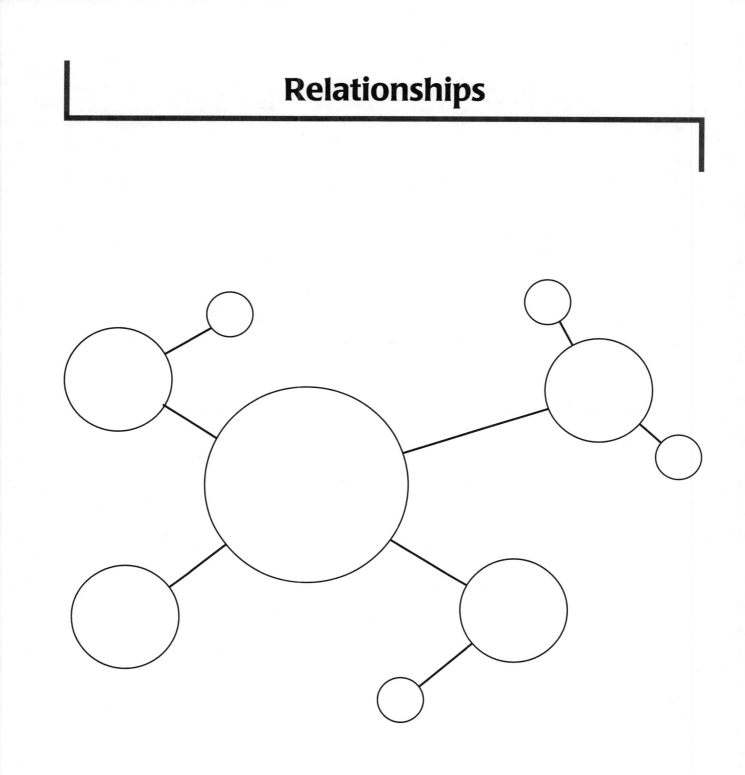

Using Context Clues to Predict Meanings for Unknown Words

Behavior Observed	The student has difficulty using context clues to predict meanings for unknown words.
Anticipated Outcome	The student will use context as one reading strategy to predict meanings for unknown words.

BACKGROUND

The words surrounding an unknown word can sometimes be used by the student to predict its meaning. When this process occurs, the student is using context clues. Such clues help students associate meaning with words that they may not be able to pronounce and can aid students in constructing the meaning of a sentence or passage.

For example, suppose a student comes across the word *yegg* in a passage. It is probable that the student will be able to pronounce the word but will not know what it means. Depending on the context, the student may or may not be able to make a reasonable guess at the meaning of the word. If the only context is "Two people saw the *yegg*," it is unlikely that the student could use the context to figure out the meaning of *yegg*. The student could determine that a *yegg* is something that can be seen, but such information is not very helpful in determining the meaning, because millions of things can be seen.

A different context might be more helpful. For example, "The *yegg*, a burglar, was seen by two people." In this sentence, the meaning is given in an appositive phrase, and the student may be able to associate the meaning with the word.

Many teachers encourage students to use context to figure out meanings for unfamiliar words.

Unfortunately, such advice often has two limitations. First, little direct instruction is given. Second, teachers need to be aware that not many words are actually defined by their context. Some words, however, can be determined solely by their context. These words will probably be found in one of the following types of sentences (two examples of each type follow the description).

- **Definition or Description:** Words are directly defined by the sentence.

 A *kingcup* is a yellow flower.

 The *commencement* or beginning of the journey was exciting.

- **Appositive Phrase:** The definition of the unknown word or the word itself is in a phrase set off by commas.

 The *kithara*, a musical instrument, was played in ancient Greece.

 The *kinglet*, a tiny bird, eats insects.

- **Linked Synonyms:** The unknown word is in a series of known words.

 His *barbarous*, cruel actions were unexpected.

 Her aim, goal, and *inclination* was to finish the book.

- **Comparisons and Contrasts:** The word can be defined by its opposite in the sentence.

 Rather than his usual lively self, today William appeared to be *ponderous.*

 Unlike the *dowdy* customer, the salesperson was neat and clean.

- **Examples:** The word can be defined by examples in the sentence.

 My family is very *musical.* My sister plays the violin; my father plays the piano; and my mother sings.

 His *machinations* to get a promotion were obvious. He bragged about his accomplishments and told his boss his colleagues were inept.

- **Classification:** The word can be defined by its relationship to known words.

The water *molecule* is comprised of two parts hydrogen and one part oxygen.

Mike was an important player on the *offensive* football team. His skills at passing the ball to any player within reach were stunning.

- **Experience:** The word can be defined by applying previous experience to the unknown word.

 As I stepped onto the diving platform, I felt *paralyzing* fear. The water surface appeared unforgiving. If I landed any way other than vertical, I could end up with a serious injury.

 He looked *deliriously* happy. As he held his new son in his arms, his eyes glowed with emotion, and his lips slowly spread into the widest grin of his life.

Section 5.2

STRATEGY 1 WHAT'S THE MEANING?

1. Develop a series of passages in which context can be used easily to help reveal the meaning of an unfamiliar word. Use a hierarchy in which context clues can be ranked informally from easy to hard.

2. Write a word on the chalkboard that the students may or may not be able to pronounce. Ask whether anyone knows the meaning of the word. If words are carefully selected, few, if any, students should know their meaning. Suppose the word is *kingcup* and a few students think they know what it means. Those students could be asked to remain quiet while the lesson continues.

3. Ask students how they might make a good prediction for the meaning of *kingcup.* Common responses include looking in the dictionary, asking someone, and seeing the word in a sentence. Stress that seeing a word in a sentence is using context.

4. Now write the unfamiliar word in a sentence where the meaning is made clear by definition or description.

 A kingcup is a yellow flower.

5. Have the students read the sentence and then identify the word or words that reveal the meaning of the unfamiliar word. Circle or underline these words.

6. Repeat this procedure with additional words. In subsequent lessons, teach other types of context clues in a similar manner. Occasionally, use an unfamiliar word in a context in which the meaning is not clear. These instances will help students realize that there are limitations to using context to determine word meanings.

STRATEGY 2 PREDICT AND CHECK*

1. Explain to the students that context clues can be important in understanding the meaning of unknown words. From a passage the students are reading, select four or five words that can be defined by their context. Write the words on the chalkboard.

2. For each word, have students apply the following questions (Sternberg & Powell, 1983).

 What information in the passage will help me figure out the meaning of the word?

 When I put together all the information that I know about the word, what word makes sense in the sentence?

 What do I know that will help me figure out this word?

3. Write down the students' guesses for each word on the chalkboard. Explain that if a word does not make sense, a different word should be tried. Try several words in the passage until students read the unknown words correctly. Discuss the meanings of the words.

4. Reflect on the strategies students used as they applied context clues to their reading. Discuss the strategies they used and suggest other strategies students could use as they try to understand the meanings of unknown words.

Practice and Reinforcement Activities

1. Watch for examples in instructional materials in which context can be used to build meanings for unfamiliar words and use these examples to help reinforce students' use of context.

2. Encourage students to consult dictionaries to find words whose meanings are likely to be unfamiliar to other students in the class. Then have students write sentences or brief passages that could be shared with other students who would attempt to identify the meanings of the words.

3. Provide brief passages that contain unfamiliar words and have students select or write the meanings of the underlined words based on the context.

4. To encourage students to use self-monitoring strategies as they read, print the following questions on a brightly-colored bookmark.

 Did what I just read make sense to me?

 Can I retell this passage in my own words?

 Are there any words I don't understand?

 Are there any sentences that confuse me?

Remind the students to ask themselves these questions as they read (Richek, Caldwell, Jennings, & Lerner, 1996).

*Gunning, 2000.

Compound Words and Affixes

Behavior Observed	The student does not use knowledge about word parts to help determine meanings of unknown words.
Anticipated Outcome	The student will use knowledge about compound words and affixes as an aid to help determine word meanings.

BACKGROUND

Compound words and affixes (prefixes and suffixes) are part of structural or morphemic analysis. In Chapter 3 (see Section 3.4) strategies were given to help students use compound words and affixes to help pronounce or decode words not known at sight. In this section, the focus is on the meanings of words, and the teaching strategies are designed to help students use compound words and affixes to make informed predictions about words' meanings.

Section 5.3

STRATEGY 1 COMPOUND WORDS

1. Refer to Chapter 3 (see Strategy 6 in Section 3.4) for ideas to develop knowledge about compound words so students can use that knowledge as an aid to pronounce words of more than one syllable.

2. Review the meaning of compound words so students understand their essential characteristic: a compound word is made up of two smaller words. In addition, the meaning of each smaller word may be retained in the compound word (*bluebird*), may be somewhat changed (*softball*), or have practically nothing to do with the meaning of the individual words (*dragonfly*).

 3. Invite students to form small groups and brainstorm a list of compound words. Students could write their words on an overhead transparency or a sheet of paper. After a few minutes, invite a student from one group to share some of the words.

4. As the words are given, be sure they are written on the chalkboard or shared using an overhead projector. Then identify each word that makes up the compound word, have a student use the compound word in a sentence, and be sure students understand the word's meaning.

5. Note that the meaning of each smaller word can sometimes contribute to the meaning of a compound word. Invite students to model this process for some of their compound words or select from the following list.

doghouse	notebook	crossroads
blueberry	cornbread	schoolwork
suppertime	blackbird	homework

6. Then share some compound words whose separate meanings are unlikely to contribute to an accurate meaning for the compound word. Model for students by saying something like the following:

I can see that two small words, goose *and* berry *make the word* gooseberry. *I know a berry is something that could be eaten, but some berries are not edible and others are poisonous. A goose is an animal that is bigger than a duck. What I don't know is whether a* gooseberry *looks a bit like a* goose. *That meaning just doesn't make sense to me. I'm pretty sure this is some type of berry, but I don't know much more. I'd better consult my dictionary.* (Look up the word and share the meaning: a spring shrub having greenish flowers and edible greenish berries.) Then say: *I was right about* gooseberry *being a type of berry that can be eaten, but it does not look like a goose. I also found out the color of the berries.*

7. Present some compound words in sentences. Have students underline the compound words and draw a line between the two words. If the meaning of the word is not known, have students consult their dictionaries. Then discuss the meanings of the compound words. Some sample sentences are provided below.

> He brought homemade cookies to the lunchroom.
>
> My grandparents gave me a notebook.
>
> The radio broadcast was about a breakthrough in medicine.
>
> The artwork and paintbrushes were in the workroom.
>
> My dad's workshop has many tools.
>
> My mom's workday is eight hours.
>
> The blueberry plants were invaded by birds.

8. Conclude the lesson by encouraging students to use their knowledge of compound words when they come across longer words in their reading. This knowledge can be used to help separate the word into pronounceable chunks and possibly help with the word's meaning. Remind students that a dictionary can also be used if the meaning is not clear or if additional clarification is desired.

9. Consult Resources for Chapter 3 for a list of compound words.

STRATEGY 2 PREFIXES

1. Explain to students that prefixes can be attached to a root word and the meanings of a particular prefix can sometimes give clues to the meaning of the word. Two lists of prefixes can be found in Resources for Chapter 5. A prefix is a separate syllable that can change the meaning of a root word completely or make meanings more specific (Fox, 2000). Provide an example of each and invite students to suggest words of each type. Several examples are provided below.

Changes meaning of root word completely	Makes meaning of root word more specific
uncover	review
disembark	repay
invisible	preview
irregular	foreground
overlook	midweek
unhappy	semicircle

2. Tell students that there are a few prefixes that account for over 58% of all prefixed words (White, Sowell, & Yanagihara, 1989). List the following prefixes on the chalkboard or an overhead transparency. Encourage students to provide examples, use those given below, or select examples from your instructional materials.

Prefix	Meaning	Example
dis	opposite	disappear
un	opposite	uncover
re	back/again	return
in (im, ir, il)	opposite	impossible

3. Help students understand that prefixes have predictable spellings and pronunciations. They can be used to help pronounce the word. Then direct students to each word and ask them if they know the meaning of the prefix as it is used in each sentence. They are likely to identify the *re* in *rewrite* to mean to write again. The *re* in *return* means to give back. The *re* in *record,* however, is just the first syllable in the word and does not mean *back* or *again*. Help students understand the three ways the prefix *re* can be used.

4. Develop a bulletin board or sheet of paper that looks like the following chart.

re		
re (means back)	*re (means again)*	*re (just the first syllable)*

Share some additional words that can be formed from the *re* prefix and have students place the words in the column where they fit best. Encourage students to use the words in sentences and, if necessary, consult a dictionary to clarify their meanings. Many possible words to select from are listed below.

react	rebellion	rebuild	recap
readjust	rebirth	rebuke	recapture
reaffirm	rebound	recall	recast
realign	rebuff	recant	recede
receipt	receive	recent	reception
recess	recharge	recital	recite
reclaim	recline	recoil	recollect
recompose	reconfirm	reconstruct	reconvert
recount	recoup	recourse	recover
recreate	recruit	recuperate	recur
recurve	recycle	redemption	redesign
redirect	rediscount	redistribute	redistrict
reduce	refect	refer	refill
refine	refit	reflect	reflex
reforest	reform	refract	refrain
refresh	refrigerator	refuel	refund
refuse	refute	regain	regard

5. After categorizing enough of the words so that students understand the three categories, have students be alert for *re* words as they read and complete assignments over the next several days. When they find a word, have them decide in which category it fits and write it on their sheet of paper or write it on a card and attach it to the bulletin board.

6. Review the words from time to time and be sure the new words are placed in the appropriate categories. Provide additional practice so students will learn the two meanings of the prefix *re*. Help them understand that prefixes can sometimes reveal a word's meaning, but students should always ask if the meaning makes sense in context. Model this strategy for students from time to time and also have students share instances when their knowledge of prefixes has helped them understand the meaning of a word.

7. See the two lists of prefixes in Resources for Chapter 5. One of the lists suggests grade levels for introducing specific prefixes.

Section 5.3

STRATEGY 3 SUFFIXES AND ENDINGS

1. Suffixes and endings are generally more complex than prefixes. Gunning (2000) suggests that *er* can be introduced in second grade and Cunningham (2000) notes that *er* is appropriate for an initial lesson. Some suffixes change the function of the word or the part of speech (*act, actor*). Two lists of suffixes can be found in Resources for Chapter 5.

2. Introduce the suffix *er* by writing it on the chalkboard. Tell students that adding this suffix to the end of certain words can change their meanings. For older students, you could say that some verbs or actions can be changed to a person who performs an action by adding *er* or *or*.

3. Write *teach* on the chalkboard and ask for a volunteer to pronounce the word. Then tell students that *teach* is an action. Next ask what you are that relates to the word *teach*. When students say *teacher,* write it under *teach* and point out that both words are related: one is an action and the other is a person who does the action.

4. Invite students to offer other words that end in *er* or *or.* The words can be placed in one of four categories. Write these categories on the chalkboard and help students place their words in the appropriate category. Some words, such as lighter, might fit in more than one category. An example is provided below.

People (who do something)	Things (that do something)	More (compares)	Leftovers (just end in er/or)
teacher preacher actor reporter painter investigator	calculator computer radiator washer	prettier smaller greater taller shorter happier faster	never winter

5. Discuss the meanings of the words, have students use them in sentences, and model how students might use this knowledge to help determine words' meanings. For example, you might say:

When you read, sometimes a word will have a suffix that will give you a clue to the meaning of a word. If you know the meaning of the word paint, *the word* painter *would probably mean a person who paints. Other words that end in* er *may be a clue that things are being compared (a dime is* smaller *than a quarter).*

6. Design other lessons using the lists of suffixes in Resources for Chapter 5.

Section 5.3

STRATEGY 4 ROOT WORDS

1. Begin with a simple word like *work* that students are able to pronounce. Tell students that additions can be made to words to make new words.

2. Invite students to suggest additions to the beginning and/or end of *work.* Write each word on the chalkboard and talk about how the meaning of each word changes. Some words that are possible are listed below.

works	overworked	workbag
worked	underworked	workbench
working	homework	workbook
workers	workable	workbox
workfare	workhouse	workload
workmanship	workout	workshop
workweek	schoolwork	groundwork
woodwork	woodworking	rework
teamwork	workmen	workable

3. Do similar exercises from time to time with other common words (*agree, play, form*). Then direct the focus of the lesson to what are called combining forms (*tri-, tele-, astro-, bi-, semi-,* and so on).

4. Select one of the forms (*bi-*) and tell students that *bi-* usually means two. Knowing the meaning of *bi-* can sometimes help determine a word's meaning.

5. Write the word *bicycle* on the chalkboard. Students will probably know that it has two wheels. Tell students that *bi-* can mean two and ask if anyone knows what a bike with one wheel and one with three wheels are called (*unicycle* and *tricycle*). Develop meanings for *uni-* and *tri-*.

6. Write *uni-, bi-,* and *tri-* on the chalkboard and give students the opportunity to suggest or find words whose meanings are likely to fit each category. Encourage students to add words to the list, then develop a chart like the one that follows.

uni-	*bi-*	*tri-*	*other*
unicycle	bicycle	tricycle	bias
unicorn	bicentennial	triacid	biological
unidirectional	biceps	triangle	trial
unilateral	bicolor	triazine	tribunal
unilingual	bicorn	tribasic	trifle
unify	bicuspid	triceps	triumph
	biennial	tricolor	
	bilingual	tricuspid	
	bimodal	trifold	
	binary	trilogy	
	binominal	trimonthly	
		triple	
		triplet	
		tripod	

7. Refer to Resources for Chapter 5 for other affixes to teach or use some of the following root words for students at and above the third grade.

Root	*Meaning*	*Example*
graph	writing	autograph
tele	distance	telemetry
port	carry	export
phone	sound	telephone
duct	lead	conduct
auto	self	autopilot
ology	study of	biology
mid	middle	midsummer
hemi	half	hemisphere
bio	life	biography

SECTION 5.4
Dictionary: Word Meanings

Behavior Observed	The student does not use a dictionary to help determine, verify, or clarify the meanings of words in context.
Anticipated Outcome	The student will be able to use a dictionary to help determine, verify, or clarify the meanings of words in context.

BACKGROUND

Look it up! Those words have been used by teachers for years—often without providing students with the skills needed to use a dictionary. In order to use a dictionary to look up the meaning of an unknown word, students need to acquire a number of prerequisite skills. Some of these skills are listed below.

1. knowing the letters of the alphabet in sequence

2. arranging several words in alphabetical order by their initial letters

3. arranging several words in alphabetical order to the second, third, and, if necessary, all the letters of a word

4. being able to locate a word in an efficient manner by knowing the general organization of a dictionary and how to use guide words

Section 3.8 presents introductory lessons for alphabetical order and guide words. Once these skills are learned, students can be taught to determine, verify, or clarify the meanings of unknown words in their reading.

The focus of dictionary use in this section is to help students locate word meanings that may be helpful in understanding words in their reading

whose meanings are unknown or uncertain. Students may begin using picture dictionaries in kindergarten through second grade. Such experiences, if carefully developed by teachers, help students learn alphabetical order and how to locate words. These dictionaries often use attractive colors, drawings, and photographs. While helpful to all students, such dictionaries may be especially useful for students of all ages who are learning to speak English. The attractive drawings and photographs may help students better understand particular words and possibly form a visual link with their experiences.

Gunning (2000) notes that students with average reading achievement are ready to use real dictionaries by third grade. The availability of hand-held electronic and CD-ROM dictionaries may be easier for students who struggle with reading. Such dictionaries may be motivational and may also pronounce the word and read its definition. Because most classrooms contain traditional dictionaries, teaching and practice strategies are given to help students use these resources to determine meanings of unknown words.

Dictionary use should not be the primary strategy students use when word meanings are unknown. Students should be encouraged to continue

reading the paragraph in which the word appears and try to determine if the context is helpful in predicting the word's meaning. Morphemic analysis (prefixes, suffixes, etc.) may also be used to construct meaning for the unknown word. If the context and morphemic analysis are not helpful, the student must then decide the importance of that particular word in constructing the overall understanding of the paragraph or passage. If the word is judged to be important, a dictionary could be consulted. Finally, if the student encounters quite a few unknown words, it is a strong indicator that the reading material is too difficult. Dictionaries should be used selectively to help students achieve their purposes while reading.

Section 5.4

STRATEGY 1

INTRODUCTORY LESSON FOR UNKNOWN WORDS

1. Remember to ensure that students know how to locate words in a dictionary or glossary. Check your classroom dictionaries for instructional ideas and practice activities. Effective dictionary use depends upon students being able to locate words efficiently. If the prerequisite skills are lacking, take the time to teach them. See Section 3.8.

2. Invite students to share what they do when they come across a word in their reading whose meaning is unknown. Write some of their responses on the chalkboard (e.g., "I skip the word," "I ask someone," "I look it up," "I try to figure out the meaning by reading the sentence").

3. Stress that many different strategies can be used when a word's meaning is unknown. Help students realize that there is not one best method to figure out an unknown word; a flexible approach is needed. For example, context and morphemic analysis may be useful to predict a word's meaning. See Sections 3.9 and 3.10 for encouraging ways to use a variety of word-identification strategies effectively.

4. Identify a dictionary as one way to help determine a word's meaning. Invite students to share their experiences with a dictionary. Note both positive and negative comments. Then help students understand that a dictionary or a glossary is one way to locate meanings of unknown words.

5. Model how you use a dictionary from time to time while you are reading. Use an example from your own reading or the following think-aloud example:

 I was reading a picture book for fun and I came across the phrase "the fronts of their tuques." I didn't know what the word tuques *meant, so I looked it up in my dictionary.*

6. Pause and a student may ask what the word means. You could then explain the meaning (a kind of knitted cap originally worn by French-Canadian trappers and farmers, but now worn by skaters and others involved in winter sports) or have students look up the word in their dictionaries. Be sure to discuss the word's meaning.

7. Conclude the lesson by inviting small groups of students to look up the meanings of several words that they don't know in sentences from their current reading. Have students share their findings with others. You might also use the following sentences.

 She saw the biffins on the table.
 He was in a ditty.
 I like the dobbin.

8. Invite students to use the dictionary when they come across unknown words in their reading. A chart like the following one could be given to students for their record keeping. Later, students could share the results of using the dictionary to help them understand unknown words.

Book: _____

Page: _____

Sentence containing unknown word: _____

Word meaning from dictionary (a phrase): _____

My new understanding of the word is now rated:

_____ very good _____ good _____ fair _____ poor _____ very poor

Book: _____

Page: _____

Sentence containing unknown word: _____

Word's meaning from dictionary (a phrase): _____

My new understanding of the word is now rated:

_____ very good _____ good _____ fair _____ poor _____ very poor

STRATEGY 2

LOCATING WORD MEANINGS
PRIOR TO READING

1. Preview a selection students have not read to identify important, difficult words. The selection may be a story, a section from a content area text, or some other genre. Materials for guided reading may also be used.

2. Select several difficult words whose meanings students are unlikely to know or are unable to determine through morphemic analysis (prefixes, suffixes, etc.) or context clues. Choose only a few words that are the most important to understand the reading selection.

3. Tell students that you have selected a few words from the selection they are about to read that they may not know. Be sure to distinguish between pronouncing words and reading or understanding words. Write the sentence containing the difficult word on the chalkboard or an overhead transparency. Underline the word and invite students to share their ideas about the meaning of the word. Remain neutral if a student shares an appropriate meaning.

4. Ask students to look up the word in their dictionaries or glossaries. Guide students through the definition(s) and invite them to share ideas about the word's meaning(s). Relate the discussion to students' earlier ideas and have them evaluate their ideas in light of the dictionary's definition. For words with multiple meanings, model how each meaning may or may not fit the context. Use a think-aloud procedure similar to the following one:

 I see that the word quarter *has two meanings in our dictionary. The sentence in the passage is talking about the third quarter of the game. I can see that one definition is a piece of money. That definition doesn't make sense unless the game involves quarters. The other definition says that many games are divided into four parts. That meaning seems to fit the passage. I guess the third quarter is the third part of the game. I'll try to keep that meaning in mind as I read.*

5. Proceed to the next word using a similar procedure. You might invite a student to guide the discussion and the exploration of the word's meaning. Ask guiding questions as needed but work toward having students take greater responsibility for the task.

6. Invite students to write a phrase on the chalkboard or an overhead transparency that defines each unknown word. These brief definitions can be referred to as students read the selection.

7. Refer, as needed, to the words initially selected in students' discussions of the selection that was read. Invite students to share their insights as well as any additional words that were unknown in the selection. Some of these words, if important to the selection, might be explored as part of the lesson or used for independent work.

8. A variation of this strategy is the Knowledge Rating Guide (Blachowicz, 1986) described in Section 5.1 (Strategy 1).

STRATEGY 3 BEST MEANING FOR THE CONTEXT

1. Tell students that many words have more than one meaning. Explain that the word *roll* has a different meaning in each of the two sentences on the chalkboard.

2. Write these two sentences on the chalkboard.

 > When Mr. Johnson called the **roll,** he learned that two students were absent.
 > My friend Beth eats one **roll** for lunch every day.

3. Ask students to read the sentences and try to determine the appropriate meaning for *roll* in each sentence.

4. Invite students to share the clues that helped them figure out the appropriate meanings for *roll*. For example, in the second sentence, Beth is eating something, and a roll is something that can be eaten.

5. Tell students that the dictionary contains the different meanings a word can have. Have everyone in the group look up the word *roll* in their dictionaries. Ask someone to read the definition that pertains to sentence one (roll: a list of names, especially of group members). Then ask a student to read the definition that pertains to sentence two (roll: a soft, round portion of bread). Ask students to read a third definition of roll (to tumble or turn over and over) to themselves. Then ask for volunteers to use it in a sentence.

6. Select an actual excerpt from students' dictionaries or use one of the examples below to help provide additional practice. Review the definitions and then provide sample sentences to match the appropriate definition. Help students see the connections. Some sample sentences follow.

 rope

 1. a strong heavy cord
 2. to catch by throwing

 Rosa tried to rope a calf.
 I tied a rope to my bicycle.

 elevator

 1. a platform or cage for carrying people and things up and down a building, mine, etc.
 2. a building for storing grain
 3. a part of the tail of an airplane that can be moved to make the airplane go up or down

 The pilot asked the mechanic to check the elevator of the plane.
 I take an elevator to my apartment.
 The farmer took a load of corn to the elevator.

 Finally, encourage students to create their own sentences using the words.

7. Invite students to suggest other multiple-meaning words. Write them on the chalkboard or an overhead transparency. Have students work in small groups to make sentences containing some of the words and then have students look up the words in their dictionaries to check the meanings. It is possible that some words may have additional meanings that could be placed in sentences. Have students share their work.

8. Tell students that when they are reading, a word may not make sense because they may be associating a particular meaning that does not fit the context. Remind students that looking up the word in a dictionary could be one strategy to consider when a word in their reading does not seem to make sense.

9. Extend the lesson by having students note other multiple-meaning words in their daily reading. These words can be discussed from time to time. You could also highlight multiple-meaning words in materials being read and discuss the meanings when appropriate. Use think alouds when appropriate. Some possible multiple meaning words to use are listed below.

| dock | dive | ditch | dolly | dot | down |
| draft | draw | drawer | drop | duck | dump |

Practice and Reinforcement Activities

1. To help students understand and work with multiple-meaning words, select a word with multiple meanings and write sentences on the chalkboard or an overhead transparency that exemplify various meanings. Then have students find the word in a dictionary and match the appropriate definition with the appropriate sentence. An example is given below.

Sentences	Corresponding Definitions
1. It is really light outside. 2. There is a light in the garage. 3. I have a very light-colored dress for the party. 4. That box is pretty light.	1. that by which we see 2. thing that gives light; cause to give light 3. pale in color 4. not heavy

Help students realize that you can get quite a different meaning from what the author intended if an inappropriate meaning is associated with the word.

2. Provide a column of words and definitions. Have students match the words with the definitions, using a dictionary when necessary. Use important words related to units or themes being studied. A general example is provided below.

_____ 1. calculate a. a special job
_____ 2. literal b. a narrow crack or opening
_____ 3. routine c. the money paid to a person for work performed
_____ 4. assignment d. beautiful in movement
_____ 5. crevice e. to inform
_____ 6. murky f. the regular act of a performer
_____ 7. notify g. exact, true, usual
_____ 8. graceful h. to answer a problem
 i. muddy, cloudy

3. Provide several sentences and definitions. Have students write the letter of the definition in the blank that matches the meaning of the word in a sentence. Similar exercises could be done with a dictionary where the number of the dictionary definition is written in the blank.

Sentences	Definitions
_____ 1. I have to go to the *store* to buy some milk.	a. Supply or stock
_____ 2. I have quite a *store* of candy.	b. Put away for future use
_____ 3. I have to find a place to *store* my clothes.	c. Place where goods are kept for sale

4. Create an interest in word study by inviting students to share words whose meanings are probably unknown to their peers. The words can be placed in a container. You can select a word several times during the week and provide guided practice in looking up the word's meaning(s) and engaging students in discussion. Students could also choose a word for independent exploration when time allows.

5. Prepare lists of words that are probably unknown to students. Invite them to answer a basic question about the words. Some sample questions without words are given below.

Which of the following words are trees?

Which of the following words are animals?

Which of the following words are sports?

6. Provide sentences with words that students are unlikely to know. Have students look up the words so that the questions can be answered correctly. Sample questions follow.

Can you eat a pierogi?

What would you do with a tuque?

Could a borscht be ridden?

Is a gilt a tree?

Where would a windrow be found?

7. Invite students to explore their dictionaries and create questions that can be answered by determining the meanings of words. The question can be placed on one side of a card and the answer on the back. The cards can be placed in a Word Explorer box. Students can create questions and answers or select questions to answer. A sample card is shown below.

What is a common word for calyx? by Jen	*leaves* that are growing at the base of the flower
Front of Card	Back of Card

8. Provide dictionary entries and sentences. Have students read the sentences and write on the lines the numbers of the entry word and the appropriate definition. An example is provided below.

page¹ (pāj), **1** one side of a sheet or piece of paper: *a page in this book.* **2** record: *the pages of history. noun.*

page² (pāj), **1** person who runs errands or delivers messages. Pages at hotels usually wear uniforms. **2** try to find (a person) at a hotel or club by having his or her name called out. **3** a youth who was preparing to be a knight. 1,3, *noun,* 2 *verb.*

palm¹ (päm), **1** the inside of the hand between the wrist and the fingers. **2** conceal in the hand: *The magician palmed the nickel.* **1** *noun,* **2** *verb.*

palm² (päm), **1** any of many kinds of trees growing in warm climates. Most palms have tall trunks, no branches, and many large leaves at the top. **2** leaf or stalk of leaves of a palm tree as a symbol of victory or triumph. *noun.*

1. The breeze moved the leaves of the tall *palms*.
 Entry Word <u>(2)</u> Definition <u>(1)</u>

2. What *page* in the book are you reading?
 Entry Word <u>(1)</u> Definition <u>(1)</u>

3. Please *page* my friend.
 Entry Word <u>(2)</u> Definition <u>(2)</u>

A variation of this activity is to invite students to find words of interest and write sentences exemplifying the various definitions.

Game

Tour the Zoo. Check students' dictionaries for unusual animals that might be found at a zoo. Write the name of the animal on the chalkboard or an overhead transparency. Have students look up the word in their dictionaries and read the definition. Then choose one student to be the guide who describes the animal to the other students. Some time also may need to be spent on using the pronunciation symbols so the word is pronounced correctly. A variation of this activity might be the Museum of Interesting Things. Consider choosing words that have an illustration. Possible words for Tour the Zoo and Museum of Interesting Things are provided below.

Tour the Zoo		Museum of Interesting Things	
aardvark	civet	abacus	breeches
eland	dingo	adz	brooch
springbok	fisher	andiron	buoy
coot	genet	ankh	burnoose
egret	guanaco	anvil	calliope
siamang	okapi	aquaplane	cameo
sloth	wallaroo	arbor	capstan
caracal	cassowary	aviary	catapult
margay	skink	awl	churn
serval	hyrax	beret	clavicle

Interest in Words

Behavior Observed	The student lacks an interest in words.
Anticipated Outcome	The student will develop an interest in words and word study.

BACKGROUND

When students have an interest in something, they will seek ways to engage in that activity. Some students enjoy games on the computer, sports, hobbies, playing with friends, and reading. Although few teachers would say many of their students have an interest in words, some of those teachers have witnessed students in the primary grades engaged in rhyming activities and even making nonsense words. As students jump rope on the playground, they often exhibit a playfulness with words. And there are some students who enjoy word games, crossword puzzles, jokes, and riddles. Finally, a few students actually spend some of their time using a dictionary or thesaurus to explore the meanings, origins, and uses of words.

We know that an interest in words can help students add words to their vocabulary in fun and meaningful ways. The strategies and ideas in this section are intended to serve as a source of activities to begin the process of helping students add to their vocabularies in more incidental ways.

These students appear to be having fun with words.

STRATEGY 1 WORD OF THE DAY

1. Prepare a piece of sturdy cardboard with a rubber band around each end to hold a word you or students select for special focus that day. Place the card where it can be seen easily by students.

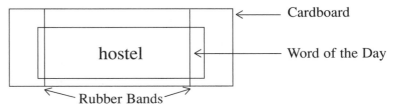

2. Introduce the Word of the Day to students. The word would relate to a unit or theme or just be a word of special interest to you or a student. Point to the word and tell students you will help them pronounce it, learn its meaning, spell it, and use it in a sentence.

3. Invite students to study the word and ask if anyone can pronounce it. Ask a volunteer to try the word. Provide assistance as necessary and point out how the word has parts similar to other words. (The word begins like <u>hos</u>*pital* and ends like *ho*<u>tel</u>.) Once the word is pronounced, have students say the word and chant the spelling.

4. Help students understand the meaning of the word (a place where travelers can stay that is not expensive; an inn). Use the word in a sentence like the following one.

 The youthful bicyclists stayed overnight at a hostel in an Italian village.

 Invite students to talk about the word and, if possible, relate it to their experiences. Contrast the meaning to other places for lodging (hotel, motel) and what would make a hostel different (hostels are mainly for youthful travelers).

5. Relate, if appropriate, the word's connection to a unit or theme of study. Encourage students to try to learn to spell, pronounce, and use the word throughout the day. You can also model the word for students. For example, say:

 I am too old to stay at a hostel meant for youthful travelers. I would prefer to stay at a bed and breakfast or hotel.

6. Develop a bulletin board for the words and invite students to write sentences, draw illustrations, or provide clues for pronouncing the words. Review the words when there are a few minutes left at the end of your lesson before recess, lunch, a special activity, or the end of the school day.

7. Invite students to suggest words for Word of the Day. Students could write the word on strips of card stock and their names on the back of the word strips. The words can be placed in a box or folder. When a student's word is selected, that student may be able to help teach the word.

STRATEGY 2

SESQUIPEDALIAN WORDS

1. Use the Word of the Day approach to introduce the word *sesquipedalian* (Dale, O'Rourke, and Bauman, 1971). The word contains the Latin *sesqui* which means one and one-half and *ped* which means foot. The word means foot and a half or very long words. Students are often challenged to learn long, distinctive, and difficult words.

2. Challenge students to locate words for the Sesquipedalian Words bulletin board. Students can be given index cards or sturdy paper for any words that might qualify for the bulletin board.

3. Model how a word card can be created. Be sure to provide the correct spelling, where the word was found, and a definition or illustration for the word.

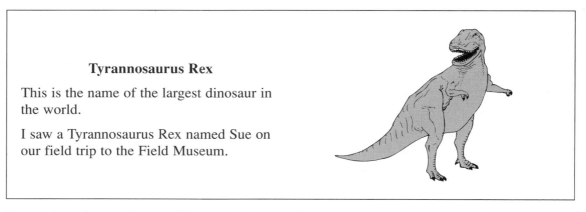

Tyrannosaurus Rex

This is the name of the largest dinosaur in the world.

I saw a Tyrannosaurus Rex named Sue on our field trip to the Field Museum.

4. Remember that students will have their own ideas about what a very long word is. The goal should be to stimulate and encourage students to find out about words. Encourage their explorations.

5. You might be interested in the longest word (45 letters) Dale, O'Rourke, and Bauman (1971) found in *Webster's Third New International Dictionary*:

pneumonoultramicroscopicsilicovolcanoconiosis

If you look at its component parts and use your knowledge of Greek, Latin, and English word parts, you may be able to pronounce the word and determine its meaning.

> pneumono/ultra/micro/scopic/silico/volcano/con/iosis
> pneumono: related to the lung (as in pneumonia)
> ultra: beyond, exceedingly, super
> micro: very small
> scopic: related to sight
> (ultramicroscopic: exceedingly small to the sight)
> silico: related to hard stone or quartz; a mineral
> volcano: related to volcanic dust; very fine particles of rock powder
> con: dust (from Greek konis)
> iosis: disease

If you are unable to determine the meaning, you might want to look it up in an unabridged dictionary.

2. A few words that might be of interest to students are listed below.

encyclopedia	convertiplane	diamondiferous
independence	conversazione	foretopmast
iconography	ichneumon	leatherback

Section 5.5

STRATEGY 3 HOMOPHONES

1. Write *homophones* on the chalkboard. Underline *homo* and tell students that it means *same*. Underline *phones* and indicate that it means *sounds*. Then tell students that homophones are words that are pronounced the same but differ in spelling and meaning.

homo + phones = homophones
(same) (sounds)

2. Invite students to suggest some words that are homophones. Write them on the chalkboard. Students will need to provide a sentence so the meaning is clear. Some sample sentences are provided below.

She went *to* the store.
I have *two* pencils in my desk.
He wants to go *too*.

Some homophones (*to, too, two, their, there, they're*) might be placed on a class word wall because they are used often by students in writing and occur frequently in printed materials. Other homophones (*carrot, carat*; *ruff, rough*; *pier, peer*) can be used for word study. There is a List of Homophones in Resources for Chapter 5.

3. Tell students that some riddles use a play on words and orally ask this riddle:

What's black and white and read all over?

Have a student volunteer to identify the word that is a homophone (*read*). Take time to explain the riddle and compare the meanings of *red* and *read*. Help students realize that such riddles are usually asked orally because the spelling would give important clues. Write the riddle on the chalkboard with *read* so students can see that the word is not a color (*red*) but an action (*read* a book).

4. Help students realize that spelling and use in a sentence are important clues to the meaning of a homophone. Say two sentences and have students share the correct spelling. See the examples below.

1. The wind *blew*.
2. The sky is *blue*.

Invite students to suggest other sentences containing homophones. Remember that dialect differences may influence the pronunciation of certain words in the List of Homophones in Resources for Chapter 5.

5. Consider using books that use homophones such as:

📖 Gwynne, F. *Chocolate Moose for Dinner*. New York: Simon & Schuster, 1988.
📖 Gwynne, F. *The King Who Rained*. New York: Simon & Schuster, 1970.

The books can be read and the sentences corrected by using the appropriate word.

6. Invite students to use their knowledge of homophones to create sentences with crazy spellings. Sentences will vary depending upon students' knowledge of homophones. The sentences with crazy spellings can be placed on the front of an index card; the back of the card should have the sentence with conventional spelling. The cards can be placed on a bulletin board, and students could be challenged to read the front of the card and then write the sentence correctly on a separate sheet of paper. What was written could be checked by comparing it to the correct spelling on the back of the card. An example card is shown below.

Aye gnu ewe wood bee hear.	I knew you would be here.
Front of Card	Back of Card

Section 5.5

STRATEGY 4 — FIGURATIVE LANGUAGE

1. Write *Look out!* on the chalkboard and ask students to explain the meaning. It should quickly become clear that the meaning is not literal. Many students, especially those whose native language is not English, will profit from some discussion of idiomatic expressions.

2. Help students realize that for some phrases in our language the meaning cannot be understood by the meanings of the individual words. Return to the sentence on the chalkboard and model for students by saying something like the following:

 The word look *can mean to see and* out *can mean the opposite of* in *or away from the inside. These meanings will not help me understand the sentence because the words have a special meaning. They are used to indicate a warning. I might say,* Look out! *if something was falling toward you, and I wanted you to get out of the way quickly. When words are used in this way, they are called idiomatic expressions.*

3. Have students share any idiomatic expressions they may know and discuss the meanings of the expressions. A few expressions are included below.

don't be a sour puss	heads up
down in the dumps	mad as a wet hen
take a bath	take a walk
piece of cake	save face
laugh my head off	bored to tears
she won hands down	lighten up

4. Be alert for idiomatic expressions in materials students are asked to read and be sure to discuss the meaning, especially if it is important to understanding.

5. Help students learn and appreciate figurative language by sharing and discussing with them Amelia Bedelia books by Peggy Parish as well as other related titles. Such books will help students learn and appreciate expressions that should not be taken literally. Two books for possible use are listed below.

 📖 Parish, P. *Amelia Bedelia*. New York: Harper & Row, 1963.
 📖 Terban, M. *Mad as a Wet Hen*. Boston: Clarion, 1987.

6. Create a bulletin board titled "Don't be Fooled" and have students place strips of paper containing idiomatic expressions and other examples of figurative language. Have students write the meaning below the phrase, as in the following example.

"That's a piece of cake."

This has nothing to do with cake.
It means that something is easy to do.

7. Additional phrases for possible use are listed below.

led by the nose	as pleased as punch
in the pink	eat crow
eat humble pie	put your foot in your mouth
turn a phrase	getting up on the wrong side of the bed
lose face	hand to mouth
wet behind the ears	stuck up
foot loose and fancy free	cold feet
shut up	give up
shot down	a long shot
a shot in the dark	fiddle around
hit the books	hit the road
a drop in the bucket	kicked the bucket
hit the hay	hit the sack
bit the dust	turn in (go to bed)
taken to the cleaners	got it for a song
step up	mixed up
down and out	in a fog
turn a new leaf	face the music
penny pincher	stretch a dollar
in the doghouse	treated like a dog
going to the dogs	hounded by someone
feeling dog tired	puppy love

Section 5.5

STRATEGY 5 SYNONYMS AND ANTONYMS

1. Write *synonym* and *antonym* on the chalkboard and ask students if anyone can give the meanings of the words. Develop the notion that synonyms refer to words having a meaning similar to that of another word. Antonyms are words of opposite meaning.

2. Have students form small groups to brainstorm some synonyms and antonyms. After students have had several minutes to develop their lists, they can write their words on the chalkboard. Select a few words for closer study. Develop the understanding that, although two words mean about the same, there are still some differences. For example, *big* and *large* are synonyms whose meanings differ slightly. Have students check the dictionary definitions and note the subtle differences in meaning.

3. Using *big* and *large,* ask students to identify some antonyms (*small, tiny, minute*). Help students realize some of the differences in the words. For example, a dime could be small but it is not minute.

4. Create a synonym web (Blachowicz & Fisher, 1996) for a word of focus. For example, if the unit of study in science is inventors, you might choose the word *invent*. Place the word in a circle and invite students to suggest synonyms for the word. Draw lines from the circle and add those words. Have students refer to a dictionary or thesaurus to find additional words. Add these to the synonym web.

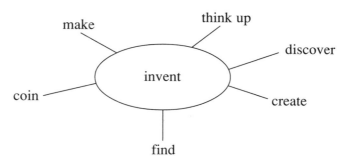

5. Ask students to consider if some of the synonyms are related to each other. For example, *make* and *create* may be more similar than *find* and *discover.* Explore the meanings of the words with students and help them revise their general synonym web to one that shows how the words may be related in meaning. See the example below.

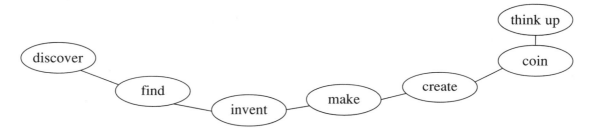

Be sure to have ample discussion so students can understand the relationships. Remember, too, that repeated opportunities to create and discuss synonym maps are likely to enhance learning.

Section 5.5

STRATEGY 6 HOMOGRAPHS

1. Ask students if they can think of any words with the same spellings that have different meanings and possibly different pronunciations. List them on the chalkboard. Tell students that such words are called homographs.

2. Help students classify the words into two groups as shown below.

Same Pronunciations Different Meanings	Different Pronunciations Different Meanings
bay	wind
palm	tear
bat	dove

3. For the first column, explore the different meanings for each word. Refer to a dictionary as needed. Learning new meanings for a known word can be difficult for students.

bay
1. part of a sea
2. long, deep barking by a dog
3. reddish-brown

bat
1. a flying mammal
2. a wooden stick
3. to wink or flutter

palm
1. part of the hand
2. a type of tree

Make the point that the words have different meanings even though they are pronounced the same.

4. Focus on the second group of words and ask students to give two pronunciations for each word. Have students use each word in a sentence. Write sentences on the chalkboard and help students see how the context clarifies how the word should be pronounced. Two examples follow.

My uncle has an old clock he must wind by hand.
I couldn't fly my kite, because there was no wind.

Invite a student to explain which clues in the sentence were helpful to get the proper pronunciation of the word.

5. Encourage students to be alert for homographs in their readings. They could add the words to a bulletin board along with new meanings and provide examples of how the context can reveal the pronunciation of a word.

tribune — an official of ancient Rome

tribune — a raised platform (He spoke to the crowd from a tribune.)

row

I will row the boat.
The plants were in a row.
The students were in a row about the game.

Older students might use a dictionary to explore the origins or etymology of words. Such explorations may help students understand the basis for word meanings.

6. Provide sentences to students that contain examples of how the same word can have different pronunciations. Have students determine the different pronunciations using the context or a dictionary (especially if the meaning is not clear). Some possible sentences are provided below.

- The bandage was wound around the wound.
- The farm was used to produce produce.
- The dump was so full that it had to refuse more refuse.
- He could lead if he would get the lead out.
- The soldier decided to desert his dessert in the desert.
- Since there is no time like the present, he thought it was time to present the present.
- A bass was painted on the head of the bass drum.
- The dove dove into the bushes.
- I did not object to the object.
- The insurance was invalid for the invalid.
- There was a row among the oarsmen about how to row.
- They were too close to the door to close it.

- A seamstress and sewer fell down into a sewer line.
- Can a farmer teach a sow to sow?
- The wind was too strong to wind the sail.
- After a number of injections my jaw got number.
- Upon seeing the tear in the painting I shed a tear.
- I had to subject the subject to a series of tests.
- How can I intimate this to my most intimate friend?

Section 5.5

STRATEGY 7 SYNONYM SUBSTITUTION*

1. Have students read a passage or chapter as a group.

2. Prepare strips of paper with "difficult" vocabulary words. Invite students to select from these words or choose their own difficult words.

3. Encourage students not to share their word with other students. They should then decide on a definition of the word using a dictionary and/or the context.

4. Have students think of a synonym for the word. For example, if the difficult word is *dagger,* a synonym might be *sword.*

5. Invite students to illustrate their selected word or present the word to other students using a dramatic presentation. The other students try to identify the word.

6. Teach students about analogies and then have students present the word in an analogy. For the word *dagger,* the analogy might be *dagger: knife:: saber: sword.*

7. Prepare a summary chart of the strategy and post it in the classroom so students can refer to the basic steps.

Synonym Substitution Procedure
1. Read the selection.
2. Select a difficult word.
3. Define the word (context or dictionary).
4. Substitute a synonym for the difficult word.
5. Illustrate or dramatize the difficult word.
6. Create an analogy for the difficult word.

*Roberts, 1999.

STRATEGY 8 SPECIAL BOOKS

1. Secure a number of books that help promote word play or explorations with words. Such books could include word histories, riddles and jokes, crossword puzzles, and related titles. Electronic books may also help promote vocabulary development (Higgins & Hess, 1999).

2. Create a special place in the classroom library for such books. Make the display attractive and inviting.

3. Introduce the special collection by telling students that the books in this particular area will provide one way to have fun with words. For example:

 This book contains information about everyday words and phrases. Here's what it says about the phrase _____." (Read the entry.) *"Here is a book of riddles and jokes about baseball. I know some of you will be very interested in this book. After you have read this book, you might want to share your favorite joke and riddle.*

4. Refer to appropriate books in the collection from time to time. For example, you might want to find a better word choice for a particular piece of writing.

5. Some possible books include the following.

 📘 Keller, C. (2000). *Best Knock-Knock Book Ever.* New York: Sterling.
 📘 Keller, C. (2000). *Kids' Funniest Riddles.* New York: Sterling.
 📘 Pellowski, M.J. (1999). *Totally Loony Riddles.* New York: Sterling.
 📘 Philips, L. (1991). *Wackysaurus: Dinosaur Jokes.* New York: Puffin.
 📘 Ryan, S. (1999). *Great Rebus Puzzles.* New York: Sterling.
 📘 Terban, M. (1989). *Superdupers: Really Funny Real Words.* New York: Clarion.
 📘 Titelman, G. (2000). *Random House Dictionary of America's Popular Proverbs and Sayings* (2nd ed.). New York: Random House.

Practice and Reinforcement Activities

1. Students should be encouraged to develop a keen interest in words and the meanings of words. Through independent word study, students can enlarge their vocabularies. One way for students to develop their word awareness is by keeping a list of words in a journal. They may want to write down where they found the word, how the word was used, and an explanation of the word's definition.

2. After students have read a story in class, ask them to discuss what words they think were interesting and what they think the words mean. They may want to look up the definitions in a dictionary to confirm their predictions.

3. Students should try to use new vocabulary words in their personal writing. Even though they may use a word incorrectly, they should continue to experiment with language by using words they have learned.

4. Provide several common words and have students try to use each word in a few sentences where it has a different meaning each time. Have students share their sentences and discuss the various meanings of the words. Possible words for such exercises are given below.

tip	part	run	cast	center
dress	circle	fly	slip	

5. Select a group of words from a content area. Divide the students into groups and ask them to find pictures of the words or objects that are associated with the words.

6. Help students learn words through their own reading by providing them with time to read. You might use one of the independent silent reading strategies found in Chapter 1. When you give students silent reading time, try to do some reading of your own. This might be a good time to catch up on reading professional journals or that mystery that you've been trying to finish. Your students will learn that you too like to read. That positive reading model will encourage them to read for pleasure themselves.

When students are given class time to read, you can catch up on your reading as well.

7. Develop a portion of your classroom library for books and games that use words in fun ways. Have a group of books that describe figures of speech and books that have riddles, jokes, and puns. These types of books show students that words can be fun. Some examples of books that you might consider follow.

Clark, E.C. (1991). *I Never Saw a Purple Cow and Other Nonsense Rhymes*. Boston: Little, Brown.

Cole, J. (1989). *Anna Banana: 101 Jump-Rope Rhymes*. New York: Morrow.

Rosenbloom, J. (1988). *The World's Best Sports Riddles and Jokes*. New York: Sterling.

Terban, M. (1989). *Superdupers: Really Funny Real Words*. New York: Clarion.

8. Ask students to keep a pencil and paper handy when they read. As they come to a word they don't know, ask them to write down the word to look up at a later date or ask someone for the word's meaning. Then they can add the word to a Word Wall or a bulletin board.

9. Read to your students, no matter what their ages. Reading interesting novels, short stories, or poems to students helps them expand their listening vocabulary. As you read, ask students to write on an index card any word that they hear that they do not know. After you have finished reading, collect the index cards. At a time convenient for you, look through the words and determine which ones you want to review with the class. The best time to review these new words is right after you have finished reading the selection. As you describe the meaning of the new word, find it in the context from which you read it. Explain the meaning of the word, read the word in its context, and then explain the meaning of the word again. Finally, have students use the new word in another sentence. After you have provided the students with this range of meanings, ask them if they can share any other meanings for the word or sentences using the word. Then add the word to a compilation of new words in a class book.

10. Once a week, write a new word on the chalkboard. Without telling the students the meaning of the word, use the word in your discussions, in directions, in conversations, and in handouts. Use the word as often as possible. Ask students to try to guess the word's meaning by your use of the word. At the end of the day, ask students to write down what they think the new word means. You may decide to tell them

the meaning of the word at this point, or you might decide to keep the students in suspense by waiting until the next day to tell them the meaning of the word. After spending so much time on one word, however, make sure the students continue hearing and reading it. Place the word on the Word Wall and encourage students to use the word in their speaking and writing.

11. If one of the words that you want your students to learn can be dramatized, ask students to create brief scenes that use the word either in conversation or in action. For example, when asked to dramatize the word *amiable,* some sixth-grade students developed this scenario.

> *Diana:* Jean, I would like you to meet my good friend, Carmel. Carmel is one of the most good-natured, kindest girls I know.
>
> *Jean:* It's good to meet you, Carmel.
>
> *Carmel:* Thank you, Diana, for describing me as *amiable.* That's one of the nicest compliments I've ever received.

12. Students, especially readers who struggle, can benefit from computer-displayed stories where unknown words can be highlighted. Explanations and pronunciations of such words may help foster vocabulary growth. The motivational aspect of computer use is another benefit that can lead to increased student engagement in reading.

13. Reading stories to students can help foster vocabulary acquisition among students in the elementary and middle schools (Elley, 1988; Layne, 1996).

Games

Tom Swifties. Older elementary students love writing Tom Swifties. Tom Swift was a character in a series of books written in the 1930s. With every utterance, Tom seemed to express himself in an unusual way. From the character came the game Tom Swifties. To play, ask students to write a sentence that has a quotation and a pun that matches what Tom says. The following are examples of Tom Swifties.

> "I'm from Texas," Tom *stated.*
> "I'll never pet that lion again," Tom said *offhandedly.*
> "I'm sick of stamping on these grapes," Tom *whined.*
> "I didn't know we derailed," Tom said *distractedly.*

You might need to begin by explaining that a pun is a word that can mean more than one thing. After students understand the meaning of a pun, try to create a list of words that could be used instead of the word *said.* Then develop a pun for each word. Some examples of words that could work as Tom Swifties follow. You can finish the sentences.

> Tom snarled.
> Tom moaned.
> Tom sputtered.
> Tom blubbered.

Palindromes. Students are fascinated with palindromes—words that can be read forwards and backwards. Words such as *mom, dad, mum,* and *did* are all palindromes. Ask students to think of as many words as they can that can be read forwards and backwards. If they are unable to think of many, ask them to use the dictionary for ideas. After they understand what a palindrome is, have students work in groups to create phrases or sentences that are palindromes. Phrases and sentences are more difficult to create

since they are not made of word palindromes but groups of words that can be read forwards and backwards, disregarding spaces. The following are examples of palindrome phrases and sentences.

Madam, I'm Adam.
A Toyota
Was it a car or a cat I saw?
Step on no pets.
Able was I ere I saw Elba.

Clues and Questions. This strategy helps students practice words that they have learned in class. Write the vocabulary word on a file card. Ask students to select several of the cards and write questions for the words. Then place the cards back in the file and divide the class into teams. One team chooses a card and asks the questions or gives clues. The opposing team tries to guess the vocabulary word.

Four Square. Students can learn the meanings of words from this strategy. Draw a square with four quadrants. In the top left quadrant, write the vocabulary word. On its right, write a personal association with the word. In the bottom left-hand square, write the word's meaning. In the bottom right, write what the word does not mean. An example follows.

Triathlete	Ironman
3 sport event	couch potato

CHAPTER 6

Promoting Comprehension

OVERVIEW

Reading is the process of making sense from print, and comprehension is the goal of all reading. Comprehension, or an understanding of the text, varies with every reader. Just think how different each of your students is. Each one has a unique set of life experiences, different experiences with print, and different abilities to process text. Since all of your students are different from each other, and they are all different from you, each one of you will understand a piece of text in a slightly different way.

> Comprehension is the goal of all reading.

Comprehension of text, or what a reader understands, is constructed by the individual reader. No two readers will produce the exact same meaning from a text, and no reader's understanding of a text will exactly match what the author had in mind while writing (Goodman, 1996). Your students, therefore, will construct different meanings from the text, some with a rich understanding of what the text could mean and some with a more superficial understanding of the text. How readers apply various strategies as they process text, however, will influence the depth of their understanding.

Good readers use strategies—
- before reading
- during reading
- after reading

Pressley (2000) suggests that there are lower-order and higher-order processes that readers use to comprehend text. Examples of lower-order processes are the skills and strategies of attending to words. Higher-order processes are activating prior knowledge, having a purpose for reading, predicting outcomes, and so on. The strategies good readers use occur before reading, during reading, and after reading (Dowhower, 1999). This chapter contains ideas for higher-order processes during the entire reading process.

Students who use few comprehension strategies while reading need instruction in ways to comprehend text. For example, students may not be making inferences while reading, or they may not be able to identify the main point. As teachers, we want our students to be able to use a variety of strategies as they read so they can construct meaning from the text. We can help them construct meaning by teaching comprehension strategies for students to use during the entire reading process.

TECHNOLOGY RESOURCES

Improving Students' Understanding of Textbook Content

http://www.Idonline.org/Id_indepth/teaching_techniques/understanding_textbooks.html
Contains online article about teaching reading using before, during, and after-reading activities

SCORE K–12 English Language Arts Cyber Guides

http://www.sdcoe.k12.ca.us/SCORE/cla.html
Contains literary lesson plans

Sample Book Ideas for Literature-Based Reading Enthusiasts

http://www.acs.ucalgary.ca/~dkbrown/yrca_samp.html
Provides lesson plans for children's literature

World of Reading

http://worldreading.org/
Provides students with online books and discussion groups

Previewing Text

Behavior Observed	The student does not preview text material before reading.
Anticipated Outcome	The student will preview text as an aid to studying and reading.

BACKGROUND

When students are assigned texts to read, many think they should begin reading with the first sentence and continue reading until the chapter is finished. Students who proceed in this manner usually are not using the most efficient means of reading. If students preview the text before reading, they can gain a better idea of the organization of the text, and they can begin to activate their prior knowledge about the subject. Understanding the text organization and making connections to what is known can help facilitate readers' comprehension as they read. You should, therefore, encourage your students to preview text material before they read.

Section 6.1

STRATEGY 1 PICTURE AND TEXT SURVEY*

1. Ask students to preview the pictures and text to get a general idea of the subject. For example, if students are going to read a chapter on insects, ask them to read the title of the chapter, the subtitles, and the first sentence and then look at each picture. As the students look at the pictures, tell them to read any captions under the pictures and think about why the picture is included.

2. Next, tell students they should organize the information in their minds by writing a sentence describing the topic. In the case of a chapter on insects, students might write a sentence similar to the following one: This chapter will discuss the life cycle of insects.

3. After organizing the information, ask students to predict questions they think the text will answer. The pictures will give them a clue. The following questions could be asked on the insect chapter.

 What are the stages of the life cycle of an insect? What happens to an insect in the egg cycle? What is larva and what does the insect look like in the larva stage? What is a pupa and what is happening to the insect in the pupa stage? How long does it take for the insect to become an adult?

*Lamberg & Lamb, 1980.

4. Before students begin reading, ask them to try to answer their questions. This helps them to access their background knowledge. As they read, then, students will be better able to comprehend the information. In the example of the life cycle of insects, students can discuss the times they have seen insect larvae. They may know something about the stages of development of frogs, and the teacher can relate this knowledge to the life cycle of insects.

5. Next, ask students to read the text to locate answers to their questions. If they have carefully formulated questions for the text, they will be able to find answers to their questions. Many times, however, students will not be able to find answers to their questions because they did not ask good questions. If students were not able to find their answers, help them revise their questions. If students are able to locate information, tell them to think about their predictions of the questions and to revise the answers they had given.

Section 6.1

STRATEGY 2 TAG: TEXTBOOK ACTIVITY GUIDE*

1. Decide on your objectives for the lesson. Then choose chapters from the text that relate to those objectives.

2. Decide which text features you want to include in the preview. Students may not need to read each passage of a chapter. Choose the ones that meet your objectives to emphasize in the TAG.

3. Choose a different task for each chapter of the guide. Even though students will be interacting with each chapter of the text, you should recommend a different strategy for each one. This will encourage students to use a variety of strategies as they read. Some strategies you might consider are predicting, reading and discussing in a small group, skimming the text (looking for the main ideas only), reading and retelling (explaining the gist of the text to a partner), and writing. Writing can take the form of a summary, a response that explains how the passage made the student feel, a fictional account of the passage, or comments on the passage in a journal.

4. Design TAGs so that students learn to interact with their texts in a variety of ways. A sample TAG follows so you can see what one looks like.

Sample Textbook Activity Guide (TAG)

1. Predict: With a partner, survey the headings on pages 20–24. Discuss what you think you will learn from the chapter.
2. Read and Discuss: Read the introduction on page 20 and discuss what you already know about the topic with your partner.
3. Skim: Skim pages 21 and 22.
4. Read and Retell: Read pages 23 and 24 and retell what you have learned to your partner.
5. Write: Write the gist of the chapter in your journal.

5. After students complete their TAGs, spend time discussing each part of the guide. Encourage students to share problems or difficulties they encountered as well as insights gained from using the guide.

*Davey, 1986.

STRATEGY 3 SCROL*

1. **S = Survey the headings.** Have students read the headings in the chapter and ask themselves what they already know about the topic. For example, if students are reading a text on the Civil War with the headings battles and generals, they may bring to mind all they already know about the topic. You might ask students to share some of their ideas. Write them on the chalkboard. List everything they say whether it is correct or not. Examples might include Grant, Sherman, Meade, Shiloh, Antietam, Gettysburg, and Vicksburg.

2. **C = Connect.** Direct students to ask themselves how the headings connect to one another. They may use key words in the headings to help them make the connections. In the example on the Civil War, students most likely will predict that the battles were battles of the Civil War and the generals were famous leaders in that conflict.

3. **R = Read the text.** Ask students to read the text, looking for words and phrases that explain the headings. As students read about the battles of the Civil War, for example, have them put the battles in order and understand their relative importance to the war as a whole.

4. **O = Outline.** Explain to your students that they should then write the headings and details under the headings that they remember from their reading. An example follows.

 Battles

 Gettysburg July 1–3, 1863
 Under General Meade
 Lee retreated
 Both sides lost about 25% of their soldiers

5. **L = Look back.** Finally, direct students to look back at the text to determine the accuracy of their outlines or notes. If they have incorrect information, they should revise what they have written. In looking at the outline for the Battle of Gettysburg, it would seem unlikely that each side lost so many men. Checking the text, however, confirms that the outline is correct.

STRATEGY 4 SQ3R**

1. Introduce the entire strategy, explaining what each step means. Just as in surveying a passage, giving the students an overview of the entire study strategy is important. Then explain to students that you will be showing them how to use the SQ3R strategy, but that eventually you will expect them to use SQ3R on their own. Provide guided practice so students can use each step of the strategy as you introduce it.

2. Introduce one step of the strategy at a time. Explain how to do each step and explain the value of the step. You may want to use the following example.

*Grant, 1993.
**Robinson, 1946.

S = Survey. Ask the students to survey the chapter by reading the opening paragraph, headings and subheadings, and the chapter summary. Surveying the chapter will give students an idea of the main points covered in the text. As they survey, direct them to ask the following questions: "From the survey, what is the chapter about?" or "What do I already know about the topic?" or "How much time do I think it will take to read and understand this material?" Explain that the value of the survey is to help students focus on the main points of the chapter. The chapter headings give the general idea, and the subtitles help students realize what is included as subpoints. Understanding what is included under the main heading is important. As students make predictions about a general topic, they may think of points that may not be included in the text. If they have not surveyed the text, they may be distracted while reading as they look for the ideas they thought might be in the chapter.

Q = Question. Tell students to convert chapter headings into questions in their head, in discussion, or in writing. Because the headings of the passage are already developed by title and subtitle, students may also write their questions in the form of an outline.

Explain that questioning before reading arouses curiosity and helps to set a purpose for reading. Questioning also helps students to focus on the material in the text by becoming actively involved in trying to answer the questions the students have formulated.

R = Read. Next, direct students to read the text, looking for the answers to their initial questions and perhaps posing additional questions. While they read, students should use comprehension monitoring strategies such as those described in Chapter 6. As they read, tell students to continue thinking about the questions they asked. If they are not able to answer their questions, they may have to reread the passage or use other fix-up strategies. They should also consider the possibility that they may have asked inappropriate questions. Explain that reading to answer self-generated questions has the advantage of holding students' attention during reading. If students are reading for the purpose of answering their own questions, they will be more attentive while reading.

R = Recite. The next step is to explain to students that they should think about the answers to their questions and recite them in their minds or write them down. They can then decide whether they answered the questions about the text and, if they had, students should decide what information is important to remember. Tell students that it is impossible to remember everything they read. After they read, they should make some judgments about prioritizing the information in the text. They may want to use memorization strategies (see Section 7.10) to process the information.

Tell students that reciting is an important aspect of SQ3R. If information is not processed, it will not be stored in the long-term memory of the student. Processing information directly after reading increases the chance that students will remember it. Tell students that reciting also helps them personalize the material by thinking about it in their own words.

R = Review. After reading, ask students to review what they have learned. Tell them that they should begin by reviewing the headings and the questions the students asked. They should look for connections between the information they read and what they already know about the topic. They should then try to recall the main points of the passage. Finally, students may want to write a brief summary (see Section 7.6).

Explain that students need to review what they have read in order to remember information. Reviewing is another way to process text so that it will be stored in students' long-term memory. Tell students that reviewing text is also valuable because they can look for relationships between the new information and their background knowledge.

3. After you have introduced one of the steps of SQ3R, demonstrate the strategy using one of the student's texts. An example of modeling SQ3R follows. If you were surveying the Identifying Words chapter from this book, you would read the chapter title, the first sentence or paragraph of the overview, and then the subtitles. You would find out which types of reading behaviors are covered in that chapter and which are not. You would then be ready to ask questions.

4. You may decide to model question-asking with the same passage or a different one. For example, you could ask:

What are some strategies recommended for helping students learn basic sight words?
or *How do I help students expand their concepts of words?*

Try to ask a question for each part of the chapter. You might even write them down.

Because the passage you surveyed is relatively long, you might want to choose one part of it to read. Let's say you have chosen the part "Identifying Sight Words." Read the part about using good reading strategies. In this instance, a good plan is to determine what teaching strategies and practice activities would be most helpful to you in your teaching. You should make a mental note of the strategies you think will be useful.

5. After reading, recite the activities you intend to put into practice. Tell yourself which ones have the highest priority and which ones you will consider at another time.

6. To review the material, reread the questions you wrote, looking for additional strategies you wish to remember. If there are activities from the text that you think would also be helpful, reread them. Then consider how the strategies you have chosen relate to what you are already doing in the classroom. For example, you may be using one of the activities, and the suggestions from the text will be added to your lesson plans. You may also be using different strategies to teach the same concept. Then you might add the strategy to your own repertoire of teaching tools.

7. An SQ3R guide follows on the next page.

Practice and Reinforcement Activities

1. Talk to students about movie previews such as "Coming Attractions" that appear before videos and movies begin. Tell students that these short clips are a preview of the movie. Discuss what previews are intended to do, such as interest people in the movie. Then have students select a book they have read. Create a poster or a PowerPoint presentation preview. Display three or four of these "Coming Attractions" each week.

2. Have students from high school or college come to your class with two or three of their textbooks. Have the older students show your class how the textbooks are organized and have them preview the books for students. Tell students that reading becomes more complex through the school years and strategies like previewing become increasingly important.

SQ3R Guide

Name _____ Date _____

Text _____ Pages _____

1. Survey the chapter. As you survey, answer the following questions.

What is the title of the chapter? _____

What are the main headings?

a. _____

b. _____

c. _____

d. _____

Describe in a sentence or two what you think the chapter will be about.

2. Question

List questions for each of the main headings and subheadings. Use who, what, when, where, why, and how in each question.

a. _____

b. _____

c. _____

d. _____

3. Read

Read one chapter of the text at a time. Think about what you have read. List any points that surprise you or that you think you don't understand.

4. Recite

Recite what you learned from the passage. Use memory techniques to remember what you learned. List what you think you need to remember here.

5. Review

Review the entire chapter. Where you able to answer your questions? If not, reread those parts. Then write the main points of the passage without looking at your text.

3. Display a web site on a projector so that all students can see. Preview the web site by scrolling through the options. Discuss the site's options with students. Ask students how many of them have spent time reading web site information that they didn't want. Tell students that they should also preview web sites to maximize their computer time.

4. Take the time to preview the books, magazines, and journals that you read. Occasionally, tell students about your reading and model your previewing techniques.

SECTION 6.2

Activating Prior Knowledge

Behavior Observed	The student does not activate prior knowledge before reading.
Anticipated Outcome	The student will activate prior knowledge before reading to enhance comprehension of text.

PERSPECTIVE AND STRATEGIES

The ability to access what you know about a subject before reading can help you understand the text with richer comprehension. Using what you know to help you connect your existing knowledge with the new knowledge from the text is called accessing prior knowledge. What students know is structured in their minds in schema, or abstract frameworks around which memory is stored. If students have knowledge about frogs and toads, for example, they will better understand the Frog and Toad stories by Arnold Lobel.

Since all students have limited background knowledge to a certain extent, because of the number of years they have lived and the experiences they have had, teachers need to help students both access their prior knowledge and develop their knowledge before they read.

This section contains several strategies that can help students access their prior knowledge before reading.

Section 6.2

STRATEGY 1 FILE FOLDERS

1. Get some file folders and ask students to share what they know about them. Help students realize that each file folder contains information about a topic or subject and that the file folders could be related to each other. For example, if you use portfolios in file folders, students would know that each student has his or her own file folder. Discuss how the information in a file folder can be used to help understand the student or topic.

2. Relate the concept of file folders to the way the human brain holds information. Stress that the brain is efficient at "filing" large amounts of information in an organized fashion and that this information is vital if we are to understand what we are reading. The important point is to use this information before, during, and after reading.

3. Use an actual file folder or have students make one and write in the folder what they know about a particular topic. Choose a topic about which practically all students have knowledge. Some possible topics include a particular animal (dog or cat), an area in the community, a sport, a game, or a famous person.

4. Give students sufficient time to write what they know about the selected topic. Stress that words or phrases, not complete sentences, can be written. Charts and/or drawings may also be used.

5. Invite students to share their knowledge; then create a master file folder on the chalkboard or an overhead transparency. As some students share, other students may say, "I knew that but I didn't write it down." These students can add the information to their file folders. Encourage all students to share their knowledge.

6. Ask students how the information in their file folders could be used if they were asked to read a story, chapter, or book about the topic. Lead students to understand that such knowledge can help them link what they already know about a topic to what they are reading. It can help them make predictions about what might be in a book or story. It can help them make sense of and raise questions about what they are reading. And it can help them evaluate, within the context of their existing knowledge, what they have read.

7. To encourage students to use their background knowledge, have them pretend to take out their file folders prior to reading about a particular topic.

Section 6.2

STRATEGY 2 BRAINSTORMING

1. Tell students that before they read they should think about what they know about the topic. Explain how you activate your own background knowledge before reading. For example, say the following:

 Yesterday, I picked up a book about a group of British mountain climbers who climbed Mt. Everest. I thought about what I already knew: Mt. Everest is the highest mountain in the world, many people have died climbing it, and British climbers are known for their skill. I remembered the books and films I had already seen about Mt. Everest. Then I previewed the book and began reading.

2. Select a book that students will be reading, such as *Owl Babies* (Waddell, 1975). Show students the book and say the following:

 Owl Babies *is a book about owls. Since the book is about owls, I'll write the word* owls *on the chalkboard. I'll draw a circle around the word so that I remember that* owls *is my topic.*

 Have students also write the word *owls* on their paper and draw a circle around it.

3. Tell students that to activate their prior knowledge they should brainstorm all the things they know about owls before reading. You can ask for ideas from the entire class or have students discuss their ideas in small groups.

4. Write the students' ideas on the chalkboard with their ideas radiating out from the center circle. Have students do the same. An example follows.

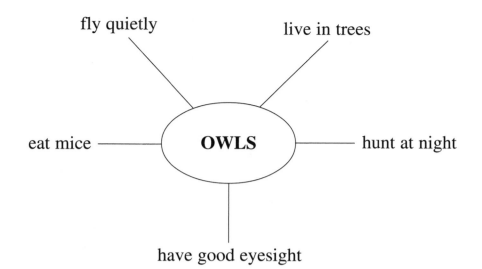

5. Encourage students to brainstorm before reading to activate their prior knowledge.

Section 6.2

STRATEGY 3 K-W-L*

1. Before beginning a topic of study or before beginning a story or book, have students complete a K-W-L chart. Tell students that before they read they should think about what they already know. Explain that a K-W-L chart prompts them to think about what they already know, what they want to know, and, after reading, what they have learned.

2. Duplicate and distribute the K-W-L chart that follows. Make a transparency of the K-W-L chart to model the strategy.

 3. Identify a topic or story that students will be experiencing. Divide the class into groups of three or four students. Ask students to think about what they already know about the topic. Provide ample time for students to think and discuss.

4. Have students share their lists with the class. Write the students' ideas on the K section of the K-W-L chart. An example follows.

| | **Planets** | |
K	W	L
(what I already know)	(what I want to find out)	(what I have learned)
Earth is a planet. *There are 9 planets.* *Planets are in space.* *Moons go around them.* *The sun is not one.*		

*Ogle, 1989.

5. Then ask students what they want to learn about the topic. Have them discuss in groups, share with the class, and list the ideas on the W section of the chart.

6. After students have read the book or the unit is complete, have students list what they have learned in the L section of the K-W-L chart. Provide additional charts so that you can include all of the things students have learned.

Name _____ Date _____

K-W-L Chart

Donna Ogle

	(title)	
K	**W**	**L**
(what I already know)	**(what I want to find out)**	**(what I have learned)**

From Ogle, D.M. (1989). The know, want to know, learn strategy. In K.D. Muth (Ed.), *Children's Comprehension of Text* (pp. 205–223). Newark, DE: International Reading Association.

Practice and Reinforcement Activities

1. Invite students to use their background knowledge (file folders) to make predictions before reading. Remind them to use the title, pictures, chapter headings, and so on.

2. Model the think-aloud strategy to show students how you use your background knowledge to make predictions about a selection to be read. For example, say the following:

> *The title of this story is 'All About Fish.' Because we are studying science, I think this is not really a story but a selection that will present some information and facts about fish. I know that fish* [you give known knowledge] . . . *and I wonder if this passage will talk about goldfish. I have two at home and* [share knowledge]. . . . *I wonder if the passage will talk about sharks. I really would like to know more about them.*

Use similar think alouds to help students learn how you link knowledge in your head with the passage while reading and after reading. Remind students to use a similar strategy while they read.

3. Develop lessons that model what you do when the information in your head is different from what you are reading or have read in the text. Sometimes you may need to go back and reread to clarify something that does not match your existing knowledge. You may have to consider whether what you know is, in fact, accurate. You may also need to go to another source (person or text) for additional information that will help clarify the conflicting information. Try to provide actual examples from your experiences for each situation.

4. Use a variety of cloze activities in which students can use their background knowledge to make reasonable predictions about the missing word(s). Help students come to understand that predictions are possible because of their background knowledge and that it is useful in reading. Discuss the various words predicted and their appropriateness. Some possible items to use follow.

> Jack and Jill _____.
> Last _____, I went to the show.
> Yesterday _____, I went to the show.
> The _____ had nearly finished building the house.
> The older person walked _____ to the car with a _____ in hand.

5. Based on the title of a book, chapter, or selection, have students brainstorm possible words that might be encountered. Discuss the reasons behind certain choices that may appear strange.

6. Use anticipation guides (see the sample titled Chomping Champs on the following page) to get students more actively involved in reading by using their background knowledge. Begin by identifying the major concepts presented in the selection. Then create a series of statements to challenge or support students' beliefs. Present the statements to students on an individual sheet, the chalkboard, or an overhead transparency. Students should work independently and then discuss their reactions to the statements (drawing on their background knowledge). Following active discussion, students should read the selection silently to verify or change their initial predictions. Post-reading assessment (see "after you read" column on Chomping Champs) and discussion provide students with an opportunity to clarify the accuracy of their predictions and to verify information. The anticipation guide on "Chomping Champs" is based on an article in the February 1982 issue of *Ranger Rick's Nature Magazine*.

Chomping Champs

Directions: The article you will be reading is about fuzzy little insects called dermestid (dur-MES-tid) beetles. Pretend you are one of these tiny beetles. Read the statements below and check the items you think are true about yourself. After reading the article go back and check those items that the author agrees with.

Before You Read

After You Read

1. I help museums save money by cleaning the bones of dead animals for their exhibits.

2. My favorite food is raw flesh.

3. I work for my room and board in museums all around the world.

4. My house is made of metal.

5. I can eat and eat and never get full.

6. After three days of eating, I spin a cocoon and turn into a butterfly.

7. Baby dermestid beetles are called dermies.

Chomping Champs*

In a dark room in a museum lie the bodies of a monkey, a fox, a deer, and fifty bats. The skeletons of these animals soon will be used for studies and displays. But first the bones must be perfectly cleaned by a team of the museum's hardest workers.

These workers, fuzzy little insects called *dermestid* (dur-MES-tid) beetles, keep busy at their job nearly 24 hours a day. Dermestids are smaller than your thumbnail, but they have mighty appetites. They can scurry in and out of a skeleton's every nook and cranny— no matter how small—leaving no flesh on the bones. Just sixty larvae can make a small bird's bones spotless in only three days.

It would take loads of time and hard work for a person to do the same job by hand. By using hungry beetles, museums save money—and get spanking-clean skeletons.

Most of the eager eaters are the beetles' young, or *larvae.* They love to feast on dried flesh and almost anything else! That's why they always must be kept in boxes made of metal.

Scientists cut most of the extra meat off an animal's body, then let the remaining meat dry. As soon as they put the body into a beetle box, the chompers get busy. Adult females lay their eggs in the dried flesh right away providing a steady supply of food from the moment the larvae hatch. After stuffing themselves for many days, they burrow into a layer of cotton on the bottom of their box, change into adults, and come out ready to lay their own eggs. (Dermestids live only about a month.)

One museum put its beetles to work on elephants and whales. Even though it will take years, they know they can count on the chomping champs.

*Adapted from Fred Johnson

Lack of Clear Purpose(s) for Reading

Behavior Observed	The student appears to approach reading tasks without purposes or goals.
Anticipated Outcome	The student will develop purposes or goals to guide his or her reading.

BACKGROUND

When students have a clear purpose for reading, comprehension is enhanced. The trouble is that many students' purposes for reading may be dominated by thinking such as "the teacher said to read this," "so I can answer the questions," or a surprising "I don't know." Although external purposes are a reality of classroom instruction, students should also learn how to set their own purposes for reading.

Recognizing that there are externally imposed purposes for reading as well as internally generated purposes in both school and life, two principles should guide your actions when asking students to read.

- First, be sure you set clear purposes and expectations for students when making reading assignments.
- Second, model how to read to fulfill purposes.

Strategies such as taking notes, summarizing, outlining, answering questions, and mapping may need to be taught, preferably within the context of your lessons. Students sometimes may be able to fuse your expectations with their purposes. The following ideas should help students develop purposes for reading. Keep in mind that students can have more than one purpose for reading even though we generally use the singular form.

Chances are this student would have high interest in a book about skateboarding.

STRATEGY 1

WHAT'S THE PURPOSE?

1. Choose one or more sports (for example, soccer and softball) and encourage students to share reasons why players participate in that sport. Students could write their responses individually or in groups. If groups are used, be sure someone serves as a recorder.

2. Invite students to share their ideas. Write their responses on the chalkboard. Some possible responses are provided below.

for fun	to be with friends	to improve skills
to win	to stay fit	to be outside

3. Help students realize that players participate in sports for different reasons. Then make the connection to reading and suggest that there are different purposes for reading.

4. Have students share purposes for reading. It may be helpful to have them think of different types of reading materials (books, stories, magazines, recipes, road signs, newspapers, television guide, and so on) when they are suggesting purposes.

5. Spend time discussing some of the advantages for setting purposes for reading. Be sure that students realize that reading can be done for different purposes and that their purposes should guide their reading.

6. Model a few situations in which you set a purpose, read, and then evaluate whether your purpose was achieved. Here is one example.

 I want to find out which movies are playing in town. I'll use today's newspaper to help me. Let's see . . . from the index on the front page, I know that the movies are in section 2, page 6. Okay, I've found the page in that section, and I can see that the following movies are playing [read movies]. *I think I might like to see _____ because I read a good review of it a few days ago. My purpose was to find out which movies were playing, and I was successful in achieving my purpose. I know I was successful because I found the movies.*

Other situations to model are listed below.

- beginning a short story
- reading a textbook
- finding a TV show
- looking up a word
- using an encyclopedia

- reading a memo
- finding a telephone number
- browsing a newspaper
- reading a magazine

7. Encourage students to think aloud and model some of the purposes they have for reading. Be sure they also explain how they went about achieving their purposes and whether they were successful.

8. Transfer purpose setting to ongoing reading activities taking place in the classroom.

STRATEGY 2

DIFFERENT BOOKS, DIFFERENT PURPOSES

1. Select a narrative book and an expository book on the same general topic (like *The Egypt Game* and *Mummies, Tombs, and Treasures*) to model setting purposes, activating background knowledge, and previewing.

2. Tell students which strategies you will be modeling and how they can help students become better readers. For example, say:

 I always have a purpose when I read. It helps me focus my attention, and I know why I'm reading. While reading, I can ask myself whether my purpose is being achieved. I also try to ask myself what I already know about the topic. Some of what I know will probably help me understand. I may also be able to link what I already know to what I'm reading. Before actually reading, I often preview the book or selection. That helps me see how the book is organized and how long the reading may take me.

3. Model a preview for a narrative book (for example, *The Egypt Game*).

 The teacher said I have to read a book for sharing with my literature circle, so I guess that's my major purpose for reading. Of course, I did have lots of books to choose from, and I chose The Egypt Game *because the title sounded interesting. I suppose I want to know what this Egypt game is. I can see that I have at least two purposes for reading, and I'll probably have more once I start reading the book. I've got to keep in mind that I'll be sharing the book in a literature circle so I need to learn about the characters and have a good idea about the major events that happened in the book. I don't really know much about Egypt, but I do know how books like this are organized.*

 Now, I'll preview the book. Wow! It's more than 200 pages long, so reading it will take me some time. I can see from the contents page in the front of the book that there are quite a few chapters, and the chapters are about 10 pages long. Perhaps I'll read a chapter or two at a time. The first chapter is called 'The Discovery of Egypt.' From the illustration on the cover of the book, I don't think the characters will discover the real country of Egypt. I think they may discover something that will eventually lead to the Egypt game. I'd better get started reading.

4. Encourage students to react to your think aloud by writing the words *setting purposes, using background,* and *previewing* to form column heads across the chalkboard. Have students recall what you did and write key words or phrases in the appropriate column. Ask students to share some of their relevant experiences and add them to the list within each column. Remember to ask questions such as, "Why is that useful?" and "How does that help you become a better reader?"

5. Model a preview for an expository selection (for example, *Mummies, Tombs, and Treasures*).

> *I'm choosing this book because I want to know about some of the secrets of ancient Egypt. That's part of the title, and I want to know more, so that's my main purpose. I know some things about mummies and tombs [describe]. As I page through the book, I see a lot of interesting illustrations and photographs. On page 40 is a real photograph of a mummy without the cloth wrappings. Under the photograph, it says that the mummy's face and shoulders are packed with sawdust. The eyes are painted stone. I'll certainly want to know more about why and how those things were done. It sure sounds strange to me. The contents page shows seven chapters. I can see from the chapter titles that the book is mostly about mummies.*

6. Elicit responses from students using a procedure similar to the one in step 5 and encourage students to relate their experiences with expository materials.

7. Guide students in using these strategies in their classroom reading assignments. Invite students to confer with you to share their successes and problems using the strategies you have taught. When appropriate, offer advice, ask questions, and help solidify the strategies taught. Remember to give recognition for effort.

Practice and Reinforcement Activities

1. Use classroom events such as daily attendance lists, lunch counts, and parents' letters to illustrate the different purposes people have for reading (Duke & Stewart, 1997).

2. Discuss the different purposes for reading. For example, you might read for pleasure, to gain information, to escape, and so on. Create a *Why Read?* chart that lists reading materials on one side and several purposes for reading on the other side as in the following example. Display the list in the classroom and add to the list when appropriate.

Why Read?	
Reading Materials	*Purposes for Reading*
Picture books	Enjoyment
Magazines	Information
Mysteries	Escape

3. Have students record their purposes for reading their self-selected reading material. After several entries, have students reflect on their most frequent purposes for reading. Encourage students to read for a variety of purposes. Have students compare lists to find their classmates' purposes for reading.

Main Point

Behavior Observed	The student has difficulty understanding the main point of a reading selection.
Anticipated Outcome	The student will understand the main point of a reading selection.

BACKGROUND

The identification of the main idea or central thought of what is read usually involves several processes. Students must distinguish between essential elements, make inferences, and make judgments—all higher-level thinking skills. Although the main idea may be stated somewhere in a passage (text explicit), it is also likely that the main idea may not be explicitly expressed, and students will need to infer it (text implicit).

Years ago, the identification of main ideas was "taught" with workbooks and skill sheets. Educators know now that these materials have limitations. Workbook exercises rarely teach main ideas or transfer to other reading materials. Such exercises may only provide practice in the task of identifying main ideas. In order for students to learn how to select or infer the main idea, the teacher should use the following teaching strategies.

Section 6.4

STRATEGY 1 FINDING THE MAIN IDEA

1. Tell students that this lesson will help them learn how to figure out the main idea of a passage. Begin by presenting lists of words (without headings) on the chalkboard. Ask students to think of a word or phrase that could be used to describe what the words are mostly about. Several lists are shown here. Be sure to select words that are appropriate for your students.

Animals	Clothes	Cars	Places to Stay
dog	shirt	Firebird	house
cat	pants	Mustang	apartment
hamster	dress	Corvette	duplex
guinea pig	shoes	RX7	trailer
horse	jeans	Ferrari	hotel

2. Discuss the words or phrases offered by the students. Stress that the words or phrases describe the topic; they tell what the words are mostly about. Relate the discussion to reading. Ask students to think of favorite books or stories and tell what the topics are. Indicate that the main idea is the most important idea given about a topic. Other pieces of information that support the main idea are called details.

3. Draw a wheel with spokes on the chalkboard and tell students that the center of the wheel represents the main idea and the spokes represent the supporting details.

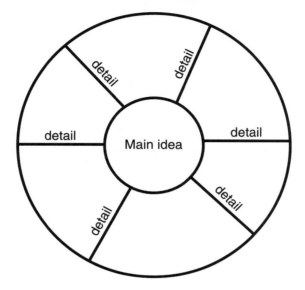

Then present a short passage and help students model how to go about finding the main idea, as in the following example.

Did you know it takes the planet Pluto over 200 years to go around the sun? Our planet, Earth, takes 365 days. Mercury, the smallest planet, only takes 88 days to go around the sun. All of the nine planets in our solar system take a different number of days or years to go around the sun.

After reading the paragraph aloud with students, think aloud to determine the main idea.

At first I thought the paragraph was going to be about Pluto, but then other planets were mentioned. In fact, one sentence says something about all nine planets . . . , so I think the paragraph is about planets, but what about planets? Each sentence gives some information about how long it takes planets to go around the sun . . . , so I'm sure the paragraph is mostly about how long it takes planets to go around the sun.

4. Then use another passage. Think aloud and explain why certain details are eliminated as the main idea. Encourage students to share their thoughts and also to think aloud as they process information in making their decisions to find the main idea. Choose a sample passage like the following one for this activity. Guide students as needed.

Owls are one of the only kinds of birds that you can see at night. That's because owls are nocturnal. They hunt at night, usually looking for small animals to eat. Owls can hunt at night because they have large eyes that can see in the dark. Their eyes are 50 times more powerful than are the eyes of humans. Owls also have extremely sensitive hearing and can hear the rustling of a mouse from high in a tree.

5. Make the point that in some passages the main idea is directly stated. In others, it is not. Also, some paragraphs may not contain a main idea, because they may be transitional paragraphs.

6. Use additional paragraphs or passages to help students learn how to figure out the main idea. Perhaps you could develop a wall chart that contains the following reminders.

Finding the Main Idea

1. What is the paragraph mostly about?
2. What is the most important idea given about the topic?
3. Look for details that tell about the main idea. If you can't locate any details, you probably don't have the main idea.
4. Remember that the main idea is sometimes right in the passage. Other times you have to use the details to figure out the main idea.

Section 6.4

STRATEGY 2 MAIN IDEA SEARCH

1. Look for the topic.
 - Read the passage.
 - Ask yourself: What is this entire paragraph, or passage about, or to what does most of this paragraph, or passage seem to refer? The answer to these questions will give you the topic.

2. Next, find the main idea or central theme.
 - Ask yourself: What is the most general statement made about the topic?
 - Go back and examine each sentence.
 - What seems to be repeated, hinted at, or emphasized in most sentences?
 - Is there one general idea in the passage that is repeated, hinted at, or emphasized in each sentence?
 - If so, that is probably the main idea.
 - If not, then you have to infer what the main idea is, because it is not stated.

3. If the strategies in step 2 didn't work, try those provided below.
 - Think of each sentence in the passage as a factor in an addition problem in math. For example, try to figure out what each of the specific statements made in the passage adds up to, or where they lead: (A specific statement) + (A specific statement) + (A specific statement) = Total: The main idea (A general statement).
 - All of the sentences in a passage might not add up to the main idea. Add up only those sentences that are connected by the same idea.
 - Ask yourself: In what direction does each of these specific points seem to lead? The answer gives you the main idea.
 - Ask yourself: Is there a general statement that applies to most of these ideas? The answer gives you the main idea.

4. If the material is really difficult and the strategies in steps 2 and 3 did not work, try those listed below. Draw a large letter T (see illustration).

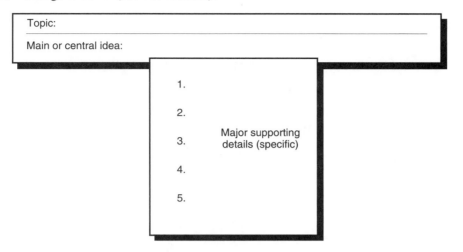

- Divide the top part in half horizontally.
- Ask yourself: What is most of this passage about?
- The answer will be the topic of the passage.
- Fill in the top part of the *T* with the topic.
- Get your answers to that question by writing, in the stem of the *T*, the sentences that seem to be connected by the same idea and seem to be specific.
- Then ask yourself: What general idea do these sentences seem to support or to what general idea do these ideas seem to point?
- The answer will be the main idea.

Practice and Reinforcement Activities

1. Pictures may be used to help students develop the notion of topic and to answer the question What is this picture mostly about? Discussions can be used to develop an understanding of main idea and important supporting details.

2. Have students read a short passage. Select the best title from several given. Students could also create their own title or write a phrase or sentence that best describes the main idea of the passage.

3. Provide several passages, each followed by four sentences. One sentence states the main idea of the passage, another is too broad, one is too detailed, and the last contains information not stated in the paragraph. After students have selected their main idea for each passage, discuss their choices as well as why other statements were not appropriate for the main idea. Guided discussion is particularly important, because it will help students clarify their thinking.

4. Read a short passage to students and have them relate, in one sentence, the main idea. Write some of their sentences on the board as a basis for discussion.

5. Cut out passages from old books or articles that are at a variety of reading levels. Fasten the passages to 5" x 8" cards. On the back of each card write several possible phrases or sentences that describe the main idea. Students should read the passage, write their answers on a separate sheet of paper, and then compare them with the answers on the back of the cards.

6. Use newspaper articles and have students underline the main idea if stated, or write it if an inference is necessary. In a different colored pencil, marker, or pen, the student can underline the supporting details.

7. To help develop the inclusive nature of a main idea, provide lists where students can practice understanding the difference between general and specific ideas. Be sure to relate the lists to the study of main ideas and discuss reasons for the best answer. Several exercises follow.

Pennies, nickels, and dimes are all _____.

Robins, sparrows, and hawks are all _____.

Circle the word that includes the others.

snow	stamps	Earth	(games)
rain	coins	Saturn	bingo
(weather)	stickers	(planets)	checkers
fog	(collections)	Jupiter	hopscotch

8. Use students' knowledge of familiar stories (such as *The Three Little Pigs, Hansel and Gretel,* and *The Gingerbread Boy*) and have them discuss their perceptions of the major thoughts in the stories.

9. Have students look through various types of reading materials to find examples of the main idea or topic sentence. Students can also write their own paragraphs using these two different types of paragraph structures.

10. Have students read a selection and draw the outline of their hand on a sheet of paper. The main idea can be written on the hand and the supporting details on the fingers.

11. List and number a series of statements on cards. Have students read the sentences. Select the one that best describes the main idea. Place the number and the main idea on the back of the card so the activity is self-correcting.

1. Bats can fly.
2. Bats are found in caves.
3. Bats are unusual animals.
4. Bats are clumsy on the ground.
5. Bats can scare people.

The main idea is 3:
Bats are unusual animals.

Front of Card Back of Card

12. Use illustrations from a story or have students draw pictures to help them understand main ideas. Begin with familiar stories. Discuss the illustrations or pictures.

13. Practice naming lists of things that are arranged in categories. Students or the teacher list four or five items, such as paper, pencils, notebooks, pens, journals. Then invite a student to offer the title of the category—how these things fit together. Give several students a chance to offer the category title. Sometimes more than one answer is acceptable.

Games

Match. Provide students with sets of six pictures and a title for them on individual strips of tagboard. Include a few additional titles that do not match the picture with the appropriate title. By writing the same number on the back of the title strip and picture, students can check their work.

Where? On 5" x 8" cards, provide reading passages in which the main idea or topic sentence is found at the beginning or the end. Also, have passages where the main idea or topic sentence is not included. Provide cards to match the passages as in the following example.

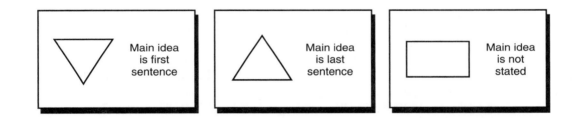

Have students match the appropriate cards with the passages. Place the appropriate geometric shape on the back of each passage to provide a means of self-checking.

Categories. Use pictures or objects from five categories (such as farm, jobs, food, colors, outdoors). Mix up the pictures or objects from the categories and have students sort them according to a logical scheme or attribute. Discuss the resulting categories and have students provide reasons for each category. Possible categories are provided below.

animals	clothing	shelters
foods	energy	musical instruments
flowers	fruits	tools
school supplies	shapes	vehicles
games	drinks	books

SECTION 6.5

Facts or Details

Behavior Observed	The student has difficulty recalling important facts or details from a passage.
Anticipated Outcome	The student will recall important facts or details from a passage.

BACKGROUND

Important facts or details often can be taught along with main ideas. Facts and details are frequently at the factual level of comprehension (text explicit) but can also be interpretive or applicative (text implicit). For example, consider the following passage and question.

> Jerry saw Beth. She was wearing a red dress.
> What color was her dress?

Most teachers would consider the question to be at the factual or literal level. The correct answer (red) is certainly explicitly contained in the passage. However, to get the answer, the student has to do a bit of inferencing and infer that the word *her* in the question refers to Beth. Although such an inference might be considered to be lower level, it is, nevertheless, an inference that is text implicit. When teachers work with facts and details, they should be alert for the higher-level comprehension strategies (interpretive and applicative) that are sometimes demanded of the student.

Section 6.5

STRATEGY 1 IDENTIFYING DETAILS

1. List several different topics on the chalkboard (for example, birds, animals, airplanes, or colors). Select one that seems to interest most of the students.

2. Write the topic on the chalkboard and have students share information they know about the topic. As students share, write sentences containing their thoughts. An example follows.

> **Airplanes**
>
> Airplanes can fly.
> Pilots fly airplanes.
> There are many different kinds of airplanes.
> Airplanes can carry people.

3. Tell students that you will ask them questions that can be answered by understanding the sentences. For example, What can airplanes carry? As the questions are answered, have students indicate which sentence provided the answer to the question. If students give correct answers that are not contained in the sentences, acknowledge the responses as correct. Then ask the students to find the answer that is given in a sentence that is written on the chalkboard. For example, if you ask "What can airplanes carry?" and the student says "Cargo," indicate that the response is correct. Then ask whether the student can also provide an answer that is contained in one of the sentences written on the chalkboard.

4. After several similar exercises, tell students they are learning how to answer questions that ask them to locate facts and details.

5. Develop another topic with sentences and encourage students to ask questions that other students who read the sentences can answer. Discuss various answers as appropriate.

6. Indicate that such questions can also be asked about the information and ideas contained in their reading. On the chalkboard, write a brief passage from a literature selection or content textbook and ask factual questions. Use a procedure similar to the one already described. A sample passage follows.

> *It was the sweetest, most mysterious place anyone could imagine. The high walls which shut it in were covered with the leafless stems of climbing roses which were so thick that they were matted together. Mary Lennox knew they were roses because she had seen a great many roses in India. All the ground was covered with grass of a wintry brown and out of it grew clumps of bushes which were surely roses if they were alive. There were numbers of standard roses which had so spread their branches that they were like little trees (Burnett, 1911/1990, p. 80).*

Section 6.5

STRATEGY 2 4 Ws

1. Write a sentence on the chalkboard. Have students read it silently and then have someone read it out loud.

 Early that morning, Brittany packed her lunch in the kitchen.

2. Tell students to use the information in the sentence to answer the questions you ask. Ask several questions (who, what, when, where) and remind students to use the information in the sentence for their answers. Tell students that the questions are checking the students' ability to identify facts and details. Remind students to ask who, what, when, and where as they read.

3. Continue this procedure with another sentence and then move to several sentences and brief passages. Encourage discussion and think aloud as necessary.

4. Use concrete objects and have students demonstrate the meaning of a sentence. For example, use several plastic animals and a small box. Have students read a sentence and manipulate or arrange objects to answer the question. Sample ideas are provided below.

Sentence:	The cat and dog are near the box.
Question:	Where are the cat and dog? (Show me.)
Sentence:	The horse is near the box and the cat is in the box.
Question:	Where are the cat and the horse? (Show me.)

Practice and Reinforcement Activities

1. During regular instructional periods ask students factual questions about the materials they are reading. Have students locate the sentences or phrases in the passage that support their answers.

2. Select a brief passage at an appropriate instructional level for your students and number each sentence. Write the passage on the chalkboard, use it on an overhead projector, or reproduce it so each student has a copy. Then have each student make individual response cards with a number that corresponds to each numbered sentence in the passage. Ask factual questions and have students hold up that card that corresponds to the sentence containing the correct answer. Discuss answers where appropriate. A sample passage with questions appears here.

Passage	Possible Questions
[1]Dennis helped his father load the mini-van. [2]It took quite a while. [3]They put in sleeping bags, a small tent, fishing rods, a pocket radio, and sacks of food, so there was enough for several days. [4]They were going camping.	1. Who is this story about? (1) 2. Where are they going? (4) 3. How much food did they take? (3) 4. What did they load? (3) 5. How long did it take? (2)

3. Provide sentences for students to read that will enable them to answer who, what, when, and where questions. Here is an example.

> Last evening, Michael left his book at the library.
>
> Who? _____
> What? _____
> When? _____
> Where? _____

4. Encourage students to write brief passages along with questions that can be answered by using information in the passages. Have students exchange their papers and answer the questions.

Game

Get the Facts. Use a world almanac, book of facts, *Guinness Book of World Records*, or another source to develop a series of sentences or short passages. Put this information on the front of a note card and put one question (with the answer) on the back of the card. Place the cards sentence-side up in front of the students.

After one student reads the sentence silently, the card is given to another student who reads the question. If it is answered correctly, the student who answered the question gets the card. Incorrectly answered questions are placed at the bottom of the pile. The correct answer should not be revealed. Questions can be developed around various themes: sports, people, movies, silly facts, celebrities, cars, TV shows, and so on. A possible list of sentences and questions related to silly facts (Sobol, 1981) follows.

Sentences	Questions
Green-yellow is the safest color for a car.	What is the safest color for a car?
The hair and skin that is seen on your body is dead.	What is dead?
Your heart weighs less than a pound, but it pumps 2,000 gallons of blood every day.	How much blood does your heart pump every day?
Cats and gorillas need 14 hours of sleep out of every 24 hours.	How many hours a day do most cats and gorillas sleep?
An elephant generally drinks about 50 gallons of water a day.	What drinks 50 gallons of water a day?
A mole can tunnel through nearly 300 feet of earth each day.	How far can a mole tunnel each day?
A bee has 5,000 nostrils and can smell an apple tree two miles away.	How many nostrils does a bee have?
The eyes of a giant squid are as large as a basketball.	How large are a giant squid's eyes?
A pig has 44 teeth.	What animal has 44 teeth?

SECTION 6.6

Sequence

Behavior Observed	The student has difficulty sequencing events.
Anticipated Outcome	The student will sequence events correctly.

BACKGROUND

Students who have difficulty retelling the events from a story in the proper order may be experiencing problems with understanding sequence. The same is true for students who have trouble following multistep directions.

Students who possess the ability to recognize or recall the sequence in a passage are often able to infer what occurred between two stated events or incidents. They can also make predictions about what might happen next in a passage based on the previous sequence of events. Sequencing demands that students use at least the literal level of comprehension. More often, however, the interpretive level as well as the applicative level must be used. In order to correctly sequence events, the students must interpret a passage of print or a series of pictures and then anticipate which event must come next (and also which cannot).

To teach sequence of events, begin with concrete experiences and then move to printed materials. In addition, consider the importance of sequence relative to the particular type of reading material and the student's purpose(s) for reading. The following strategies are helpful in teaching sequence.

Section 6.6

STRATEGY 1 SEQUENCING

1. Gather a series of objects that can be put in order. Some examples follow.

pencils of varying lengths	paper of different sizes
straws of different lengths	books of different sizes
balls of various sizes	chalk of varying lengths

2. Use a series of objects (such as three pencils of varying lengths) and have students arrange them from shortest to longest. Tell students that they are arranging the pencils in a particular order or sequence. Repeat this process with other objects (nested dolls or other toys also work well). Have students give directions for ordering or arranging the objects in a particular sequence.

3. Transfer the notion of sequence by using a series of three pictures. Have a student arrange the pictures in sequence. Then discuss the reasons for a particular sequence. Have students make up a brief story that explains the sequence and have them share it aloud. Two possible sets of pictures are given here.

4. Help students become aware of sequences in their daily activities by discussing the order of the letters in their names, how a book is read (left to right and top to bottom), eating (breakfast, lunch, and dinner), getting dressed (socks before shoes, shirt before coat), and coming to school. Stress that the sequence or order observed in these activities also occurs in reading.

5. Use an activity like brushing teeth and have students list the major steps in the sequence. Write these steps on the chalkboard and encourage discussion.

6. To begin the transfer to reading, present sentence strips that relate to a particular sequence and have a student arrange them in proper order. Vary the number and complexity of the sentences for the group being taught. Think aloud and discuss the arrangement. Tell the students that during reading there is often a sequence or order to the story, as in the following example.

_____ Mario and Mike raked the leaves.

_____ Dad asked if the two boys wanted to earn some money.

_____ They put the piles into large brown bags.

_____ Dad looked out the window and saw the lawn covered with leaves.

_____ The boys counted the money they had earned.

Read the sentences with students and demonstrate how to choose the correct sequence by thinking aloud. "I wonder which thing happened first. Well, Mario and Mike didn't rake the leaves first because I think someone asked them to do that job. It was Dad who asked the boys to rake the leaves so the boys could earn some money. That's right, but something came before that. . . . Oh, Dad must have seen a lot of leaves first and maybe he didn't have time to rake. So, the fourth sentence down is the first thing that happened. Next, Dad must have asked the two boys if they wanted to earn some money. That's the second one down. Then the boys raked and put the leaves into the brown recyclable bags. Then they got paid for their work and counted their money . . . , so the sentences are numbered 3, 2, 4, 1, 5." Read the sentences in order with the students and ask them whether they agree. Encourage suggestions.

7. Retell several familiar stories (such as *The Three Little Pigs, Snow White, Peter Pan*) and ask students questions about the sequence of the events. Use words that help signal sequence (*first, then, later, next, finally*) and highlight these words through discussion.

8. Give students a brief passage at their instructional level that contains several events and a list of the major events in scrambled order. After students have read the passage, have them number the events in the order in which they happened. Discuss their answers.

Section 6.6

STRATEGY 2 ACTIVITY LIST

1. Tell students that in stories they read events usually happen in a particular order or sequence. Invite their sharing based on books they have read or TV programs or movies they have seen. Stress that a series of events can often show the progression of time.

2. Ask students to think about events in their daily lives like getting up, dressing, eating, going to school, going home, playing, doing homework, and going to bed.

 Encourage discussion and then provide a chart on which the day's activities in school can be listed. An example is provided below.

Time	Events/Activities
8:40	Arrive at school
8:50	School begins
8:50–9:00	Attendance, lunch count
9:00–9:30	Science

3. After activities at school have been listed, encourage students to share events that take place before and after school. Distribute the following chart that they can complete with events in their daily routines.

When	Time	Events/Activities
Before school		
At school		
After school		
At bedtime		

4. After students have completed their charts, help them to get a sense of events over a 24 hour period. A circle should help students see the sequence and repeated events in their daily routines.

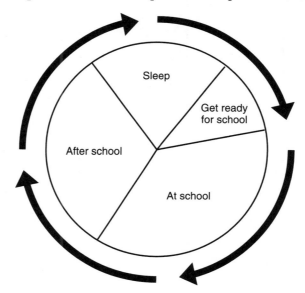

5. Stress that stories have a sequence of events. Relate important events in history or in the lives of famous people. Have students think about their own lives and construct a time line of their lives.

6. Conclude the lesson by reading aloud a short story with a clear sequence. Folktales and fairy tales often are short stories with obvious sequences. Then discuss and list the important events on the chalkboard.

Practice and Reinforcement Activities

1. Students who need practice in acquiring the concept of sequence should be given various concrete objects and instructed to order them according to size, length, shape, and so forth.

2. Provide comic strips or stories told through pictures that are presented in a mixed-up order. Have students arrange the pictures in the order in which they happened and retell the story. Use the following example or create your own pictorial story.

3. Give students three or four letters of the alphabet and have them place the letters in correct sequence.

4. Provide an oral set of directions for the students to carry out several specific actions. Use words to help signal sequence (*first, then, last*). Other signal words include *yesterday, today,* and *tomorrow.*

5. After students have read a selection, ask them questions about the order of events.

6. List the major events of a selection in a scrambled order on the chalkboard. Instruct students to rewrite the list in the correct order or number the events in the order in which they happened. Have students discuss their answers.

7. After a selection has been read, students can draw pictures to illustrate the order of major events or write sentences that describe them.

8. Scrambled sentences can be arranged in proper order and discussed. An example follows.

_____ Thomas Edison worked hard and invented electric lights.

_____ Once there were no electric lights.

_____ Today we have electric lights in our homes.

9. Have students arrange sentence strips that go with pictures to tell the story in the proper sequence.

10. Prepare paragraphs that have a sentence missing and provide two to four alternative sentences that could be the missing sentence. Ask students to select the sentence that best fits within the sequence of the paragraph. Discuss why the other sentences are less likely choices.

_____. Use strong twine, sticks, and paper for the kite. Tie rags together for the tail. Wait for a windy day to try to fly your kite.

1. You can buy a kite at the store.
2. You need several things to make a kite.
3. Flying a kite is not easy.

11. Provide activities where students can practice the correct sequence of events. See the example below.

1. noon
2. sunrise
3. sunset

123 132 ⟨213⟩

1. fruit
2. flower
3. bud

312 123 ⟨321⟩

1. get dressed
2. get up
3. go to school

231 ⟨213⟩ 312

12. Prepare sentences or brief passages that have a sequence of events or activities. Have students answer the questions posed and then discuss how they arrived at their answers.

> Bill took out the garbage after he cleaned his room.
>
> What did Bill do first? _____
>
> What did Bill do next? _____
>
> What helped you decide on the sequence?
>
> Jessica left home before Katie.
>
> Who left last? _____
>
> What helped you decide on the sequence?

13. Have students develop lists of words that may give clues to sequence (such as *later, soon, tomorrow, yesterday, in the future, in the evening*). Discuss these words and have students write short selections that include some of them. Students can also write or ask questions that focus on sequence.

14. Have students list important times or events in their lives. Then help them arrange the events in order by years. Stress the notion that the events have been placed in a time sequence.

15. Have students list step-by-step instructions for cooking, making something, doing a magic trick, and so on. Other students can follow the directions as written in sequence.

16. Read stories to your students that have a clear sequence of events. Create story cards of the events and place them in random order on the table. Ask students to place the events in the order of the story. An example of story cards from *If You Give A Moose A Muffin* (Numeroff, 1991) appears on the following page.

Games

Scramble. Prepare several sets of the same five sentence strips that can be formed into a paragraph. Divide the group into several teams and give each an envelope containing the sentence strips. The first team that arranges the sentence strips into a logical paragraph wins. One variation of the game uses a sentence that has been cut into words or phrases. A sequence of pictures also can be used.

How Is It Ordered? Develop a series of paragraphs that vary in how the reading is sequenced, such as time, events, directions, actions of the main character, or which ingredient comes next. Make note cards with the various sequences as headings. Place the paragraphs on note cards and have students draw a card, read it, and place it under the correct heading.

Going to New York. The first student says "I went to New York and took my _____." The next student repeats the object named and adds another. Subsequent students do the same, naming the objects in the proper order. The game can be played by a single group of students or by several students taking alternate turns. Help transfer the game to reading by telling students that there is a sequence in reading selections that needs to be remembered. Alternate names for the game can be used (I went for a walk and saw a (an) _____).

Directions: Enlarge the story squares and label them on the back with the title of the story, *If You Give a Moose a Muffin*. Read the book to your students, and then place the story cards in random order. Ask students to place the story cards in the order of the story.

a muffin	blackberry bush	cardboard and paints
jam	needle and thread	a sweater
socks	a sheet	soap
Muffin Mix		

Making Predictions

Behavior Observed	The student has difficulty predicting outcomes while reading.
Anticipated Outcome	The student will learn to make predictions before and during reading to improve comprehension.

BACKGROUND

Providing students with prediction strategies helps increase their comprehension of text (Hansen, 1981). When students predict before reading a story, they activate their prior knowledge and form purposes for reading. During reading, prediction strategies allow students to generate many possibilities for meaning they can confirm or discard as they find more information. The teaching strategies and activities that follow were developed to encourage students to predict before and/or during reading. Teaching students a variety of prediction strategies can eventually help students become better comprehenders of text.

Section 6.7

STRATEGY 1

DIRECTED READING-THINKING ACTIVITY*

1. Select a story or a passage that students have not read. Show students the title of the story and ask "What do you think this story will be about?" Encourage students to draw upon their background knowledge to make predictions about the story. Write the students' predictions on the chalkboard or on chart paper.

2. Select a portion of text for students to read. Choose a stopping point after students have read enough of the story to have a sense of the problem but before the climax. Have students silently read the first portion of text. Tell students to stop at the predetermined point. Encourage students who finish early to think about the story thus far. (You can also copy the text on overhead transparencies to prevent students from reading ahead.)

*Stauffer, 1969a.

3. Write the following questions on the chalkboard or on an overhead transparency.

What has happened thus far in the story?

What do you think will happen next?

Why do you think so?

4. Duplicate and distribute the Thinking Chart that follows. Have students discuss what has happened in the story up to the point they have read and write their ideas on the chart.

5. Then have students generate ideas about what they think will happen next in the story. Encourage students to think of as many possibilities as they can. Have students list their ideas on the Thinking Chart.

6. Tell students that their predictions should be based on evidence from the story thus far. Have students justify their predictions with evidence from the story. Then have groups of students share their predictions with justifications.

7. Repeat the DR-TA procedures one or two more times during the story. Have students use the Thinking Chart for their ideas.

8. Encourage students to use the DR-TA thinking process as they read independently.

Thinking Chart

Story Title	What has happened?	What will happen next?	Why do I think so?

From Jerry L. Johns and Susan Davis Lenski, *Improving Reading: Strategies and Resources* (3rd ed.). Copyright © 2001 Kendall/ Hunt Publishing Company (1-800-247-3458, ext. 5). May be reproduced for noncommercial educational purposes.

STRATEGY 2 STORY IMPRESSIONS*

1. Develop a list of key ideas from a story that the students have not read. Write the words in a vertical list with arrows connecting the words. A partial list from the first chapter of *Little House in the Big Woods* (Wilder, 1932) follows.

girl
↓
Wisconsin
↓
deer
↓
moon
↓
Pa
↓
swift
↓
hinges
↓
chopping
↓
smoke
↓
coming
↓
venison

2. Write the list on the chalkboard, chart paper, or an overhead transparency. Have students read the list of words in order.

3. Divide the class into groups of three or four students. Have students look for relationships and connecting concepts between the words to develop a story from the words. Tell students that they are predicting the chapter or passage by creating their own story.

4. After students have created a story, have them write the story down or tell it to their classmates.

5. Have students read the chapter or passage. Tell them to think about the ways in which their predicted story is like or unlike the actual story.

*McGinley & Denner, 1987.

STRATEGY 3 PREDICT-O-GRAM*

1. Select a story that the students haven't heard or read. Choose several key words from the story.

2. List the words on the chalkboard, chart paper, or an overhead transparency.

3. Duplicate and distribute the Predict-O-Gram chart that follows. Make a transparency and use it to model the strategy for students.

4. Tell students to predict what will happen in the story by placing the words from the list in the boxes of the chart. Model how to use the Predict-O-Gram by writing two or three words on the chart and telling students why you have made these decisions. An example of a partially filled Predict-O-Gram for *Clean Your Room, Harvey Moon* (Cummings, 1991) follows.

Saturday Harvey doom clean broom marched
dirty lunch creature dripping found sticky

Setting	Characters	Goal or Problem
Saturday	*creature* *Harvey*	*clean*
Action	**Resolution**	**Other Things**

5. Give students time to write all the words on their Predict-O-Gram. Take a few minutes to have students discuss reasons for their choices. Then have students read the story.

6. Following reading, have students refer to their Predict-O-Grams to find out how their predictions compare with the text. Tell students they may move words to the correct places on their charts.

*Blachowicz, 1986.

Predict-O-Gram

Camille L.Z. Blachowicz

Directions: What do you think these words will be used to tell about? Write them on a square on the Predict-O-Gram. You may have more than one word on a square.

Predict-O-Gram for _____

Setting	Characters	Goal or Problem
Action	**Resolution**	**Other Things**

From Blachowicz, C.L.Z. (1986). Making Connections: Alternatives to the vocabulary notebook. *Journal of Reading, 29,* 643–649.

STRATEGY 4 WHAT IF?

1. Write several What if? questions on index cards. Some examples follow.

 ? What if you only say two words, up and down?

 What if everything you touched turned to marshmallow?

 What if you were suddenly seven feet tall?

 What if you couldn't remember your name?

 What if your skin turned green?

2. Read the cards to students. Divide the class into groups of three or four students. Give several blank index cards to students and ask students to write several additional What if? questions.

3. Place all of the cards into one pile. Have one student from each group select a card. Have students discuss answers to their What if? questions.

4. Encourage students to share their What if? questions and their answers. Help students recognize how answering What if? questions leads them to predict various outcomes.

5. Remind students that as they read they need to make frequent predictions.

Practice and Reinforcement Activities

1. Select a picture book with a text that has a plot and characters. Cover the text of the picture book and display the book on a table. Have students look at the illustrations and predict the contents of the text.

2. Ask students to choose one piece of writing from their writing folders. Then divide the class into pairs. Have each student tell the other student the title of the piece of writing. Then have the student predict the other student's story. After the student has made predictions, he or she should begin reading the piece of writing.

3. When students participate in paired reading, have them stop after each page or section and make predictions to share with their reading buddy.

4. Select an object, photograph, or picture that is connected to a story or book that students will be reading. Tell them that this object has "mysterious possibilities" (Stephens & Brown, 2000). Have students predict what those mysterious possibilities could be. Write the students' ideas on the chalkboard, on chart paper, or on an overhead transparency. After students have listed many ideas, show students the book that they will be reading.

Making Inferences

Behavior Observed	The student has difficulty making inferences during reading.
Anticipated Outcome	The student will learn to make inferences during reading to improve comprehension.

BACKGROUND

Much of the meaning that readers construct is based on their own prior knowledge combined with the text. Using textual information along with prior knowledge is called drawing inferences. Drawing inferences is required when part of the knowledge necessary to understand a passage is found in the text but some is not. That's what we know as reading between the lines. Many students have difficulty drawing inferences. The following strategies and activities can help students learn to draw inferences in order to improve reading comprehension.

Section 6.8

STRATEGY 1 WRITER AND ME QUESTIONS*

1. Explain to students that there are two kinds of information: information in books and information in their heads. Explain that at times students will have to combine the information from the text with their own knowledge to understand a story.

2. Select a story or passage that has some subtlety—that doesn't explicitly explain everything that happens. Read the story or passage with students or have them read it independently.

3. Have students develop Writer and Me Questions and write them on index cards. These questions should not be able to be answered from information from the text alone. An example of questions from *The Magic School Bus Lost in the Solar System* (Cole, 1990) follows.

- What do you think Ms. Frizzles' class was studying in science class?
- Had the children been on the bus before? How do you know?

*Raphael, 1984.

4. Collect the questions and ask the appropriate ones to the class. Encourage students to use the story as well as their own information to answer the questions.

5. Encourage students to ask and answer Writer and Me Questions as they read.

Section 6.8

STRATEGY 2 GETTING TO KNOW MY CHARACTER*

1. Duplicate and distribute the Getting to Know My Character chart on page 316. Explain to students that this strategy will help them comprehend fictional stories more easily.

2. Display the following summary of *The Balancing Girl* by Bernice Rabe (1981) on an overhead projector or write it on the chalkboard. Read the passage aloud and ask students to follow along.

> *Margaret was good at balancing. She could balance a book on her head while gliding along in her wheelchair. She could balance herself on her crutches too. One day Margaret went to a quiet corner in the classroom. She worked hard all morning and made a big domino castle. When Margaret came back to the classroom after lunch, she saw that her castle had been knocked down. "I DIDN'T DO IT!" shouted Tommy. Margaret yelled, "Yes, you did Tommy, and you better never knock down anything I balance again, or YOU'LL BE SORRY!" Later, Margaret made a new domino castle. When she finished, six dominoes fell down. "Oh no!" she thought, but just then, the dominoes stopped falling. "Thank goodness," Margaret thought to herself.*

3. Tell students that the author provides some important facts about Margaret in the story. Ask students to identify some of these facts. As students identify important facts, highlight the appropriate portions of the passage on the overhead projector. Ask questions as needed to help students identify facts.

4. After the important facts have been identified, place a blank copy of the Getting to Know My Character chart on an overhead projector. Fill out the facts section of the chart. Guide students to make inferences about Margaret based on the facts presented in the summary. You can do this by asking questions such as "Why do you think Margaret balances books on her head?" or "Why might Margaret be in a wheelchair?"

5. Tell students that the author also helps the reader learn about Margaret by describing her actions. Guide students through locating portions of the passage that provide descriptions of Margaret's actions. Highlight these portions on an overhead transparency.

6. Record on an overhead transparency the information that describes Margaret's actions. Guide students to make inferences about Margaret by considering her actions. Model how you make inferences to aid students in making their own inferences. For example, you might say:

> *The story says that Margaret "worked hard all morning and made a big domino castle." That makes me think that Margaret was a careful, hard worker who had a lot of patience. I know that making something from dominoes can be very hard and take a lot of concentration and patience.*

Encourage students to make other inferences by using information about Margaret.

*Richards & Gipe, 1993.

7. Discuss how authors also tell readers about a character by use of the character's words and thoughts. Tell students that you can also draw inferences about the character by examining these words and thoughts.

8. Duplicate and distribute the Getting to Know My Character chart that follows after students have read fictional selections to help them make inferences.

Name _____ Date _____

Getting to Know My Character Chart

Story _____

My Character _____

Facts about my character	My character's actions
My character's conversations	**My character's thoughts**

Adapted from Richards, J.C., & Gipe, J.P. (1993). Getting to know story characters: A strategy for young and at-risk readers. *The Reading Teacher, 47*, 78–79.

STRATEGY 3 CHARACTER INTERVIEWS

1. Select a novel or section of text that students will be reading. The text should involve a number of people, including a strong, central character.

 2. Divide the class into groups of three or four students. Have each group read the novel or passage from the text. Because the novel will take much longer to read, you may want to have the students read it prior to meeting as a group. During their first meeting, students could skim back though the book to review the characters and story line.

3. After the selection or novel has been read, have students develop a list of main characters. An example for *Where the Red Fern Grows* (Rawls, 1961) follows.

Characters identified
Billy Coleman Mama Papa Grandpa

4. Have students generate questions for each of the people identified. If this strategy is being used with a novel, several characters could be identified. Groups of students should develop a set of questions for each character. The questions should require thoughtful responses, not merely yes-no answers. Explain to students that these are the interview questions. Then have students write the questions on colored strips of paper. Sample questions for Billy Coleman follow.

- You worked to save your money for your dogs for two years. How did you feel each time you added coins to the can?
- Were you ever tempted to give up and spend the money on other things for your family?
- What role did your grandfather play during your childhood?
- How would you describe your relationship with your dogs?

5. Have groups of students share their interview questions with the entire class. Provide extra colored strips for questions that are generated during discussion. Set aside duplicate questions. Have students add any new questions to their original list.

6. Within each group, have students assume the role of the different characters or people involved. Students can choose a character to portray for the interview by choosing a "prop" that represents the person. For example, a pair of empty eyeglass frames, costumes, or hats may be used. You will need to consider ahead of time what props to provide.

7. Tell students to take turns being interviewed as the character or person of their choice. Other students from the group should take turns as the interviewer and ask the "character" two or three questions. If enough characters are identified, each student in the group can assume a different role.

8. Tell students who are being interviewed to consider the character's actions, traits, and motives to evaluate how they think the character would respond to a question.

9. Upon completion of the interview process, have students discuss the responses different characters provided. Students should discuss whether they agree or disagree with how the characters answered the questions.

*Swindall & Cantrell, 1999.

Practice and Reinforcement Activities

1. Write down on index cards several well-known sayings, such as

 "A penny saved is a penny earned."

 Divide the class into groups of two or three students. Have students choose a card. Tell students that they will be pantomiming the saying for the rest of the class. Provide students with time to practice. Then have them pantomime the saying and have the other students guess the saying.

2. Select a wordless picture book to show to students. Read the title and show students the illustrations. Then have students make up a story based on the illustrations.

3. Collect a variety of advertisements. Display the advertisements on chart paper. Read the advertisements with students and help students read between the lines of the ads.

4. Make sure that you vary your questions during discussions and on tests so that some questions encourage students to draw inferences.

5. Have students make a character doll (Hughey & Slack, 2001). Character dolls are pictures of the main character of a story with an explanation of the character's qualities. To have students make a character doll, have them draw an image of the character's face on a piece of paper and draw a circle for the body. On the circle place lined paper for students to write about the character's qualities. Encourage students to draw clothes on the character that are representative of the time period and place in which the character lived.

Visualizing

Behavior Observed	The student does not visualize while reading.
Anticipated Outcome	The student will visualize while reading to improve comprehension.

BACKGROUND

In recent years, educators have renewed their interest in mental pictures and how they can be used to aid comprehension. Making mental pictures can facilitate the ongoing comprehension of text. Gambrell and Jawitz (1993) suggest using mental pictures along with text-relevant illustrations as complementary reading comprehension strategies. They also can be used by the strategic reader when comprehending is difficult, and the student activates the "read, picture; read, picture" strategy. Try some of the following ideas with students who could benefit from forming mental pictures while reading.

These students may be using the visualizing strategy while reading this book.

STRATEGY 1 FORMING MENTAL PICTURES

1. Introduce the concept of forming mental pictures by telling students that mental pictures can help them comprehend what they read. Be sure they understand that the lesson is focused on how mental pictures can aid comprehension.

2. Explain why making pictures is useful. For example, say:

 When we read, we can sometimes make pictures in our minds about what we're reading. Pictures of characters, where the story takes place, or what's happening can help us understand and remember what we read.

3. Model the strategy by thinking aloud and telling how you would use the strategy. For example, explain:

 I am going to read two sentences and try to make pictures in my mind about what I read. The air was warm and fragrant with the perfume of flowers. There were roses of various colors and fire bush. *In my mind, I am picturing some red, pink, and white roses. The name fire bush makes me think of fire, and I picture a bush that is red or yellow.*

4. Use some brief passages (see Practice and Reinforcement Activities) with students and encourage them to describe their pictures. Discuss how their pictures of the same material are similar and different.

5. Introduce other brief passages and give students opportunities to use mental pictures independently. Encourage students to help locate passages that are good for using mental pictures.

6. Several good guidelines for using mental pictures have been suggested by Cramer (1992).

 • Expect wide variation in students' pictures.
 • Explain that pictures are likely to be "hints and flashes." Rarely will students' pictures be as complete as motion pictures or TV.
 • Foster appreciation and tolerance for students' unique pictures.

STRATEGY 2 MAKING A PICTURE

1. Tell students that good readers may picture what they are reading in order to understand and remember text. You may want to use the idea of taking pictures with a camera or camcorder. Picturing or visualizing is probably best done with books rich in description.

2. Invite students to share some of the things that they have pictured in their minds. Make the point that recalling pictures can help students remember something that may have taken place long ago.

3. Write a short, evocative passage on the chalkboard or overhead projector that is likely to foster discussion and create pictures in the students' minds. Use the following example or write your own passage.

It was noon and the sun was at its hottest. The sand was scorching my bare feet. I could see nothing but dust and glaring sand for miles and miles. I was all alone.

4. After students have read the passage, have them elaborate on the scene using their five senses. Ask questions such as the following ones.

How do you feel?

What do you smell?

Where are you?

What are you going to do next?

After each response, have the students expand on it. If Barbara says she feels thirsty, have the class focus on thirst and how it feels. The idea is to help students physically experience being in the setting. You may want to use other selections such as an experience at a beach, in the middle of a deep forest, a musty barn, or a crowded city street, or attempting to climb a rocky cliff.

5. Tell students that you are going to read them a passage and you want them to try to picture the scene in their minds. They should be told that this is a strategy they can use during reading. Have students listen carefully as you read.

I slept late again today. My mom was at my grandmother's house next door, so the house was quiet—so quiet that I could hear the refrigerator humming. I was just about to roll over and get a few more hours of sleep when I heard a soft whining noise. I sat up on my elbow and tried to listen, but I didn't hear it again. Then I heard a scratching sound. I thought of mice and winced, burrowing my head under the covers. Finally, I heard the whining noise again and a short bark. I remembered. I was supposed to let the new puppy outside this morning.

6. Engage students in a discussion to share all that they can remember about the passage. Write their thoughts on the chalkboard. Then discuss how creating a picture of what you read can aid comprehension. Remember that not all students organize, store, and retrieve information in the same way.

7. Conclude the lesson by discussing the types of material for which thinking of pictures may work best and encourage students to consider creating pictures in their minds during reading to help them understand and remember. Tell students that there are no "correct" answers and that pictures vary depending on prior knowledge and experience.

Section 6.9

STRATEGY 3 CREATING COMIC STRIPS*

1. Identify an excerpt from a text or story for students to read. The section should include events or ideas that are new to students. A math story example follows.

Seven children are on the swings.
Two children got off.
How many children are left?

*Sherman & Wright, 1999.

2. Model how to visualize the story by saying the following:

> *As I was thinking about this story problem, I visualized a teacher watching students on swings at recess. I named the teacher Marty Math. As the teacher was watching the children, a beautiful butterfly flew by the swings. Two of the children got off the swings to look at the butterfly. Five children were left on the swings. They continued swinging.*

3. Present three frames or panels using the chalkboard, an overhead transparency, or chart paper. Explain that you have invented a comic character who is watching the action and telling the story. Draw a simple face for students.

4. Show students how to place the comic figure in each frame with a "talking bubble" above its head. Also, show students how to leave room in the frame to illustrate the action. An example follows.

5. Fill in the "talking bubbles" with comments by the comic figure as in the following example.

6. Show students how to fill in the rest of the action of the picture. Think of ways to add a little humor as in the following example.

7. Have students read the text that you selected for them. While students are reading, have them visualize the information presented.

8. Explain that there are several ways to visualize material after reading a passage. Have students think of mental images that represent the information in the text.

9. Divide the class into groups of two or three students. Have students discuss the text that they just read including their mental pictures.

10. Duplicate and distribute the comic frames that follow. Have students create a comic strip that expresses the ideas from the reading.

11. Conclude the activity by having groups share comic strips with at least two other groups. Then discuss different approaches to the comic strips. Emphasize the visualization that occurred to help students understand the text that was read.

Comic Strips

By

STRATEGY 4

OPEN-MIND PORTRAITS*

1. Select a story or a passage from a novel that has a well-described main character.

2. Have students read the story or passage. Ask students to identify the main character in the text.

3. After students have identified the main character, tell them that they can understand the story better by visualizing the main character. Explain to students that the strategy Open-Mind Portraits can help them visualize the main character and understand the main character's actions.

4. Tell students that to create an Open-Mind Portrait they need to draw and color a portrait of the head and neck of a main character. Give students time to finish their portraits.

5. Then have students cut out the portraits and attach them with brads or staples on top of other sheets of drawing paper.

6. Have students lift the portraits and draw and write about the character's thoughts on the second page. Students can add several extra sheets of paper to show the character's thoughts at key points in the story. An example of an Open-Mind Portrait of Leigh from *Strider* (1991) follows.

7. Then have students share their portraits with classmates and talk about the words and pictures they have chosen to include in the mind of the character.

*Tompkins, 1998.

Practice and Reinforcement Activities

1. From a catalog, cut out the pictures and descriptions of various sets of articles (bikes, games, jewelry, clothes, and so on). Pass out the descriptions of one particular set of items (for example, bikes) to a group of students. Each student should have a different description of some similar item. Instruct students to read the description and to form a picture of the article in their minds. After they have fixed the description firmly in their minds, ask students to go to a table containing cutout pictures of similar articles. Their task is to match their picture of the item with the appropriate cutout picture.

2. Take advantage of what may be on your students' minds. For example, 10 minutes before lunch, have them read about food. Tear out food articles from magazines accompanied by pictures. Have students discuss their favorite menu selections from the assortment of articles. The rationale for this activity is that because students are hungry it will be easy for them to imagine food. Associating reading with their already-present pictures may help reinforce the habit of using mental pictures during reading.

3. Be prepared for unusual days by having an appropriate story or poem on hand. If it is a rainy, windy day, read your students a relevant story or poem. Try to take advantage of whatever may be on their minds by reinforcing it with a complementary reading passage. If a field trip is planned, be sure to read something related to the trip both before and after the excursion.

4. Use selected passages from literature to give students an opportunity to practice forming mental pictures. For example, *Charlotte's Web* (White, 1952) contains an excellent description of a barn, and *A Wrinkle in Time* (L'Engle, 1962) offers a rich description of a kitchen. Share with students parts of your reading that are appropriate for mental pictures. Here are two examples we have used with students (sources unknown).

> *I allowed myself to walk out back yesterday afternoon when I returned to the farm. The air was warm and fragrant with the perfume of flowers, and I hoped that I wasn't too late to see the blooming of what Ozarkers call fire bush. All over these hills there are foundations of long-gone cabins—overgrown stone walls that show where families lived back in the days when the big timber was cut in this part of the country. Beside most of them, like the one at the back of my place, there are also flowers. Iris, bridal bush, and fire bush were planted, I think, by women who put them there to brighten their harsh homesteading lives.*

> *Early in the morning, after making a fire in the wood stove, I step outside my cabin while the bacon is frying to get a feel for the day in the darkness before dawn. There are no clouds in the sky, and the last stars are shining brightly. The day promises to be fair. It is too cool to have my breakfast outside and watch the sun rise, so I sit near the wood stove on an old rocking chair and watch the eastern sky through the large, inviting kitchen window.*

5. Have students draw pictures based on something you have read from the pictures they formed in their minds as you read. Students can talk about their pictures in small groups. You can also have students draw pictures of a scene from a book or story they have read recently.

6. Have students imagine that they are involved in a particular activity and describe it (for example, reading a book in a comfortable location; flying a kite; swinging in the park).

7. Ask one student to leave the classroom. Ask the remaining students to describe the student in writing (clothes, physical attributes, interesting details like rings, and so on). When the student comes back into the classroom, the other students should compare their descriptions to the actual student.

8. Remember to have students use text-relevant illustrations along with mental pictures as complementary strategies.

Drawing Conclusions

Behavior Observed	The student has difficulty drawing conclusions after reading.
Anticipated Outcome	The student will draw conclusions about the text.

BACKGROUND

Drawing conclusions and making inferences may be thought of as predicting outcomes and involves using material that is implicit or not directly stated in the text. This level of comprehension—interpretive—requires more reasoning skill on the part of the reader than factual recall. When a student draws a conclusion, the main idea, supporting details, and sequence of events in a passage often are used as the basis for the conclusion. A conclusion can be regarded as a reasoned deduction or inference. Although fine distinctions can be made between the two terms, teachers may assume that the terms describe students' attempts to infer a reasonable prediction of outcomes or conclusions based on the available information.

Section 6.10

STRATEGY 1 PREDICTING CONCLUSIONS

1. Explain to students that in much of their reading they are able to use the information presented to predict conclusions. Tell students that conclusions are based on what is stated in the story or text as well as what they already know.

2. Give students an opportunity to predict a conclusion after several facts are given. See the following example.

 Fact 1: The sun did not shine on Saturday.
 Fact 2: There were many clouds in the sky.
 Fact 3: The grass, houses, roads, and sidewalks were wet.
 Fact 4: Our picnic was canceled.

 Then ask students to predict a conclusion or make an inference. Discuss the basis on which the conclusion or inference is made.

3. Present a series of events and several possible conclusions, as in the following example.

 Event: It snowed all night, and by Friday morning there was more than a foot of snow on the ground.

 Possible Outcomes: We went swimming in our outdoor pool.

 We shoveled the sidewalk and driveway.

 We didn't have school.

 We put the top down on our convertible.

 Be sure to discuss the reasons why some conclusions are more probable than others.

4. Give students part of a selection to read. At the end of the reading, have students consider the facts and events that have been presented in order to infer what will happen next. After listing the students' predictions on the chalkboard, read students the remainder of the selection and then discuss whether any of their predictions were right.

5. Help students realize that they draw conclusions based on the information they have gained by reading and from their own personal experiences that may relate to the passage they are reading.

Section 6.10

STRATEGY 2 PROBLEM-SOLUTION CHART

1. Duplicate and distribute copies of the Problem-Solution Chart that follows. You may also want to make a transparency of the chart to place on an overhead projector.

2. Present the class with a problem that needs to be solved. The problem could be one facing our country, your community, school, or classroom. It could also be a problem from a story the class is reading. For example, a problem facing your class might be that your class gerbil is not eating.

3. Write the problem on the chart in the section labeled *Problem*. Discuss the problem with students.

4. Tell students that you also want them to generate possible solutions to the problem. Guide students through a discussion of possible solutions. Have students vote on three of the most promising solutions. Record the solutions on the chart.

5. Divide the class into three groups. Have each group select one of the possible solutions. Ask group members to evaluate each possible solution by listing the pros and cons. (Explain the meanings of the words *pro* and *con* if necessary.)

6. Have groups share their evaluations of the solutions with the class. Have the class discuss each of the solutions and choose one solution for the problem.

7. Record the solution to the problem on the chart and give the reasons for the decision.

8. Tell students that when they read they are often faced with a problem with many possible solutions. Explain to students that to draw conclusions they need to entertain many potential ideas. Encourage students to think of many options as they draw conclusions during reading.

Problem-Solution Chart

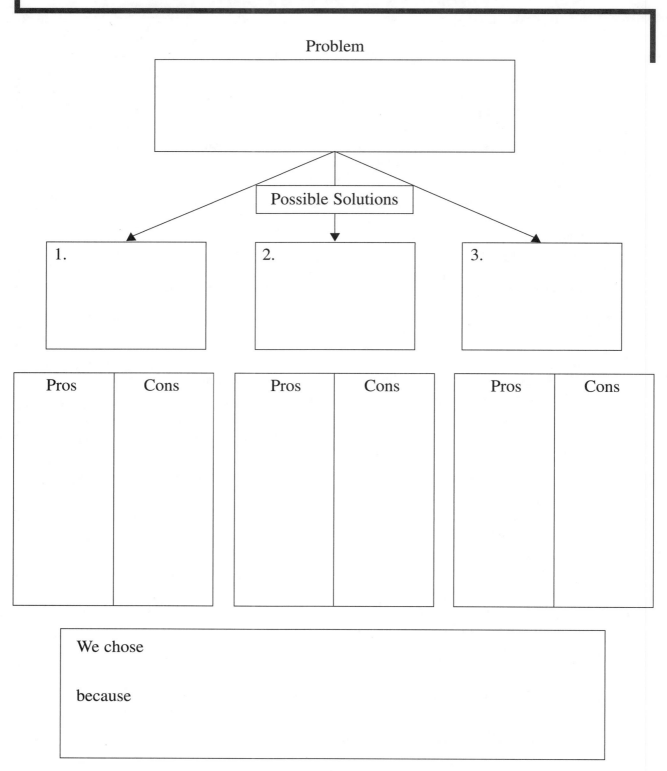

Problem

Possible Solutions

1.

2.

3.

Pros	Cons

Pros	Cons

Pros	Cons

We chose

because

Practice and Reinforcement Activities

1. Students who have difficulty seeing relationships may also have trouble drawing conclusions, making inferences, and predicting outcomes. These students often can be helped to see relationships through classification exercises. Present objects (concrete objects, pictures, or words) and have students identify the one that does not belong as well as explain why the others do belong. See the examples provided below.

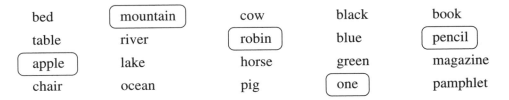

2. Provide reading materials at the students' instructional level and ask questions that encourage the students to use information in the passage to draw conclusions. Take time to discuss the basis for the conclusions that were drawn.

3. Provide questions for which students are asked to give logical conclusions. An example follows.

? What would happen if you—

. . . didn't sleep for two days?

. . . had to stay in bed for a week?

. . . had a birthday every month?

. . . ate a pound of candy?

. . . crashed into a tree on your bicycle?

4. Give students brief passages where a conclusion must be drawn.

 Bill was reading about the sun, the moon, and Mars.
 It was a book about the _____ (planets, solar system).

5. Provide pictures or illustrations and have students classify them under one or more of the following categories.

 Animals Sports Seasons
 Large Small Football Golf Soccer Summer Fall Winter Spring

6. When students are reading a selection that lends itself to inference-making, stop them at the appropriate point and ask them to write their predictions about what will happen next or how they think the story will end. Discuss their predictions, the basis for their judgment, and the supporting evidence in the story. Then let students read to the end of the story to see whether their predictions were right.

7. Provide students with pictures, illustrations, or verbal descriptions of events. Encourage them to list possible causes of the event and then select those that seem most appropriate. Sample events are listed below.

- a soccer player being congratulated near the opponent's goal
- a child who has just blown out the candles on a cake
- a boy and girl with sad expressions on their faces looking out their front window and seeing that it's raining
- a patient sitting in a doctor's office

8. Provide sentences where students use the information given to answer a question. Stress that the answer isn't stated, so students must reason it out or infer it. Discuss students' answers.

At recess the students got their gloves, bats, and balls. What were they likely to do?

 During a very severe storm, the electricity went off. Dad lit a match. What did he probably want to find?

Maria had a day off school. She looked in the newspaper to find the best sales. Then she left the house. Where did she probably go?

A variation of this activity is to provide possible answers and have students select the best one.

Jesse and his father went walking on a warm spring day. There was a nice breeze in the air. What might Jesse and his father do to have fun?

_____ rake leaves _____ fly a kite _____ watch TV

Be sure to discuss students' answers and their reasons for choosing them.

CHAPTER 7

Expanding Comprehension

OVERVIEW

Readers who achieve a deep comprehension of text apply a variety of strategies as they construct meaning. First, active readers use their knowledge of organization of texts to identify relationships between ideas. Fiction is organized in different ways from nonfiction. Readers who want to expand their ability to understand texts will apply what they know about text organization as they construct meaning from the text. Good readers also are able to monitor their comprehension, interpret charts and graphs, summarize as they read, make connections while reading, process text after reading, evaluate the ideas in the text, and remember what was read. All of these strategies help readers comprehend text.

Many factors influence the use of strategies. Some factors include the teacher's theory of learning, the teacher's theory of the student, the student's response history, and the demands of the text (Lenski & Nierstheimer, in press). Choosing which of the strategies to teach students is the first step. Let's say your students are having difficulty remembering what they have read. You might choose the strategy DRAW (Agnew, 2000). To teach students how to use DRAW, you should first model the strategy. Af-

ter modeling, provide students with opportunities to use the strategy with support. After students have several experiences with DRAW, you can expect them to use the mental processes to remember what they have read. Students need to see how strategies are applied, and modeling gives them a verbal picture of the processes that occur in the mind.

Teaching comprehension strategies tends to help students become better comprehenders. However, the modeling of teaching strategies is just the beginning. The goal of teaching comprehension strategies is to have students become self-regulating readers (Pressley, 2000). Self-regulating readers have a repertoire of skills and strategies that they use flexibly and appropriately as they approach printed materials. Therefore, it's also important that you give students the feeling of ownership when teaching comprehension strategies. Students need to understand that these strategies must have a prominent place in their reading routines.

The goal of teaching comprehension strategies is to have students become self-regulating readers.

Helping students expand comprehension is challenging. The teaching of the strategies and the use of the activities provided in this chapter will help students become better comprehenders of text.

TECHNOLOGY RESOURCES

RHL School

http://rhlschool.com/links.htm
Contains reading activities, games, and brainteasers

Gifted Readers and Reading Instruction

http://indiana.edu/~eric_rec/ieo/digests/d101.html
Summary of research about gifted readers

Read *Write* Now!

http://www.parentsplace.com/readroom/education/rwnintr.html
Provides reading and writing activities and ideas

Doucette Index K–12 Literature-Based Teaching Ideas

http://www.educ.ucalgary.ca/litindex/
Contains lesson plans for works of literature

Understanding Fictional Text Structure

Behavior Observed	The student does not understand how fictional texts are organized.
Anticipated Outcome	The student will apply knowledge of fictional text structure during studying.

BACKGROUND

Texts are written in a variety of organizational patterns, depending on the author's purpose. Authors may write a fictional story that is narrative (a sequence of events leading to a solution of a problem). Readers who can identify the elements in narrative text and who can discern the organizational pattern in expository text will have an easier time comprehending the selection and studying it.

When you teach text structure, first review the information yourself. Then model how you identify text organization and help students recognize organizational patterns. Finally, ask students to write text with different organizational structures. Only after students have had instruction and practice with different text structures can you expect students to use text structure as a tool for studying.

Narrative text is a more formal name for a story. Stories have seven main elements: beginning-middle-end, repetition, plot, setting, characters, theme, and point of view (Tompkins, 2001).

✎ **Beginning-middle-end.** All stories have a beginning, a middle, and an end. Often the beginning contains information about the characters

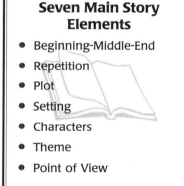

Seven Main Story Elements

- Beginning-Middle-End
- Repetition
- Plot
- Setting
- Characters
- Theme
- Point of View

and the setting. A problem or a conflict is also introduced in the beginning. In the middle of the story, events are described that advance the conflict until it is finally resolved at the end of the story.

✎ **Repetition.** Repetition is a writing device to make stories more interesting. Books for young children often use repetition to advance the plot. See Appendix C for a list of pattern books.

✎ **Plot.** The plot is the sequence of events that happen in the story. The characters in the story have a conflict (problem), and that conflict is explained by a series of events. The plot includes all of the events that take the characters through the conflict to the resolution.

✎ **Setting.** The setting is the story's time and place. The time may be past, present, or future. The setting can be real or imaginary.

✎ **Characters.** The characters are the people or animals in the story.

✎ **Theme.** The theme is the main point of the story, the idea the author wants to get across to the reader.

- **Point of View.** Stories are written from various points of view. Two common points of views authors use are first person and the omniscient. First-person viewpoint tells the story through the eyes of the author. In the omniscient viewpoint, the author knows everything about the characters and action.

Section 7.1

STRATEGY 1 NARRATIVE TEXT

1. Collect stories that illustrate each element. You might use some of the following children's books as examples of the story elements (adapted from Tompkins & Hoskisson, 1991).

 📖 **Repetition**

 Anderson, H. C. (1979). *The Ugly Duckling*. New York: Harcourt.
 Gag, W. (1956). *Millions of Cats*. New York: Coward.
 Sendak, M. (1963). *Where the Wild Things Are*. New York: Harper and Row.

 📖 **Plot**

 Galdone, P. (1973). *The Little Red Hen*. New York: Seabury.
 Kellogg, S. (1985). *Chicken Little*. New York: Morrow.
 McGovern, A. (1967). *Too Much Noise*. New York: Scholastic.

 📖 **Characters**

 McCloskey, R. (1969). *Make Way for Ducklings*. New York: Viking.
 Van Allsburg, C. (1981). *Jumanji*. Boston: Houghton-Mifflin.
 White, E. B. (1952). *Charlotte's Web*. New York: Harper and Row.

 📖 **Theme**

 Lobel, A. (1970). *Frog and Toad Are Friends*. New York: Harper and Row.
 Piper, W. (1953). *The Little Engine That Could*. New York: Platt and Munk.
 Van Allsburg, C. (1985). *The Polar Express*. Boston: Houghton Mifflin.

 📖 **Point of View: First Person**

 Howe, D., and Howe, J. (1979). *Bunnicula*. New York: Atheneum.
 MacLachlan, P. (1985). *Sarah, Plain and Tall*. New York: Harper and Row.
 Viorst, J. (1977). *Alexander and the Terrible, Horrible, No Good, Very Bad Day*. New York: Atheneum.

 📖 **Point of View: Omniscient**

 Grahame, K. (1961). *The Wind in the Willows*. New York: Scribner's.
 Lewis, C. S. (1981). *The Lion, the Witch, and the Wardrobe*. New York: Macmillan.
 Steig, W. (1982). *Doctor De Soto*. New York: Farrar.

2. Read stories to the class, explaining which story element is emphasized. For example, if you had read the book *The Little Engine That Could* (Piper, 1953) to the class, you might say:

 This story is a fun story, but it also tells us something important. When an author writes a story, he or she usually wants to convey a point to the readers. The point the author is conveying is told through a story, but it's up to the reader to try to understand. In The Little Engine That Could, *the author is trying to tell us that if we think we can accomplish something and try really hard, we can. That main point is called the theme of the story.*

3. Read another story to the class and ask students to identify the specific story element. For example, if you read *Frog and Toad Are Friends* (Lobel, 1970), you should ask students some possible main ideas that the author wanted to convey. Students should be able to answer something about the value of friendships.

4. Create a chart listing the seven story elements (e.g., point of view, plot, theme) as you teach them. Under the story elements, write information from the books you discuss. The partial chart that follows is an example.

Story	Setting	Characters
Make Way for Ducklings	Boston	Mr. and Mrs. Mallard
Frog and Toad Are Friends	Forest	Frog and Toad

5. After students read narrative passages, discuss the elements of the story. You may want to choose from the following questions (adapted from Tompkins & Hoskisson, 1991) to form the basis for the discussion.

Beginning-Middle-End

- What kinds of information does the author include at the beginning of the story?
- What happens in the first part of the story?
- Does the author add new characters in the middle of the story?
- What happens to the story at the end?
- How do you feel about the end of the story?

Repetition

- What words are repeated in the story?
- Is an event repeated?
- How does the repetition make you feel?

Setting

- What is the setting?
- Is the setting described in detail?
- Does weather play an important role in the story?
- Could the characters be found in other kinds of settings?
- Does the author use the setting to provide important action?

Characters

- What is the character's goal?
- What problems do the characters face?
- Are there minor characters in the story?
- What do the characters look like?
- What do the actions of the characters tell us about them?
- Are the actions of the characters consistent throughout the story?

Theme

- What does the story mean?
- Is the main idea stated in the story?
- How does the author get the theme across?

Point of View

- Who is telling the story?
- Do we know what the characters are thinking?
- Does the story have a narrator?

Section 7.1

STRATEGY 2 STORY MAP

1. Tell students that they can map the events in pieces of fiction by completing a story map. Explain that a story map is an outline of the elements of the story. Tell students that when they map a story they are identifying key story elements.

2. Review the elements of fiction with students if necessary. Remind students of the definitions of the terms *title*, *setting*, *characters*, *problem*, *events*, and *solution*.

3. Select a piece of literature that clearly illustrates the elements of fiction. Read the selection with students or have students read the story independently.

4. Divide the class into groups of three or four students. Ask students to identify fictional elements: *title*, *setting*, *characters*, *problem*, *events*, and *solution*.

5. Select one of the story maps reproduced in the resource section of this chapter. Choose a story map that best fits the events of the story.

6. Duplicate and distribute the story map that you have selected. Make an overhead transparency of the story map.

7. Model for students how to complete the story map by filling in the sections listed on the map. Tell students that the story map you have selected for this story may be used for different information from other stories.

8. Have students independently complete the story map for the piece of literature you have selected.

9. Use other types of story maps as you reinforce the organizational pattern of fictional text. Model how to use each story map before having students complete it.

Section 7.1

STRATEGY 3 STORY FRAMES

1. Select a story frame from the resource section in this chapter that fits a piece of literature students have read.

2. Duplicate and distribute the story frame. Make a transparency of the story frame to use on an overhead projector.

3. Read the story frame with students. Tell students that they can learn about the organizational pattern of fiction by focusing on a specific story element. For example, if you chose the story frame Character Comparison, you would be analyzing the similarities and differences between two characters.

 4. Divide the class into groups of three or four students. Tell them the title of the story frame and have them brainstorm ideas that they think will apply. For example, if you are using the story from Character Comparison, have students identify two characters in the story, list their character traits, and discuss the similarities and differences between the characters.

5. After students have discussed ideas, have them complete the story frame independently.

6. Use other story frames when you want students to think about specific elements of fiction. Model how to use each story frame before students complete it.

Section 7.1

STRATEGY 4 STORY PYRAMID

1. Select a fictional story that has a clear plot outline. Read the story to students or have them read it independently.

 2. Divide the class into groups of three or four students. Have students identify a character, the setting, and the events in the story.

3. Duplicate and distribute the blank story pyramid that follows. Make a transparency copy to use on an overhead projector.

4. Tell students to think of one word that names a character in the story. Have them write the name of that character on the first line.

5. Then have students think of two words that describe the setting. Tell students that they must use two words, no more and no fewer. Ask students to write the two words on the next two lines.

6. Complete the directions on the story pyramid by having students write three words that describe the character, four words in a sentence that describe one event, and five words in a sentence that describe another event.

7. After students have completed the story pyramid, have them share their work with classmates.

8. Modify the story pyramid by adding additional lines and have students write six words describing the resolution and seven words that describe the theme.

9. Duplicate additional copies of the story pyramid for students to use after reading fictional texts.

10. A sample story pyramid follows.

Story Pyramid

1. Phoebe

2. Confused, guilty

3. Present, small, town

4. Mick's sudden unexpected death

5. The fight over a tattoo

6. Zoe says Mick can be everywhere.

7. Phoebe speaks at the assembly about Mick.

8. Phoebe writes **Mick Harte Was Here** in cement.

9. Phoebe realizes that Mick's accident was no one's fault.

Directions:
1. Name of the main character
2. Two words describing the main character
3. Three word describing the setting
4. Four words stating the problem
5. Five words describing one event
6. Six words describing a second event
7. Seven words describing a third event
8. Eight words describing a final event
9. Nine words stating the solution to the problem

From Park, B. (1996). *Mick Harte was here*. New York: Scholastic.

Name _____ Date _____

Story Pyramid

Directions:
1. Insert 1 word that names a character.
2. Insert 2 words that describe a character.
3. Insert 3 words that describe the setting.
4. Insert 4 words in a sentence that describe one event.
5. Insert 5 words in a sentence that describe the problem.

You can also adapt the story pyramid by adding more lines such as the resolution or conclusion.

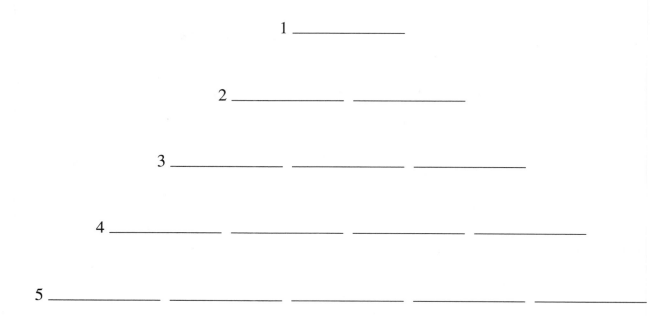

Practice and Reinforcement Activities

1. Encourage students to read widely. Provide a classroom library with books and stories representing a variety of genres and levels.

2. When planning stories, have students draw storyboards to show the major story elements. For example, students can draw the main character, the setting, the problem situation, important events, and the solution. Older students can write phrases and details on their storyboards to prepare for writing the story. Once students have prepared their storyboards, they can tell their story to a partner to confirm effective use of story elements, clarity, and details. Students can then write a draft of their story.

3. Prepare a set of cards that contain information about story elements. Have students tell a story using the elements presented on the cards. Encourage them to add details and consider the sequence of events. Students can then write stories using the story line they have created from the cards. To show students how story elements are related to each other within a story, substitute one of the cards. Ask students how the story will be changed. Sample story element cards are shown below.

Setting: A small town in the United States	**Main Character:** A shy, quiet boy named Billy
Problem: Billy's best friend has moved away, and Billy is very lonely.	**Solution:** Billy learns he has a special talent that helps him make new friends.

4. Use wordless picture books to help students "read" pictures to discover the story line and identify the main story elements. Wordless books with clear, familiar patterns and story lines such as *Deep in the Forest* (Turkle, 1976), a modification of the "Three Little Bears," work well with younger or struggling students. After identifying the elements, younger students may dictate the story. Older students may write their own stories based on the pictures. Students can then analyze their stories and their peers' stories to determine if major story elements are present and used effectively in the story. A list of wordless picture books is provided in Appendix A.

5. Ask students to retell a story, emphasizing one of the story elements. You may choose a story that you have read to the entire class or one that students have read independently.

6. Ask students to dramatize stories with puppets or by acting out a play. They may want to focus on making the characters believable, on making the setting realistic, or on any combination of story elements.

7. Have students compare the beginning, middle, and end of different versions of the same story. Fairy tales are especially appropriate.

8. Have students use the strategy zigzag to identify fictional elements (Wisendanger, 2001). After students have read a story, draw the zigzag model on the chalkboard or on an overhead transparency. For students to complete the zigzag, have them write on the lines words from the story that represent a main concept. For example, students should write the name of the main character on the first line, a word describing the setting on the second line, and so on. After students have completed the zigzags, have them display their work in the classroom.

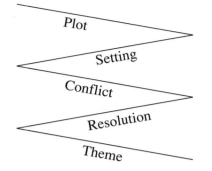

9. Draw a bookworm similar to the example that follows. On each circle, list an element of fiction that students know. You might draw a circle for the title, author, setting, characters, problem, events, and solution. Have students write the element of fiction on the circles. Connect the circles and draw a face on the first one. Display the bookworms in your class.

Bookworm

1. Title

Author

TAB

2. Setting

TAB

3. Characters

TAB

4. A Problem and Solution

TAB

5. Events

TAB

Understanding Nonfiction Text Structure

Behavior Observed	The student does not understand how nonfiction texts are organized.
Anticipated Outcome	The student will learn how nonfiction texts are organized.

BACKGROUND

The majority of texts that young readers read are fictional texts (Yopp & Yopp, 2000). Typically, students in second or third grade begin reading many more nonfiction texts. Nonfiction texts are texts that are true, including textbooks. Nonfiction texts have a text organizational pattern that is unlike that of fictional texts. Nonfiction texts typically are organized in five patterns: description, sequence, comparison, cause-effect, and problem-solution. Knowing how texts are organized can increase comprehension. The following teaching strategies and activities can help students learn how to read nonfiction texts.

Nonfiction Organizational Patterns

- Description
- Sequence
- Comparison
- Cause-effect
- Problem-solution

Understanding nonfiction text structure is important as second and third graders move from fiction to nonfiction texts.

STRATEGY 1 GRAPHIC ORGANIZERS

1. Tell students that there are five types of nonfiction organizational patterns: description, sequence, comparison, cause-effect, and problem-solution. Explain to students that knowing the types of nonfiction organizational patterns can help them comprehend texts better.

2. Duplicate and distribute the graphic organizers that follow. Tell students that the graphic organizer depicts how information could be organized in nonfiction texts.

3. Have students read the descriptions of the organizational patterns that accompany the graphic organizers. Help them note the differences between the types of nonfiction writing patterns.

4. Locate five short passages that fit the five types of organizational patterns. Divide the class into groups of three or four students. Have students match the passage with the text organizations.

5. Encourage students to think about how texts are organized as they read. Refer, as appropriate, to a particular graphic organizer when it is demonstrated in a particular nonfiction text.

Description. The author of descriptive writing lists characteristics, features, and examples to describe a subject. Clue words for description include *for example* and *characteristics*. To map a descriptive passage, you might use the following graphic organizer.

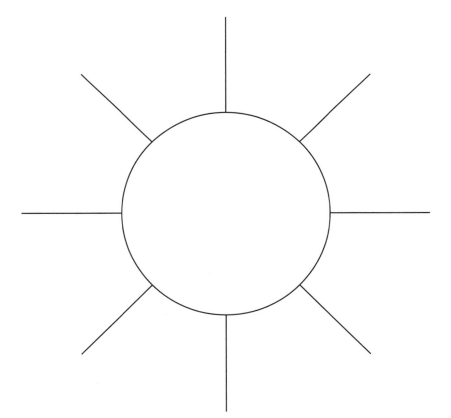

Sequence. Writers who use sequence in a text list events in chronological or numerical order. Some clue words are *first, second, third* or *next, then,* and *finally.* To map a sequential passage, you might use the following graphic organizer.

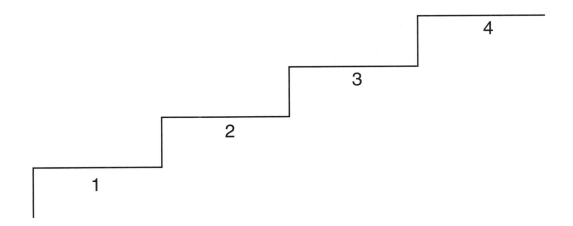

Comparison. In comparison text, the writer is explaining how things are alike or different. Clue words include *different, in contrast, alike, same as,* or *on the other hand.* The following graphic organizer best depicts a comparison passage.

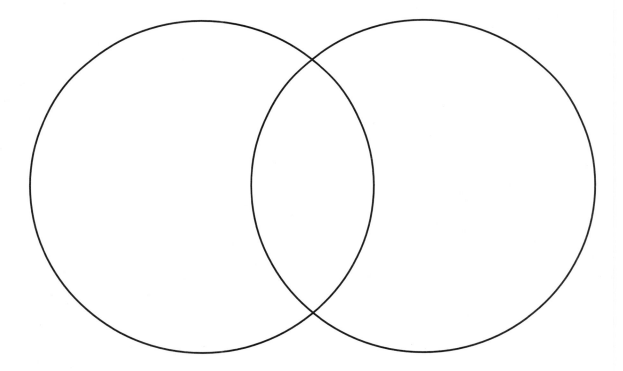

Cause and Effect. The author describes a cause and the resulting effect. Clue words are *reasons why, if . . . then, as a result, therefore,* and *because.* The following is the most common graphic organizer used in cause and effect writing.

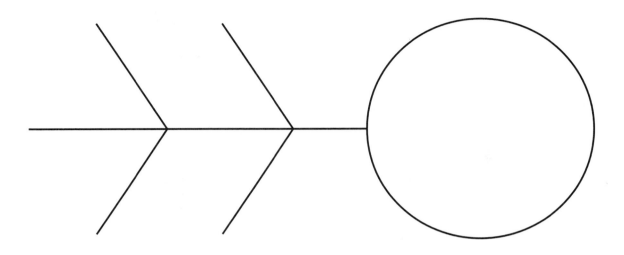

Problem and Solution. The author describes a problem and lists solutions for that problem. Some clue words are *the problem is, solved,* and *the dilemma is.* A graphic organizer used for problem and solution texts follows.

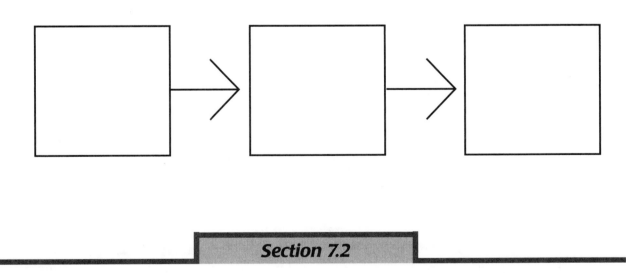

Section 7.2

STRATEGY 2 PROBABLE PASSAGES*

1. Select a nonfiction text that students have not yet read. Identify the text organizational pattern.

2. Locate words in the passage that are important for text comprehension. Write the words on the chalkboard under their text categories. An example using a problem/solution text follows.

*Wood, 1984.

Problem		Solution
scurvy	→	nutrients
beriberi		diet
pellegra		carbohydrates
disease		vitamins
		minerals
		balanced diet
		thiamine
		niacin

3. Explain how the terms are used and what the problem and solution mean in this situation. Then ask students to write a Probable Passage, or a passage that makes sense, that contains the text structure and the identified words.

4. After students have completed their Probable Passage, have them read the original text.

5. After students have read the text, have them edit their own passage to reflect missing or contradictory information they learned from the passage.

Section 7.2

STRATEGY 3 EXPOSITORY TEXT

1. Identify texts with different structures that are at the appropriate reading levels for your students. To teach expository text structure, choose a passage that exemplifies the type of structure you want to teach. The following is an example of description.

> *People have always been fascinated by gold. Gold is one of the metallic elements. Because it is found in such small quantities on earth, gold is very expensive. In fact, its rarity gave rise to the practice of alchemy, the object of which was to turn base metals into gold. Throughout history, gold has been the preferred substance for money and jewelry. Other examples of its use are that it has been woven into fabric and hammered thin for bracelets, drinking vessels, and body coverings such as breastplates.*
>
> *As a metal, gold has some unique characteristics. Because it does not react with oxygen, it will neither rust nor corrode. It has a low melting point, so it can be heated and then reshaped. Although gold is heavy, it is very soft. This makes it easy to work with. However, gold's softness makes it impractical for use. Therefore, gold is often combined with other metals that give it strength and help to prevent scratching.*

2. Explain that you will be discussing the descriptive text structure. Tell students that descriptive writing is when an author lists characteristics, features, or examples of a topic.

3. Ask students to read the passage about gold. Model how you would identify the text structure of this passage. You may say something like the following:

As I read the first sentence, I saw that the topic of the passage was gold. Because the main idea seems to be the fascination people have with gold, I'm going to predict that the author will be describing gold. The first paragraph does describe gold. Another clue I find in the second paragraph is the word examples. *Often, descriptive writing uses examples. As I continue to read, I find out the characteristics of gold. Again, the word* characteristics *is a clue that the passage is descriptive.*

4. Ask students to discuss other clues from the text that might signal text structure.

Section 7.2

STRATEGY 4 IDEA-MAPPING*

1. Select a passage that you want students to read. Determine the organizational pattern of the text. Select the appropriate Idea-Map for the text. Examples of Idea-Maps can be found in the Resources for Chapter 7.

2. Tell students that you will be demonstrating how to use a strategy called Idea-Maps to help them understand how nonfiction texts are organized.

3. Explain that there are five main patterns for organizing nonfiction texts: description, sequence, comparison, cause-effect, and problem-solution. Write these words on the chalkboard or an overhead transparency.

4. Model the Idea-Map strategy using the following example. You might find it useful to make a transparency of the example to show students.

Topic: **Moving Ice Changes the Land**
Details:
Glaciers are snow piles that melt and refreeze.
Glaciers become mounds of ice.
Rocks become frozen to the bottom of the ice.
Weight of ice makes glaciers move.
Rocks on the bottom of the glacier cut into rocks.
Glaciers can pick up rocks and carry them away.
Main Idea: **A glacier is a sheet of moving ice.**

5. Have students identify the main points of other passages using the appropriate Idea-Map. You may need to identify the text structure for your students initially and provide them with the appropriate Idea-Map to use as they read. After students have used Idea-Maps for a while, they should be able to identify the structure of each text themselves.

*Armbruster, 1986.

Practice and Reinforcement Activities

1. Have students write text passages using the different organizational patterns of nonfiction text.
2. Have students work in groups to find out the text structure of a selected passage. Ask them to underline words or phrases that give them clues about the pattern.
3. Give students a blank graphic organizer and ask them to organize other information they know into the same pattern. Then ask them to write a passage similar to the passage they had read.
4. Have students diagram a passage using the graphic organizer suggested for the specific text pattern. A partial example from a passage on gold follows.

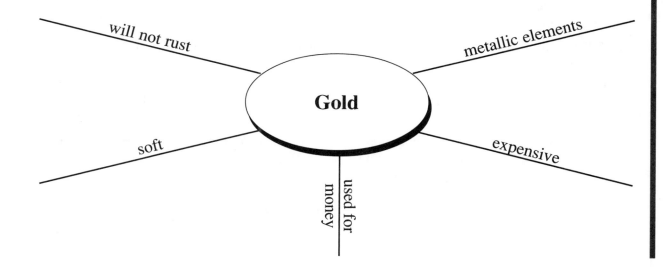

Charts and Graphs

Behavior Observed	The student has difficulty interpreting charts and graphs.
Anticipated Outcome	The student will use graphic aids to study.

BACKGROUND

Graphs and charts are an integral feature of most texts because they can communicate information quickly, effectively, and persuasively. For some students, graphs and charts are a mystery rather than a source of information. Teachers need to be certain that students have the proper background in the interpretation of graphs and charts. The following strategies may provide some assistance.

Section 7.3

STRATEGY 1 INTERPRETING CHARTS

1. Explain that charts are ways of simplifying data to make it easy to read at a glance. Then hand out individual-size bags of M&M candies to each student. Let them open the bags and put the candy on their desks. Ask them to think about the aspects of the candies (weight, color, number).

2. Hand out a blank chart and ask students to record their data for the different colors and the number of each. An example is provided below.

blue candies	3
green candies	5
brown candies	6
yellow candies	4
orange candies	7
red candies	4
Total	29

3. Discuss the importance of developing a descriptive title for the chart. Ask students to suggest titles for the M&M chart. Some students' responses might include M&Ms, Number of M&M Candies, and Types of M&M Candies. Explain that someone reading the chart needs to know exactly what information is listed. Then ask students to write a title for their chart (perhaps Number of Colors in a Bag of M&Ms).

4. Ask students to compare their charts with each other, noting similarities and differences.

5. Synthesize the individual charts into a class chart. Discuss the information that the class found.

6. Explain that information listed on a chart can also be expressed in a pictorial form using a graph. Show students an example of a bar graph and ask them whether they are able to understand the information given more readily than by using a chart. Explain that many people find graphs a quick method of understanding information.

7. Create a bar graph on the chalkboard or an overhead transparency from the information gathered from the class chart on M&M candies. As you write, explain the different features of the graph.

From the example that follows, for instance, you could say something like this:

This bar graph has its title at the top. The title tells me exactly what I can find on the graph. I see that this graph compares the numbers of individual colors of M&M candies that were gathered from our class project. I see the numbers of candies is on the left side of the graph and the colors are listed at the bottom. Looking at the graph, I can see that the most colors found in the class were brown. We had a total of 56 brown candies. The next highest number was 50 orange. We had 45 green candies, 44 yellow candies, 40 red candies, and 35 blue candies.

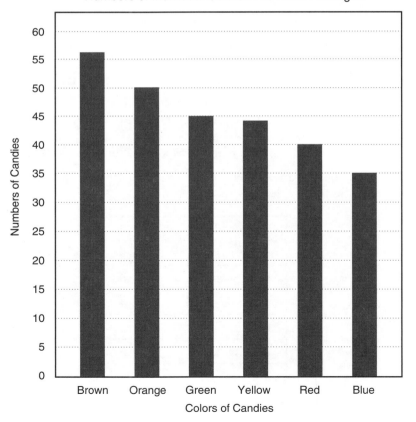

Numbers of Individual Colors in 10 M&M Packages

8. Provide students with graph paper and ask them to create a bar graph for their individual data. They may want to color the bars in the graphs with colored pencils or markers for effect.

9. Ask students to share their graphs with each other. Discuss the similarities and differences among the graphs.

10. Then groups of students could combine their data into group bar graphs. The final activity could be a single bar graph for the total group data.

11. Refer to a bar graph in your text and help students transfer their skills. Guide students through an interpretation of the graph by asking questions and thinking aloud. Model how you go about understanding a portion of the graph and invite students to share their thinking.

Section 7.3

STRATEGY 2 CHARTS AND GRAPHS

1. Explain to students that graphs and charts are visual methods of presenting information, making comparisons, and showing relationships, rather than using lots of words.

2. Brainstorm the similarities and differences between charts and graphs. Answers might include that charts show the relationships among several parts. They may show the order in which things happen or the cause and effect, but they always show how one part relates to the others. Graphs are similar to charts in that they show relationships, but they use points and lines rather than pictures or symbols.

3. Create a chart and a graph illustrating the months when students have birthdays.

4. Demonstrate how to read the chart and graph.

5. Ask questions for which the students will have to use the graphic aids to answer, for example, Which month has the most birthdays?

Section 7.3

STRATEGY 3 INTERPRETING LINE GRAPHS

1. Explain that a line graph is another way of arranging information that can be read at a glance. Ask students whether they have seen graphs other than bar graphs in their readings. Discuss the kinds of graphs students have seen.

2. Show students an example of a line graph on an overhead projector. Tell students about the features of the line graphs including the title, the numbers, the lines, and the labels. An example of a line graph follows.

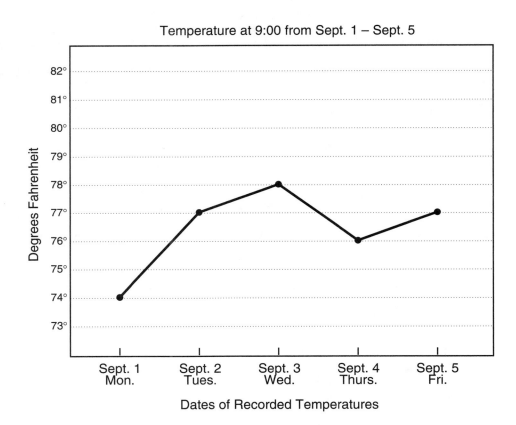

Temperature at 9:00 from Sept. 1 – Sept. 5

Degrees Fahrenheit

82°
81°
80°
79°
78°
77°
76°
75°
74°
73°

Sept. 1 Mon. Sept. 2 Tues. Sept. 3 Wed. Sept. 4 Thurs. Sept. 5 Fri.

Dates of Recorded Temperatures

3. Ask the students to discuss the information they found on the graph. Some guiding questions and answers follow.

> *Teacher:* What does this graph tell us?
>
> *Student:* The temperature.
>
> *Teacher:* Where did you find that information?
>
> *Student:* From the title.
>
> *Teacher:* What else do we know from this graph?
>
> *Student:* How hot it was during the last week.
>
> *Teacher:* Can you tell me how hot it was last Wednesday?
>
> *Student:* Yes, it was 78 degrees.

4. Provide students with graph paper and help them construct a sample line graph using information from the birthday charts. See Strategy 2.

5. Ask students to compare line graphs with each other noting similarities and differences. Give them an opportunity to discuss how effective they think line graphs are at representing information.

STRATEGY 4 INTERPRETING PIE CHARTS

1. Remind students that graphs and charts are visual ways of presenting information, comparisons, and relationships using few numbers and words. Explain that one of the uses of charts and graphs is to give information in a brief form and help students visualize the data without a great deal of reading.

2. Tell students that they will be learning a new kind of chart, a pie chart. Put an example of a pie chart on an overhead projector. Tell students that the information from the chart was gathered from the class family heritage unit. An example of a pie chart follow.

Mr. Thompson's Class
Percentage of members from different cultural groups

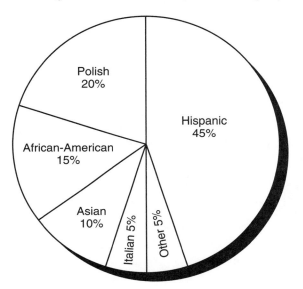

3. Ask students whether they have seen a pie chart in their reading or on television. Give students a chance to discuss the pie charts they have seen. If possible, refer to a pie chart in one of their texts.

4. Ask students what information they found on the pie chart. Remind them of the features of any graph or chart: the title, the labels, and the numbers.

5. Model for the students how you would read a pie chart for information. You might say something like this:

> *The first thing I look for when I see a chart is the title. This title says that the chart is the percentages of classroom members from different cultural groups. From looking at the chart, I see the largest area on the graph is made up of Hispanics. We see that 45% of the class has Hispanic origins. The second largest ethnic group in the class is made up of students of Polish ancestry. There are 20% of students who make up this group. We also see 15% of students who have African-American backgrounds; 10% of students with Asian backgrounds; 5% of students with Italian backgrounds; and 5% in a category that says other.*

6. Ask students whether they were able to understand the information from the pie chart. Provide students with an opportunity to discuss difficulties they had with interpreting the chart. Students may ask about the category *other* on the chart. Explain that when there are too few members in a group to be represented on the chart, they may be placed together in one category.

Practice and Reinforcement Activities

1. Ask students to think of some information they would like to know. It might be how many students wear a certain brand of clothes, the ways students get to school, or the number of rabbits in their backyards. Have students record their data for a period of time, several days at least. Ask students to make a graph for their data. All the points on the graph should be neatly plotted and connected. Share the data with the class by writing a story about it or explaining it to other students.

2. Divide the class into groups of two. Distribute two graphs to each pair of students. Ask each student to read one graph with the purpose of explaining that graph to his or her partner. Give the students time to read and think about the graphs. Then ask them to share what they have learned. After the discussions are finished, ask students whether they have questions about the information on the graphs that they were unable to understand. Answer any questions students might have.

3. Ask students to look for bar graphs, line graphs, and pie charts in newspapers and magazines. Invite them to bring samples of these graphs to class. Give students an opportunity to explain the graphs either to the entire class or to a small group. Post the graphs on a poster or bulletin board.

4. Locate information from the texts used in class that would be appropriate to chart or graph. Ask students to develop a graph for the information.

5. Convert some of the information you record on a daily or weekly basis into a graph. For example, you might graph the number of books the students have read, the number of books they have written, or the number of sunny days in the month. Ask a group of students to chart the information and another group to graph it on poster board for the class.

6. Integrate graph learning activities with the ongoing curriculum. Pay particular attention to graphic aids in textbooks.

Inflexible Rate of Reading

Behavior Observed	The student does not vary rate of reading.
Anticipated Outcome	The student will vary reading rate to match his or her purposes.

BACKGROUND

Proficient readers have a flexible silent reading rate that is determined by their purposes. Rate of reading is better thought of as rate of comprehension to achieve the reader's purposes. It does little good to consider rate apart from comprehension; moreover, comprehension may suffer when rate is too fast or too slow. For many students experiencing difficulty in reading, lack of automaticity in identifying words may require so much of students' attention that meaning suffers. One teacher observed that it takes Jada so long to decode that she forgets what the beginning of the sentence is about by the time she gets to the end. Jada may be preoccupied with decoding. Another student is excellent at decoding but does not have the slightest idea what the passage is about. This student is a word caller. Between these two extremes are students who seldom practice flexibility in reading—quite possibly because it was never an instructional focus.

Strategic readers know that there are several factors that help determine the rate at which they read, and they know how to take these factors into account while they are reading.

Major Factors That Determine Reading Rates

- purpose
- type of material
- familiarity with content and/or background knowledge
- motivation and/or mood (for example, preparing for a test, relaxing with a novel)
- reading environment (for example, light quality, presence or absence of distractions)
- size of type, amount of figures, illustrations, and so on

These factors influence each of the major kinds of reading such as study-type reading, rapid reading (like skimming and scanning), and technical reading. Within each of these major types of reading, rate may sometimes be faster or slower. The important point to keep in mind is whether the readers' purposes are being achieved.

STRATEGY 1 — DIFFERENT RATES

1. Be sure students understand that meaning is what reading is all about.

2. Ask students to name some of the reasons they read and to offer examples of that kind of reading. A chart similar to the following might be developed on the chalkboard.

What We Read	Why We Read
Clifford books	For fun
Our own stories	To read better
	To learn words
Lunch menu	To see what we will eat
Science book	To learn things

3. Use the chart to help students realize that they read for different purposes, especially for fun and to learn things.

4. Tell students that good readers know why they are reading something and that they should always know why they are reading a book or story. Refer to the chart as necessary and use other examples as appropriate.

5. Then tell students that sometimes they will read faster and sometimes they will read slower. Help students develop a list of times when they might speed up or slow down. See the following example.

 I speed up my reading when I—
 - already know the story.
 - am reading a story I've already practiced.
 - understand the meaning of the story.

 I slow down my reading when I—
 - don't understand.
 - am mixed up.
 - encounter unfamiliar words.

6. Spend time helping students realize that good readers will reread if they are not understanding. They also stop reading and try to get help if they are not understanding.

7. Use subsequent lessons or instructional opportunities to foster a greater awareness and understanding that everything is not read at the same speed.

STRATEGY 2 — READING RATE CHART

1. Begin by inviting each student to compile a list of the various kinds of reading accomplished within the last day or two and the purposes for reading. A chart like the following one might be helpful.

Day	Time	What Was Read	Why It Was Read (Purpose)

2. After students have had sufficient time for individual reflection, have them form small groups to compare their answers. Ask them to identify both common and unique items. Each group can list common and unique items on an overhead transparency or on the chalkboard.

3. Engage students in a group activity in which volunteers can share overhead transparencies or write responses on the chalkboard.

4. After responses are shared, lead students in a discussion about the rate at which the reading occurred to fulfill the intended purpose(s). Help students realize that there is a connection between purpose and rate. For example, Roger may have used a television program guide to find out whether any TV movies were showing Tuesday evening at eight o'clock. He said it took him longer to find the guide than to find out the titles of the movies by scanning the guide. Ami not only located the movies in her guide but she also read the brief blurbs about each of them. Actually, she didn't read the entire blurb for a movie once she decided that she wasn't interested. After her initial reading, she went back and reread one of the movie blurbs because she thought it might be worth watching.

5. Use the previous example or a similar one to help develop the notion of a flexible rate of reading that is governed by purpose. For example, both Roger and Ami scanned the guide to find specific information to fulfill their purposes for reading. Once the information was found, Roger and Ami read. Roger read the movie titles; Ami read the titles and blurbs and even reread one of the blurbs. Both students' reading was successful because their purposes were achieved.

Practice and Reinforcement Activities

1. Give students a newspaper article and develop a purpose for reading the article (to find who, what, when, where, or why). Have students read at a rate that is comfortable to fulfill purposes. After reading, determine whether those purposes were achieved. Invite individual students to share insights about their reading. Several examples follow.

"I just skimmed to find each of the answers."

"I reread the questions so I'd know what to read for."

"I only had trouble remembering the answer to one of the questions so I scanned the article for that specific information. Then I reread that sentence."

2. Use a selection from one of your classroom texts and model how you set purposes for reading and read flexibly to achieve those purposes.

3. Secure classroom quantities of various reading materials (telephone books, driver's license study manuals, product information sheets, maps, and so on). Identify some of the major purposes for reading each type of material and how the material might be read to fulfill particular purposes. Then have students use the material to fulfill one or more of the purposes. Share how the material was read.

4. Have students share their anticipated rate of reading prior to reading one of the materials mentioned in activity 3. Then have the students think aloud to share what they will do. Model the process by saying the following:

> *I want to know the phone number for Sports of All Sorts. I'll look toward the back of the phone book and find the* s. *Then I'll use my knowledge of guide words to find the right page. I'm not really very good at using guide words, so I'd better take my time. I'll look on that page until I find the entry and phone number. If I can't find it, I might try the Yellow Pages under sports or sporting.*

Then have a student actually perform the task and think aloud. Use this general procedure with other types of reading materials.

5. Give students opportunities to write down some of their insights about reading rate. For example, the following chart might be developed.

I can usually speed up my reading when—

- it is easy and I'm understanding.
- I already know a lot about the topic.
- the book is repeating what was said before.
- the information is not related to my purposes.

I should usually slow down my reading when—

- the information is related to my purposes.
- the book has ideas that I'm interested in.
- I'm confused.
- the writing is complicated.

6. Timed silent reading exercises with comprehension questions may give students opportunities to see whether they are able to comprehend information at a faster rate. After scoring the comprehension questions, have students reinspect the text to find the correct answer or the information that formed the basis for the inferences or conclusions that they drew.

7. Remember to keep your instruction on various rates of reading linked to purpose. Helping students practice flexibility in their reading is the key.

Monitoring Reading

Behavior Observed	The student does not monitor comprehension.
Anticipated Outcome	The student will monitor comprehension while reading.

BACKGROUND

Monitoring reading involves the concepts of strategic reading and metacomprehension. Both concepts are complex; therefore, the ideas we present are concrete and visual in an effort to help students begin to grasp the concept of monitoring.

You should feel free to adapt the ideas and substitute actual examples from students or from your experiences to make the concept clear and relevant. Remember to keep your students' maturity in mind.

Section 7.5

STRATEGY 1 MONITORING

1. Tell students that you are a good reader and that good readers still experience difficulty in reading. If possible, select an actual example from your own reading that represents a genuine instance of monitoring. You may also want to begin developing a file of such ideas to help with appropriate strategy lessons.

2. Share areas in which you have had difficulty, such as failing to understand a text or mispronouncing a word. Invite students to share difficulties they have experienced during reading, and write their ideas on the chalkboard.

3. Encourage discussion of the ideas presented and help students realize that:

 - All readers (not just poor readers) experience difficulty in reading.
 - Better readers keep watch over their reading to make sure they are understanding.
 - Readers fix up their reading to ensure understanding.

4. Ask students to share some of the things they do to keep watch over their reading. Encourage specific examples and discussion. Then share an example from your own reading. You could also use the following example. The actual words in the newspaper article are in italics.

5. Print *Lewis slows up; so do admirers* on the chalkboard and say something like the following: "I read the title to the newspaper article you see and then began reading the article. *Carl Lewis appeared Friday at the Olympic Village, nearly starting a riot in the food court. He was reading his messages on a computer when a mob of 100 athletes and passersby surrounded him for autographs and photos.* As I finished that part of the article, I thought there were quite a few people around Carl Lewis. The headline had said that admirers had slowed up because Carl Lewis had slowed up. Although I was a bit confused because of all the people around Lewis, I continued reading. *"Carl, Carl," the controlled mob screamed, following Lewis out the double doors of the Olympic Village.* At this point I was quite certain that the title and the article were not telling me the same thing. I decided to check over my reading by going back to the title. As I reread the title, I saw my mistake; I had initially read *slows* instead of *shows*. When I read the headline correctly, the content of the article made sense. I was watching over my reading and realized that the title and the article did not seem to agree. I then decided to go back and read the title again. That's when I found my mistake. Now the article makes sense."

6. Take time to discuss this example with students and be sure they understand that rereading is one strategy that good readers sometimes use to overcome a difficulty in understanding. Use the items from number 2 and invite students to share what they have done to overcome or resolve their problems.

7. Remember that numerous lessons and modeling are needed to develop the concept of monitoring. One follow-up activity invites students to record their actual encounters with difficulties in reading. Such examples could be shared and discussed by volunteers in large or small groups to further develop the concept of monitoring.

Book or story _____ Name _____			
Page/Paragraph	*Problem I Had*	*What I Did*	*How It Worked*

Section 7.5

STRATEGY 2 WHAT'S A MONITOR?

1. Write the word *monitor* on the chalkboard and ask students to share meanings and examples of the word.

2. Explore various definitions of *monitor* by using class dictionaries or an overhead transparency with the definitions, or by distributing the definitions. A thesaurus may also be useful. Have students verify their definitions with those you provide and add new definitions. Some definitions, like a computer monitor or hall monitor, may be common. Other definitions for monitor, like a lizard or a heavily ironclad warship, may broaden students' understanding of the word.

3. Ask students to focus on what it might mean to monitor one's reading and help them identify appropriate words or phrases from the various definitions. Some examples follow.

- keep track of
- check
- keep watch over
- control
- oversee
- supervise

4. Invite students to share what actions they take to monitor their reading to ensure that they are understanding the text. Add appropriate examples from your own reading or the example used in Strategy 1.

5. Help students realize that a characteristic of good readers is that they monitor their reading. Many poor readers are under the mistaken notion that good readers always know the words, read fast, and never encounter difficulty in comprehension. Take time to list some of the more important actions students can take to monitor their reading. Specific items from the list could become the focus of future lessons.

6. Consider using a sheet similar to that in Strategy 1 (number 7) so students can begin to see concrete examples of how they monitor reading. These examples could also be used in future lessons and discussions.

Section 7.5

STRATEGY 3 THE CRITTER

1. Use the notion of a "critter" to help get students thinking visually about the concepts of strategic reading and metacomprehension. Enlarge and present a critter on an overhead transparency (or draw one of your own).

2. Tell students that similar critters were drawn by students who used the picture to help them remember that there is something in their heads to help them understand what they are reading. The term "inner voice" may be helpful to students.

3. Invite students to visualize a critter that they have in their heads to help them read. You may wish to give students time to draw and color their critters. You could also draw your own critter on an overhead transparency or use the sample provided.

4. Use your critter to help develop important questions with the class. Some possible questions your critter asks to help your reading make sense are listed below.

> **?** Do I understand what I'm reading? If yes, great! If no, what should I do about it?
>
> What do I already know about this topic?
>
> How is this chapter organized?
>
> How can I figure out this unknown word?
>
> What is my purpose for reading?
>
> Have I achieved my purpose for reading?

5. A single question could be the focus of one or more lessons to develop important ideas related to strategic reading. Have students add the questions and strategies to the sheet containing their critters. For example, if the answer to "Do I understand what I'm reading?" is "no," some possible actions could include:

 - I need to concentrate on what the author is trying to tell me and visualize the message.
 - I'll reread the last paragraph.
 - I'm tired so I'll take a short break.
 - I need to ask someone for help.
 - I think I need to look up the meaning of a word.

6. Remind students to use the important ideas their critters are telling them so they understand what they are reading. The important point is for students to take control of their reading and to monitor their comprehension. A critter may help provide a concrete, visual image toward that end.

Section 7.5

STRATEGY 4 MONITORING AND FIX-UPS

1. Tell students that good readers monitor their reading. Although each of the following strategies will be dealt with, you may want to use separate lessons for particular strategies so that they are fully developed.

 - Summarize
 - Identify confusions
 - Look back or reread confusing parts
 - Read ahead to possibly clarify confusions
 - Ask myself questions
 - Use *like a*

Write the strategies on the chalkboard and explain each of them briefly. Encourage students to share specific instances from their reading when they might have used the strategies. Have students share why the strategy did or did not work. Most of the strategies are probably familiar except *like a* (Davey, 1983). In this strategy, the reader links part of the text with something from his or her background. For example, the student might say, "The mummy being described in the text is *like a* mummy I saw when I was at the museum last summer." The *like a* approach helps the student relate relevant background experiences to better comprehend the text.

2. Tell students that you are going to use some or all of these strategies as you read *The Saga of Shakespeare Pintlewood and the Great Silver Fountain Pen* (Lehman, 1990). Thanks to the kindness of the author and illustrator, the title page and two actual pages have been reproduced here in black and white. You may make copies or overhead transparencies for classroom use. The actual words in the story are in regular print. You might want to audiotape or videotape yourself modeling the strategies and then use the tape for the lesson. It can be replayed to help make your major points.

3. Begin by reading the title and thinking aloud.

> *The title is* The Saga. . . . *Wait a minute; I don't know what saga means, but I'll read ahead to see if I get any help . . .* of Shakes-peare/Shakespeare Pin-tle-wood/ Pintlewood. *Let's see, I think this is a story about Shakespeare Pintlewood, so perhaps* saga *means story. I could look it up in the dictionary, but I'll just read on for now. I can look it up later if I can't figure it out soon. I'll finish the title . . .* and the Great Silver Foun-tain/Fountain Pen. *I can see from the picture that there is an ant holding a pen. I guess that must be a fountain pen. It looks like a pen my dad has. It's not like the ball-point pen I use. My dad even has a bottle of ink he uses to fill the pen when it runs out of ink. From the title and picture, I think this is a story about an ant named Shakespeare Pintlewood who might use the pen. I know ants can't write, so this story is not real. I have heard the name Shakespeare before, but I don't know much else. Maybe my mom will know.*

4. Give students an opportunity to identify and comment on the strategies you have used. If necessary, replay parts of the tape to help clarify the discussion. Note specific strategies on the chalkboard and take time to explain why you used a particular strategy. The chart on the chalkboard might look something like the following one.

Summarize	Identify Confusions	Look Back; Reread	Read Ahead	Ask Questions	Use Like a
what is known based on the title and picture	saga unknown some words	sentence with garage	when saga wasn't known	about saga about garage	fountain pen like Dad's

5. Continue reading the title page (which lists the author and illustrator) and then move on to the text.

> Once upon a time there was an ant who made up stories for children. *I know from 'once upon a time' that this is not a true story. Another thing is that real ants do not make up stories.* His name was Shakespeare Pintlewood, but all the other ants called him Shakey for short. *I'm glad the ant has a nickname, because I have trouble saying his name.*

Because he was very small, Shakey saw things the way little girls and boys do. To him people looked like giants and gar-āge doors. . . . *No, that's not right; I've never heard of gar-āge doors. Let me finish the sentence . . .* looked like castle gates, and so he was able to make up good stories. *Now, what kind of doors look like castle gates and begins with 'gar'? It has to be a big door because castle gates are big. At our house, we have a front door, but that isn't the word because front doesn't begin the same way as the word in the book. We also have a garage door and it begins the same way as the word in the book. I'll reread the sentence to see whether it makes sense [reread sentence]. Yes, the word makes sense. So far, I know this is a story about an ant named Shakey who was able to make up good stories for children. I think I'm understanding everything so far.*

6. Refer students to the chart and discuss the reading. As they tell you appropriate behaviors from your think aloud, fill in the chart. Point out that all your thinking aloud actually happens very quickly when you are reading. This might also be a good time to refer students to the critter developed in Strategy 3. It is your critter or inner voice that helps you monitor or keep track of your reading.

THE SAGA OF
Shakespeare Pintlewood

AND THE

GREAT SILVER FOUNTAIN PEN

by James H. Lehman

illustrated by Christopher Raschka

O nce upon a time there was an ant who liked to make up stories for children. His name was Shakespeare Pintlewood, but all the other ants called him Shakey for short.

Because he was very small, Shakey saw
things the way little girls and boys do. To him
people looked like giants and garage doors
looked like castle gates, and so he was able to
make up good stories.

7. Develop subsequent lessons in which you expand and refine the strategies using materials being read by your students. Plenty of carefully guided opportunities are needed to make the strategies automatic. Ultimately, students need to value the strategies and use them independently. Some possible questions for students to ask themselves are provided below.

Before Reading

What are my purposes for reading?

Why am I reading this?

What will I be doing with the information?

What do I already know about this topic?

What do I think I will learn?

What are my predictions?

What reading strategies will I have to use to read this?

How is this selection organized?

During Reading

Am I meeting my purposes for reading this?

Am I understanding what I am reading?

Does my reading make sense?

Do I have a clear picture in my head?

Is this what I had expected?

What parts are similar to or different from my predictions?

What can I do to increase my understanding?

Do I agree with the author?

After Reading

Have I learned what I wanted to learn?

Should I go back and reread portions of the selection for better understanding?

What new information did I learn and how does it fit with what I already know?

Should I get another point of view? What else do I still need to know about this topic?

How do I feel about what I read? Do I agree or disagree? Why? Do I like it or not? Why?

Practice and Reinforcement Activities

1. Ask students to take out a book that they have just read and to think about the strategies they used as they read. To find out how aware students are of their reading strategies, you may want to interview them individually or reproduce the Reading Strategies Questions below and have students answer on separate sheets.

Reading Strategies Questions

Before I began reading, I _____

When I got stuck on a word, I _____

When I didn't understand what was happening, I _____

After I finished reading, I _____

2. After students have answered the above questions about their reading, ask them to read their answers and write goals for improving their monitoring. If they are not sure of the goals they could choose, use some of the suggestions from the following example and write them on the chalkboard. Then ask students to discuss their reading goals in small groups and with you. An example appears below.

Emily was a voracious reader of easy books but was not able to verbalize any strategies for understanding reading. Before she read a book, she looked at the title and began reading. You might suggest that Emily also do any of the following activities.

- look to see how hard or easy the book is
- read the book jacket
- preview the pictures or chapter titles
- make a prediction about the book
- look to see what genre the book is

Because Emily usually chooses easy books, she rarely comes to a word she doesn't know. When she does come to a word she doesn't know, Emily just skips it and reads ahead. You might suggest that Emily do any of the following activities.

- skip the word, read to the end of the sentence, then go back to the beginning and try again
- read ahead to connect the word with other ideas
- try to use word parts she knows
- substitute a word that makes sense
- use a picture clue
- reread and connect the word to the sense of the sentence
- ask someone what the word is
- look up the pronunciation of the word in a dictionary
- cross check by asking if it sounds right, if it makes sense, and if it looks right

Sometimes Emily does not have a high degree of comprehension when she reads. However, she normally continues reading without using any fix-up strategies. You might suggest that Emily do the following.

- reread the confusing part
- use pictures or subheadings to make sense of the text
- read ahead and try to connect the information
- use signal words in the text to understand

After reading, Emily usually writes the name of the book in her book log, but does little else to process the text. You might suggest that she do the following.

- tell a friend about the book
- videotape a book talk
- read the book again
- look for a similar book
- write about the book in her journal
- write a letter to the author

3. Help students monitor their reading by providing them with self-check lists. A variety of self-report lists can be found in the Resources for Chapter 7. Use the information to inform your instruction.

Summarizing Ideas

SECTION 7.6

Behavior Observed	The student has difficulty summarizing ideas during and after reading.
Anticipated Outcome	The student will learn how to summarize ideas during and after reading.

BACKGROUND

Effective readers summarize as they read. Think what you do when you read. As you read, you stop occasionally and briefly rehearse what you have read. In essence, you are summarizing. As a reader, you also summarize when you come to the end of a text. You think back to the text in its entirety and review what it said. Again, you were

> Effective readers summarize as they read.

summarizing. You can teach students the same type of summarization strategies you use. When students use summarization strategies, they become better comprehenders of text. The teaching strategies and activities in this section emphasize summarizing both during reading and after reading.

Section 7.6

STRATEGY 1 · WRITING SUMMARIES

1. Provide students with short passages at their instructional level of reading. An example follows.

 Zebras are one of the most attractive animals in nature. Zebras come from the horse family so they look much like horses you would see at a farm or zoo. Just like horses, baby zebras are called foals, and mothers are called mares. The difference between horses and zebras, of course, is their appearance. Zebras have black and white stripes, unlike domesticated horses. Their stripes cover their entire body including their mane. Each zebra has its own unique pattern of stripes.

2. Guide students to underline the main idea of the passage and to cross out unimportant or redundant information. An example follows.

Zebras are one of the most attractive animals in nature. Zebras come from the horse family so ~~they look much like horses you would see at a farm or zoo. Just like horses,~~ baby zebras are called foals and mothers are called mares. ~~The difference between horses and zebras, of course, is their appearance.~~ Zebras have black and white stripes, ~~unlike domesticated horses. Their stripes cover their entire body including their mane.~~ Each zebra has its own unique pattern of stripes.

3. Help students make a graphic organizer with the remaining information. See the following example.

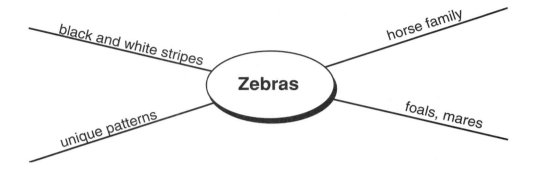

4. Together, write a short paragraph from the information on the graphic organizer, as in the following example.

 Zebras come from the horse family. Babies are called foals, and mothers are called mares. Each zebra has its own pattern of black and white stripes.

5. Review the procedure and provide students with an appropriate passage so they can begin to gain competence with the strategy. After they have completed their summaries, go through each of the above steps and discuss students' strategies. Provide guidance as needed.

Section 7.6

STRATEGY 2

GRASP: GUIDED READING AND SUMMARIZING PROCEDURE*

1. Provide students with a short passage at their instructional level of reading. Explain that the students will be writing a summary of the passage. If your students do not understand the term *summary,* explain that a summary is a brief description of a longer text.

2. Ask students to read the passage independently with the purpose of remembering all that they can. After they are finished reading, they should put the passage on their desk and wait for others in the group.

3. After all students have finished reading, ask them to tell you what they remembered. List on the chalkboard all of the items they suggest.

4. Ask students to reread the passage with the purpose of making additions to and deletions from the list on the board.

*Hayes, 1989.

5. After rereading, have the class suggest changes to the list on the chalkboard. Revise the list as needed.

6. Then ask students to suggest categories for the information. List the categories and ask students to divide the items on the list into the categories.

7. Using the outline generated by categorizing the information, write the summary. You might suggest that students begin with a main idea statement for the first main heading with details as the subheadings. An example of the GRASP strategy based on an adapted encyclopedia entry follows.

Otters are aquatic or semiaquatic carnivores of the weasel family. The body of the otter is lithe and muscular and covered with thick fur. Their paws are generally webbed. Otters often shut their nostrils and eyes to swim underwater. Their prey consists of small fish, eels, crayfish, and frogs. The sea otter's diet is more specialized. They have powerful teeth that are perfect for crushing sea urchins, abalones, and mussels. The sea otter floats on its back, breaking open the urchin—or mussel—shell on a stone anvil balanced on its chest. Unlike most other wild animals, otters remain playful as adults.

Teacher: Today we are going to read a paragraph about otters. I'd like you to read it carefully trying to remember as much of the passage as you can. After you're done reading, put your paper on your desk and wait for the other students.

Teacher: Now that you have finished reading, what can you remember from the passage?

Students:

Otters like to play.	Otters eat snakes.	Otters are weasels.
They have fur.	They swim underwater.	They eat fish and frogs.
Sea otters eat seaweed.	Sea otters eat sea animals.	Their paws are webbed.

Teacher: Now reread the paragraph and think if you would like to add any more ideas, erase some of them, or change some of them.

Student: Otters shut their eyes underwater just like we do!

Teacher: Let's add that one to the list.

Student: We have some wrong things on the chalkboard. Otters don't eat snakes or seaweed.

Teacher: What do you think, class? Raise your hands if you agree that otters don't eat snakes or seaweed. I see everyone's hand is up, so I'll erase those two ideas. Now let's try to put some of the information into categories. What categories can you think of?

Student: How they look.

Teacher: What would fit under How Otters Look?

Student: They have fur and webbed feet.

Teacher: Let's make an outline with categories and information under them.

Otters in General
weasels
swim under water with eyes shut
like to play

How Otters Look

fur

webbed feet

What Otters Eat

fish

frogs

sea animals

Teacher: Let's try to write a summary using this information.

Otters are playful weasels who like to swim under water with their eyes shut. They have fur and webbed feet. Otters like to eat fish, frogs, and sea animals.

Section 7.6

STRATEGY 3 SUMMARY MICROTHEME*

1. Explain to students that a summary microtheme is a short sentence (or two) that expresses the main point of a text or a lecture. A microtheme can be used to help students know whether they are understanding a passage.

2. After students have read a paragraph or two, ask them to think about the main idea of the passage. You might ask students to refer to the title and/or subheadings of the text to help them understand the main idea.

3. Distribute large index cards to each student and ask students to write the main idea on the card in a sentence or two. For example, regarding the preceding paragraph about otters, a main idea sentence can be one of the following statements.

 Otters are in the weasel family but they can swim underwater.

 Otters are playful animals who like to swim.

4. Ask students to evaluate their responses by determining whether they understood the main point of the passage. Those students who are unsure whether they have an accurate summary should reread the text.

5. After the students have completed a final reading of the text and have written a summary sentence, give them an example that does not express the main idea of the text but is one of the details. An example might be *Otters eat frogs.*

 Explain that this is one of the details of the passage and that students sometimes confuse details with main ideas. Then write an example that is too broad, such as *Otters are wild animals.*

 Explain that, although students need to think in general terms, students should also try to have some specific information in their summary microtheme.

6. Invite students to make changes in their responses if needed to express the summary of the text in a sentence or two.

*Brozo & Simpson, 1991.

Practice and Reinforcement Activities

1. After teaching all three summary writing strategies, give students a passage and ask them to use all three strategies. After they have finished, ask them which strategy they preferred, which was most useful, and when they could use each one.

2. When students are studying for tests, ask each student to summarize two important sections from the chapter. Combine the chapters into a booklet that students could use for study purposes.

3. Give students five minutes to discuss their hobbies with a partner. Then ask them to write down a summary of what their partner said. Share the summaries with the class.

4. Ask students to summarize their favorite television program. Give them an opportunity to read their summaries to a partner.

5. Have students listen to a story on tape by a storyteller. Then have them summarize the story. They can share their summaries with the class by illustrating them and placing them on a bulletin board.

Making Connections

Behavior Observed	The student does not make connections while reading.
Anticipated Outcome	The student will make connections while reading.

BACKGROUND

Students who make a wide variety of connections during reading have more possibilities for meaning making. Therefore, students who make connections to their personal experiences and to other texts as well as making connections within the text will have a richer range of ideas as they construct meaning from text. Although making connec-tions is natural, students need to be encouraged to integrate knowledge they have from outside school with school learning. When students are guided to make connections, they generally do so. The teaching strategies and activities in this section can help students as they learn to make an expanding range of connections as they read.

Section 7.7

STRATEGY 1 THINKING HATS*

1. Make Thinking Hats for each of the students in your class using six different colors of construc-tion paper. Use the pattern for Thinking Hats on page 382 to make the hats. Duplicate one sheet of hats per color. Cut out the Thinking Hats.

2. Attach each Thinking Hat to a craft stick. On the back of each hat, write one of the following types of connections: personal experiences, school subjects, other books, community, general knowledge, and people.

3. Select a story or a passage at students' independent reading level. Provide students with ample time to read the selection.

4. Divide the class into groups with six students in each group. (One group may have fewer stu-dents than six.)

*Moore, 1998.

5. Give a different colored Thinking Hat to each student in a group. Be sure students understand what is meant by the word on their hats. Then tell students that the Thinking Hat that they have been given will be their focus for discussion about the story. You might say the following:

 Each of you has a different color Thinking Hat. On the back of each hat is your discussion topic today. You might have a hat that has the word personal experiences *on the back. You should tell the group what personal experiences you remembered as you read the story.*

6. Give students time to discuss the story using their Thinking Hats. After they have discussed the story in small groups, have them share their ideas by topic. For example, ask all of the students who had a hat with *other books* written on it to tell the class what other books they thought of as they read the story. Emphasize the different types of discussions that the Thinking Hats generate.

7. For variety, give each group the same kind of Thinking Hat so that one group has a *school subjects* hat, one group has a *personal experiences* hat, and so on.

From Jerry L. Johns and Susan Davis Lenski, *Improving Reading: Strategies and Resources* (3rd ed.). Copyright © 2001 Kendall/ Hunt Publishing Company (1-800-247-3458, ext. 5). May be reproduced for noncommercial educational purposes.

STRATEGY 2

THINK SHEET

1. Select a story or a passage that students will be reading. Formulate an issue about the topic to be studied, such as the Industrial Revolution.

2. Duplicate and distribute the Think Sheet that follows. Make a transparency of the Think Sheet to use to model the strategy.

 3. Divide the class into groups of three or four students. Invite students to generate questions about the Industrial Revolution. Have groups share their ideas and write them on the section labeled questions on the Think Sheet. Some sample questions about the Industrial Revolution follow.

> What was the biggest social change during that time period?
>
> Who were the people who made up the middle class?
>
> Who were the people of the working class?
>
> What were some of the good points and bad points of the Industrial Revolution?

4. Tell students that the second column of the Think Sheet focuses on what students know about the issue before reading the text. Ask students to list their ideas about the changes of the Industrial Revolution before they read the text.

5. Explain to students that they should read the text to find answers to their questions and also to determine whether their ideas are supported by the text. Ask students to record as they read facts to answer their questions.

6. After students have completed the reading, have them share what they learned from the text. Guide students to make connections among their questions, ideas, and ideas in the text. A partial example of a Think Sheet about the Industrial Revolution follows.

Think Sheet		
Central Issue: *What were the changes that occurred during the Industrial Revolution?*		
My questions	*My ideas*	*Text ideas*
What was the biggest social change?	More money More freedom	The growing importance of the middle class
Who were the people in the middle class?	The middle class was composed of people who had some money but weren't rich.	The middle class was made up of business people who owned factories, mines, and banks.

Name _____ Date _____

Think Sheet

Think Sheet		
Central Issue:		
My questions	My ideas	Text ideas

STRATEGY 3

DIRECTED READING-CONNECTING ACTIVITY*

1. Select a story or a passage that students have not read. Show students the title of the story and ask, "What do you think this story will be about?" Encourage students to draw upon their background knowledge to make predictions about the story. Write the students' predictions on the chalkboard, on chart paper, or on an overhead transparency.

2. Select a portion of text for students to read. Choose a stopping point after students have read enough of the story to have a sense of the problem but before the climax. Have students silently read the first portion of text. Tell students to stop at the predetermined point. Encourage students who finish early to think about the story thus far.

3. Write the following questions on the chalkboard or on an overhead transparency.

 What other books does this story remind you of?

 How does this story relate to what you've learned in school?

 How does this story remind you of yourself?

4. Duplicate and distribute the DR-CA Chart that follows. Have students discuss what has happened in the story up to the point they have read and write their ideas on the chart.

5. Then have students generate ideas about what they think will happen next in the story. Encourage students to think of as many possibilities as they can. Have students share their ideas.

6. Tell students that their predictions should be based on evidence from the story thus far. Have students justify their predictions with evidence from the story. Then have small groups of students share their predictions with justifications.

7. Repeat the DR-CA procedures one or two more times during the story. Have students use the Thinking Chart for their ideas.

8. Encourage students to use the DR-CA thinking process as they read independently.

*Lenski, 1999.

DR-CA Chart

Story Title	
Connections to other books	
Connections to school learning	
Connections to self	

Practice and Reinforcement Activities

1. Books on CD-ROM are ideal for having students make connections (Labbo, 2000). Have students read and listen to a talking book on CD-ROM; then ask students to recall how events in the story are similar to other stories or to their personal experiences.

2. Create a Character Home Page (Stephens & Brown, 2000) from a book students have read. Have students identify an individual character from the story. Then have the students assume the character's identity. Help students design the Character's Home Page with the following information: personal information, characteristics, interests, hobbies, and so on. Encourage students to think of a wide variety of connections.

3. Gather students together in a literature circle. Give students the same book to read. Tell students that as they read you want them to make connections to other books, to personal experiences, and to school subjects. Encourage students to discuss the book and think of ways they can connect their story to other things.

4. Have students bring family photographs to class. Tell students to place their photographs on their desks or tables and think of the many stories the photographs represent. Model using a photograph of your own. For example, say the following:

Teachers need to be familiar with web sites suggested for students.

> *This is a picture of my family camping in Alaska. We set up our tent right next to that stream. We thought it was a wonderful camping site, but what we didn't know was that the Grizzlies in the area liked to come to that stream to catch fish. We were walking back to the tent when we saw four Grizzlies circling our tent. It didn't take us long after that to move our campsite.*

After telling one story, remind students that any memory can trigger many more memories. Continue making connections such as the following:

> *When I see that picture I think of the videos we have at home of Alaska. I also think about a book I read about the gold rush in Alaska.*

Provide students with ample time to make connections using their photographs.

Processing Text

Behavior Observed	The student does not process text after reading.
Anticipated Outcome	The student will use text-processing strategies to enhance comprehension.

BACKGROUND

In order for students to have a rich comprehension of text, they need to process the information in the text in an elaborate fashion. After students have finished reading, they need to think about the text, talk about the text, manipulate the ideas, and make connections to their existing knowledge. As they work with the text, students can continue learning more about the story or passage and improve their comprehension.

Section 7.8

STRATEGY 1 CHARACTER TRAITS MAP

1. Have students select a character from a story they have read.

2. Tell students that they can infer character traits from events in the story.

3. Duplicate and distribute copies of the Character Traits Map that follows.

4. Have students place the name of a character in the box.

 5. Divide the class into groups of three or four students. Have students think of a character trait of the character they have chosen. For example, a character might be courageous.

6. Then have students list events from the story that provide evidence for that specific character trait.

7. Repeat the directions with a second character trait.

8. Have students share their thoughts with others in the class. Point out the similar and different perspectives students have about the same character.

Name ——————————————————— Date ———————————

Character Traits Map

Directions: Choose a character from the story. Examine his/her actions to decide how to describe the character. Fill in two of the character's traits and the events from the story that led to your conclusions.

Name of Character

Trait 1

Trait 2

Events Supporting Trait

Events Supporting Trait

From Jerry L. Johns and Susan Davis Lenski, *Improving Reading: Strategies and Resources* (3rd ed.). Copyright © 2001 Kendall/Hunt Publishing Company (1-800-247-3458, ext. 5). May be reproduced for noncommercial educational purposes.

STRATEGY 2 RETELLING

Retelling is a strategy to help students summarize, organize, and recognize elements in all types of printed materials. However, retellings are generally applied to literature selections and often used in the lower grades. Students having difficulty in reading can be helped to remember story sequence and character elements in the story by using words such as *first, next, last, then,* and *finally.* Although retellings can be written, they are most often thought of as an oral activity.

Refer to the following procedures and guidelines for helpful suggestions for retelling narrative and expository text. Additional retelling suggestions can be found in Johns (2001).

Retelling Procedure for Narrative Passages

1. Ask the student to retell the passage by saying, "Tell me about (name or title of passage) as if you were telling it to someone who has never heard it before."

2. Use the following prompts only when necessary.

 What comes next?

 Then what happened?

 If the student stops retelling and does not continue with the prompts, ask a question about the passage that is based on that point in the passage at which the student has paused. For example, "What did the boys do after raking the leaves?"

3. When a student is unable to retell the story, or if the retelling lacks sequence and detail, prompt the retelling step by step. The following questions may help you.

 Who was the passage about?

 When did the story happen?

 Where did the story happen?

 What was the main character's problem?

 How did he (or she) try to solve the problem? What was done first/next?

 How was the problem solved?

 How did the story end?

Retelling Expectations for Expository Passages

Independent level retelling will generally reflect:

* the text structure
* organization of how the material was presented
* main ideas and details contained in the text

Instructional level retelling will generally reflect:

* less content than at the independent level
* some minor misrepresentations and inaccuracies
* organization that differs from the actual text

Frustration level retelling will generally be:

- haphazard
- incomplete
- characterized by bits of information not related logically or sequentially

STRATEGY 3 HERRINGBONE

1. Tell students that the Herringbone pattern helps them organize information.

2. Duplicate and distribute the Herringbone pattern that follows or draw a Herringbone pattern on the chalkboard or on an overhead transparency.

3. Point out the features of the Herringbone pattern. Point to the horizontal line and say something like the following:

 This line is for the main idea of the story. Think about the story we just have read. What do you think was the main idea? Write it on the horizontal line.

4. Have students share their main ideas with others. Give students a chance to modify their original thoughts.

5. Show students the angled lines off the main idea.

6. Write the following words on a copy of the Herringbone pattern as in the example that follows: who, what, where, when, why, and how.

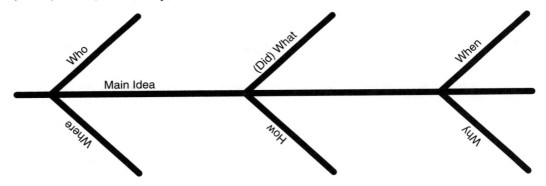

7. Have students answer the following questions on the angled lines in the Herringbone pattern.

 ? Who is the passage about?

 What is the passage about?

 Where did the passage take place?

 When did the action happen?

 Why did the action happen?

 How did the action happen?

8. Provide students with ample time to answer the questions and share their ideas with others.

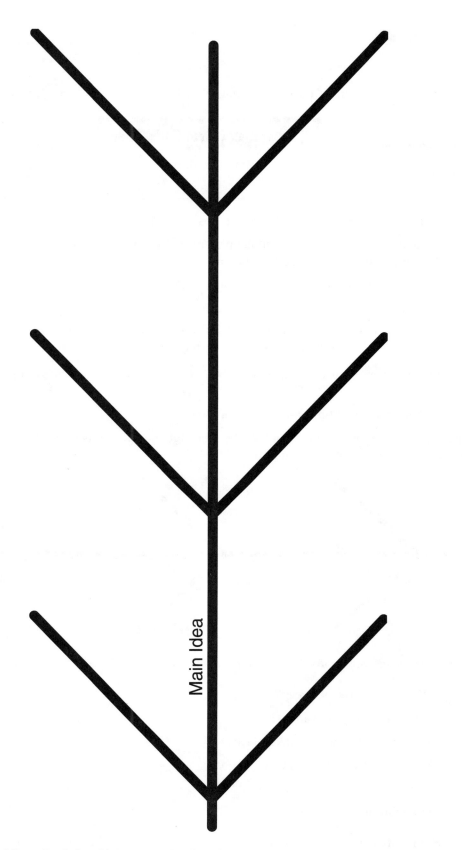

Main Idea

From Jerry L. Johns and Susan Davis Lenski, *Improving Reading: Strategies and Resources* (3rd ed.). Copyright © 2001 Kendall/Hunt Publishing Company (1-800-247-3458, ext. 5). May be reproduced for noncommercial educational purposes.

Practice and Reinforcement Activities

1. Locate a roll of adding machine paper and cut strips about three feet long. Have students divide the paper into as many sections as there are chapters in a book. Include an additional section for their names, the title of the book, and the name of the author. Have students draw a picture on each section illustrating the events of the chapters. Encourage students to include a caption under the picture. Make a slit in a small box and run the strip through the slit so that the pictures show through the opening of the box.

2. Have students bring to school large paper sacks. Slit the sack down the front and add arm holes and a scooped neck. Have students design and color the vest to represent a story that they have read.

3. Implement learning logs so students can reflect on their reading. Leaning logs can be used in conjunction with any area of the curriculum. Teachers may provide daily or weekly opportunities for students to write in their learning logs. A list of learning log prompts is provided below.

- Something important I learned is . . .
- I don't understand . . .
- I want to learn more about . . .
- I wonder why . . .
- I get confused by . . .

4. Have students participate in a paraphrase passport (Faltis, 2001). After students have read a story or a passage from a text, divide the class into groups of three or four students. Ask one student to begin to retell the story or passage. After the first student has begun the retelling, ask a second student to paraphrase the words of the first student. Then the second student should continue retelling the story, and a third student should paraphrase the second student's words and continue retelling the story and so on until the story has been completely retold.

5. After students have read a passage of text, lead a discussion to promote deep thinking. Consider the following as you prepare questions for discussions after reading (Roe, Stoodt, & Burns, 2001).

What are the important ideas in this selection?

What ideas and concepts do I want the students to remember from this selection?

What questions will lead students to understand these ideas and concepts?

What thinking abilities have students already developed?

What thinking abilities do students need to develop?

6. Incorporate informational trade books into the content areas. Trade books are generally more appealing to students than textbooks. In addition, most trade books provide more complete treatments of topics and concepts than textbooks. Book lists such as *A to Zoo* (Lima & Lima, 1998) and *Adventuring with Books* (Jett-Simpson, 1989) are arranged by subject and can be helpful in locating appropriate informational trade books for use in the classroom.

7. Students can become editors and experts on a specific topic by creating skinny books (Epstein, 1996). Individually or in small groups, students select a specific topic related to the unit of study in the classroom. Students gather articles, pamphlets, pictures, interviews, letters, and other resources related to their topic. They identify key ideas related to their topic and develop an outline or semantic map to organize their material. They become the editor of their book as they cut, paste, write headlines, create head-

ings and subheadings, write introductions, and create connecting information for their skinny book. Students can also highlight key vocabulary words and create a glossary, develop a table of contents, and make an index for their skinny book. Students can add illustrations, charts, graphs, tables, and other graphics to clarify their topics. Students can do presentations on their topics, and their skinny books can be added to the classroom library.

8. Encourage students to write "wish you were here" letters to clarify their learning about new places, important events, and important people. For example, students could write "wish you were here" letters about meeting with Abraham Lincoln after hearing the Gettysburg Address, traveling to Jupiter, visiting the rain forest, or participating in the Battle of the Alamo.

Evaluating Written Materials

Behavior Observed	The student has difficulty evaluating written materials.
Anticipated Outcome	The student will use information from text to evaluate written materials.

BACKGROUND

The ability to read between and beyond the lines is regarded as higher-level comprehension and is often referred to as critical reading or problem solving. It involves the ability to judge, analyze, or evaluate what is read. Implicit task demands of the reader at this level include distinguishing fact from opinion; recognizing propaganda techniques; evaluating the author's bias, competence, accuracy, and viewpoint, and reacting to what has been written on the basis of one's background and experience.

Reading instruction and classroom questions have focused on the lower levels of comprehension. This emphasis is shortsighted and prevents readers from reaching their full potential. However, there are actions teachers can take to help students evaluate and react to what is read. Several strategies are presented here.

Section 7.9

STRATEGY 1 — DISTINGUISHING FACT FROM OPINION

1. Ask students whether they believe everything they read and encourage students to share their reasons. Look for the opportunity during this discussion to use the words *facts* and *opinions*.

2. Discuss the differences between facts and opinions. You may look up the words in the dictionary and discuss their meanings. List attributes of facts and opinions that are derived from each word's meaning.

Facts	Opinions
things known to exist	beliefs
real or true	judgments
actual events	personal attitudes
you can prove them	what someone thinks about something

3. Write the following sentence on the chalkboard: *Greg looks outside and sees that it is raining.* Have students decide whether *it is raining* is fact or opinion. Help them decide that it is a fact because Greg can see it raining.

4. Now have students assume that they asked three different people "What's the weather?" and the following responses are given.

 Tiffany: Rainy
 Roman: Great
 Esther: Terrible

 Ask students to identify each response as fact or opinion and to offer possible explanations for the two opinions. For example, Roman said the weather was "great" and may be a farmer who knows a recent planting needs rain. Esther said the weather was "terrible" because she may have planned a picnic and is disappointed.

5. Take time to stress that a person's background, feelings, attitudes, and beliefs can influence how events, actions, and even facts are interpreted. Relate these factors to the reading done by students.

6. Provide a brief passage and have students decide which statements are facts and which are opinions:

 Pennsylvania is the best state. Its capital is Harrisburg. Pennsylvania became a state on December 12, 1787. It is one of the oldest states. Almost everyone likes Pennsylvania.

 Be sure to allow ample time for students to share reasons why they identify a sentence as fact or opinion. Stress that some writers state their opinions as if they were facts.

Section 7.9

STRATEGY 2 DISCUSSION GRID*

1. Provide students with a story to read or a passage from a content area textbook. Tell students that as they read they should think about the ideas from the text that interest them.

2. Duplicate and distribute copies of the Discussion Grid that follows. If possible, make a transparency of the Discussion Grid to project on an overhead projector. Use the transparency to model how to use the Discussion Grid.

3. Point out to students the sections of the Discussion Grid. Tell students that the section *Ideas from text* should be used as they read. Explain to students that when reading they should pay attention to facts in the text that are of interest to them.

4. Model how to take note of ideas from the text as in the following:

 I am going to read a section from our science book titled Creatures of the Night. *First, I'll preview the section. As I preview the text, I find that the author writes about raccoons, bats, flying squirrels, and opossums. After previewing the text, I begin to read. One thing I notice right away is that raccoons sleep during the day. I know from experience that raccoons often forage at night, but I never really thought about them sleeping during the day.*

*Taylor, 1998.

5. Write *raccoons sleep during the day* in the first box of the Discussion Grid as in the following example.

Discussion Grid				
Ideas from the text	*Your response*	*Comments of others*		
Raccoons sleep during the day.		Name_____	Name_____	Name_____

6. Continue reading the passage and write other ideas from the text in the additional boxes in that section.

7. Then tell students that while reading they should be thinking about the facts they have identified. Model how to write a response to the facts as in the following example. Say:

> *As I was thinking about raccoons sleeping during the day, I wondered where they sleep and if the light and noise during the day bother them.*

8. Add your sample response to the box titled *Your response*. An example follows.

Discussion Grid				
Ideas from the text	*Your response*	*Comments of others*		
Raccoons sleep during the day.	I didn't know this. I wonder where they sleep.	Name_____	Name_____	Name_____

9. After the students have read the passage, have them fill out the first two sections of the Discussion Grid. After students have listed ideas from the text and their responses, divide the class into groups of three or four students. Have students take turns sharing an idea and response. After one student has told the group an idea, have the group member make comments. Have the student who expressed an idea record the comments on the Discussion Grid.

Discussion Grid

Ideas from the text	Your response	Comments of others		
		Name_____	Name_____	Name_____
		Name_____	Name_____	Name_____
		Name_____	Name_____	Name_____

STRATEGY 3 CHARACTER REPORT CARD

1. Tell students that when they read fictional books they can form judgments about the characters in the story. Explain that forming judgments about fictional characters helps readers expand their comprehension by relating in positive or negative ways to the character.

2. Select a story or a novel for students to read that gives details about a character. Provide ample time for students to read the selection.

3. Divide the class into groups of three or four students and ask students to discuss the character. Encourage students to provide factual details about the character's actions, statements, and thoughts. Then ask students to share their opinions about the character.

4. Read the Character Report Card that follows and modify it if needed. Duplicate and distribute the Character Report Card to students.

5. Have the groups of students discuss each of the character traits and assign the character a grade. Tell students that the group's grade should be unanimous.

6. After students have assigned a grade, have them discuss the reasons for the grade. Then have students list several of their reasons below the grade.

7. Ask students to complete the entire Character Report Card. After the groups have finished, have them share their grades with their classmates.

Character Report Card

Name of character _____

Title of book _____

Friendship Grade _____

Reasons: _____

Courage Grade _____

Reasons: _____

Intelligence Grade _____

Reasons: _____

Compassion Grade _____

Reasons: _____

Responsibility Grade _____

Reasons: _____

Group members: _____

STRATEGY 4 DISCUSSION WEB*

1. After students have read a passage from the text, introduce a central question. The question should be one that lends itself to opposing viewpoints. Write the question on the chalkboard or on an overhead transparency. For example, ask students the following question after they have read *Where the Red Fern Grows* (Rawls, 1961).

 Should Billy have cut down the big old sycamore tree in order to get to the coon?

2. Divide the class into groups of three or four students. Ask students to brainstorm at least three reasons for answering *yes* to the central question. Then have students generate at least three reasons for answering *no* to the central question. When students have written their reasons for answering the question in the affirmative and the negative, ask them to volunteer some of their ideas. Write the ideas in two separate columns as listed below.

Yes	**No**
He shouldn't disappoint his dogs.	It would take a long time to grow.
His dogs worked for it.	When it fell it could hurt something.
He said he would.	It's part of nature.
He felt he had to.	It was his favorite tree.

3. Discuss both sides of the question as objectively as possible. Then encourage students to take a position either for or against the issue. Some students will want to take both sides. Tell them that, although they understand both sides of the issue, they need to take one position.

4. Ask students to come to conclusions independently, defending the side they have chosen. Have them write their conclusions on index cards. Collect the index cards when students are finished and use them to learn which conclusions students have chosen. An example of a conclusion follows.

 Conclusion

Billy should have cut down the tree because he wanted to keep his word.

5. A blank Discussion Web follows. Duplicate and distribute the Discussion Web for students to use with another reading selection.

*Alvermann, 1991.

Discussion Web*

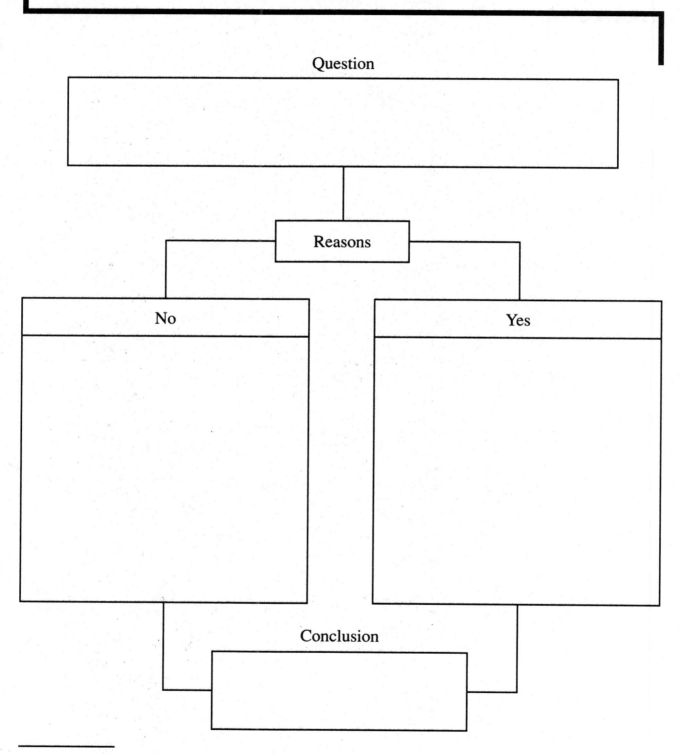

Question

Reasons

No

Yes

Conclusion

*Alvermann, 1991.

Practice and Reinforcement Activities

1. Provide sentences and have students identify them as facts (F) or opinions (O). Some sentences may require research. Take time to discuss students' responses and reasons for their decisions. An example follows.

F	Charles Lindbergh made the first solo flight across the Atlantic Ocean.
O	Lindbergh's plane is nice.
F	Amelia Earhart was the first woman to fly solo across the Atlantic Ocean.
F	Earhart wrote a book called *Soaring Wings*.
O	I read her book and liked it.
O	Generally, airplanes are the best way to travel.

2. Prepare questions for a selection and have students decide whether their answers are facts or opinions. Have students discuss their responses.

3. Present a problem and have students suggest as many solutions to the problem as possible. Then evaluate the proposed solutions and select the ones that appear to be the most workable. Use this same technique with problems in stories.

4. Additional resources for the facts-and-opinions exercises can be found in newspaper articles, advertising, editorials, columns, and cartoons.

5. Challenge students to write their own persuasive paragraph or advertisements using one of the persuasive propaganda techniques discussed. Volunteers can share them with the class.

6. After presenting a nonfiction text, have students evaluate that text (Glazer, 2000). Tell students that nonfiction text should have a clear organizational pattern. Have students identify patterns such as a chronological approach, or a pattern of general to specific, and so on. After students have identified the organizational pattern, have them look for an accurate presentation of facts in the text. In order for students to find out whether the author presented facts accurately, have students select facts from the piece to verify in a reference book. Finally, have students evaluate the text to determine whether the text has current information. Again, have students identify information and verify its accuracy. Tell students that they should evaluate texts as they read them.

These students can be asked to evaluate the books they are reading.

Remembering

Behavior Observed	The student has difficulty remembering what was read.
Anticipated Outcome	The student learns strategies to remember what was read.

BACKGROUND

Part of reading is remembering. Good readers remember much of what they read and are able to recall needed information. But remembering isn't always easy. Some students have difficulty remembering and, for those students, memory strategies are helpful. Of course, students won't remember everything they read, but a few strategies can help them remember more than they did before learning the strategies.

> Part of reading is remembering.

Will this student remember what she is reading?

STRATEGY 1 MEMORIZATION TECHNIQUES

1. Tell students they will need to remember parts of their reading.

2. Explain that the first thing students should do is plan to remember. Tell them that their minds will react differently to information that they have consciously intended to commit to long-term memory. To model how you would plan to remember, you might try the following:

 I've got to read this section in my science book on the habitat of dolphins. I know Ms. Linder said this section was important both for our test and for a project we will be working on. I'm going to remember this information as I read it and not just gloss over it.

3. Remind students that they need to schedule time for remembering. Many students prefer to memorize information and facts last in their schedule. Ask students to write down when they will be studying and to write in times for memorizing information and facts.

4. Tell students that as they memorize they should read the entire chapter that discusses the points they want to remember. This will help them understand the relationship of the facts to other information they know.

Working with a partner is one strategy for remembering facts.

5. Give students a chance to talk about the things they want to remember. During science class, for example, provide students with several minutes to discuss the ideas that they have been memorizing with a partner.

6. Explain the use of mnemonic devices. A mnemonic device is a memory strategy that helps you retain bits of information. The following are examples of mnemonic devices that you can teach to your class.

Mnemonic Devices

Rhyme	Create a rhyme or a song that includes the points you have to learn. *"Thirty days hath September . . ."*
Acronyms	Form words by using the first letter from each of the words to be recalled. *HOMES (Names of the Great Lakes: Huron, Ontario, Michigan, Erie, Superior)*
Pegwood	Memorize a short rhyme and then create the images that link the nouns in the rhyme with the items to be remembered.
Method of Loci	Select a spatial layout, such as your home. Mentally place the items to be recalled in each room.
Clustering	Memorize the material in categories and learn them as a pattern.
Silly Sentences	Make up a silly sentence from the first letter of each word to be remembered. *Even After Dinner, Giraffes Bend Easily (guitar strings E, A, D, G, B, E).*
Numbering	When you are memorizing a group of words, remember how many items there are to avoid missing any when you need to recall them.

Section 7.10

STRATEGY 2 DRAW*

1. Choose a short article, story, or content area chapter to read to your students.

2. Prepare a series of numbered questions about the selection at the literal, inferential, and applied levels of comprehension.

3. Distribute question sheets to students or to small groups of students.

4. Tell students that they will DRAW the passage. Explain that DRAW stands for Draw, Read, Attend, and Write.

5. Taking the sheet of questions about the passage, cut the sheet into strips so that one question is on each sentence strip. Mix up the question strips and have each individual or group draw one question.

6. Tell students that their group will be responsible for the question that they have drawn. Then have students read the passage.

7. After students have read the passage, ask a student to read and answer his or her question to the class. Ask the other students whether they agree or disagree with the answer to the question. Encourage students to pay attention to the class discussion. Explain that they will need to remember what they read and what other students said during the class discussion.

8. When all of the questions have been answered and discussed, gather the question slips to use as a quiz. Read the questions to the students and have students write the answers. Have students correct their responses to determine how much they remembered from the text.

*Agnew, 2000.

STRATEGY 3

REACTION GUIDE

1. Select a passage of text that students haven't read. Look for the most important facts that you want students to remember. An example of a passage about pyramids follows. Use the passage as a guide for this strategy.

2. Develop a series of sentences based on information from the passage. Print the sentences similar to the example that follows called Reaction Guide for Pyramid Article. The sentences should have a before reading column and an after reading column. Each of those columns should have the words *true* and *false*.

3. Duplicate and distribute the Reaction Guide to students before they have read the passage.

4. Tell students that sometimes you will alert them to the things they should remember from the text. Tell them that you would like them to predict the answers to the statements on the Reaction Guide. Have students answer *true* or *false* for each of the statements.

5. Ask students to read the passage and look for the correct answer to the statements. As they read, remind students to remember what they have learned.

6. After students have finished reading, have them complete the second column. Determine from their answers which students are having difficulty remembering what was read.

Pyramids

The Ancient Egyptians built many pyramids, but the most famous of these are the three pyramids of Giza, near Cairo, the capital of Egypt. Over the years, the city has gradually crept closer. Now there are new houses almost at the feet of the pyramids. But if you look at the pyramids across the city, they still rise up, silent and mysterious, on the edge of the great desert. For more than four thousand years, they have stood there, barely changed by the passage of time.

The largest of the three pyramids was built by King Khufu or King Cheops, to use his Greek name. This is called the Great Pyramid. It was the first to be built at Giza, in about 2500 B.C. The second largest is only a few feet lower and was built by Khafre (or Chephren in Greek), the son of Khufu. The third pyramid in this group is much smaller and was built by King Menkaure (or Mycerinus in Greek). All three pyramids were built in the space of about 80 years.

The Great Pyramid is made of limestone and is the same color as the sand and rock of the desert around it. There are no trees or other plants on this plain—just dry, open spaces. The pyramid soars to 137 meters above this—about as high as a 40-story modern skyscraper. A total of 2,300,000 blocks of stone, weighing between $2\frac{1}{2}$ and 5 tons each, were used to build the Great Pyramid. It is still the biggest stone building in the world. Assuming that the pyramid was completed within Khufu's 23-year reign, this means that some 100,000 of these huge blocks of stone had to be prepared and put into position each year—or 273 every day. The Great Pyramid was the most ambitious of the pharaoh's many great building works; in view of its huge size it is not surprising that is has been called "Pharaoh's Mountain."

Enormous though this monument is, the stone blocks are so accurately cut and so carefully fitted together (without mortar) that in many cases the joints will not allow even a sheet of paper to be inserted. The actual position of the Great Pyramid is also remarkably precise: its sides face almost exactly north, east, south and west. How was all this done? How could a people who lived so long ago and who only had very simple tools plan and carry out such a great project?

Reaction Guide for Pyramid Article

Directions:
- Before you read the article on pyramids, read each statement below. Depending on what you believe, circle true or false for each statement.
- After you read the article, decide if the statement is true or false based on the article. Circle the word to the right of each statement.

Before Reading				**After Reading**	
True	False	1.	Some pyramids are located near Cairo.	True	False
True	False	2.	The pyramids are over 10,000 years old.	True	False
True	False	3.	The three pyramids of Giza are quite famous.	True	False
True	False	4.	The Great Pyramid is called Khafre.	True	False
True	False	5.	The Great Pyramid is made of granite and is the biggest stone building in the world.	True	False
True	False	6.	There are over 3 million blocks of stone in the Great Pyramid.	True	False
True	False	7.	The blocks of stone weigh between $2^{1}/_{2}$ and 5 tons each.	True	False
True	False	8.	The Great Pyramid is taller than the Leaning Tower of Piza.	True	False
True	False	9.	Mortar was used to hold the blocks of stone together.	True	False
True	False	10.	The sides of the pyramid face almost exactly north, south, east, and west.	True	False

Practice and Reinforcement Activities

1. Encourage students to use a variety of memory devices. Ask them to use several different devices on the same information. Explain that different students will find some strategies more effective than others. Ask them which ones they thought worked best for them and why.

2. Have students keep Memory Journals. Tell students to record in their Memory Journal things they especially want to remember. Provide time for students to share special memories from their journals.

3. Tell students that a location often triggers memory. Provide an example similar to the following:

> *I was trying to remember the author of a book I had just read. I just couldn't remember. Then I thought about the book and pictured where it was located on my bookshelf. As I pictured the book, I remembered how the title page looked, and I thought of the author.*

Ask students to share times they used a location for memory. Encourage students to try this strategy when they are trying to remember what they read.

4. Tell students to use Post-It notes to write down things they want to remember as they read. Explain that thoughts can leave our memory if they are not written down. Provide students with Post-It notes when they read independently.

CHAPTER **8**

Involving Parents to Improve Reading

OVERVIEW

Parents and caregivers play an important role in the development of their children's reading achievement. They are their children's first teachers. From the moment of their children's birth, parents consciously and unconsciously model the values and knowledge they want their children to learn. Parents spend a great deal of time with their children, showing them how to develop into successful adults who can care for themselves, earn a living, function in society, and read (Purcell-Gates, 2000).

The vast majority of parents care very much about their children's learning, and all parents contribute to the language and literacy development of their children (Goldstein, 2000). Even in homes where parents themselves are not highly literate, spoken language and written language are used to negotiate daily life. Most parents from all walks of life read print texts such as signs, billboards, lists, notes, advertisements, and newspapers. Many parents also read to their children and experience other types of reading activities with them. Since children spend only 9% of their time in school and 91% of their time outside school under the guidance of parents, the reading and writing activities children experience in the home are of the utmost importance (Kearns, 1993).

Some parents, however, are unfamiliar with schooling and the language of schooling. An increasing number of parents who have had little or no schooling and who may have low literacy levels will be part of the schools of the coming decade (Meier, 2000). However, "when parents are welcomed as partners in their child's 'educational team,' a bridge connecting the child's home and school environment is created, which empowers parents to be active participants in their child's development" (Morningstar, 1999, p. 693). Involving parents in the schooling of their children can improve children's reading achievement.

There are many things that parents can do to help their children become better readers. Parents can help their children recognize the connection between the reading they do at school and the reading they do at home. Parents can provide their children with more experiences with books, and they can help motivate their children to read. Parents can also help their children learn how to decode words, read fluently, comprehend text, become more interested in reading, and complete schoolwork at home. Many parents are already involved in helping their children improve reading in these ways. The strategies and activities in this chapter can provide additional ideas for ways to involve parents in order to improve the reading achievement of your students.

Note: The term *parents* is used throughout this chapter, but our intention is that the term *parents* can include other adults who act as caregivers for children.

Parents are their children's first teachers.

TECHNOLOGY RESOURCE

Internet Public Library Reading Zone–Picture Books

http://www.ipl.org/cgi-bin/youth.out.pl?sub=rzn2000
Contains illustrated stories for young children

Experiences with Books

Behavior Observed	The student has had few experiences with books.
Anticipated Outcome	Parents will provide their child with additional experiences with books.

BACKGROUND

Students who have had many experiences with books in their early years will have a greater likelihood of becoming proficient readers (Purcell-Gates, 2000). Students come to school with a variety of early literacy experiences—the difference can be thousands of hours. Therefore, when teachers conclude that students seem to have had few experiences with books, they should ask the parents of those students to become involved in the students' schooling by providing the children with additional literacy experiences.

One of the best services that a school can offer parents is suggestions about how they can make their homes conducive to reading. At this time, there is no other societal structure that assists parents in helping their children learn. Perhaps the need for home literacy experiences is

more important to this generation than it was in the past. Many families in our society do not know what to do to support their children's learning, because they did not experience it during their formative years (Field & Spangler, 2000). The literacy demands for students today, however, are much higher than they were for the parents of your students, and by the time your students graduate from high school, the demands for reading, writing, speaking, and using technology will have increased even more. To help students in classrooms meet the literacy demands of our present society, we need to offer suggestions to parents about ways to provide their children with additional literacy experiences.

This section presents strategies and activities to help parents provide their children with additional experiences with books.

STRATEGY 1 READING AT HOME

1. Remind students that they read books at school and that they should also read books at home. Provide an example of a book students have read in school. Include examples of books that you have read aloud to them, that students have read in small groups, and that students have read as an entire class. Say something like the following:

 We've read many books so far in school this year. Sometimes I have read aloud to you; sometimes you have read with other students; and sometimes you have read books alone. I know that sometimes you look through books without reading every word. That's all right. The more times you look through books and read some or all of the words, the better reader you will be.

2. Tell students that they are going to make a list of reading ideas that they can use at home with their parents. Explain to students that they should be reading books at home every day and that reading at home can consist of having a parent read to them, reading with friends and/or relatives, and reading alone. Say something like the following:

 Just as we read in many ways at school, you can read in lots of ways at home. You should be reading books at home every day. Remember, even if you can't read every word in a book, you are practicing reading.

3. Ask students about their experiences reading at school. Provide them with examples such as the following ones.

 > We read many different kinds of books.
 > We read in different places in the classroom.
 > We read aloud as a group.

4. Have students generate their own ideas. Write them down on the chalkboard or on an overhead transparency. Revise the list as needed.

5. Tell students that you will be sending home a letter to their parents that gives their parents suggestions about reading at home. Tell students that you will be adding their ideas to the list.

6. Type or print the students' ideas on the lines next to the title, *Ideas From Your Child.* Older students may want to type their own lists for the letter. Revise the letter as needed to adapt to your teaching situation.

7. Tell students that they can use any font and ink color to print the letter. Check the students' work, help them correct any mistakes, and then send the list home to parents in decorated envelopes. A sample letter follows.

Dear Parents,

Children need a great deal of practice reading. Whenever someone learns something new, he or she needs to learn new techniques and then practice, practice, practice. At school, I spend time teaching your child reading skills and there is time to read, but not nearly enough. It would help tremendously if you would provide a time and place for your child to read at home. Enclosed are some suggestions about ways you can accomplish reading at home.

Sincerely,

Reading At Home: How Parents Can Help

- ✓ Read aloud to your children, young and old, every day.
- ✓ Alternate parents reading aloud with your children so both male and female models are given.
- ✓ Read and write often for authentic purposes to serve as a model for your children.
- ✓ Read a novel to your children on long car trips or tape-record books for them to listen to during the ride.
- ✓ Set up a neighborhood Reading Circle where parents and children get together to read and discuss their favorite books.
- ✓ Encourage your children to select books by interest and not necessarily by reading level. Children who are interested in a particular topic may enjoy a book on that subject that they might otherwise consider too easy or too difficult.
- ✓ Discuss books with your children.
- ✓ Encourage your children to write a journal or diary from the perspective of the main character in the book being read.
- ✓ Have your children make hand puppets and act out a book they have read.
- ✓ Encourage your children to explore answers to questions by using informational books.

Ideas from your child_____

From Jerry L. Johns and Susan Davis Lenski, *Improving Reading: Strategies and Resources* (3rd ed.). Copyright © 2001 Kendall/ Hunt Publishing Company (1-800-247-3458, ext.5). May be reproduced for noncommercial educational purposes.

STRATEGY 2 CREATING A READING HOME

1. Tell students that you often read books at home. Tell students how often you read at home, where you read, and the kinds of books you read. Provide examples of the books that your read at home. For example you might say something like the following:

 When I go home from school, I'm usually pretty tired. As soon as I get home, I get a drink of juice and sit in my recliner for 20 minutes reading a book. I usually read books from the library, but sometimes I buy books from a discount store. I set my timer for 20 minutes and just enjoy the book for that amount of time. After 20 minutes are up, I begin my household chores. I also read before and after I put my own children to bed. Before their bedtime, I read stories to them. I let them pick their own stories most nights. After the children are in bed, I read magazines and professional journals for at least 45 minutes. After that I begin correcting the papers you have completed in school that day.

2. Ask students how often they read books at home. Allow time for students to respond.

3. Then discuss where you like to read. Tell students that they can read in many different places and that they do not have to sit at a desk to read. For example, say:

 When it's nice outside, I read on the porch swing or in a hammock in our backyard. When it's cold or rainy, I sit in a beanbag chair in the family room.

4. Ask students where they like to read at home. Allow time for students to respond.

5. Explain to students that most good readers spend time reading at home and that they will become better readers if they read every day. Tell them that having several comfortable places to read at home will help them want to read.

6. Provide students with suggested amounts of times to read at home. You might recommend that younger students read 10 minutes daily and older students might read 30 minutes.

7. Tell students that their parents can help create *A Reading Home* to help them as they develop a reading routine. Explain to students that you have prepared a letter that is in the form of a quiz for their parents that asks them about their reading areas.

8. Duplicate the letter that follows, sign your name, and distribute it to your students. Ask students to take the letter to their parents and remind students that they need to read at home every day.

Dear Parents,

One of the best ways you can help your child in reading is to make your home a place for reading. I've listed some ideas for you to consider.

Please read this list and circle "yes" for those you have and "no" for those you do not have. Then think about which ones you would want to add to your home routine. You should try to do as many as possible, but I know that there are times when some of them probably won't work in your family situation. You should consider your home a Reading Home if you are able to accomplish many of the items on this list. I welcome any other ideas you may have so our list can grow.

Sincerely,

Creating a Reading Home

Does the place where you live have

✓	an inviting area or corner for reading?	Yes	No
✓	a wide variety of books and magazines for all family members?	Yes	No
✓	a regular time for reading?	Yes	No
✓	a collection of "how to" books?	Yes	No
✓	shelves, crates, or boxes for storing books?	Yes	No
✓	places for writing messages?	Yes	No
✓	places to display notes, writings, and drawings?	Yes	No
✓	different kinds of paper for writing?	Yes	No
✓	crayons, markers, pencils, and pens?	Yes	No
✓	comfortable chairs for reading?	Yes	No
✓	a library card for checking out books?	Yes	No

STRATEGY 3 BACKPACK ACTIVITY

1. Fill a brightly colored backpack with items that promote reading and writing activities. These could include a variety of short books, paper, pencils, crayons, colored pencils, colored chalk, and construction paper.

2. Write a letter to parents telling them how to use this backpack with their child or use the sample letter that follows.

3. Duplicate and sign the letter and place it in an envelope inside the backpack.

4. Tell students that you have a special surprise for them. Explain to students that they need to read more at home and that you have compiled a backpack with reading and writing materials for them to use at home. Tell students that they will be able to take the backpack home for a few nights and use the materials. Encourage students to bring to school any writing they have completed or artwork they have drawn to show the rest of the class.

5. Ask a student who needs more experiences with books to take the backpack home. Have the student identify which day would be best. Give the student two or three days to read the books in the backpack, use the writing materials, and enjoy the experience.

6. When the backpack is returned, have the student share any writing or artwork with the class. Ask the student to talk about one of the books in the backpack. Then give the backpack to another student to take home. Replace materials and add appropriate books as needed.

Dear Parent,

In this backpack are all of the supplies you need to have a fun literacy experience with your child. Please feel free to use any of the supplies in the backpack to create a story, picture, or piece of art. Included in this backpack are some short books that you and your child could read together. Enjoy the books and materials, and please have your child return the backpack to school in two or three days.

Sincerely,

STRATEGY 4

READING ACTIVITIES

1. Tell students that they engage in many activities at home that use reading and writing. Explain to students that, when they do simple reading and writing tasks at home, they are practicing literacy and becoming better readers.

2. Provide several examples of reading and writing activities that students may be engaged in at home. Write the activities on the chalkboard, an overhead transparency, or chart paper. Some examples follow.

> writing to friends and relatives
>
> reading letters from friends and relatives
>
> keeping score at a sporting event
>
> playing word games
>
> writing messages

3. Ask students to share additional types of reading and writing activities that they do at home. Write down the students' suggestions under your own ideas.

4. Tell students that their parents can benefit from the ideas from the entire class. Explain to students that you have a letter that includes several reading activities for children of various grade levels and that you will be adding suggestions from the class to the list.

5. Revise the letter that follows to include your own ideas and ideas from the students. Then duplicate, sign, and distribute the letter to students. Suggest that students display the letter in a prominent place in their home. Occasionally, remind students to engage in reading activities at home.

Dear Parents,

Many of you have more than one child at home, and you have been asking me about appropriate reading activities for children of different ages. Enclosed is a list of suggestions of reading activities for children of different ages. I've decided to send this letter home with every child in my room. There are many good ideas on this list that you might find useful.

Sincerely,

Reading Activities

Preschoolers
- ✓ Read a bedtime story.
- ✓ Read the same books over and over.
- ✓ Give your child markers or paper and pencils.
- ✓ Give your child a chalkboard and chalk.
- ✓ Write messages to your child.
- ✓ Label your child's possessions.
- ✓ Put magnetic letters on the refrigerator.

Five and Six Year Olds
- ✓ You read to me and I'll read to you.
- ✓ Fill in the blanks. Read poetry and verse that rhymes and stop before the end of the line, having your child fill in the blank.
- ✓ Play sound games. A simple starter is, "Riddle, riddle, ree. I see something you don't see and it starts with T."
- ✓ Create a newspaper.
- ✓ Write a wish list.
- ✓ Make a calendar.
- ✓ Write a fill-in-the-blank story.
- ✓ Write a biography or autobiography.
- ✓ Make a board game.
- ✓ Start a memory box.
- ✓ Cook from a book.

Seven and Eight Year Olds
- ✓ Write a book about something real or imagined.
- ✓ Keep a journal.
- ✓ Write a thank-you letter.
- ✓ Write your own cards.
- ✓ Keep score at sports events.
- ✓ Start a scrapbook.
- ✓ Explore your family's letters and albums.

Nine and Ten Year Olds
- ✓ Read riddles.
- ✓ Play thinking games.
- ✓ Work on projects.
- ✓ Support scout activities.
- ✓ Write fractured fairy tales.
- ✓ Create a camera story.
- ✓ Write a text for wordless books.

Eleven and Twelve Year Olds
- ✓ Put a book in your child's room.
- ✓ Tell about a book you enjoyed.
- ✓ Start your child on a new series.
- ✓ Share newspaper articles.
- ✓ Keep a journal.
- ✓ Discuss materials read.

Practice and Reinforcement Activities

1. Send home short books in plastic bags every night that students have already read. Tell students to read them with their parents or to someone at home. Explain to students that often adults are busy, and they can read their books to a stuffed animal or toy if no one has the time to hear them read. Remind students that reading at home will help them become better readers.

2. Send home information about obtaining library cards and events at bookstores.

3. Develop lists of Books Too Good to Miss several times during the year. Send home lists for parents to use.

4. Initiate a Family Read Aloud program. Encourage the family to pick a book at the child's level and set time aside, either at night or on the weekend, when the whole family sits down together and reads the book. Encourage discussion and possible extension activities using the questions that follow.

? Did this story turn out the way you thought it would? Why or why not?

What made this book interesting?

Is the main character someone you would like to have as a friend?

If you were the author, how would you have changed the ending?

Is this a book you would recommend to a friend?

In which other events would you like to see the main character involved?

How would the story change if it took place in our town?

Have you ever experienced some of the events or feelings that the main character had experienced?

Would you enjoy reading other books by this author?

What do you think would happen in a sequel to this book?

5. Encourage parents to have a book bag in their car with library or paperback books. Explain to parents that students having quick access to books will encourage them to read at various times. Ask parents to remind their children to read while waiting in the car.

6. Invite parents to send in pictures of their children at various ages. Attach the pictures to folded construction paper and have students write stories about the pictures. Have a blank page after each story for parents to use for writing. Cut the folded pieces of paper into a book. On the final page, suggest that parents write stories on the blank pages. Send the book home and encourage students to read it with their parents.

Some students get excited about reading books on CD-ROMs.

7. Recommend lists of books on CD-ROMs that parents can use at home. Some students would rather read books on the computer. Reassure parents that reading books on the computer can provide students with quality practice in reading.

8. Encourage students to write and make their own books. Circulate them within the classroom. In the front cover have a note that explains that this book was written by a student in your class, that it should be read and reread at home, and that it should be returned to school the next day. Then develop a library of student-authored books that students can check out and take home to read. Several suggestions on ways to make books at home follow. Duplicate and distribute to parents the following pages as appropriate.

Ideas for Publishing Student Writing

Students can make individual bound books to take home, put in the classroom or school library, present to a special person as a gift, or donate to a younger student or class.

Book Binding Formats

Type of Book	Directions	Sample
Shape Book	Make pages and cover in the shape of object. For example, make a fish shape for a book about fish. Fasten together with staples, duct tape, or yarn.	THE PUMPKIN PATCH / FUN FACTS / The Day I Turned Into a Pencil!
Ring Book	Punch holes in pages and cover and fasten together with chicken rings (available at a feed supply store), shower curtain rings, or metal binder rings (available at office supply stores).	OUR POEMS
Stapled Book	Staple together pages and cover. Then use duct tape along the spine for added strength and durability.	**Outer Space Race**
Flip Book	Fold three sheets of 8½" x 11" paper so one sheet has a 3-inch flap, one has a 4-inch flap, and one has a 5-inch flap. Line up the folds and use a long-arm stapler to fasten the pages.	
Fold-out Book	Fold paper accordion style. Then staple or glue to covers.	My number Book 1 2 3 4 5

Making a Book

Materials Needed

2 pieces of heavy cardboard

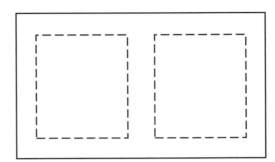

1 piece of fabric
(allow 1" on all sides)

Pieces of white paper (slightly
smaller than the 2 cardboards
laid together).

**Button
thread**

2 pieces of drymount (one
slightly smaller than the fabric
and one slightly smaller than
the white paper pages) or
rubber cement.

Procedure

1.

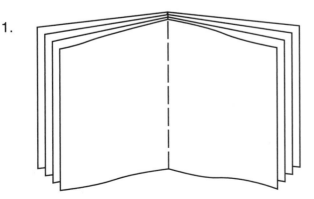

Fold sheets of white
paper in half.

Sew together with button
thread on the fold.

From Jerry L. Johns and Susan Davis Lenski, *Improving Reading: Strategies and Resources* (3rd ed.). Copyright © 2001 Kendall/
Hunt Publishing Company (1-800-247-3458, ext. 5). May be reproduced for noncommercial educational purposes.

Making a Book (continued)

2.

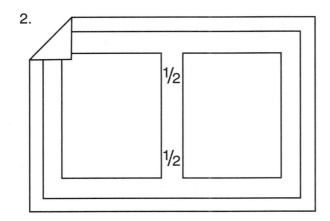

Cover of Book

Lay drymount on the fabric, then place cardboard pieces on the drymount. Leave about 1/2" space between the cardboard pieces.

Fold corners down, as illustrated, and press with a warm iron. Next, fold the four sides over and press onto cardboard. Turn and press on the other side.

After pressing

3.

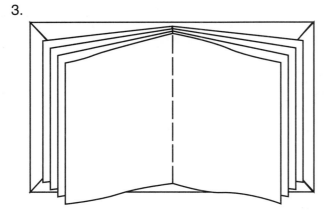

Place another sheet of drymount between cover and first and last pages. Press.

Fold to make a book.

Word-Solving Skills

Behavior Observed	The student does not know word-solving skills.
Anticipated Outcome	Parents practice word-building and word-solving activities with their child.

BACKGROUND

When readers encounter a word they don't know, they face a problem that must be solved. That's word solving. Word solving is the ability to recognize words, take them apart, and put them together in order to read (Pinnell & Fountas, 1998). Some students learn word-solving skills easily, but others need a great deal of practice, more practice than you have time for in school. Parents can provide their children with the types of word-building activities that give readers clues when reading. These clues can help them solve words. Parents can also help their children solve words when the children are reading aloud. When the children come to an unknown word, parents can ask questions that will help their children figure out that word. Word-building and word-solving activities can help students who experience difficulty in reading.

Section 8.2

STRATEGY 1 WORD-SOLVING BOOKMARK

1. Tell students that, when they come across a word that they don't know, they can use a variety of strategies to solve the word. Provide students with an example of the strategies you use to solve words. For example, say the following:

 I was reading a book last night and I came across the word locution. *I had never seen the word before, but I was able to use what I know about the sounds represented by the letters and word chunks to say the word. Once I said the word, I realized that I had heard it before, and I was able to figure out what it meant.*

2. Tell students that there are a variety of strategies they can use to solve words. Explain that you used two strategies to figure out a word but that there are many others.

3. Adapt the bookmarks on the following page as needed and duplicate them on sturdy paper. Distribute bookmarks to students.

Problem Solving
Unknown Words

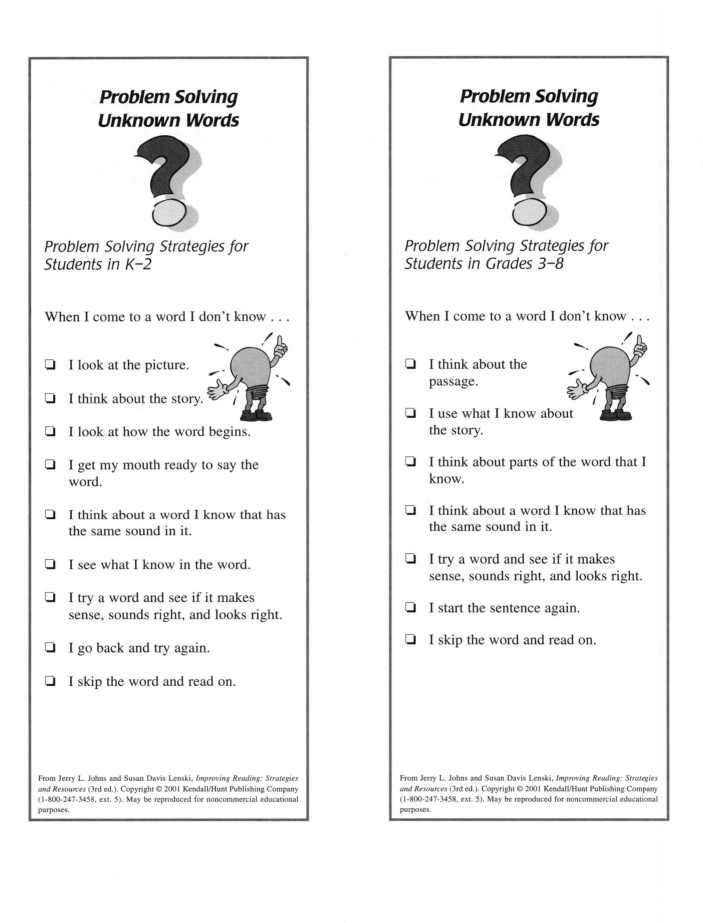

Problem Solving Strategies for Students in K–2

When I come to a word I don't know . . .

❏ I look at the picture.

❏ I think about the story.

❏ I look at how the word begins.

❏ I get my mouth ready to say the word.

❏ I think about a word I know that has the same sound in it.

❏ I see what I know in the word.

❏ I try a word and see if it makes sense, sounds right, and looks right.

❏ I go back and try again.

❏ I skip the word and read on.

Problem Solving
Unknown Words

Problem Solving Strategies for Students in Grades 3–8

When I come to a word I don't know . . .

❏ I think about the passage.

❏ I use what I know about the story.

❏ I think about parts of the word that I know.

❏ I think about a word I know that has the same sound in it.

❏ I try a word and see if it makes sense, sounds right, and looks right.

❏ I start the sentence again.

❏ I skip the word and read on.

4. Tell students that the Problem Solving Unknown Words bookmarks contain strategies students can use to figure out unknown words. Read the strategies with students and explain as necessary.

5. Have students take their bookmarks home to use as they read with their parents or as they read alone. Tell students to show the bookmarks to their parents and have students explain the strategies they should use to solve unknown words.

6. Tell students that their parents can remind them of word-solving strategies as they read with their parents.

Section 8.2

STRATEGY 2 SOUND WHEEL

1. Duplicate on sturdy paper the Sound Wheel on the following page.

2. Cut out the Sound Wheel and make a spinner by attaching a slightly open paper clip. Push the point of the paper clip through the center of the Sound Wheel to make a spinner.

3. Place the sound wheel on a table. Spin the paper clip. When the spinner stops, say a word that begins with that sound combination. For example, say something like the following:

 My spinner landed on sp *so I need to think of a word that begins with* sp. *Here's one: spinner!*

4. Have students spin the paper clip. Say the sound of the letter combination indicated by the spinner. Then encourage students to think of a word that begins with that sound.

5. Repeat the game until students are comfortable with the rules.

6. Place the Sound Wheel with its spinner in a bag. Have students take home the Sound Wheel to play with their parents. Tell students to play the Sound Wheel frequently.

7. After several days, send home a new Sound Wheel with different letter combinations in the spaces.

Sound Wheel

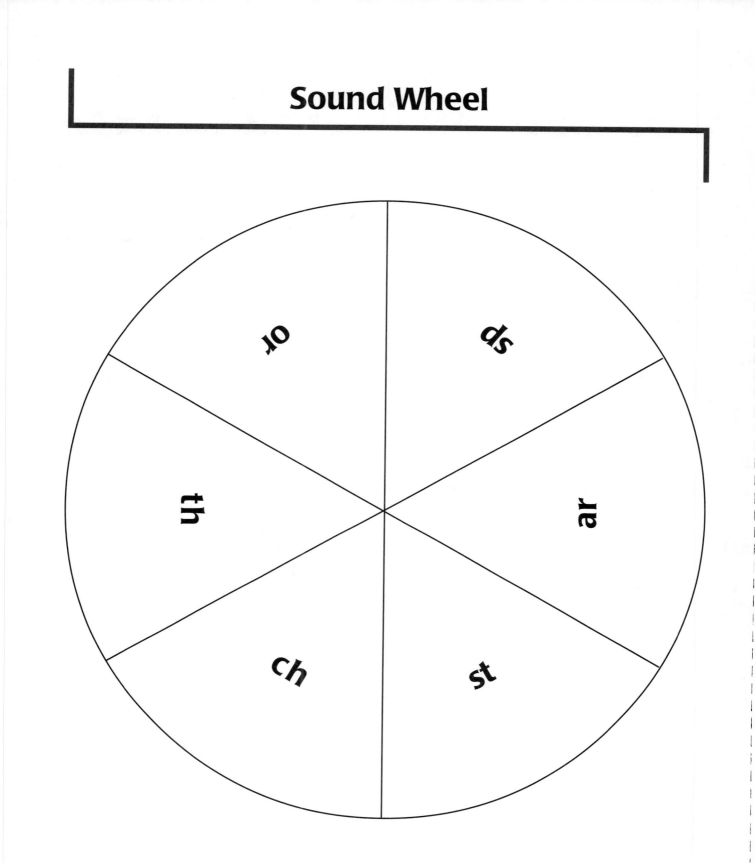

STRATEGY 3 FIVE BY FIVE*

1. Duplicate on sturdy paper the Five by Five grid and the letters. Cut out the individual letters.

2. Distribute copies of the grid and the letters to students.

3. Place the letters face up on the table in front of you. Have students also turn their letters face up.

4. Think of a word that has five or fewer letters, for example, *jam*. Place the word in the first line, using one letter per square.

J A M

5. Tell students what you have done by saying something like the following: "I was thinking about the breakfast I ate this morning. I had toast and jam, so I thought of the word *jam*. I put the *J* in the first box, *A* in the second box, and *M* in the third box."

6. Have students think of a word to fit in the first line of their Five by Five grid.

7. Then think of a word for the second line with the remaining letters, for example, *curb*. Model how you thought of the word. Place this second word under the first word.

<p align="center">J A M
C U R B</p>

8. Have students think of a word for the second line on their grid.

9. Continue the game until you have listed five words, as in the example that follows. (It will become increasingly more difficult to think of words since you cannot repeat any of the consonant letters.)

J A M
C U R B
F I L E
T O E
K I N D

10. Have students fill their cards with five words.

11. After students have finished, encourage them to try to find words made by their letter combinations. Have them identify hidden words as in the example that follows.

12. After students understand how to play the game, place the grids and letters in a bag. Have students take home the game to play with their family.

*Hall, 1997.

Five by Five

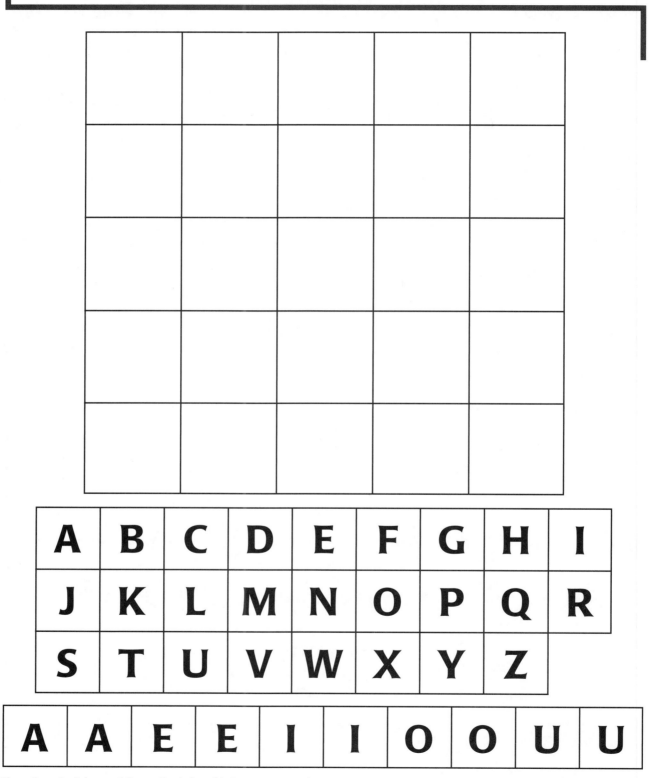

A	B	C	D	E	F	G	H	I
J	K	L	M	N	O	P	Q	R
S	T	U	V	W	X	Y	Z	

A	A	E	E	I	I	O	O	U	U

Practice and Reinforcement Activities

1. Label items in your classroom such as your desk, the chalkboard, and so on. Print the labels in different colors. Have students "read the room" by pointing to all the labeled items and reading the words on the labels. Then have students list items in their rooms at home that could be labeled. Write the labels at school and give them to students to take home. Remind the students to have their parents help them read their rooms at home.

2. Write a word ladder for students by creating new words in a vertical column. Write one word, such as cat. Add, delete, or change one letter in the word to make a new word, such as car. Continue the process until you have written several words as in the example below. Have students read the words with you and then have students read them independently. Send the word ladder home. Ask parents to create a similar word ladder to read with their children.

Word Ladder	New Word Ladder
cat	fit
car	
care	
card	
yard	
lard	
laid	
paid	
pain	

3. Develop a word stair with students. Ask students to think of a word. Write the word on an unlined piece of paper. Using the original word, build a new word on one of the letters. Continue the process. Have students read all of the words. You may need to read the words with students before they read them independently. Have students take the word stair home to read with their parents. Encourage parents to make word stairs with their children.

4. Play recordings of songs, chants, rhymes, and jingles with students. Have students sing along with the recordings using a printed text. Emphasize how words sound when they rhyme. When the students know the songs or rhymes well, have students bring home the recordings to practice. Give students several days to practice.

5. Find a small box. Label the box "wild-word cage" (Cicciarelli, 1997). Draw bars on the box to make it look like a cage. Write words the students have solved in school on cards and place the cards in the box. Have students take the box home over the weekend to practice with parents.

6. Play a variety of rhyming games with children such as rhyming concentration, rhyming bingo, sorting rhyming words, inventing rhymes, and reading books of rhymes (Bear, Invernizzi, Templeton, & Johnston, 2000). Rhyming words can give students knowledge of sounds of words. Encourage students to play those rhyming games with their children.

7. Write on a piece of cardboard sentences that students can read. Include one "new" word that students should be able to solve independently. Cut the words apart and place them in an envelope. Have the students take the envelope home to work with their parents to put the words together in a sentence and read the sentence.

8. Gather together several magazines and a large sheet of construction paper. Write a letter on the sheet such as the letter *t*. Say several words that begin with *t*, such as top, table, and tinsel. Have students repeat the words with you and say other words that begin with the letter *t*. Then look through magazines, saying the names of the items represented on the pages of the magazine. When you say the name of an item that begins with *t*, have the students cut out that picture and paste it on the construction paper. Repeat with one or more additional pictures. When students have a few pictures on the page, have students take home the construction paper and find several more pictures to place on the page. Send home the magazine, blunt-edged scissors, and paste so students can work with their parents to add more pictures to the page.

9. Have magnetic letters or plastic letters available for sale in the school store or at a school bazaar. Have ideas for solving words on a sheet to give to parents who purchase the letters.

10. Help children figure out words in context by reading sentences with words left out. For example, read the sentence:

The small puppy wagged its _____.

Tell students that they can figure out the word by the rest of the sentence. Provide sentences with a key word left out for students to read at home. Remind students that they can solve the word by using the rest of the sentence (Wilson, Hall, Leu, & Kinzer, 2001).

Reading Fluency

SECTION
8.3

Behavior Observed	The student does not read fluently.
Anticipated Outcome	Parents practice reading with their child to help build fluency.

BACKGROUND

Many students are able to read words, but they do not read fluently. These students' reading may be disjointed and choppy, and they may have difficulty comprehending the story because of their lack of reading fluency. Becoming fluent takes time and practice, and it is a perfect skill for students to build at home.

Many parents are able to help their children build reading fluency at home. However, some parents have limitations that prevent them from doing as much as they would like to help their children. Some parents feel insecure about their own reading ability, either because they have difficulty themselves with reading or they cannot read English. Asking parents to provide their children with reading practice that builds fluency can help those parents who have shaky reading skills while they are helping their children (Edwards, 1995).

Section 8.3

STRATEGY 1 ECHO READING

1. Choose a book that you think the student will be able to read independently. The book should be easy enough so that the student can read practically all of the words easily.

2. Sit next to and slightly behind the student. Place the book in front of the student so that both of you can read it.

3. Tell the student that you will be reading with him or her. Say something like the following:

 As you read this book, I'll be reading with you. Sometimes I'll whisper the words, sometimes I'll read in a regular voice, and sometimes I'll be quiet as you read. If you come across a word you don't know, you can listen to the way I figure out the word. This kind of reading is called Echo Reading.

4. Place your mouth directly behind a student's ear. Read with the student. When the student has difficulty with a word, stretch out the word so that the student can hear the word parts and the sounds in the word. Read with expression.

5. Tell the student that this type of reading practice can build reading fluency.

6. After the student is familiar with Echo Reading, suggest that the student Echo Read with his or her parents. Say something like the following:

 You can read with your parents like you do in school. Your parents can also help you listen for word parts and word sounds as you read. You already know how to Echo Read. I'm going to send a letter about Echo Reading home with you so that your parents can Echo Read with you.

7. Revise the following letter to fit your classroom situation. Then duplicate, sign, and distribute the letter to parents. Remind students to try Echo Reading with their parents, and when you communicate with parents, reinforce the need for this practice.

Dear Parents,

One of the ways your child is learning to read fluently is by reading with a more skilled reader using a strategy called Echo Reading. In school, your child reads with me and other readers. Reading along with a more skilled reader is both fun for your child and a good learning experience. Echo Reading is described below. Try it and enjoy.

1. Choose a book that your child can read easily. To find out whether your child can read a particular book, open the book and have your child read a randomly chosen page aloud. If your child stumbles on more than one word out of every 10 words, select an easier book.

2. Place your child on your lap or near you. Hold the book together with your child.

3. Read the book with expression in a soft voice. Have your child read with you. Encourage your child to read with expression.

4. As your child's reading becomes more fluent, decrease the volume of your voice until the child is reading alone.

5. Congratulate your child on his or her reading. Remember, your child is learning to read and may make many errors. It's the practice that counts.

 Sincerely,

STRATEGY 2 STORY-READING IDEAS

1. Make a book for parents using ideas that develop reading fluency. Use the ideas on the following page or write your own ideas. Cut out each statement and affix it to a page in a book made of construction paper.

2. Show students the book that you have made. Tell students that they will be making a similar book and taking it home to their parents. Say something like the following:

 This book contains ideas for your parents to help you become a better reader. You will be making a book like this one. After you've finished your book, you can take it home and give it to your parents. Remind your parents to use the book as they help you read.

3. Provide students with the numbered pages of their book. Have the words already on the pages.

4. Read the pages to the students and then instruct them to illustrate each page of the book, showing the idea on the page.

5. Have students make front and back covers for the book. When the covers are complete, use the book publishing station in your classroom or learning center to put books together.

6. Have students share their books with each other; then send them home.

7. Remind students to read their books with their parents.

Story-Reading Ideas

1. Select a book that your child can read with few errors. (Only one of every 20 words should be unknown.)

2. Read the book to your child.

3. Read the book again, asking your child to read with you.

4. Ask your child to read the book alone.

5. Read the book again, this time with expression.

6. Encourage your child to read the book with expression.

7. Leave the book in a place where your child can read it independently.

8. Encourage your child to read the book on a tape recorder, to a friend, or to a relative.

STRATEGY 3 READING CALENDAR

1. Tell students that you will be making a Reading Calendar with reading activities on each date for them to take home.

2. Have students brainstorm ideas that they feel should be on the calendar that month. Provide students with suggestions such as read with parents, read to pet, read or look at the newspaper, read recipes in a cookbook, and so on.

3. Write the students' ideas on the chalkboard or on an overhead transparency. Revise the students' list as needed and add suggestions of your own.

4. Discuss with students which activities should be on the different days of the month and list the activities in order.

5. Prepare and distribute a blank calendar to each student. Use a transparency of the calendar on an overhead projector to fill in the activities and the dates.

6. Have students number the days of the calendars. Then ask students to fill in reading activities for each day.

7. Let students decorate the calendars with crayons, markers, stickers, or stamps. Send the calendars home with students.

8. Remind students to complete the reading activities on their reading calendars.

Practice and Reinforcement Activities

1. Write a sentence each day on sentence strips. Have the student read the sentence several times. Then send the sentence home with the student to practice reading at home.

2. Make audiotapes of the student's favorite books. Play the audiotape and read the book with the student. Then have the student read alone with the tape. After the student experiences success reading the book fluently, place the audiotape and the book in a large plastic bag and have the student take it home. Remind the student to read the book with the tape several times during the next several days.

3. Have a Listening Pet Day where students take home books to read to pets. Explain to students that they can read to a pet, or, if they don't have a pet, they can create an imaginary pet to read to. After Listening Pet Day, have students draw pictures of their pets and write a bit about the book.

4. Have students read and reread a favorite book. Then have students make up some music for the words to the book. Encourage students to "sing the book" at school. When they feel ready, encourage them to take the book home and sing for their parents.

5. Have a small group of students tell an "add-on" story in class. Tape-record your activity. Begin the story with "Once upon a time," and then have the next student in line add another section to the story. After everyone in the group has contributed a part of the plot, conclude the story with an appropriate ending. Transcribe the audiotape onto lined paper and duplicate copies for students. Have students take the story home to read to their families. Then encourage the students to create an "add-on" story at home.

6. Watch students during recess and listen for repeated sayings or rhymes. Transcribe the rhymes onto chart paper. Tell students that you have written some rhymes on chart paper that will be familiar to them. Have students read the rhymes several times until their reading is fluent. Tell students that they are reading fluently. Then copy the rhymes on paper or have students copy them. Have students take home their rhymes and read them to their parents.

7. Have a What a Character party in your class. Have students select a book with a main character whom the other students would recognize. Ask students to choose a portion of the book to read aloud to the class. Encourage students to practice fluent reading of the passage at home. Request that each student dress like the character or bring one prop that would identify the character. At the What a Character party, have students take turns sharing their selected passages with other students.

8. Gather lined paper and construction paper and assemble a book for every student. Have students write *Family Stories* on the cover of the book. Ask students to take the book home for family members to use to record stories. Have students select a story from their Family Stories to practice reading fluently. Then have students share their stories with a small group of classmates.

Understanding While Reading

Behavior Observed	The student does not understand what is read.
Anticipated Outcome	Parents will work with their child to increase understanding while reading.

BACKGROUND

The goal of reading is comprehension, or constructing meaning from text. Students who are able to pronounce words but who have little or no understanding of what was read need to develop better comprehension skills and strategies. The bulk of comprehension instruction should be conducted at school. However, involving parents in developing their children's comprehension is also a way to promote learning.

- Parents can provide their children with reading activities to give them additional practice reading.
- Parents can encourage their children to think about the story by asking key questions.
- Parents can also guide their children toward greater understanding of the structure of stories.
- Parents of children who have difficulty understanding text should be encouraged to use the activities that follow.

Section 8.4

STRATEGY 1	**PARENT CHECKLIST**

1. Tell students that there are many reasons why people have difficulty understanding what they read. Explain that there are times that you have difficulty understanding some text. Provide an example of a text that is difficult for you. An example follows.

 I was trying to read the directions on how to assemble a new computer table. As I was reading, I found that I had to reread many sections, stop and look up a few words in a dictionary, and carefully read the graphics. I found the reading very challenging.

2. Have students tell you about texts that are difficult for them. Allow ample time for discussion.

3. Tell students that their parents can help them understand reading, but that parents need to become aware of the components that help promote good reading understanding.

4. Read the Parent Checklist that follows and revise it as needed. Duplicate and distribute the checklist to students. Have the students give the checklist to their parents.

Parent Checklist

Name _____

Grade _____

Date _____

> **Directions:** Please indicate your observation of your child's learning in the following areas and comment where appropriate.

	Yes	No	Comments
My child likes to listen to me read to him or her.			
My child likes to read to me.			
My child attempts to read in daily situations, that is, signs, labels, and other print.			
My child understands books I read to him or her.			
My child attempts to figure out words.			
My child sometimes chooses to write.			
My child shares what he or she writes.			
My child is provided with the opportunity to visit the public library often.			

STRATEGY 2 STORY-READING IDEAS

1. Choose a book to read to your students. Before reading the book, show students the title and the illustrations, discuss what you already know about the topic, and ask the students to predict what will happen in the story. Then begin to read.

2. During reading, encourage students to visualize the story and ask them to predict what will happen. If the book has illustrations, have the students talk about the illustrations.

3. After you have finished reading, ask students to retell the story or to retell the story from the point of view of one of the characters.

4. Explain to students that when reading they should think about the story before, during, and after reading. Then tell students that they can use these same techniques when reading at home.

5. Duplicate the letter that follows, sign each letter, and distribute them to students. Tell students that the letter for their parents explains the before, during, and after reading steps that they should follow as they read. Send the letters home.

Dear Parents,

Many of you are reading with your child at home. There are a few techniques that will make your reading time even more beneficial for your child. At school, when I read a story, I use special techniques to help students understand the story. I'd like to share these story-reading ideas with you.

Sincerely,

Story-Reading Ideas

Before reading

✓ Look at the title and illustrations together. Predict what the story will be about.

✓ Discuss what you both already know about the topic of the story.

✓ Read the first page and then ask your child to predict what might happen next.

During reading

✓ Encourage your child to picture in his or her mind what is happening in the story.

✓ Ask what might happen next in the story.

✓ Have your child change his or her predictions as the story provides new information.

✓ Ask how a character might feel.

✓ Talk about the illustrations.

After reading

✓ Have your child retell the story and create a new ending together.

✓ Retell the story from another character's point of view.

✓ Let your child illustrate his or her favorite part of the story.

✓ Discuss the story together.

STRATEGY 3 PLOT RELATIONSHIPS CHART*

1. Pick a story that has clear plot elements: characters, goal, problem, and solution. *Jamaica Tag-Along* by Juanita Havill (1990) works well for this strategy.

2. Read the story aloud to students, asking them to predict, confirm, and change their predictions throughout the story.

3. Make a transparency of the plot relationships chart (Schmidt & Buckley, 1991) on the following page. Tell students they will be using this chart to help them learn the parts of a story and how the parts fit together.

4. Guide students in identifying the key story elements of main character, goal, problem, and solution. Use the cue words *somebody, wanted, but,* and *so* to prompt students to identify the elements. You may ask questions, such as "Who is the important somebody in this book?" When students answer, Jamaica, write it on the chart. To elicit the goals, present the statement, "In the story, Jamaica wanted" Follow this pattern of using the cues and students' responses to identify the problem and solution in the story.

5. Explain to students that there are special words to tell the parts of a story. They are main character (somebody), goal (wanted), problem (but), and solution (so). Write these words on the chart below the cue words.

6. Discuss with students how these important elements of stories fit together so the reader can understand the story.

7. Make additional copies of the plot relationships chart for students to take home. Encourage students to complete the chart using the books that they read with their parents.

*Schmidt & Buckley, 1991

Plot Relationships Chart

Somebody	Wanted	But	So

From: Schmidt, B., & Buckley, M. (1991). Plot relationships chart. In J.M. Macon, D. Bewell, & M. Vogt (Eds.). *Responses to literature: Grades K–8*. Newark, DE: International Reading Association.

Practice and Reinforcement Activities

1. Identify films or videotapes that are made from a book that is at the students' reading level. Compile and duplicate the list for parents along with a letter recommending that their children view the film or videotape before reading the book. Then suggest that the parents read the book with their children and discuss ways in which the film or videotape differs from the book.

2. Tell students one of your own family stories. Explain to students that all families have stories that are recycled for generations. Write your story on the chalkboard or on chart paper. Have the students read the story with you. Remind students that most stories have a beginning, a middle, and an end and identify those story elements in your family story. Then have students tell their own family stories in small groups. (You might set some ground rules on the types of stories that are appropriate in school and the types that are not appropriate.) After students have told family stories, have them share the beginning, middle, and end of their own stories. When you think students are able to identify the basic story structure, ask them to gather additional family stories from their parents. You might say something like the following:

> Please talk with a parent or family member this weekend and have them tell you another family story. You might need to hear the story several times. Tell your parent or family member that you need to identify the story's beginning, middle, and end for school. Have a parent or family member help you if needed. When some students have heard family stories and are able to identify the story structure, have them tell the stories to the class. (Remember that family stories in some cultural groups may have a different story structure. If this is the case with the students in your class, identify the structure of the story for students to apply as they listen to their own family stories.)

3. Bring a mail order catalog to school. Show students how to read the information given under each item. Ask students to find mail order catalogs at home. Encourage students to read the catalogs with parents.

4. Encourage students to write about what they know best—themselves. Tell students that they should complete these projects at home with their parents' help, if necessary. Younger students can write and illustrate All About Me books which include parts devoted to favorite foods, books, colors, and television programs. Students' All About Me books can be bound, shared, and displayed in the classroom. Older students can write autobiographies that also make predictions about their futures. Photographs and illustrations can be incorporated into the autobiographies. Have students discuss their books or autobiographies in small groups.

5. Establish a pen pal program with students in other schools, cities, states, or countries. College undergraduate students studying to become teachers make excellent pen pals for students. Initially, provide class time for students to write to their pen pals. Then encourage students to work with their parents to continue the correspondence. Tell students that when reading a pen pal letter they need to pay close attention to the meaning of the writer. Encourage students to talk with their parents about the content of their letters to increase their comprehension.

6. Ask students to close their eyes as they listen to you read a descriptive passage aloud. Tell students to visualize or picture the image that the words paint for them. Younger students can draw the picture they "see" in their mind's eye. Next, reread the text and ask students to identify words, phrases, and literary techniques that help create pictures and images for students. Encourage students to show their parents this visualizing technique and have them practice visualizing text as they read at home.

7. Cut out several short articles from newspapers or magazines that would be of interest to your students. Cut the headlines from the articles. Place the articles in random order on a table. Divide the class into groups of two students. Ask students to read the articles and predict the headlines based on the meanings of the articles. Then place the headlines in random order on the table. Have students try to match the headlines with the articles. Explain to students that, when matching headlines to articles, they are determining the main point of the article, which is an important reading comprehension skill. Ask students to try this activity at home by having parents find articles to use.

8. Gather several comic strips or have students bring in comic strips from a newspaper at home. Cut the segments of the strips apart and mix up the segments. Place the name of the comic strip on an envelope and place the cut segments inside the envelope. Have students take the envelopes home and work with parents to sequence the comic strip correctly.

Motivation for Reading

Behavior Observed	The student is not motivated to read.
Anticipated Outcome	Parents will work with their child to increase motivation.

BACKGROUND

Parents can make a difference in how motivated students are to read. In one study, young children who were highly motivated to read had parents who read to them daily and who had more books in their homes than unmotivated students did (Morrow, 1983). Certainly, some students who are not motivated to read have parents who already have tried to interest their children in reading. However, parents who have unmotivated children usually can do more to help their children love to read.

Typically, parents of young children are targeted for home activities to motivate their children. However, we shouldn't ignore the influence parents have on older children. When children reach early adolescence, they may be ambivalent toward their parents, but they still rely on their parents for encouragement and support (Baker, 2000). Parents of children of all ages can help increase their children's motivation to read.

Section 8.5

STRATEGY 1 ATTITUDE SCALE FOR PARENTS

1. Explain to students that reading is a skill to be learned and that having a good attitude about reading is important. Draw parallels between reading and other skills by saying something like the following:

 What kinds of activities are you engaged in? I play soccer whenever I can, and I also like to play the cello. Do you have a sport or a skill that you play?

 Allow ample time for students to discuss the kinds of activities they enjoy.

2. Choose one of the activities the students have suggested, such as basketball. Then have students visualize a basketball player with a good attitude and a basketball player with a poor attitude. Have students discuss the differences between the two players without mentioning any names. Guide students to understand that those basketball players with good attitudes can more easily become better at the activity.

3. Continue drawing the parallel between reading and other learned skills by having students discuss activities that require a coach or a teacher. For example, say something like the following:

> *When you play basketball, you often have an older player who teaches you new moves and shots and who gives you suggestions. This person is your coach or your teacher. Have you ever heard a coach tell players to improve their attitudes? How do you think the coach knows the players have poor attitudes?*

Allow time for discussion and help students understand that coaches observe, evaluate, and assess players' attitudes as well as skills.

4. Tell students that you, as their teacher, other teachers they have, and their parents are their reading coaches. Remind students that you and other teachers often observe their attitudes toward reading. Tell students that having their parents also make observations about their attitudes will help them become good readers.

5. Revise as appropriate the Attitude Scale for Parents that follows. Duplicate and distribute the survey along with an envelope for its return.

6. Have students give the survey to their parents to complete. Request that the survey be returned in two days. After the surveys are returned, use the information to help gain additional information about students to help motivate their reading.

Attitude Scale for Parents

Child's Name: _____ Date: _____

> **Directions:** Please indicate your observation of your child's reading growth since the last report. Feel free to comment where appropriate.
>
> A = Strongly agree C = Disagree
> B = Agree D = Strongly disagree

My child

1.	Understands more of what he or she reads.	A	B	C	D
2.	Enjoys being read to by family members.	A	B	C	D
3.	Finds time for quiet reading at home.	A	B	C	D
4.	Sometimes guesses at words, but they usually make sense.	A	B	C	D
5.	Can provide a summary of stories read.	A	B	C	D
6.	Has a good attitude about reading.	A	B	C	D
7.	Enjoys reading to family members.	A	B	C	D
8.	Would like to get more books.	A	B	C	D
9.	Chooses to write about stories.	A	B	C	D
10.	Is able to complete homework assignments.	A	B	C	D

Strengths I see: _____

Areas that need improvement: _____

Concerns or questions I have: _____

 Signature

From Fredericks, A.D., & Rasinski, T.V. (1990b). Involving parents in the assessment process. *The Reading Teacher, 44,* 346–349.

STRATEGY 2 READING ALOUD

1. Tell students that people of all ages like to hear stories. Tell students about ways our culture values stories in all aspects of life. For example, say something like the following:

 I love to hear stories. At family gatherings my grandfather tells stories about farming with horse-drawn cultivators. After my grandfather tells a story or two, my aunts and uncles tell stories about the mischief they caused when they were young. Then my cousins tell stories about their children, and the children tell stories about school. Our family spends hours telling stories when we are together.

2. Explain to students that when one person tells a story others tend to follow suit. Tell students that listening to and telling stories can be interesting.

3. Discuss ways in which telling stories is similar to listening to books being read aloud. Explain to students that books are written stories that follow a specific structure. Have students talk about ways books they have heard or read are similar to stories that they have heard.

4. Remind students that you read them stories aloud frequently. Tell them that even older students should have the opportunity to listen to books being read aloud in school and out of school (Sanacore, 2000).

5. Talk about your own experiences with reading aloud, when you were a child or as a parent. Provide students with specific examples, such as the following one.

 My wife or I read to our children every night. We try to alternate nights of reading, but sometimes my wife is at meetings late at night, so I read to the children more often than she does. Our children are ages 7, 9, and 13. I try to read a book that would be of interest to all of the children. Right now I'm reading a long chapter book, so I also read a short picture book every other night. All of our children like to listen to my wife or me read to them.

6. Tell students that their parents should also read to them. Explain to students that listening to books helps them improve their own motivation to read.

7. Explain to students that parents frequently request information about reading aloud to their children. Tell students that you will be distributing a letter to their parents that explains ways to read aloud.

8. Revise the following letter as appropriate. Duplicate, sign, and distribute the letter to students. Ask students to take the letter home and give it to a parent or other family member.

9. Occasionally, ask students whether their parents are reading aloud to them at home. For those students whose parents are not reading aloud to them, contact the parents and remind them of the importance of reading aloud. Provide tips for reading aloud and possible books or audiotapes for parents to use.

Dear Parents,

Children love to listen to stories, even older children. And it's fun to read stories to children. You can read books your child has brought home, or you can borrow books from your public library. In any case, it would be good for your child to listen to you read aloud at least three times each week. I have included reading aloud techniques that I thought you might enjoy.

Sincerely,

Reading Aloud Techniques

✓ Select books that you'll enjoy and that will spark your child's interest.

✓ Read unfamiliar stories silently first to note places that may need special effects to create drama.

✓ Don't read too fast and adjust your pace to the story and your child.

✓ Be responsive to your child's actions.

✓ Encourage your child's participation in the reading session—joining in repeating phrases, making comments, asking questions, predicting what will happen, or actually reading parts of the material.

✓ Allow time after reading for a relaxed discussion. This should involve sharing reactions, not quizzing on facts.

✓ Both parents should take turns reading aloud. Both fathers and mothers are important models, too. Make sure your child sees you read for pleasure.

✓ Never withdraw reading aloud as a punishment. That may destroy all the positive effects of reading aloud.

Strategy 3

Motivating Your Child

1. Tell students that their parents can be very influential in their beliefs about schooling. Talk with students about your experiences with your parents and schooling. For example, say something like the following:

 I grew up with my mother, grandmother, and brother. My grandmother never finished high school, but she made sure my mother did. My mother had to work two jobs, so my grandmother spent most evenings with my brother and me. Every night my grandmother asked me whether I had homework. Sometimes I would tell her I had finished my homework at school, but she never believed me. She thought I should do at least an hour of homework every night. Grandma told me many times that, to get ahead in life, I had to do well in school. She really motivated me to get good grades even when I didn't care very much.

2. Have students share their own stories about family members who have motivated them to do well in school. Do not expect every student to contribute to the conversation.

3. Talk with students about ways in which their parents subtly motivate them to do well in school. For example, say something like the following:

 I didn't see my father very often as a child. He lived in another state, and I only saw him twice a year. He called me once a month and on my brother's birthday and my birthday. He never talked about school, but every time he talked to me, he asked me about college. Even when I was in first grade, I remember my father saying that I would be going to college before I knew it. I guess my father was motivating me to do well in school even though I didn't realize it at the time.

4. Have students share their own stories about family members, friends, and others who have motivated them to do well in school.

5. Help students realize that sometimes parents don't know many ways to motivate their children to do well in school. Tell students that you have a letter for their parents that will give them some ideas.

6. Revise the letter titled Motivating Your Child to Succeed in School, duplicate it, sign it, and distribute the letter to students. Have students take the letter home to their parents.

Dear Parents,

One of the most important qualities of a good student is high motivation. I know your child may be motivated to do many things well, and I want your child also to be highly motivated at school. There are many things you can do at home to increase your child's motivation. I know you do many of these already, but please think about adding a few more to what you already do. You can play a major role in increasing your child's motivation to succeed in school.

Sincerely,

Motivating Your Child to Succeed in School

- ✓ Show interest in your child's learning. Ask about what is happening in school. Ask to see papers and projects.

- ✓ Work with your child on setting daily goals that are attainable. Write the goals and post them in a prominent place.

- ✓ Help your child envision and formulate long-term goals.

- ✓ Instill in your child the idea that achievements are usually the result of persistence and hard work, not luck or ability.

- ✓ Show caring and love if your child makes a mistake or fails and help him or her see mistakes as opportunities to learn and grow.

- ✓ Use words and actions to demonstrate faith in your child's ability to learn and achieve.

- ✓ Look for successes in your child's efforts and acknowledge them.

- ✓ Recognize, praise, and celebrate your child's successful completion of a goal.

- ✓ Model for your child language that conveys positive expectations, such as *I can, I will, I want to, I understand, my goal is,* and so on.

- ✓ Frequently stress to your child the importance of learning and education.

STRATEGY 4 SELF-ESTEEM

1. Tell students that how they feel about themselves is called self-esteem. Explain that thinking well of yourself can provide the boost that enhances motivation. Give an example, such as the following one.

 When I feel good about myself, I believe that I can succeed, and I try harder. One of the things that I'm trying to learn is Spanish. Sometimes I feel discouraged, and I feel as if everything I do is wrong and that I will never learn how to speak Spanish. At those times I don't practice very much. On some days, I feel like I'm really doing well. On those days, I'm speaking Spanish much of the time, and I feel like I will accomplish my goal.

2. Explain to students that their parents can help them develop their self-esteem, and, in turn, they can become better readers. Tell students that some parents are looking for ways to help their children develop positive self-esteem and that you have some ideas for them.

3. Revise the letter titled Helping Children Develop Healthy Self-Esteem as appropriate. Duplicate the letter, sign it, and distribute it to the students. You could also have the letter available during open house or conferences.

Dear Parents,

Your child is an important person, but many children don't realize how special they are. Everyone struggles with uncertainty about themselves at some time in their lives; it's part of being human. But the better children feel about themselves, the more attention they can give to learning. Children who have low self-esteem often are so worried about themselves that they do not do as well as they could in school.

As a parent, you can help your child have healthy self-esteem. Having healthy self-esteem doesn't mean your child will be conceited. It just means that your child will be able to take pride in his or her accomplishments, make good decisions, and be responsible.

Here are ways to help your child develop healthy self-esteem. I know you do many of these already, but try to add a few more. It will help your child in school.

Sincerely,

Helping Children Develop Healthy Self-Esteem

✓ Seek out opportunities to praise and encourage your child.

✓ Recognize the things your child does well.

✓ Treat your child with love, respect, and courtesy.

✓ Nurture a positive attitude in all situations.

✓ Give your child opportunities to assume responsibility appropriate for his or her age.

✓ Encourage your child to participate in activities that will be successful.

✓ Listen attentively to your child's ideas, fears, feelings, and concerns.

✓ Reward good behavior and accomplishments.

✓ Encourage decision making whenever possible.

✓ Spend time together and share favorite activities.

Practice and Reinforcement Activities

1. Invite parents, other adults, older students, and possibly published authors to come to school to read and share their enthusiasm about books.

2. Spend time talking with and observing students to determine their reading interests. Then tap into those interests when reading books or recommending possible books for outside reading.

3. Display books that a particular student enjoys in a prominent place for several days. Encourage other students to interview the chosen student. Make the books available for checkout.

4. Encourage students to participate in one of the currently popular book clubs.

5. Encourage students to develop a bulletin board that features topics on subjects they enjoy. These students and others could then try to locate reading materials on these subjects. Provide titles and/or create a display of relevant materials.

6. Have students look in the library for the "ugliest" book cover they can find at their approximate reading level. It will probably be a good book but very old. The student then reads the book at home and decides on a "new" cover to spice up the book. The cover should include the name of the author and/or illustrator with a byline—new cover by _____. When the cover is completed, have a contest and let the class vote to select the best covers. Put the books in your class library where your students have the first opportunity to check them out. Then place them in your school library again so other students can read them.

7. Spend a few minutes each day talking about the books you read. Tell students that you read many books at home and that you like to talk about the books you have read. Then have students talk with their parents or family members about books and other materials they have read. Have students share the book titles and types of materials that their family members read at home.

8. Encourage students to talk about books and authors they like and dislike. Share your own opinions about books. If students do not like a particular book, ask them to tell you the reasons for their dislike. Explain to students that all readers have favorite books and authors and also books and authors they dislike. Then have students talk with their parents about their favorite and not-so-favorite books and ask their parents to talk about their own book preferences.

9. Decorate a bag and send it home with the following directions: "Find an item from home that will fit in the bag. Write three clues about the object on the index card you will find in the bag. Bring the bag and object back to school." Have a special table to display the bag and the clues. Let the children look at the bag and read the clues during the day. Then let them write what they think the object is and why. Have the class share their ideas and allow the student to reveal what is in the bag.

10. Create attractive flyers about books that students have enjoyed hearing you read. On the flyer suggest that parents read the books at home with their children. Use the Mail Merge function on your computer to personally address the newsletters to parents and students in your class (Anderson & Speck, 2001).

Reading Outside of School

Behavior Observed	The student does little or no reading outside of school.
Anticipated Outcome	Parents will encourage their child to read outside the classroom.

BACKGROUND

Many students don't pick up a book outside of the school day. Instead, students' time is filled with television, video games, MTV, the Internet, sports, and other activities. The competition for students' free time is fierce. However, the amount of reading students do outside of school is important, because students who read outside of the school day tend to have better reading achievement.

Sometimes it's all a teacher can do to encourage students to read during the school day without worrying about what a student does outside of school. But here's where parents can help. There are many things that a parent can do to help children to read at home. A successful approach to encouraging outside reading often begins by helping students become aware of the pleasure and satisfaction that can be attained from reading. The following strategies and activities can be useful.

Section 8.6

STRATEGY 1 INTEREST CHART

1. Tell students that people are naturally interested in different things. Talk with students about your interests. For example, say something like the following:

 I've always been interested in history, especially about the lives of pioneers. I've read lots of books about the Oregon Trail and other settlers. I like to imagine what it was like for pioneers to see an uninhabited land.

2. Contrast your interests with someone else's interests. For example, say something like the following:

 My children have never been interested in history. Both of my children, however, love science fiction. They like to imagine what life would be like in the future. My interests and my children's interests are very different.

3. Tell students that most people prefer to read about topics that interest them. Talk about books that you have read recently.

4. Tell students that their parents have been trying to encourage them to read outside of school and that identifying the students' interests can be helpful.

5. Duplicate and distribute the Interest Chart that follows. Have students take the Interest Chart home for parents to administer to them.

6. Remind parents in newsletters or phone calls to keep checking on their children's interests. Tell parents that helping their children find books that interest them can encourage students to read outside of school.

Interest Chart

Music I Like	Sports I Like to Play	Other Interests I Have
Things I Like to Do	**My Hobbies**	**Books I Have Read**
Places That Interest Me	**Animals of Interest**	**Heroes**

STRATEGY 2

PARENT/STUDENT BOOK CLUB

1. Tell students that you will be forming book clubs in your class and that these book clubs will consist of two students and two parents.

2. Divide the class into pairs. Ask each pair of students to choose a book to read from a list of recommendations. You might give a brief introduction to each of the books on the list.

3. Obtain at least four copies of the books. Give each pair of students two copies of their chosen book, one for the students and one for the parents.

4. Communicate with parents about the Parent/Student Book Club. Tell parents that your goal is for students to increase the amount of reading they do outside of the school day and that Parent/Student Book Clubs are one of the strategies you will be using to accomplish the goal. Tell parents that each student and parent will be asked to read one chapter of the book each day and that the students should discuss the book with their parents after reading.

5. Assign students to read one chapter of their chosen book each day. Tell students that their parents will also be reading that chapter and that they should discuss the chapter with their parents after reading.

6. After students and parents have read several chapters, ask students to tell you about the plot of the book.

7. After students and parents have finished reading a book, invite the parents to your classroom to participate in a class discussion.

8. Duplicate and distribute the parent letter that follows describing the Parent/Student Book Club.

Dear Parents,

One way for students to strengthen their reading achievement is to read at home. You can help by participating in our Parent/Student Book Club. You will find how to participate by following the steps below. Thanks for helping your child in this way.

Sincerely,

Parent/Student Book Club

1. Your child will give you a copy of the book he or she is reading.

2. You and your child should each read a chapter a day.

3. Set aside a few minutes to talk about the chapter together. Some of the things you might discuss include the following.

 ✓ what the characters are doing

 ✓ major events in the chapter

 ✓ interesting words or phrases

 ✓ words that might be difficult for your child

 ✓ predictions about what might happen next

 ✓ your child's reactions to what was read

 ✓ problems or challenges the characters are facing

 ✓ how the story relates to your child

STRATEGY 3 INTERNET READING

1. Tell students that there are many ways to read outside of school, and one way is on the computer. Remind students that when they are reading web sites on the Internet they are reading text that is presented in different ways.

2. Identify a list of web sites that complement a topic you are teaching. For example, if you are teaching a science unit on the rain forest, search for web sites that deal with the rain forest. Preview all web sites and their links.

3. Access the Internet in your classroom. Show students how to find appropriate web sites about a topic that you are teaching. Explain to students how text is organized on web sites, how to scroll through the text, and how you decide when to stop and read. Allow students to practice reading the web sites.

4. Tell students that you know of many more web sites that would help them learn about topics that you will be teaching. List several web sites for students. Duplicate and distribute the list for students.

5. Ask students who have Internet access at home to work with their parents on Internet Reading by accessing one of the web sites on your list.

6. Have students who were able to read one of the web sites discuss in class what they have learned.

Practice and Reinforcement Activities

1. Maintain a well-stocked classroom library in which books and other reading materials are rotated regularly. Involve students in setting up the library and developing a system to check out the materials. Encourage students to check out books, brochures, magazines, and related items to be read at home.

2. Have students list the kinds of reading that their families do. Then have students interview each family member who can read and ask them about the types of reading material they usually read. Reading materials may include things like cookbooks, car manuals, labels on cans, magazines, newspapers, and so on. Have students bring their lists to school. Compile a master list of things people read and post the list in a prominent place in the classroom.

3. Have each student bring three kinds of reading materials to school from home. These materials may include coffee mugs, T-shirts, cereal boxes, and so on. Have students place their reading materials on a large table. Guide students to think about their various reading experiences outside school.

4. Ask students to talk with their parents about their cultural background. Encourage students to find at home cultural artifacts that use print such as books, magazines, letters, brochures, and so on. Tell students that when they find a cultural artifact to read it with their parents. Then invite students to bring these cultural artifacts to school and tell the class about their backgrounds.

5. Keep lists of books that you would like to read or to purchase for yourself in a prominent place in your classroom, such as on the chalkboard. Tell students that this list is your "Books I Want to Read." Tell students that readers often have lists of books that they want to read. Provide each student with a paper with the title "Books I Want to Read." When new books are introduced, ask students if the book might possibly interest them. If so, have them record the book on their lists. In addition, when you think of a book that might be of interest to a particular student, suggest that the student add the book to his or her list. Periodically, send the book list home with a cover letter suggesting that parents obtain copies of the book for their child to read at home. In the letter, include the location and hours of the public library.

6. Write a Class Diary together (Lenski & Johns, 2000). Have students record class events and write their reactions to those events in a big book, a small notebook, or on construction paper. An example of a Class Diary entry follows.

> Event: On Tuesday a local cab driver came to class and told us a story. He told us about his home country of Kenya. He told us about his family of 10 brothers and sisters, and he described the animals commonly found in his home country—lions, elephants, and hippopotamuses.

> Responses:
> Wow, I can't imagine walking down a trail and hearing a lion!
> —Samuel

> I didn't know where Kenya was located, so I had to look it up on a map.
> —Tanya

After a week or more, have students take home the Class Diary to read with their parents. Suggest that students write a Home Diary with their parents and bring it to school. On the front cover, provide an explanation of the Class Diary and suggest that parents write a Home Diary with their children.

7. Remind students that they are reading when they write and send e-mail messages. Have students write several e-mail messages that they would like to send. As students write their messages, ask them to read or reread their writing before they send it. Explain that writers read as they write. Model writing an e-mail message by saying something like the following:

Provide an opportunity for your students to practice reading and writing by sending e-mails.

> *I'm going to write a message to my brother to find out whether he can come to a birthday dinner at my house later this month. Here's the first few sentences of my message.* Hey, Dave, how's it going? Ready to celebrate your birthday? How about a birthday bash at my house in two weeks? *Now that I've written several sentences, I need to read them to determine whether the message says what I want it to say. After reading them over, I think I'll change* in two weeks *to* on the 20th. *That way he'll know the exact date.*

Have students reread and revise their own messages. If you have e-mail access in your school, have students send the messages from school or send them from another computer. (Remember to include each student's home e-mail address so replies don't come back to school.) Then send an e-mail message to parents similar to the following one.

Dear Parents,

In class, we have been discussing ways in which sending and receiving e-mail is a good example of reading outside school. I have encouraged your child to view e-mail as a reading/writing activity. Although e-mail should not be the only type of reading your child does outside school, it is one reading/writing activity. Please reinforce this message by having your child keep track of the amount of time spent on e-mail. Remind your child that e-mailing is one way to read outside of school.

Thank you,

Schoolwork

SECTION 8.7

Behavior Observed	The student does not complete work in school.
Anticipated Outcome	Parents monitor the student's schoolwork at home.

BACKGROUND

One of the most frustrating aspects of teaching can be getting students to finish schoolwork, both during school and at home. Students who do not finish their work in school are in danger of falling behind other students and frequently receive poor grades. There are many reasons why some students do not finish their work. One reason is that students who have difficulty reading may not have time in school to finish their assignments. Another reason may be that some students have poor time-management skills. A third reason may be that some stu-

dents use schoolwork as a way to exert control over their teacher and parents.

When students do not complete work at school, parents can help. Actually, teachers need parents to work with them to find the causes for the students' inability to finish their work. And parents can help their children develop the dispositions and abilities to change their behavior and learn how to complete work during school time. The following suggestions may help parents who have agreed to monitor their children's schoolwork.

Section 8.7

STRATEGY 1 HOMEWORK TIPS

1. Tell students that an important component of school is finishing work in school and as homework. Explain to students that the work that you give them in school helps them practice reading skills and also lets you know what they know and can do.

2. Draw a parallel between schoolwork and other types of skill practice. For example, say something like the following:

 When you are learning a skill, you have to practice. Recently, I've been learning how to blade. I've never skated with in-line blades before. I had roller-skated as a child, but in-line skating was new. To learn, I had a neighbor teach me how to turn and stop, and together we skated in our neighborhood until I felt secure. Then I continued practicing in our neighborhood for weeks. Now I think I'm ready for a more challenging trail.

3. Ask students about sports, music, and other activities in which they have recently become involved. Provide ample time to discuss the students' activities. Guide the discussion toward activities that take practice to learn.

4. Remind students that reading is a skill that they are learning. For younger students, show them picture books and chapter books and explain that they need to practice reading in order to progress to the longer books. For older students, discuss the kinds of reading they will do in secondary school. For example, bring in a science or social studies textbook and show students the text's difficulty. Explain to students that they will be able to read the more difficult text in the future if they practice reading at their level now.

5. Tell students that some of their reading practice will take place in school and some will take place at home. Explain to students that when they are doing schoolwork at home their parents need to monitor their work.

6. Tell students that you have written a letter for their parents titled Homework Tips for Parents that provides parents with information about helping their children with schoolwork.

7. Revise the letter that follows so it is appropriate for your situation. Then duplicate the letter, sign it, and distribute it to your students to share with their parents.

Dear Parents,

Your child will be receiving homework this year. I would like your support by asking you to help your child do the homework, but not to do it for him or her. I need to see your child's best work. There are some things you can do to encourage your child to finish the homework. I would like to share these homework tips with you. Attached you will also find an Assignment Sheet that your child may use to know which homework assignments need to be completed when.

Sincerely,

Homework Tips for Parents

✓ Set aside daily family time when each family member is engaged in quiet activities while your child does homework. Starting quiet time when children are young establishes the expectation for doing homework and gets them into the routine of studying.

✓ Establish a time and place where homework is to be done. Make sure the table or desk is in a well-lighted area and that needed materials such as paper, pencils, and crayons are available.

✓ Make sure your child understands all assignments. If needed, work through the first question or problem together. If your child does not understand an assignment and you are unable to help, have him or her call a friend or a homework hot line, if available, for help.

✓ For elementary children, check over the completed assignment. You may need to sign and date it.

✓ Each day ask whether there is any homework. Even when there isn't any, the simple act of asking conveys that you consider homework to be an important responsibility. If no specific homework is due, this is a golden opportunity to read together, write a story, take a walk, or just talk together.

✓ Don't forget to praise your child for homework efforts.

STRATEGY 2

ASSIGNMENT SHEET

1. Tell students that one of the most difficult aspects of completing schoolwork at home is in listing assignments, knowing when they are due, and taking home the correct materials. Explain that people of all ages and in all types of occupations need organizational ability.

2. Talk with students about your own organizational methods. For example, say something like the following:

 Because I plan some of my lessons at home and often correct papers at home, I need to remember which books and papers to take home every night. To remember, I have a basket on my desk at school that I use to gather the things I will need at home. When there is an assignment that I know I will grade at home, I put those papers in my at-home basket. I also place the books I will need in that basket. That way when I'm ready to go home I don't need to try to remember what materials I will need; they're all right there in my basket.

3. Tell students that many businesses train their employees in work management skills. Remind students that many of the skills they are learning at school will be useful for them when they enter the workplace. Tell students about one of your management techniques. For example, say something like the following:

 I carry an index card in a special pocket in my purse that I use to remind myself of the things I need to accomplish that day. I use one side for things I need to do at school and the other side for things I need to do at home. When I am at school and I think of something I need to do at home, like calling my sister to ask her to baby-sit, I write it on the "home" side of the card. When I am at home and I think of something I need to accomplish at school, like talking with the maintenance people about setting up the science fair, I write it on the "school" side of the card. At the end of the day, I reread my index card and transfer any items I didn't finish to the next day's card. Then I throw the old card in the recycling bin. This technique helps me organize my work.

4. Talk with students about the organizational strategies they currently use. Allow ample time for discussion.

5. Remind students that parents can play a key role in their school learning by helping them organize their assignments and by monitoring their work. Tell students that most workers have one or more bosses that monitor their work. Talk with students about the role your school administrator plays in monitoring your work. For example, your school administrator might look at your lesson plans,

Familiarize your students with the assignment sheet to help them organize their homework.

observe you teach, and analyze your students' test scores. Then explain the roles of additional administrators in schools, such as a superintendent and school board. Tell students that their parents hold a supervisory role, possibly similar to a school board, and that they should do some of the monitoring of the students' work.

6. Tell students that you have developed an assignment sheet as an organizational tool for them to keep track of the work they need to do at school and the materials they need to take home.

7. Revise the assignment sheet that follows to fit your teaching situation. Duplicate the assignment sheet and explain its parts to students. Then have students use the assignment sheet to organize their school assignments and their homework.

Day_____ Month _____ Date _____ 20_____

Subject	Assignments	Date Due
☐ Reading		
☐ Language		
☐ Spelling		
☐ Math		
☐ Science		
☐ Social Studies		
☐ Writing		
☐		

Things to Take Home

1._____

2._____

3._____

4._____

5._____

Things to Bring to School

1._____

2._____

3._____

4._____

5._____

Parent's Signature

STRATEGY 3 TEST-PREPARATION CHECKLIST

1. Tell students that they will be taking many tests during the school year and that they can prepare for tests by knowing *about* the test as well as information *for* the test. Remind students that there are many types of tests and that their test preparation should be appropriate for the type of test they will be taking.

2. Provide students with examples of the types of tests you will be giving during the school year. For example, you might give spelling tests, vocabulary tests, multiple-choice tests, and so on. Show students what each of these tests looks like.

3. Remind students that their parents can help them prepare for tests by asking them questions *about* the test. Make a transparency or copy of the Test-Preparation Checklist that follows. Read each question with your students, making sure that they understand the meanings of the questions.

4. Tell students that you would like their parents to review the Test-Preparation Checklist with them at home before major tests.

5. Several days before a test, reread the Test-Preparation Checklist and revise it to fit your teaching situation. Then duplicate the checklist and distribute it to students. Ask students to take the checklist home and to have parents use it to help students prepare for tests.

Test-Preparation Checklist

Directions: Here are some tips to help you get ready for a test. Circle *yes* or *no* for each item. If you are able to answer *yes* to each question, then you are probably ready for the test. Work on those areas where you have circled *no*.

1. Do I know what type of test I'll be taking? (multiple choice, essay, matching, etc.) Y N

2. Do I know which subject areas will be covered? Y N

3. Have I studied a little at a time, not waiting until the last minute? Y N

4. Have I reviewed my notes carefully? Y N

5. Have I looked up hard vocabulary words in order to understand them? Y N

6. Do I know important words that are printed in **bold** or *italics*? Y N

7. Have I skimmed chapter headings to recall the overall ideas in each chapter? Y N

8. Can I recall the main ideas listed in the chapter summaries? Y N

9. Have I looked at charts, diagrams, or illustrations for important information? Y N

10. Can I answer the questions at the end of the chapter? Y N

I can find out more information about the test by doing the following:

STRATEGY 4 HOMEWORK SCHEDULE

1. Tell students that they need to schedule homework just as they schedule other activities. Explain to students that, if they don't have homework scheduled, they may not find time to finish the work they need to do for school.

2. Discuss with students the types of activities in which they are engaged after school is over. Many students will have very full schedules with sports practices, lessons, and so on.

3. Tell students that your life is also very busy, but that you schedule time to do schoolwork at home. For example, say something like the following:

 After school is over, I often have a committee meeting. At 4:45, I leave school and drive to after-school care to pick up my children. I'm home by 5:30. At that time, I talk with my children about their day while I begin preparing our evening meal. My husband is usually home by 6:00. We eat at 6:30. My husband clears the dishes while I read to the children and help them with their homework. By 7:30 the children are working independently and I begin grading papers. At 8:00 the children are usually finished with their homework, and I am finished with my chores. Then, we all watch television together or we play a game. The children go to bed at 9:30. From 9:30–10:30 I finish grading papers and preparing for school, or I read a book. Then I go to bed around 11:00.

4. Remind students that people can't do everything they want to do. For example, tell students something like the following:

 When I was in school, I played the clarinet in the band. I still love playing the clarinet, and I try to practice for 20 minutes in the morning before I leave for work. If I had more time in my schedule, I'd practice much longer and I would play in the community band. However, right now I have children at home and don't have time to play as much as I'd like. Even though I'd really like to play my clarinet for hours, I don't shirk correcting papers and planning lessons in order to play.

5. Have students discuss their typical afternoons and evenings. Talk about things students would like to do that they don't have time for. Discuss ways to prioritize activities. Allow ample time for discussion.

6. Revise the Homework Schedule that follows, duplicate it, and distribute it to students. Tell students that they should take the schedule home and complete it with their parents.

7. Tell students that they should write in their lessons, practices, and meetings first. Then they should include family time such as eating with their family or watching television. After these items are scheduled, they should block out between 30 and 60 minutes every day for homework.

8. Have students complete the Homework Schedule with parents at home. For some students, you might ask them to bring you a copy of their schedule, so you can remind them of the time they need to complete homework.

9. When you communicate with parents, remind them to monitor their children's scheduled homework time.

Homework Schedule

Time	Monday	Tuesday	Wednesday	Thursday	Friday
3:00					
3:30					
4:00					
4:30					
5:00					
5:30					
6:00					
6:30					
7:00					
7:30					
8:00					
8:30					
9:00					

Practice and Reinforcement Activities

1. Tell students that they should develop study and homework goals with their parents. Provide examples of homework goals such as a targeted amount of time to study, a grade to improve, and so on. Give students an index card and have them write *Homework Goals* on the top of the card. Have them take the card home and develop homework goals with their parents.

2. Have students create study plans with parents at home. Tell students that a study plan is a detailed plan of their homework period. Provide an example of a study plan such as the following one.

7:00–7:05	Develop day's study plan with parents
7:05–7:25	Read novel for class
7:25–7:30	Break
7:30–7:45	Study vocabulary words
7:45–8:00	Write response to literature in journal

3. Have students study vocabulary words with parents by using their vocabulary notebook to identify words that parents and students could use in conversations. Encourage students to apply these targeted vocabulary words when talking at home. Have parents take note of words their children have used, and ask the students to take note of words their parents have used.

4. Have students develop sample test questions with parents at home. Encourage students to create lists of possible questions for tests with their parents.

5. Remind students that homework needs to be "neat." Show examples of papers that are neatly done, of papers that are acceptable, and of papers that are unacceptable. Send home short excerpts of these papers so that parents know your "neatness standards." Tell students that they should ask parents to determine whether the completed homework meets your standards for neatness.

6. Provide students with a list of materials needed for projects that you expect will be completed at home. For example, if you ask students to create book covers on construction paper, develop a list that might include 9" x 11" construction paper, markers, and so on. Send home the list of materials in advance of the project so that parents can have the materials available at the correct time.

7. Some students need extrinsic motivation and a mention of consequences to complete homework. Send home suggestions of rewards and consequences that you feel are appropriate for the student and the situation. Suggest that parents use these rewards and consequences until the student learns how to complete homework without them.

8. Remind students that many of their homework assignments can be organized and completed on a computer. When appropriate, tell students to complete certain assignments on their home computer. An example of an appropriate assignment might be for students to develop a flyer publicizing a book. Have students with home computers work with their parents to complete the assignment. Some students will need permission to use the home computer, others will need assistance with a computer application, and others may teach parents how to use a computer application.

SECTION
8.8 School and Home Literacies

Behavior Observed	The student does not understand the connection between school and home literacies.
Anticipated Outcome	Parents help their child understand the connection between school and home literacies.

BACKGROUND

Some students do not see the need for school. These students may think that their home life and their school life are totally separate entities. They may even consider home "the real world" and school a place where they are forced to go during the day. These students need to understand that there is a connection between school literacy and home literacy.

Teachers often try to merge home and school through various activities. These activities generally are useful in helping students connect school literacy learning with home life. Parents can also be terrific partners in helping their children make the connection between home and school literacies. The following suggestions can help you involve parents so their children will draw connections between home and school.

Section 8.8

STRATEGY 1 PARENT INTEREST SURVEY

1. Explain to students that there are many ways that their parents can be involved in their education. For example, say something like the following:

 There are many ways in which your parents can support your school learning. All of your parents want you to do well in school, and many of your parents tell you how important school is. Some of your parents read with you at home, and others volunteer in the school. Several of your parents may have even donated items for school sales. I appreciate all of the ways your parents help in the school.

2. Tell students that you will be sending a Parent Interest Survey home with them for their parents to complete and return to school. Copy the survey on a transparency and read the items to the students. Ask students if there are other ways their parents can work with the school. Provide students with several minutes to discuss additional school activities for their parents.

3. Add the students' ideas to the Parent Interest Survey that follows and revise the survey to fit your teaching situation. Read the survey with students to clarify items as necessary. Revise the survey again if appropriate. Then duplicate and distribute the survey to students.

4. Send the Parent Interest Survey home with students and ask students to return the survey in two days. When the surveys are returned, read them carefully and try to involve parents in as many ways as possible.

Parent Interest Survey

1. How interested are you in being a room mother/father?

 Very interested Somewhat interested Not interested
 X X X

2. How interested are you in reading to our class?

 Very interested Somewhat interested Not interested
 X X X

3. How interested are you in listening to students read to you?

 Very interested Somewhat interested Not interested
 X X X

4. How interested are you in coming on a field trip?

 Very interested Somewhat interested Not interested
 X X X

5. How interested are you in talking to the class about your job?

 Very interested Somewhat interested Not interested
 X X X

6. How interested are you in planning and helping with our parties and special events?

 Very interested Somewhat interested Not interested
 X X X

7. How interested are you in donating treats for our parties and spacial events?

Very interested Somewhat interested Not interested
 X X X

8. How interested are you in donating merchandise for our monthly sale?

Very interested Somewhat interested Not interested
 X X X

_____ _____
 Parent's Name Phone Number

 e-mail address

Additional ideas: _____

STRATEGY 2 REAL READING AT HOME

1. Have students brainstorm the many different reading materials they have in their homes. List the ideas on chart paper or an overhead transparency.

2. Tell students that they will be writing a letter to their parents that will make them aware of the different kinds of reading materials they already have at home.

3. Using chart paper or an overhead transparency, model a letter you have written that shows students the kinds of things that can be included in their letter. Use the letter that follows as an example.

4. Assist students who need help with their letters.

5. When the letters are complete, have students decorate an envelope and take home the letter to their parents.

Give students time in class to brainstorm reading materials found in their homes.

Dear Parents,

There are many ways you can help your child read at home. Your home is filled with reading material. You might be surprised how much we all rely on reading. You might read directions when you cook, clip coupons from the newspaper, read cards or letters from friends, and read junk mail. You read all of the time! And the reading you do is important. It is reading for a real purpose. For example, you need to read the directions to microwave popcorn correctly or you will burn the popcorn. Your child needs to know that reading outside school is still reading.

Invite your child to read with you during reading times at home. At least once a day, think about one of these reading events and ask your child to join you. Read the directions (or whatever) to your child and then ask your child to read them with you. Finally, ask your child what the words are saying. This will help your child on the road to reading!

Sincerely,

Real Reading at Home

- ✓ write family diaries
- ✓ cook together and read recipes
- ✓ collect grocery coupons
- ✓ read video game directions
- ✓ design cards and invitations
- ✓ write letters to relatives
- ✓ videotape family events
- ✓ read TV guide and discuss good choices
- ✓ make a pictorial biography
- ✓ read and discuss news articles
- ✓ write thank you notes
- ✓ prepare a calendar of activities
- ✓ create original stories

- ✓ write messages to each other
- ✓ read bulletins from school
- ✓ create photo album captions
- ✓ sing together
- ✓ write and file addresses
- ✓ write a family history
- ✓ make shopping lists
- ✓ read menus
- ✓ read bus schedules
- ✓ write a family vacation journal
- ✓ create a family bulletin board
- ✓ tape-record stories
- ✓ read cartoons in newspapers

STRATEGY 3 — COOK TOGETHER

1. Tell students that they will have a different kind of homework assignment this week. Explain to students that there are times when accomplishing household tasks also furthers their literacy.

2. Tell students that they will be working with a parent, caregiver, older sibling, or older friend to read the directions of a favorite recipe in order to cook something.

3. Talk with students about their family situations in order for them to identify a responsible adult or older friend with whom to cook. Be sensitive toward all family situations. For example you might say the following:

 Some of you have a parent at home after school who will have time to complete this project. However, many of your parents work either during the day or in the evening, and some of them will be too busy to cook with you. In that case, ask another adult or an older sibling to do this project with you. Make sure you have the permission of a parent, though, to cook with another adult or an older sibling.

4. Tell students that they will be reading a cookbook or a recipe to prepare food for their families. If students speak a language other than English at home, reassure students that they can either read a recipe in English or a recipe in their home language. If students do not have a cookbook or a recipe at home, you can duplicate and distribute the recipe that is included with the directions on the following page.

5. Duplicate and distribute the instruction sheet that follows. Read the instructions with students. Remind students that, although this is a homework assignment, their parents also need to agree to participate. Provide an alternate assignment for students who do not secure parental permission.

6. Give students several days, including the weekend, to complete their homework. After the students have cooked at home, discuss their experiences with them.

 Cooking Together

Instructions

1. Find a recipe that you and a parent or adult can make at home some time this week or use the recipe that follows.

2. Have your parent read the recipe to you; then read it again together.

3. Create a list of ingredients needed for the recipe. Write the ingredients on the grocery list. Make sure you have included the amounts of ingredients on the list.

4. Shop for the food with a parent. Make sure all of the food on the recipe is ready before you cook.

5. Read and reread the recipe as you put ingredients together.

6. While the food is cooking or after you have finished, make a list of five interesting or new words you found in the recipe. Write these words on a sheet of paper and define each word. (For example, you may not have known exactly what the word *blend* means.)

7. Write about your cooking experiences in a journal and/or draw a picture of yourself cooking at home.

8. Bring the list of words, their definitions, and a drawing of the food you made to show the class at school.

Recipe

Cracker Bars

1 cup brown sugar	soda crackers
1 cup butter	6 oz. chocolate chips

Place soda crackers on foil in a 8" x 8" pan. After boiling brown sugar and butter 3 minutes, pour mixture over crackers. Bake at 375° for 5 minutes. Remove and sprinkle chocolate chips over top. Sprinkle with nuts if desired. Cut into squares before completely cool.

STRATEGY 4 MAGAZINES FOR CHILDREN

1. Bring to class several examples of magazines from home, the school library, or the public library. Talk with the students about the reasons why you subscribe to magazines and why there are magazines in libraries. Say something like the following:

 At home my family subscribes to six different magazines. Because my husband is interested in traveling, we subscribe to two travel magazines. My hobby is bicycling, so we subscribe to one bicycling magazine. Our family also likes to keep current with the news, so we subscribe to a news magazine. My children like sports, so we subscribe to two sports magazines.

2. Explain that school and public libraries contain a section on magazines. Show students samples of the magazines in the libraries or have a librarian discuss the magazine collection.

3. Explain to students that people read magazines to learn more about a topic, interest, or hobby. Ask students whether they have magazines at home. Have students share the names or topics of the magazines at home.

4. Show students several magazines and explain that there are different types of articles. Show examples of feature articles, commentaries, short articles, and so on.

5. Tell students that there are a variety of magazines written especially for students their age. Compile a list of appropriate magazines or use the example that follows.

6. Duplicate and distribute the letter that follows or revise the letter to fit your purposes. Read the letter with students.

7. Tell students that this letter to their parents is for information only. Explain that magazine subscriptions cost money and that it is the parents' decision whether or not to use their money to subscribe to magazines. Remind students that subscribing to a magazine is not a homework assignment and is not required for your class.

8. Tell students that magazine subscriptions make a great gift for themselves and for other family members. Suggest that students consider a magazine subscription when they have the opportunity to request a gift or when they buy gifts for others.

Bicycling magazines for children offer biking safety tips. (Corbis)

Dear Parents,

One of the most important ways you can help your child become a better reader is to have reading material at home that is appropriate for your child. You can get books and other reading materials from your public library. You might also choose to purchase magazines that are written with children in mind. Many parents have asked me what magazines they could get for their children. In response to that question, I have devised a list. If you do not wish to use this list, please pass it on to another parent who may be interested.

Sincerely,

Magazines for Children

Child Life
1100 Waterway Blvd.
Indianapolis, IN 46202
12 issues a year
Ages 5–12
Stories, poems, arts and crafts

Creative Kids
P.O. Box 637
Holmes, PA 19043-9937
8 issues a year
Poems, stories, photos, artwork by children

The Electric Company Magazine
P.O. Box 2926
Boulder, CO 80322
12 issues a year
Activities for beginning readers

Highlights for Children
P.O. Box 269
Columbus, OH 43272
11 issues a year
Ages 5–12
Stories, poems, arts and crafts, activities

Jack and Jill
P.O. Box 567B
Indianapolis, IN 46206
12 issues a year
Ages 8–12
Stories, poems, art

Sesame Street Magazine
P.O. Box 52000
Boulder, CO 80321
10 issues a year
Ages 3–7
Stories, games, and activities

Ranger Rick
National Wildlife Federation
1400 16th Street N.W.
Washington, D.C. 20036-2266
12 issues a year
Stories, photos, activities about animals and wildlife

Sports Illustrated for Kids
P.O. Box 830
Birmingham, AL 35282-9487
12 issues a year
Ages 8–14
Sports articles and photos

Your Big Backyard
National Wildlife Federation
1400 16th Street N.W.
Washington, D.C. 20036-2266
Ages 3–5
Stories, puzzles, games, arts and crafts; photos about animals and nature

Practice and Reinforcement Activities

1. Encourage parents to complete a project with their children where some directions need to be read.

2. Maintain dialogue journals with students that focus on the outside reading students are doing. After students have read a portion of a book at home, have them write their responses to the story in a notebook. After students have written responses at home, have them read their responses to their parents and discuss the story with their parents. Then ask students to bring their notebooks to school. Read the entries and respond with your own reactions to the story. Some questions for student responses follow.

What is the best or most memorable thing about this book?

What is the worst thing about this book?

How do you feel about the main character?

Why do you think the book ended this way?

How is the author's style of writing like other authors you have read?

Why do you think the author selected the title?

What are some of your favorite words, phrases, or sentences from the book?

3. Secure books with audiotapes and make them available for home use.

4. Ask students about trips they have taken and list them on the chalkboard. Find as many books as you can about the places students have been and arrange the books on a large table.

5. Provide parents with a refrigerator magnet with the school phone number. Encourage them to call the school with any compliments or concerns.

6. Tell students about the kinds of reading you do as a teacher. Explain to students that many types of jobs require a great deal of reading. Have students ask their parents about the amount and types of reading required on their jobs. Have students share with the class the kinds of reading parents do on their jobs. Create a chart with categories for the types of jobs, the amount of time spent reading, and the kinds of reading done.

7. Contact parents in your class to find local businesses who support community involvement. Have parents organize special speakers who will come to your class to discuss the types of reading and writing they do in their businesses. For example, if you live in a rural area, you might have parents invite local farmers to discuss the reading they need to do about fertilizers, insecticides, environmental issues, and crop production. If you live in a suburban or urban area, you might find managers of local fast food franchises or restaurants. Have speakers discuss the amount of schooling they need for their jobs and the types of reading and writing that they do.

8. Encourage students to maintain learning logs at home. Learning logs are journals for students to record and reflect what they are learning (Tompkins, 2000). Ask students to list the kinds of things they have learned at home. For example, students might have learned how to operate a lawn mower. Tell students to become aware of their learning at home and encourage students to keep a learning log about home learning.

9. Remind students that the actors and actresses they see on television and in the movies read from scripts. Obtain or develop a script for a short play or a commercial. Read the script with the students and then have students volunteer for a part in the script. Read the script as a play or a commercial with different students reading different parts. After students experience a script, ask them to watch television with a parent or older family member for several hours over a week's time. Ask them to identify one or more commercials that are repeated several times during that week. Have students share the words of the commercials in class. (At this point, remind students that commercials are developed to sell something or to share information. Make sure students are aware of the purposes for commercials. If the commercial is designed to sell something, talk with students about ways to resist the commercial's message.) After identifying one or more commercials, ask the students to write the commercial script with their parents at home. After students have written the scripts, ask them to bring the scripts to school to place in a binder. Have students occasionally read the commercial scripts and remind students that when they watch television or movies the actors and actresses have memorized something they read from a script.

Books without Words

OVERVIEW

Driving down a typical road, it is evident that understanding visual clues is crucial to reaching a destination. According to Debes (cited in Smith & Read, 1982), 80% of information must be comprehended visually. Visual literacy is a term used to describe actively using past visual experiences with incoming visual messages to obtain meaning (Sinatra, 1987). Books without words provide a meaningful way for children to become visually literate by perusing the material and telling their own versions of the stories.

One tends to think of books without words as being only appropriate for prereaders; however, such books can benefit *all* age levels and abilities. Non-English-speaking children can "read" these books without the burden of print. Young children can develop expressive verbal skills as they retell the stories repeatedly. Many children will also notice the left-to-right progression of stories as they follow the story line. Nurss, Hough, and Goodson (1981) suggest using books without words to develop a sense of story in young readers. When a child's version of a story is transcribed, it will become apparent that speaking, writing, and reading are interrelated. If the story is then read to an audience, the listening factor is added.

Reading strategies required to comprehend text can also be represented in books without words. Smith and Read (1982) list these concepts addressed in books without words: sequence, details, main idea, inferences, conclusions, cause and effect, and judgments. Also, story elements such as characterization, plot, and imagery are represented in the illustrations of books without words.

Books without words are available in two forms: concept and story. Concept books such as Tana Hoban's *Of Colors and Things* (1989) focus on one idea such as color. Other ideas covered may be shapes, numbers, or letters. The other type of wordless book is a story. In this form, a plot is revealed as the reader follows the progression of the illustrations. In Brinton Turkle's *Deep in the Forest* (1976), a variation of *Goldilocks and the Three Bears* unfolds as the "reader" follows a small bear through a house.

Activities for Books without Words

Provided here are a few activities adapted from a list by Raines and Isbell (1988) to use with books without words. All the suggestions can easily be adapted to fit the needs of students at various age and grade levels.

PREREADERS

- Dictate a version of the story to an adult.
- Act out a favorite scene.
- Label pictures in concept books.
- Tape-record a retelling of the story using a bell when the page is turned.
- Pretend to be a specific character for a friend.
- Make pictures in sequence for a wordless book.
- Name the actions of a character.

BEGINNING READERS

- Write a caption for the most exciting pages.
- Retell the story to a group of classmates.
- Write a new ending for the story.
- Describe your favorite character.
- Write a group story.
- Write dialogue for the story.
- Make a story map.
- Provide words or sentences on cards and match them to a page in the book.

FLUENT READERS

- Remove a character from the story and write a new story about the character.
- Create a wordless book for a younger reader.
- Role play a new scene to be added to the wordless book.
- Discuss how the main idea is shown in a picture book.
- Discuss art elements expressed.
- Create a talking mural in a small group.

Alexander, Martha. *Bobo's Dream.* New York: Dial, 1970.

———. *Out! Out! Out!* New York: Dial, 1968.

Aliki. *Go Tell Aunt Rhody.* New York: Macmillan, 1974.

Amoss, Berthe. *By the Sea.* New York: Parents' Magazine, 1969.

Anderson, Laurie. *The Package.* Indianapolis: Bobbs-Merrill, 1971.

Angel, Marie. *The Ark.* New York: Harper & Row, 1973.

Anno, Mitsumasa. *Anno's Italy.* New York: Philomel, 1984.

———. *Anno's Flea Market.* New York: Philomel, 1984.

———. *Anno's U.S.A.* New York: Philomel, 1983.

———. *Anno's Britain.* New York: Philomel, 1982.

———. *Anno's Journey.* Cleveland, Ohio: Collins-World, 1978.

———. *Anno's Counting Book.* New York: Crowell, 1977.

———. *Anno's Alphabet.* New York: Crowell, 1975.

———. *Dr. Anno's Magical Midnight Circus.* New York: Weatherhill, 1972.

———. *Topsy-Turvies.* New York: Walker/Weatherhill, 1970.

Ardizzone, Edward. *Look What I Can Do.* New York: Scribner's, 1971.

———. *The Wrong Side of the Bed.* New York: Doubleday, 1970.

Arnowsky, Jim. *Mouse Letters: A Very First Alphabet Book.* New York: Clarion, 1999.

Asch, Frank. *In the Eye of the Teddy.* New York: Harper & Row, 1973.

———. *The Blue Balloon.* New York: McGraw-Hill, 1971.

Baker, Jeannie. *Window.* New York: Greenwillow, 1991.

Bang, Molly. *The Grey Lady and the Strawberry Snatcher.* New York: Four Winds, 1980.

Banyai, Istvan. *REMI Rapid Eye Movement.* New York: Viking, 1997.

———. *Re-Zoom.* New York: Viking, 1995.

Barton, Byron. *Elephant.* New York: Seabury, 1971.

Baum, Willi. *Birds of a Feather.* Reading, MA: Addison-Wesley, 1969.

Bollinger-Savelli, Antonella. *The Mouse and the Knitted Cat.* New York: Macmillan, 1974.

———. *The Knitted Cat.* New York: Macmillan, 1972.

Bonners, Susan. *Just in Passing.* New York: Lothrop, Lee & Shepard, 1989.

Briggs, Raymond. *The Snowman.* New York: Random House, 1978.

———. *Father Christmas.* New York: Coward, McCann & Geoghegan, 1973.

Brinckloe, Julie. *The Spider Web.* New York: Doubleday, 1974.

Brown, Craig. *The Patchwork Farmer*. New York: Greenwillow, 1989.

Burton, Marilee R. *The Elephant's Nest*. New York: Harper & Row, 1981.

Carle, Eric. *My Very First Book of Colors*. New York: Crowell, 1974.

————. *My Very First Book of Shapes*. New York: Crowell, 1974.

————. *I See a Song*. New York: Crowell, 1973.

————. *A Very Long Tail*. New York: Crowell, 1972.

————. *The Very Long Train*. New York: Crowell, 1972.

————. *Do You Want to Be My Friend?* New York: Crowell, 1971.

————. *One, Two, Three to the Zoo*. Cleveland, OH: Collins-World, 1968.

Carrick, Donald. *Drip, Drop*. New York: Macmillan, 1973.

Carroll, Ruth. *The Dolphin and the Mermaid*. New York: Henry Z. Walck, 1974.

————. *Rolling Downhill*. New York: Henry Z. Walck, 1973.

————. *The Witch Kitten*. New York: Henry Z. Walck, 1973.

————. *The Chimp and the Clown*. New York: Henry Z. Walck, 1968.

————. *What Whiskers Did*. New York: Henry Z. Walck, 1965.

Carroll, Ruth, and Latrobe, Carroll. *The Christmas Kitten*. New York: Henry Z. Walck, 1970.

Collington, Peter. *A Small Miracle*. New York: Knopf, 1997.

————. *The Tooth Fairy*. New York: Knopf, 1995.

————. *The Midnight Circus*. New York: Knopf, 1992.

————. *On Christmas Eve*. New York: Knopf, 1990.

————. *Angel and the Soldier Boy*. New York: Random House, 1983.

Craig, Helen. *Mouse House Months*. New York: Random House, 1981.

Crews, Donald. *Truck*. New York: Tupelo, 1997.

Day, Alexandra. *Follow Carl!* New York: Farrar Straus Giroux, 1998.

————. *Carl's Birthday*. New York: Farrar Straus Giroux, 1995.

————. *Carl's Masquerade*. New York: Farrar Straus Giroux, 1992.

————. *Carl's Christmas*. New York: Farrar Straus Giroux, 1990.

De Groat, Diane. *Alligator's Toothache*. New York: Crown, 1977.

De Paola, Tomie. *Sing Pierrot, Sing*. New York: Harcourt, 1983.

————. *Flicks*. New York: Harcourt, 1981.

————. *The Hunter and the Animals*. New York: Holiday, 1981.

————. *Pancakes for Breakfast*. New York: Harcourt, 1978.

Elzbieta. *Little Mops and the Butterfly*. New York: Doubleday, 1974.

———. *Little Mops and the Moon*. New York: Doubleday, 1974.

———. *Little Mops at the Seashore*. New York: Doubleday, 1974.

Emberley, Ed. *Birthday Wish*. Boston: Little, Brown, 1977.

Espenscheid, Gertrude. *Oh Ball*. New York: Harper & Row, 1966.

Ets, Marie Hall. *Talking Without Words. I Can. Can You?* New York: Viking, 1968.

Felix, Monique. *The Further Adventures of the Little Mouse Trapped in a Book*. La Jolla, CA: Green Tiger, 1983.

Fuchs, Erich. *Journey to the Moon*. New York: Delacorte, 1969.

Gabrielle, Vincent. *A Day, A Dog*. Asheville, NC: Front Street, 1999.

Gilbert, Elliot. *A Cat*. New York: Holt, 1963.

Gill, Madelaine. *The Spring Hat*. New York: Simon & Schuster, 1993.

Giovannetti. *Max*. New York: Atheneum, 1977.

Goodall, John S. *Creepy Castle*. New York: Simon & Schuster, 1998.

———. *Shrewbettina's Birthday*. New York: Simon & Schuster, 1998.

———. *Little Red Riding Hood*. New York: MacMillan Child Group, 1988.

———. *Above and Below Stairs*. New York: Atheneum, 1983.

———. *Lavinia's Cottage*. New York: Atheneum, 1983.

———. *Paddy Finds a Job*. New York: Atheneum, 1981.

———. *Shrewbettina Goes to Work*. New York: Atheneum, 1981.

———. *Victoria Aboard*. New York: Atheneum, 1981.

———. *An Edwardian Season*. New York: Atheneum, 1980.

———. *An Edwardian Christmas*. New York: Atheneum, 1978.

———. *An Edwardian Summer*. New York: Atheneum, 1976.

———. *Paddy Pork's Holiday*. New York: Atheneum, 1976.

———. *Creepy Castle*. New York: Atheneum, 1975.

———. *Naughty Nancy*. New York: Atheneum, 1975.

———. *The Midnight Adventures of Kelly, Dot and Esmeralda*. New York: Atheneum, 1973.

———. *Paddy's Evening Out*. New York: Atheneum, 1973.

———. *Jacko*. New York: Harcourt, 1972.

———. *The Ballooning Adventures of Paddy Pork*. New York: Harcourt, 1969.

———. *The Adventures of Paddy Pork*. New York: Harcourt, 1968.

Graham, Alastair. *Full Moon Soup*. New York: Dial, 1991.

Hamburger, John. *A Sleepless Day*. New York: Four Winds, 1973.

———. *The Lazy Day*. New York: Four Winds, 1971.

Hefter, Richard. *The Strawberry Word Book*. New York: Larousse, 1974.

Heller, Linda. *Lily at the Table*. New York: Macmillan, 1979.

Henstra, Frisco. *Mighty Mizzling Mouse*. Philadelphia: Lippincott, 1983.

Hoban, Russell, and Selig, Sylvie. *Crocodile and Pierrot*. New York: Scribner's, 1977.

Hoban, Tana. *Of Colors and Things*. New York: Greenwillow, 1989.

———. *Round and Round and Round*. New York: Greenwillow, 1983.

———. *A, B, See*. New York: Greenwillow, 1982.

———. *Take Another Look*. New York: Greenwillow, 1980.

———. *Is It Red? Is It Yellow? Is It Blue?* New York: Greenwillow, 1978.

———. *Dig, Drill, Dump, Fill*. New York: Greenwillow, 1975.

———. *Circles, Triangles and Squares*. New York: Macmillan, 1974.

———. *Over, Under and Through*. New York: Macmillan, 1973.

———. *Count and See*. New York: Macmillan, 1972.

———. *Push Pull, Empty Full*. New York: Macmillan, 1972.

———. *Where Is It?* New York: Macmillan, 1972.

———. *Look Again!* New York: Macmillan, 1971.

———. *Shapes and Things*. New York: Macmillan, 1970.

Hoest, William. *Taste of Carrot*. New York: Atheneum, 1967.

Hogrogian, Nonny. *Apples*. New York: Macmillan, 1972.

Hutchins, Pat. *Changes, Changes*. New York: Macmillan, 1971.

Keats, Ezra Jack. *Clementina's Cactus*. New York: Viking, 1982.

———. *Pssst! Doggie*. New York: Franklin Watts, 1973.

———. *Skates*. New York: Franklin Watts, 1973.

Kent, Jack. *The Scribble Monster*. New York: Harcourt, 1981.

———. *The Egg Book*. New York: Macmillan, 1975.

Knobler, Susan. *The Tadpole and the Frog*. Commack, NY: Harvey, 1974.

Krahn, Fernando. *Amanda and the Mysterious Carpet*. New York: Clarion Books, 1985.

———. *The Secret in the Dungeon*. New York: Clarion, 1983.

———. *The Biggest Christmas Tree on Earth*. Boston: Little, Brown, 1978.

————. *Catch That Cat!* New York: Dutton, 1978.

————. *Earth.* Boston: Little, Brown, 1978.

————. *The Great Ape.* New York: Viking, 1978.

————. *A Funny Friend from Heaven.* Philadelphia: Lippincott, 1977.

————. *The Mystery of the Giant Footprints.* New York: Dutton, 1977.

————. *Little Love Story.* Philadelphia: Lippincott, 1976.

————. *Sebastian and the Mushroom.* New York: Delacorte, 1976.

————. *Who's Seen the Scissors?* New York: Dutton, 1975.

————. *April Fools.* New York: Dutton, 1974.

————. *The Self-Made Snowman.* Philadelphia: Lippincott, 1974.

————. *A Flying Saucer Full of Spaghetti.* New York: Dutton, 1970.

————. *How Santa Claus Had a Long and Difficult Journey Delivering His Presents.* New York: Delacorte, 1968.

————. *Journeys of Sebastian.* New York: Delacorte, 1968.

Lisker, Sonia. *Lost.* New York: Harcourt, 1975.

————. *The Attic Witch.* New York: Four Winds, 1973.

Lustig, Loretta. *The Pop-Up Book of Trucks.* New York: Random House, 1974.

McCully, Emily. *New Baby.* New York: Harper & Row, 1988.

————. *School.* New York: Harper & Row, 1987.

————. *Picnic.* New York: Harper & Row, 1984.

McTrusty, Ron. *Dandelion Year.* Commack, NY: Harvey, 1974.

Maizligh, Lisa. *The Ring,* New York: Greenwillow, 1996.

Mari, Iela, and Mari, Enzo. *The Apple and the Moth.* New York: Pantheon, 1970.

————. *The Chicken and the Egg.* New York: Pantheon, 1970.

Massie, Diane Redfield. *Cocoon.* New York: Crowell, 1983.

Mayer, Mercer. *Oops.* New York: Dial, 1977.

————. *Ah Choo.* New York: Dial, 1976.

————. *Hiccup.* New York: Dial, 1976.

————. *The Great Cat Chase.* New York: Four Winds, 1975.

————. *One Frog Too Many.* New York: Dial, 1975.

————. *Frog Goes to Dinner.* New York: Dial, 1974.

————. *Two Moral Tales.* New York: Four Winds, 1974.

————. *Two More Moral Tales*. New York: Four Winds, 1974.

————. *Bubble Bubble*. New York: Parents' Magazine, 1973.

————. *Frog on His Own*. New York: Dial, 1973.

————. *Frog, Where Are You?* New York: Dial, 1969.

————. *A Boy, a Dog, and a Frog*. New York: Dial, 1967.

Mayer, Mercer, and Mayer, Marianna. *A Boy, a Dog, a Frog and a Friend*. New York: Dial, 1971.

Mendoza, George. *The Inspector*. Garden City, NY: Doubleday, 1970.

————. *And I Must Hurry for the Sea Is Coming In*. Englewood Cliffs, NJ: Prentice Hall, 1969.

Meyer, Renate. *Hide-and-Seek*. Scarsdale, NY: Bradbury, 1972.

————. *Vicki*. New York: Atheneum, 1969.

Miller, Barry. *Alphabet World*. New York: Macmillan, 1971.

Olschewski, Alfred. *Winterbird*. Boston: Houghton, 1969.

Ormerod, Jan. *Moonlight*. Wooster, OH: Lathrop, 1982.

————. *Sunshine*. Wooster, OH: Lathrop, 1981.

Peddle, Daniel. *Snow Day*. New York: Doubleday, 2000.

Prater, John. *The Gift*. New York: Viking Kestrel, 1986.

Ramage, Corinne. *The Joneses*. Philadelphia: Lippincott, 1975.

Rathman, P. *Goodnight Gorilla*. New York: Scholastic, 1994.

Reiss, John J. *Shapes*. Scarsdale, NJ: Bradbury, 1974.

Ringi, Kjell. *The Winner*. New York: Harper & Row, 1969.

————. *The Magic Stick*. New York: Harper & Row, 1968.

Rockwell, Anne. *Albert B. Club and Zebra*. New York: Harper Children Books, 1987.

Rohmann, Eric. *Time Flies*. New York: Crown, 1994.

Ross, Pat. *Hi Fly*. New York: Crown, 1974.

Schick, Eleanor. *Making Friends*. New York: Macmillan, 1969.

Schubert, Dieter. *Where's My Monkey*. New York: Dial, 1987.

Schweninger, Ann. *A Dance for Three*. New York: Dial, 1979.

Simons, Ellie. *Family*. New York: David McKay, 1970.

————. *Cat*. New York: David McKay, 1968.

————. *Dog*. New York: David McKay, 1967.

Sis, Peter. *Dinosaur!* New York: Greenwillow, 2000.

————. *Ocean World*. New York: Greenwillow, 1992.

Spier, Peter. *Dreams*. New York: Doubleday, 1986.

———. *Christmas*. New York: Doubleday, 1983.

———. *Rain*. New York: Doubleday, 1982.

———. *Noah's Ark*. New York: Doubleday, 1977.

Steiner, Charlotte. *I Am Andy*. New York: Knopf, 1961.

Sugano, Yoshikatsu. *The Kitten's Adventure*. New York: McGraw-Hill, 1971.

Sugita, Yutaka. *My Friend Little John*. New York: McGraw-Hill, 1973.

Tafuri, Nancy. *Follow Me*. New York: Greenwillow, 1990.

———. *Junglewalk*. New York: Greenwillow, 1988.

———. *Do Not Disturb*. New York: Greenwillow, 1987.

Tanaka, Hideyuki. *The Happy Day*. New York: Atheneum, 1983.

Turk, Hanne. *Happy Birthday Max*. Natick, ME: Neugebauer, 1984.

———. *Max Packs*. Natick, ME: Neugebauer, 1984.

———. *Goodnight Max*. Natick, ME: Neugebauer, 1983.

———. *A Lesson for Max*. Natick, ME: Neugebauer, 1983.

———. *Max the Artlover*. Natick, ME: Neugebauer, 1983.

———. *Merry Christmas Max*. Natick, ME: Neugebauer, 1983.

———. *Rainy Day Max*. Natick, ME: Neugebauer, 1983.

———. *Raking Leaves With Max*. Natick, ME: Neugebauer, 1983.

———. *Max Versus the Cube*. Natick, ME: Neugebauer, 1982.

———. *The Rope Skips Max*. Natick, ME: Neugebauer, 1982.

———. *A Surprise for Max*. Natick, ME: Neugebauer, 1982.

Turkle, Brinton. *Deep in the Forest*. New York: Dutton, 1976.

Ueno, Noriko. *Elephant Buttons*. New York: Harper & Row, 1973.

Ungerer, Tomi. *One, Two, Three*. New York: Harper & Row, 1964.

———. *One, Two, Where's My Shoe?* New York: Harper & Row, 1964.

———. *Snail, Where Are You?* New York: Harper & Row, 1962.

Van Allsburg, Christopher. *The Mysteries of Harris Burdick*. Boston: Houghton, 1984.

———. *Ben's Dream*. Boston: Houghton-Mifflin, 1982.

Van Soelen, Philip. *A Cricket in the Grass*. New York: Scribner's, 1981.

Vasiliu, Mircea. *What's Happening?* New York: John Day, 1970.

Ward, Lynd. *The Silver Pony*. Boston: Houghton, 1973.

Weatherbee, Holden. *The Wonder Ring.* New York: Doubleday, 1979.

Wezel, Peter. *Good Bird.* New York: Harper & Row, 1966.

Wiesner, David. *Sector 7.* New York: Clarion, 1999.

————. *Tuesday.* Boston: Houghton, 1991.

————. *Free Fall.* New York: Lothrop, 1988.

Wildsmith, Brian. *Whose Shoes?* Oxford: Oxford University Press, 1984.

————. *The Apple Bird.* Oxford: Oxford University Press, 1997.

————. *The Nest.* Oxford: Oxford University Press, 1983.

————. *The Trunk.* Oxford: Oxford University Press, 1982.

————. *Animal Tricks.* Oxford: Oxford University Press, 1981.

————. *Brian Wildsmith's Circus.* New York: Franklin Watts, 1970.

Wilson, April. *Magpie Magic.* New York: Dial, 1999.

Winter, Paula. *Sir Andrew.* New York: Crown, 1980.

————. *The Bear and the Fly.* New York: Crown, 1976.

Wondriska, William. *A Long Piece of String.* New York: Holt, 1963.

Young, Ed. *Up a Tree.* New York: Harper & Row, 1983.

Alphabet Books

OVERVIEW

When *The New England Primer* was published in 1683, the intent was to present letters of the alphabet as well as to teach the moral strictures of early American Society (Camp & Tompkins, 1990). During this period, reading was a serious subject, not to be considered interesting or fun. Alphabet books have evolved considerably in content and form over the last 300 years; they are a pleasurable literary genre that benefits *all* age levels.

As adults share alphabet books, prereaders can learn several concepts about print that are crucial to emergent literacy:

1. differences between letters and words

2. directionality

3. orientation of letters

4. distinctive graphic features

5. sound-symbol relationships

6. beginning word sounds

7. symbolic differences between numbers and letters (Smolkin & Yaden, 1992).

Alphabet books are represented in several formats, varying from uppercase and lowercase letters accompanied with pictures to complex rhymes discussing a specific topic. In *A Is for Angry* (Boyton, 1983), a simple phrase describes the actions of the animal in the picture, which also helps form the letter. Graeme Base's *Animalia* (1986) uses alliteration to describe a scene representing each letter, as well as several fantastic illustrations. *Chicka Chicka Boom Boom* (Martin & Archambault, 1989) tells a rhyming story of letters racing to the top of a coconut tree. When the tree topples over, the reader sees the letters in different positions and predicaments. Illustrations and paragraphs describe 26 African concepts in Musgrove's (1976) Caldecott-winning *Ashanti to Zulu: African Traditions.*

Activities for Alphabet Books

The following are extension activities for alphabet books. Although the activities are arranged by type of reader, they can be adapted to any age or ability level.

PREREADERS

- Name pictures or objects in the book.
- Talk about your favorite letter page.
- Share an alphabet book with a friend.
- Tell the story to an adult.
- Draw a picture that shows your favorite letter.

BEGINNING READERS

- Make an alphabet book about yourself.
- Make an alphabet book with a group describing your favorite foods.
- Tell three differences between two alphabet books.
- Tape-record your reading of an alphabet book for a younger student.
- Write a rhyme about your favorite letter.
- Make an alphabet name book of classmates and friends.

FLUENT READERS

- Make an alphabet book for a young child.
- Describe an object using alliteration.
- Write riddles to represent letters. Use *Q Is for Duck* (Elting & Folsom, 1980) for ideas.
- Make an alphabet book in a group that describes a historic event.
- Write about a science topic using the ABC form.

Recommended Alphabet Books

Agard, John. *The Calypso Alphabet.* New York: Henry Holt, 1989.

Alexander, Martha. *A You're Adorable.* Cambridge, MA: Candlewick Press, 1994.

Anglund, Joan Walsh. *In a Pumpkin Shell, A Mother Goose ABC.* San Diego: Harcourt, 1960.

Anno, Mitsumasa. *Anno's Magical ABC: An Anamorphic Alphabet.* New York: Philomel, 1981.

————. *Anno's Alphabet: An Adventure in Imagination.* New York: Crowell, 1975.

Ashton, Elizabeth Allen. *An Old-fashioned ABC.* New York: Viking, 1990.

Aylesworth, Jim. *Old Black Fly.* New York: Holt, 1992.

Azarian, Mary. *A Gardener's Alphabet.* Boston: Houghton Mifflin, 2000.

————. *A Farmer's Alphabet.* Boston: Godine, 1981.

Barsam, Richard Meran. *A Peaceable Kingdom: The Shaker Abecedarius.* New York: Puffin, 1982.

Base, Graeme. *Animalia.* New York: Harry N. Abrams, 1986.

Baskin, Leonard. *Hosie's Alphabet.* New York: Viking, 1972.

Bayer, Jabe. *A, My Name is Alice.* New York: Dial, 1984.

Bender, Robert. *The A to Z Beastly Jamboree.* New York: Lodestar, 1996.

Bernhard, Durga. *Alphabeasts: A Hide & Seek Alphabet Book.* New York: Holiday House, 1993.

Blake, Quentin. *Quentin Blake's ABC.* New York: Knopf, 1989.

Bourke, Linda. *Handmade Alphabet: A Manual ABC.* Reading, MA: Addison-Wesley, 1981.

Boynton, Sandra. *A Is for Angry.* New York: Workman, 1983.

Bridwell, Norman. *Clifford's ABC.* New York: Scholastic, 1983.

Brown, Judith Gwyn. *Alphabet Dreams.* Englewood Cliffs, NJ: Prentice Hall, 1976.

Brown, Marcia. *All Butterflies: An ABC.* New York: Scribners, 1974.

Burningham, John. *John Burningham's ABC.* Bellevue, WA: Bobs, 1967.

Carle, Eric. *All About Arthur: An Absolutely Absurd Ape.* Chicago: Watts, 1974.

Carlson, N. *ABC Like Me!* New York: Penguin, 1997.

Carter, Angela. *Comic & Curious Cats.* New York: Harmony Books, 1979.

Chandra, Deborah. *A is for Amos.* New York: Farrar, Straus and Giroux, 1999.

Chess, Victoria. *Alfred's Alphabet Walk.* New York: Greenwillow, 1979.

Coletta, Irene. *From A to Z: The Collected Letters of Irene and Hattie Coletta.* New York: Prentice Hall, 1979.

Crowther, Robert. *The Most Amazing Hide and Seek Alphabet Book.* New York: Viking, 1977.

Downie, Jill. *Alphabet Puzzle.* New York: Lothrop, 1988.

Duke, Kate. *The Guinea Pig ABC.* New York: Dutton, 1983.

Duvoisin, Roger. *A is for Ark*. New York: Lothrop, 1952.

Ehlert, Lois. *Eating the Alphabet: Fruits and Vegetables from A to Z*. San Diego: Harcourt, 1989.

Eichenberf, Fritz. *Ape in a Cape*. San Diego: Harcourt, 1952.

Elting, Mary, and Folsom, Michael. *Q Is for Duck: An Alphabet Guessing Game*. New York: Clarion, 1980.

Ernst, L. *The Letters are Lost*. New York: Penguin, 1996.

Feelings, Muriel. *Jambo Means Hello: Swahili Alphabet Book*. New York: Dial, 1974.

Fisher, Leonard Everett. *Alphabet Art*. New York: Simon and Schuster, 1984.

Gag, Wanda. *ABC Bunny*. New York: Coward, 1933.

Garten, Jan. *An Alphabet Tale*. New York: Random House, 1964.

Geddes, Anne. *Down in the Garden Alphabet Book*. San Rafael, CA: Cedco, 1997.

Geisert, Arthur. *Pigs from A to Z*. Boston: Houghton Mifflin, 1986.

Girnis, Meg. *ABC for You and Me*. Morton Grove, IL: Whitman, 2000.

Grover, Max. *The Accidental Zucchini: An Unexpected Alphabet*. New York: Harcourt Brace, 1993.

Hague, Kathleen. *Alphabears: An ABC Book*. New York: Henry Holt, 1984.

Hepworth, Cathi. *Antics! An Alphabet of Ants*. New York: Putnam & Sons, 1992.

Hoban, Tana. *A, B, See!* New York: Greenwillow, 1982.

Horenstein, Henry. *A Is For . . .: A Photographer's Alphabet of Animals*. New York: Gulliver/Harcourt Brace, 1999.

Houget, Susan. *I Unpacked My Grandmother's Trunk*. New York: Dutton, 1985.

Hughes, Shirley. *Alfie's ABC*. New York: Lothrop, Lee and Shepard, 1998.

Isadora, Rachel. *City Seen from A to Z*. New York: Greenwillow, 1983.

Jernigan, Kathleen. *Agave Blooms Just Once*. Tucson: Harbinger House, 1984.

Johnson, Audean. *A to Z Look and See*. New York: Random House, 1989.

Johnson, Stephen T. *Alphabet City*. New York: Viking, 1995.

Jordon, Martin and Tanis. *Amazon Alphabet*. New York: Kingfisher, 1996.

Kellogg, Steven. *Aster Aardvark's Alphabet Adventures*. New York: Mulberry Books, 1987.

Kitamura, Satoshi. *What's Inside: The Alphabet Book*. New York: Farrar, 1985.

Kitchen, Bert. *Animal Alphabet*. New York: Dial, 1984.

Knowlton, Jack. *Geography from A to Z: A Picture Glossary*. New York: Crowell, 1988.

Lear, Edward. *A Was Once an Apple*. Cambridge, MA: Candlewick Press, 1992.

————. *Nonsense ABC's*. Philadelphia: Running Press, 1991.

————. *An Edward Lear Alphabet.* New York: Lothrop, 1983.

Leedy, Loreen. *The Dragon ABC Hunt.* New York: Holiday House, 1986.

Leonard, Marcia. *Alphabet Bandits.* Mahwah, NJ: Troll, 1990.

Lester, Mike. *A is for Salad.* New York: Putnam & Grosset, 2000.

Linscott, Jody. *Upon A to Z: An Alphabet Odyssey.* New York: Doubleday, 1991.

Lionni, Leo. *The Alphabet Tree.* New York: Dragonfly Books, 1968.

Lobel, Anita. *Alison's Zinnia.* New York: Greenwillow, 1990.

Lobel, Arnold. *On Market Street.* New York: Greenwillow, 1981.

Macdonald, Suse. *Alphabetics.* New York: Bradbury Press, 1986.

McPhail, David. *Animals A to Z.* New York: Scholastic, 1989.

Martin, Bill, Jr., and Archambault, John. *Chicka Chicka Boom Boom.* New York: Simon and Schuster Books for Young Readers, 1989.

Matthiesen, Thomas. *ABC: An Alphabet Book.* New York: Platt, 1966.

Micklethwait, Lucy. *I Spy.* New York: Greenwillow, 1992.

Miles, Miska. *Apricot ABC.* Boston: Little Brown, 1969.

Miller, Jane. *Farm Alphabet Book.* New York: Scholastic, 1981.

Munari, Bruno. *Bruno Munari's ABC.* Chicago: World, 1960.

Musgrove, Margaret. *Ashanti to Zulu: African Traditions.* New York: Dial, 1976.

Neumeier, Marty, and Glaser, Byron. *Action Alphabet.* New York: Greenwillow, 1984.

Obligado, Lilian. *Faint Frogs Feeling Feverish & Other Terrifically Tantalizing Tongue Twisters.* New York: Viking, 1983.

Oxenbury, Helen. *Helen Oxenbury's ABC of Things.* Chicago: Watts, 1972.

Pallotta, Jerry. *The Extinct Alphabet Book.* Watertown, MA: Charlesbridge Publishing, 1993.

————. *The FROG Alphabet Book.* Chicago: Children's Press, 1990.

————. *The Yucky Reptile Alphabet Book.* Watertown, MA: Charlesbridge Publishing, 1989.

————. *The FLOWER Alphabet Book.* Boston: Quinlan Press, 1988.

Paul, Ann Whitford. *Eight Hands Round: A Patchwork Alphabet.* New York: HarperCollins, 1991.

Preller, J. *NBA Action from A to Z.* New York: Scholastic, 1997.

Rankin, Laura. *The Handmade Alphabet.* New York: Dial, 1991.

Robinson, M., San Jose, C., & Richmond, M. *The Timbertoes ABC Alphabet Book.* Honesdale, PA: Boyds Mills Press, 1997.

Rockwell, Anne. *Albert B, Cub, and Zebra.* New York: Harper, 1977.

Ruben, Patricia. *Apples to Zippers.* New York: Doubleday, 1976.

Rubin, Cynthia Elyce. *ABC Americana from the National Gallery of Art.* San Diego: Gulliver Books, 1989.

Sanved, K. *The Butterfly Alphabet.* New York: Scholastic, 1996.

Sardegna, Jill. *K is for Kiss Goodnight.* New York: Delacorte Press/Doubleday, 1994.

Sendak, Maurice. *Alligators All Round.* New York: Harper, 1962.

Shannon, George. *Tomorrow's Alphabet.* New York: Greenwillow, 1996.

Shelby, Anne, and Trivas, Irene. *Potluck.* New York: Orchard, 1991.

Simmonds, Posy. *F-Freezing ABC.* New York: Knopf, 1995.

Slate, Joseph. *Miss Bindergarten Gets Ready for Kindergarten.* New York: Dutton/Windmill, 1996.

Sloat, Teri. *From Letter to Letter.* New York: Dutton, 1989.

Steig, Jeanne, and Steig, William. *Alpha Beta Chowder.* New York: HarperCollins, 1992.

Stock, Catherine. *Alexander's Midnight Snack: A Little Elephant's ABC.* New York: Clarion, 1988.

Sullivan, Charles. *Alphabet Animals.* New York: Rizzoli, 1988.

Tarlow, Nora. *Halloween Alphabet.* New York: Putnam, 1999.

Tryon, Leslie. *Albert's Alphabet.* New York: Atheneum, 1991.

Tudor, Tasha. *A Is for Annabelle.* New York: Walck, 1954.

Van Allsburg, Chris. *The Z Was Zapped.* Boston: Houghton Mifflin, 1987.

Walters, Marguerite. *The City-Country ABC: My Alphabet Ride in the City, and My Alphabet Ride in the Country.* New York: Doubleday, 1966.

Watson, Clyde. *Applebet: An ABC.* New York: Farrar, Straus & Giroux, 1982.

Wildsmith, Brian. *Brian Wildsmith's ABC.* Chicago: Watts, 1963.

Williams, Jenny. *Everyday ABC.* New York: Dial, 1991.

Wilner, Isabel. *A Garden Alphabet.* New York: Dutton Children's Books, 1991.

———. *B is for Bethlehem: A Christmas Alphabet.* New York: Dutton Children's Books, 1990.

Wojtowycz, David. *Animal ABC.* London: Winchester House, 1999.

Yolen, Jane. *All in the Woodland Early.* New York: Collins, 1979.

Pattern Books

OVERVIEW

Students who are just learning to read are exposed to a number of different approaches, and print awareness is probably the first skill emergent readers will need to develop. As teachers begin exposing students to print awareness concepts, whole class or small group instruction is helpful. The use of pattern books, along with a combination of language experience and big books, should enable students to become aware of the purposes and functions of print. Observing early contact with print allows teachers to collect information about students' awareness of important concepts related to reading.

Rhodes (1981) defines a predictable book as one having text that, at times, is either sufficiently repetitive or so predictable that students can chant the text with the teacher after it has been read once or twice. One major distinction of pattern books is the language in the books. Some teachers confuse predictable materials in the books with consistent spelling patterns: Pat sat on that mat. Predictable language is much different from consistent spelling patterns, mainly because such sentences are an unnatural example of the way we speak.

Certain predictable language can be found in a student's speech; the distinction is that the student's pattern and rhythm of language contain a message that is also memorable. Most students find it easy to recall information that is repetitive, meaningful, and can be chanted or read along with the teacher or other students.

Pattern books and other predictable materials are available in a variety of forms. *Brown Bear, Brown Bear* (Martin, 1970) uses catchy rhythm and rhyme to entice the reader, making recall of the material rather simple. Other books use repeated phrases and plot to hold the attention of students. An example of this type of pattern book is *Alexander and the Terrible, Horrible, No Good, Very Bad Day* (Viorst, 1972). Students can relate to the story line of this book, and their anticipation heightens throughout the story as they gain appreciation for the way Alexander copes with his problems and catastrophes. Opitz (1995) recommends strategies and activities for teaching with predictable books and provides a resource of over 800 predictable books.

With some pattern books, students can use the rhyming language to hypothesize what the author might say next. Reading will help confirm predictions as well as strengthen new knowledge of the familiar print encountered. Structured language patterns allow beginning readers to use their predictive abilities for successful reading. Modeling and role playing are essential to the success of using pattern books in the classroom.

Uses for Pattern Books

Following are a few ideas for using pattern books to develop fluent, natural reading with beginning readers. The ideas may also be adapted for use with other, more experienced readers.

- Ask students to predict what the book will be about once they have heard the title of the book and have seen the cover.
- After you have read three or four pages to them, ask students what they think will happen or what a specific character will say.
- Have students explain the reasons for their predictions.
- Allow students to confirm, reject, or revise their predictions once you have read the part of the story that pertains to their predictions.
- Read the rest of the story and ask students to join in when they can.

Activities Involving Pattern Books

- Match sentence strips to lines from the actual story. Matching individual words with target words from the story can also be done.
- Do a cloze activity with the students based on the predictable language found in the story. Omit key words from the story that would complete a phrase, thought, or rhyme.
- On a subsequent day, read the story to the students again, giving them opportunities to join in as well as to say the next line before you read it.
- Using a large wall chart, have students take turns pointing to words you read again from the story.
- When students have learned the story well, let them take home booklets that contain a copy of the story to practice reading to friends or family members.
- Have students dictate patterned language of their own to you for the composition of student-generated literature. Stress, as appropriate, the importance of familiarity of language and the use of rhythm and/or rhyming. Students will want to read books they have made and will want to share this material with parents, teachers, and other students.
- Change the outcome of the story.
- Have students draw a new picture that could be added to the story, following the pattern or prediction. Students could work individually or in groups.
- Change one or two words and create a new pattern book. Rewrite the story as a class activity.

Ahlberg, Janet, and Ahlberg, Allen. *Each Peach Pear Plum.* New York: Scholastic, 1978.

Alain. *One Two Three Going to Sea.* New York: Scholastic, 1964.

Alborough, Jez. *Where's My Teddy?* Cambridge, MA: Candlewick, 1992.

Aliki. *My Five Senses.* New York: Crowell, 1962.

Anholt, Catherine, and Anholt, Laurence. *What I Like.* New York: Putnam, 1991.

Archambault, John, and Bill Martin, Jr. *A Beautiful Feast For a Big King Cat.* New York: Harper Collins, 1989.

Asch, Frank. *Monkey Face.* New York: Parents' Magazine, 1977.

———. *Just Like Daddy.* New York: Prentice Hall, 1961.

Aylesworth, Jim. *My Son John.* New York: Aladdin, 1994.

Baer, Gene. *Thump Thump Rat A Tat Tat.* New York: Harper & Row, 1989.

Baker, Keith. *Who is This Beast?* New York: Voyager/Harcourt Brace, 1990.

Balian, Lorna. *Where in the World Is Henry?* Scarsdale, NJ: Bradbury, 1972.

Barrett, Judi. *Animals Should Definitely Not Act Like People.* New York: Antheneum, 1980.

———. *Animals Should Definitely Not Wear Clothing.* New York: Antheneum, 1970.

Bauer, Marion Dane. *Sleep, Little One, Sleep.* New York: Simon & Schuster, 1999.

Baurn, Arline, and Baum, Joseph. *One Bright Monday Morning.* New York: Random House, 1962.

Beaton, Clare. *One Moose, Twenty Mice.* New York: Bearfoot, 1999.

Becker, John. *Seven Little Rabbits.* New York: Scholastic, 1973.

Beckman, Kaj. *Lisa Cannot Sleep.* New York: Franklin Watts, 1969.

Bonsall, Crosby. *The Case of the Cat's Meow.* New York: Harper & Row, 1965.

Borden, Louise. *Caps, Hats, Socks & Mittens.* New York: Scholastic, 1989.

Brandenberg, Franz. *A Robber, A Robber.* New York: Greenwillow, 1976.

———. *I Wish I Was Sick, Too.* New York: Greenwillow, 1976.

———. *I Once Knew a Man.* New York: Macmillan, 1970.

Brooke, L. Leslie. *Johnny Crow's Garden.* New York: Fredrick Warne, 1903.

Brown Marcia. *The Three Billy Goats Gruff.* New York: Harcourt, 1957.

Brown, Margaret Wise. *The Important Book.* New York: Parents' Magazine, 1964.

———. *Four Fur Feet.* New York: William R. Scott, 1961.

———. *Home for a Bunny.* New York: Golden Press, 1956.

———. *Where Have You Been?* New York: Scholastic, 1952.

———. *Goodnight Moon.* New York: Harper & Row, 1947.

Brown, Ruth. *A Dark, Dark Tale.* New York: Dial, 1981.

Bulla, Clyde Robert. *The Chalk Box Kid.* New York: Random House, 1987.

Bunting, Eve. *Flower Garden.* New York: Harcourt Brace, 1994.

Burningham, John. *Would You Rather?* New York: Crowell, 1978.

———. *Mr. Gumpy's Outing.* New York: Holt, 1970.

Burton, Marilie. *Tail, Toes, Eyes, Ears, Nose.* New York: Harper & Row, 1988.

Butler, Dorothy. *My Brown Bear Barney.* New York: Greenwillow, 1988.

Byars, Betsy. *Hooray for the Golly Sisters!* New York: Harper & Row, 1990.

Cairns, Scharlaine. *Oh No!* Crystal Lake, IL: Rigby Education, 1987.

Carle, Eric. *The Very Busy Spider.* New York: Philomel, 1985.

———. *The Grouchy Ladybug.* New York: Crowell, 1977.

———. *The Mixed-Up Chameleon.* New York: Crowell, 1975.

———. *Have You Seen My Cat?* Saxonville, MA: Picture Book Studio, 1973.

———. *Rooster's Off to See the World.* Saxonville, MA: Picture Book Studio, 1972.

———. *Do You Want to Be My Friend?* New York: Harper & Row, 1971.

———. *The Very Hungry Caterpillar.* Cleveland, OH: Collins-World, 1969.

Cazet, Denys. *Nothing At All.* New York: Orchard, 1994.

Charlip, Remy. *Fortunately.* New York: Parents' Magazine, 1969.

———. *What Good Luck! What Bad Luck!* New York: Scholastic, 1969.

Cherry, Lynne. *Who's Sick Today?* New York: Dutton, 1988.

Coerr, Eleanor. *Chang's Paper Pony.* New York: Harper & Row, 1986.

Cohen, Caron Lee. *Three Yellow Dogs.* New York: Greenwillow, 1980.

Cohen, Miriam. *First Grade Takes a Test.* New York: Greenwillow, 1980.

Cole, Brock. *The King at the Door.* New York: Doubleday, 1979.

Cole, Joanna, and Calmenson, Stephanie. *Ready . . . Set . . . Read! The Beginning Reader's Treasury.* New York: Doubleday, 1990.

Collicutt, Paul. *This Train.* New York: Farrar, Straus & Giroux, 1999.

Conover, Chris. *Six Little Ducks.* New York: Crowell, 1976.

Cook, Bernadine. *The Little Fish That Got Away.* Reading, MA: Addison-Wesley, 1976.

Cowley, Joy. *Greedy Cat.* New York: Richard C. Owen, 1988.

———. *Meanies.* Bothell, WA: The Wright Group, 1987.

———. *Mrs. Wishy-Washy.* Bothell, WA: The Wright Group, 1987.

———. *Number One.* New York: Richard C. Owen, 1987.

———. *The Jigaree.* Bothell, WA: The Wright Group, 1987.

———. *The Red Rose.* Bothell, WA: The Wright Group, 1987.

Cuyler, Margery. *That's Good, That's Bad.* New York: Holt, 1991.

DePaola, Tomie. *The Comic Adventures of Old Mother Hubbard and Her Dog.* New York: Harcourt, 1981.

Recommended Pattern Books

De Regniers, Beatrice Schenk. *May I Bring a Friend?* New York: Atheneum, 1972.

———. *Catch a Little Fox.* New York: Seabury, 1970.

———. *Willy O'Dwyer Jumped in the Fire.* New York: Atheneum, 1968.

———. *The Day Everybody Cried.* New York: Viking, 1967.

———. *How Joe the Bear and Sam the Mouse Got Together.* New York: Parents' Magazine, 1965.

———. *The Little Book.* New York: Henry Z. Walck, 1961.

Demers, Jan. *What Do You Do With a . . .?* Pinellas, FL: Willowisp, 1985.

Deming, A. G. *Who Is Tapping at My Window?* New York: Dutton, 1988.

Dodds, Dayle Ann. *Wheel Away.* New York: Harper Trophy, 1989.

Domanska, Janina. *Din, Dan, Don, It's Christmas.* New York: Greenwillow, 1975.

Dragonwagon, Crescent. *This Is the Bread I Baked for Ned.* New York: Aladdin, 1999.

Ehlert, Lois. *Feathers for Lunch.* New York: Harcourt Brace, 1990.

Ehrlich, Amy. *Leo, Zack, and Emmie.* New York: Dial, 1981.

Einsel, Walter. *Did You Ever See?* New York: Scholastic, 1962.

Emberly, Barbara. *One Wide River to Cross.* Englewood Cliffs, NJ: Prentice Hall, 1966.

Emberly, Barbara, and Emberly, Ed. *Drummer Hoff.* Englewood Cliffs, NJ: Prentice Hall, 1967.

Emberly, Ed. *Klippity Klop.* Boston: Little, Brown, 1974.

Ets, Marie Hall. *Elephant in a Well.* New York: Viking, 1972.

———. *Play With Me.* New York: Viking, 1955.

Evans, Katie. *Hunky Dory Ate It.* New York: Dutton, 1992.

Field, Rachel. *General Store.* New York: Greenwillow, 1988.

Flack, Marjorie. *Ask Mr. Bear.* New York: Macmillan, 1932.

Fleming, Denise. *In the Tall, Tall Grass.* New York: Holt, 1992.

Fox, Mem. *Shoes from Grandpa.* New York: Orchard, 1990.

Gage, Wilson. *Squash Pie.* New York: Greenwillow, 1976.

Galdone, Paul. *The Teeny, Tiny Woman.* Boston: Houghton, 1984.

———. *The Gingerbread Boy.* New York: Seabury, 1975.

———. *The Little Red Hen.* New York: Scholastic, 1973.

———. *The Three Billy Goats Gruff.* New York: Seabury, 1973.

———. *The Three Bears.* New York: Scholastic, 1972.

———. *The Three Little Pigs.* New York: Seabury, 1970.

———. *Henny Penny.* New York: Scholastic, 1968.

Gelman, Rita Golden. *I Went to the Zoo.* New York: Scholastic, 1993.

Gilman, Phoebe. *Jillian Jiggs.* New York: Scholastic, 1985.

Gerstein, Mordicai. *Roll Over!* New York: Crown, 1984.

Ginsburg, Mirra. *Good Morning, Chick.* New York: Greenwillow, 1980.

———. *The Chick and the Duckling.* New York: Macmillan, 1972.

Goennnel, Heidi. *My Day.* Boston: Little, Brown, 1988.

Goss, Janet L., and Harste, Jerome. *It Didn't Frighten Me!* New York: Scholastic, 1988.

Graham, John. *I Love You, Mouse.* New York: Harcourt, 1976.

———. *A Crowd of Cows.* New York: Scholastic, 1968.

Green, Robyn, Pollock, Yevonne, and Scarffe, Bronwen. *When Goldilocks Went to the House of the Bears.* New York: Scholastic, 1987.

Greenberg, Polly. *Oh Lord, I Wish I Was a Buzzard.* New York: Macmillan, 1968.

Greenly, Valerie. *White Is the Moon.* New York: Macmillan, 1990.

Griffith, Helen V. *Alex and the Cat.* New York: Greenwillow, 1982.

Guarino, Deborah. *Is Your Mama a Llama?* New York: Scholastic, 1989.

Hamm, Diane. *Rockabye Farm.* New York: Half Moon/Simon Schuster, 1992.

Hays, Sarah. *The Grumpalump.* New York: Clarion, 1990.

Hellen, Nancy. *Old MacDonald Had a Farm.* New York: Orchard, 1990.

———. *The Bus Stop.* New York: Orchard, 1988.

Hennessy, B.G. *Jake Baked the Cake.* New York: Viking, 1990.

Higgins, Don. *Papa's Going to Buy Me a Mockingbird.* New York: Seabury, 1968.

Hill, Eric. *Where's Spot?* New York: Putnam, 1980.

Hoban, Lillian. *Arthur's Prize Reader.* New York: Harper & Row, 1978.

Hoberman, Mary Ann. *A House Is a Home for Me.* New York: Viking, 1978.

Hoffman, Hilde. *The Green Grass Grows All Around.* New York: Macmillan, 1968.

Hogrogian, Nonny. *One Fine Day.* New York: Macmillan, 1971.

Hopkins, Lee Bennett, selector. *Good Books, Good Times.* New York: Harper & Row, 1990.

Hutchins, Pat. *The Doorbell Rang.* New York: Greenwillow, 1986.

———. *The Wind Blew.* New York: Macmillan, 1974.

———. *Good-Night, Owl!* New York: Macmillan, 1972.

———. *Titch.* New York: Collier, 1971.

———. *The Surprise Party.* New York: Collier, 1969.

———. *Rosie's Walk.* New York: Macmillan, 1968.

Johnson, Crockett. *A Picture for Harold's Room.* New York: Harper & Row, 1968.

Joslin, Sesyle. *What Do You Say, Dear?* Reading, MA: Addison-Wesley, 1958.

Kalan, Robert. *Jump, Frog, Jump.* New York: Mulberry, 1981.

Keats, Ezra Jack. *Over in the Meadow.* New York: Four Winds, 1972.

Kent, Jack. *The Fat Cat.* New York: Scholastic, 1971.

Kessler, Leonard. *Kick, Pass, and Run.* New York: Harper & Row, 1966.

Kirk, David. *Miss Spider's Tea Party.* New York: Scholastic, 1994.

Klein, Leonore. *Brave Daniel.* New York: Scholastic, 1958.

Kochenmeister, Cherryl. *On Monday, When It Rained.* Boston: Houghton, 1989.

Kraus, Robert. *Where Are You Going, Little Mouse?* New York: Greenwillow, 1986.

———. *Leo the Late Bloomer.* New York: Windmill, 1971.

———. *Whose Mouse Are You?* New York: Collier, 1970.

Krauss, Ruth. *The Carrot Seed.* New York: Scholastic, 1984.

———. *What a Fine Day for. . . .* New York: Parents' Magazine, 1967.

———. *The Happy Day.* New York: Harper & Row, 1949.

———. *Bears.* New York: Harper & Row, 1948.

Langstaff, John. *Oh, A-Hunting We Will Go.* New York: Atheneum, 1974.

———. *The Golden Vanity.* New York: Harcourt, 1972.

———. *Soldier, Soldier, Won't You Marry Me?* New York: Doubleday, 1972.

———. *Gather My Gold Together: Four Songs for Four Seasons.* New York: Doubleday, 1971.

———. *Over in the Meadow.* New York: Harcourt, 1957.

Larranga, Ana Martin. *The Big Wide-Mouthed Frog.* Cambridge, MA: Candlewick, 1999.

Lawson, J. *Kate's Castle.* Toronto: Stoddart, 1997.

Lexau, Joan. *Crocodile and Hen.* New York: Harper & Row, 1969.

Lindbergh, Reeve. *There's a Cow in the Road.* New York: Dial, 1993.

Lobel, Anita. *King Rooster, Queen Hen.* New York: Greenwillow, 1975.

Lobel, Arnold. *On Market Street.* New York: Greenwillow, 1981.

———. *Mouse Soup.* New York: Harper & Row, 1977.

———. *A Treeful of Pigs.* New York: Greenwillow, 1975.

Long, Earlene. *Gone Fishing.* Boston: Houghton, 1987.

Lyon, George Ella. *The Outside Inn.* New York: Orchard, 1991.

Mack, Stan. *10 Bears in My Bed.* New York: Pantheon, 1984.

Mandel, Peter. *Red Cat, White Cat.* New York: Henry Holt, 1994.

Maris, Ron. *Is Anyone Home?* New York: Greenwillow, 1985.

Martin, Bill, Jr. *Polar Bear, Polar Bear, What Do You Hear?* New York: Holt, 1990.

———. *Chicka Chicka Boom Boom.* New York: Simon and Schuster, 1989.

———. *Monday, Monday, I Like Monday.* New York: Holt, 1983.

————. *Brown Bear, Brown Bear, What Do You See?* New York: Holt, 1970.

————. *Fire! Fire! Said Mrs. McGuire.* New York: Holt, 1970.

McDonald, Megan. *Is This a House for Hermit Crab?* New York: Orchard, 1990.

McGovern, Ann. *Too Much Noise.* New York: Scholastic, 1967.

McMillan, Bruce. *Play Day: A Book of Terse Verse.* New York: Holiday, 1991.

Melser, June, and Cowley, Joy. *Grandpa, Grandpa.* Bothell, WA: The Wright Group, 1987.

————. *Hairy Bear.* Bothell, WA: The Wright Group, 1987.

————. *In a Dark Dark Wood.* Bothell, WA: The Wright Group, 1987.

————. *Lazy Mary.* Bothell, WA: The Wright Group, 1987.

————. *Sing a Song.* Bothell, WA: The Wright Group, 1987.

————. *Yes Ma'am.* Bothell, WA: The Wright Group, 1987.

Memling, Carl. *Ten Little Animals.* New York: Golden Press, 1961.

Merriam, Eve. *Do You Want to See Something?* New York: Scholastic, 1965.

Miller, Margaret. *Big and Little.* New York: Greenwillow, 1998.

————. *Who Uses This?* New York: Greenwillow, 1990.

Minarik, Else Holmelund. *Little Bear.* New York: Harper and Row, 1957. (Others in the Little Bear series: *Father Bear Comes Home,* 1959; *Little Bear's Friend,* 1960; *Little Bear's Visit,* 1961; *A Kiss for Little Bear,* 1968.)

Moffett, Martha. *A Flower Pot Is Not a Hat.* New York: Dutton, 1972.

Moore, Lilian. *I'll Meet You at the Cucumbers.* New York: Atheneum, 1988.

Numeroff, Laura Joffe. *If You Give a Moose a Muffin.* New York: HarperCollins, 1991.

————. *If You Give a Mouse a Cookie.* New York: Harper & Row, 1985.

Parkes, Brenda. *Who's in the Shed?* Crystal Lake, IL: Rigby Education, 1986.

Patrick, Gloria. *A Bug in a Jug and Other Funny Rhymes.* New York: Scholastic, 1970.

Peppe, Rodney. *The House That Jack Built.* New York: Delacorte, 1970.

Pigdon, Keith, and Marilyn Woolley. *Is There Room For Me?* Cleveland, OH: Modern Curriculum Press, 1989.

Pinczes, Elinor. *One Hundred Hungry Ants.* Boston: Houghton Mifflin, 1993.

Pizer, Abigail. *It's a Perfect Day.* Philadelphia: Lippincott, 1990.

Polushkin, Maria. *Mother, Mother, I Want Another.* New York: Crown, 1978.

Porte, Barbara Ann. *Harry in Trouble.* New York: Greenwillow, 1989.

Preston, Edna Mitchell. *Where Did My Mother Go?* New York: Four Winds, 1978.

Quackenbush, Robert. *Too Many Lollipops.* New York: Scholastic, 1975.

————. *She'll Be Comin' Round the Mountain.* Philadelphia: Lippincott, 1973.

Roe, Eileen. *All I Am.* Scarsdale, NJ: Bradbury, 1990.

Recommended Pattern Books

Root, Phyllis. *One Duck Stuck.* Cambridge, MA: Candlewick, 1999.

Rosen, Michael, reteller. *We're Going on a Bear Hunt.* New York: Macmillan, 1989.

Rowe, Jeannette. *Whose Ears?* New York: Little, Brown, 1999.

Rylant, Cynthia. *Henry and Mudge and the Happy Cat.* Scarsdale, NJ: Bradbury, 1990.

Sawyer, Ruth. *Journey Cake, Ho!* New York: Viking, 1953.

Scheer, Jullian, and Bileck, Marvin. *Upside Down Day.* New York: Holiday House, 1968.

————. *Rain Makes Applesauce.* New York: Holiday House, 1964.

Sendak, Maurice. *Where the Wild Things Are.* New York: Scholastic, 1963.

Serfozo, Mary. *Who Said Red?* New York: Macmillan, 1992.

Seuss, Dr. *Fox in Sox.* New York: Random House, 1965.

————. *Green Eggs and Ham.* New York: Random House, 1960.

————. *The Cat in the Hat Comes Back.* New York: Random House, 1958.

————. *The Cat in the Hat.* New York: Random House, 1957.

Shapiro, Arnold. *Who Says That?* New York: Dutton, 1991.

Shaw, Charles B. *It Looked Like Spilt Milk.* New York: Harper & Row, 1947.

Shaw, Nancy. *Sheep Take a Hike.* Boston: Houghton Mifflin, 1994.

————. *Sheep Out to Eat.* Boston: Houghton Mifflin, 1992.

————. *Sheep in a Jeep.* Boston: Houghton, 1989.

————. *Sheep on a Ship.* Boston: Houghton, 1989.

Shulevitz, Uri. *One Monday Morning.* New York: Scribner's, 1967.

Simon, Mina, and Simon, Howard. *If You Were an Eel, How Would You Feel?* Chicago: Follett, 1963.

Skaar, Grace. *What Do the Animals Say?* New York: Scholastic, 1972.

Slobdkina, Esphyr. *Caps for Sale.* New York: Scholastic, 1968.

Spier, Peter. *The Fox Went Out on a Chilly Night.* New York: Doubleday, 1961.

Stickland, Paul, and Stickland, Henrietta. *Dinosaur Roar!* New York: Dutton, 1994.

Stover, JoAnn. *If Everybody Did.* New York: David McKay, 1960.

Tafuri, Nancy. *Spots, Feathers, and Curly Tails.* New York: Greenwillow, 1988.

————. *Have You Seen My Duckling?* New York: Greenwillow, 1984.

Titherington, Jeanne. *A Child's Prayer.* New York: Greenwillow, 1989.

Tolstoy, Alexei. *The Great Big Enormous Turnip.* New York: Franklin Watts, 1968.

Van Laan, Nancy. *Possum Came a-Knocking.* New York: Knopf, 1990.

————. *The Big Fat Worm.* New York: Knopf, 1987.

Van Leeuwen, Jean. *Oliver and Amanda's Christmas.* New York: Dial, 1973.

Viorst, Judith. *Alexander and the Terrible, Horrible, No Good, Very Bad Day.* New York: Atheneum, 1972.

Watanabe, Shigeo. *How Do I Put It On?* Cleveland, OH: Collins, 1977.

Weiss, Nicki. *On a Hot, Hot Day.* New York: Putnam & Sons, 1992.

―――. *Where Does the Brown Bear Go?* New York: Greenwillow, 1989.

Welber, Robert. *Goodbye, Hello.* New York: Random House, undated.

Wellington, Monica. *All My Little Ducklings.* New York: Dutton, 1989.

Wells, Rosemary. *Noisy Nora.* New York: Dial, 1989.

―――. *A Lion for Lewis.* New York: Dial, 1982.

Wescott, Nadine Bernard. *I Know an Old Lady Who Swallowed a Fly.* Boston: Houghton, 1980.

Winter, Jeanette. *Follow the Drinking Gourd.* New York: Knopf, 1988.

―――. *Hush Little Baby.* New York: Pantheon, 1984.

Winter, Susan. *I Can.* New York: Dorling Kindersley, 1993.

Wondriska, William. *All the Animals Were Angry.* New York: Holt, 1970.

Wood, Audrey. *The Napping House.* New York: Harcourt, 1984.

Zaid, Barry. *Chicken Little.* New York: Random House, undated.

Zemach, Harve. *The Judge.* New York: Farrar, 1969.

Zemach, Margot. *Hush, Little Baby.* New York: Dutton, 1976.

―――. *The Teeny Tiny Woman.* New York: Scholastic, 1965.

Zolotow, Charlotte. *It's Not Fair.* New York: Random House, 1976.

―――. *If It Weren't for You.* New York: Harper & Row, 1966.

―――. *Someday.* New York: Harper & Row, 1965.

―――. *Do You Know What I'll Do?* New York: Harper & Row, 1958.

Literacy-Related Web Sites

There are many web sites that relate to literacy. The sites we have listed provide an overview of the wealth of information that can be accessed through the internet. Once a site is located, there are often numerous links to related areas.

Teachers know that there is a growing need to evaluate information from the internet. Consider the following criteria, adapted from Greenlaw (2001), when evaluating internet sites.

Criteria for Evaluating Internet Materials*

1. Make sure the lesson plan you find on the Internet matches your teaching goals.

2. If the lesson is for students, make sure the reading level is appropriate for the students' reading ability.

3. Site links are appropriate.

4. Activities are online or able to be downloaded.

5. Journal articles include complete references.

*From Greenlaw, J. (2001). *English Language arts and reading on the Internet: A resource for K–12 teachers.* Upper Saddle River, NJ: Prentice Hall.

Literacy-Related Web Sites

ERIC Clearinghouse on Reading, English, and Communication

http://www.indiana.edu/~eric_rec/
Provides links to lesson plans, bibliographies, and Web resources

ISLMC Children's Literature and Language Arts Resources

http://falcon.jmu.edu/~ramseyil/childlit.htm
Contains links to children's literature sites, curriculum resources, chat rooms, and keypal organizations

National Council of Teachers of English (NCTE)

http://www.ncte.org/
English and language arts resources such as journals, books, standards, and discussion lists

Reading Online

http://www.readingonline.org/home/html
Electronic reading journal of the International Reading Association in hypertext format

Learning to Read

http://toread.com/
Includes information about reading instruction

The Whole Language Umbrella

http://www.ncte.org/wlu/about.shtml
Contains information about the philosophy and practices of Whole Language

Sixty Years of Reading Research—But Who's Listening?

http://pdkintl.org/kappan/kzem9903.html
Discusses why research describing progressive approaches to reading has not produced consensus among reading educators

The Big "R"—Reading

http://www.Idonline.org/Id_indepth/reading/tutor_tips.html
Information about the importance of reading instruction

From Greenlaw, J. (2001). *English Language arts and reading on the Internet: A resource for K–12 teachers.* Upper Saddle River, NJ: Prentice Hall.

Literacy-Related Web Sites

Helping Children Overcome Reading Difficulties

http://www.indiana.edu/~eric_rec/ieo/digests/d72.html
Summary of research about teaching students with reading difficulties

Reading Across the Curriculum

http://www.scholastic.com/instructor/curriculum/index.html#langarts
Contains online articles about teaching reading and writing

Room 108

http://netrover.com/~kingskid/108.html
Music, stories, and games for students

Standards for the English Language Arts

http://www.ncte.org/standards/thelist.html
Provides standards document

Technology and Learning Online

http://www.techlearning.com/
Contains information about developing a website for your class or school

Web66: International School Web Site Registry

http://web66.coled.umn.edu/schools.html
Contains home pages of schools worldwide

Proteacher

http://proteacher.com
Provides teachers with reading articles and activities

From Greenlaw, J. (2001). *English Language arts and reading on the Internet: A resource for K–12 teachers.* Upper Saddle River, NJ: Prentice Hall.

CHAPTER 1

RESOURCES

Interest Inventories

- About Me
- Sentence Completion

Reading Attitude Inventories

- Reading and Me
- My Ideas About Reading
- Class Summary Sheet for Reading Attitude Survey
- Self-Report Reading Scale
- Motivation to Read Profile: Conversational Interview
- What Are Some of Your Ideas About Reading?

Teacher Resource

- Checklist for Student's Attitudes and Personal Reading

Name _____ Date _____

About Me

1. My name is _____
 _____.

2. I like to _____
 _____.

3. I feel good when _____
 _____.

4. I feel happy when _____
 _____.

5. I feel important when _____
 _____.

6. I worry when _____
 _____.

7. I don't like to _____
 _____.

8. I don't like it when _____
 _____.

9. I think _____
 _____.

10. I would like to be _____
 _____.

11. Some of my favorite things are _____
 _____.

12. My favorite TV shows are _____
 _____.

13. Reading is _____
 _____.

Name _____ Date _____

Sentence Completion

Directions: I am going to begin certain sentences for you. I want you to finish each sentence with the first idea that comes to your mind.

1. My idea of a good time is _____ .

2. When I have to read, I _____ .

3. I wish my parents knew _____ .

4. I can't understand why _____ .

5. I wish teachers _____ .

6. I wish my mother _____ .

7. People think I _____ .

8. I especially like to read about _____ .

9. To me, homework _____ .

10. I hope I'll never _____ .

11. I wish people wouldn't _____ .

12. When I finish school, _____ .

13. When I take my report card home, _____ .

14. Most brothers and sisters _____ .

15. I feel proud when _____ .

16. I wish my father _____ .

17. I like to read when _____ .

18. I am really interested in _____ .

19. I often worry about _____ .

20. I wish someone would help me _____ .

From Boning, T., & Boning, R. (1975). I'd rather read than. . . . *The Reading Teacher, 10*, 196–200.

Reading and Me

Directions: The 10 statements that follow will be read to you. After each statement is read, circle either yes or no, depending on what you believe.

Yes No 1. I can read as fast as good readers.

Yes No 2. I like to read.

Yes No 3. I like to read long stories.

Yes No 4. The books I read in school are too hard.

Yes No 5. I need more help in reading.

Yes No 6. I worry quite a bit about my reading in school.

Yes No 7. I read at home.

Yes No 8. I would rather read than watch television.

Yes No 9. I am not a very good reader.

Yes No 10. I like my parents to read to me.

Name _____ Date _____

My Ideas About Reading

Directions:	The 10 statements that follow will be read to you. After each statement is read, circle the response that tells what you feel or believe.

Agree ? Disagree 1. Reading is a good way to spend spare time.

Agree ? Disagree 2. Most books are too long and dull.

Agree ? Disagree 3. There should be more free reading in school.

Agree ? Disagree 4. Reading is as important as watching television.

Agree ? Disagree 5. Reading is boring.

Agree ? Disagree 6. Reading is rewarding to me.

Agree ? Disagree 7. I think reading is fun.

Agree ? Disagree 8. Teachers ask me to read books that are too hard.

Agree ? Disagree 9. I am not a very good reader.

Agree ? Disagree 10. My parents spend quite a bit of time reading.

Class Summary Sheet
for Reading Attitude Survey

Teacher _____ Grade _____ School _____

| Student | Date Administered _____ | | Date Administered _____ | |
	Score	Comments	Score	Comments

From Jerry L. Johns and Susan Davis Lenski, *Improving Reading: Strategies and Resources* (3rd ed.). Copyright © 2001 Kendall/ Hunt Publishing Company (1-800-247-3458, ext. 5). May be reproduced for noncommercial educational purposes.

Self-Report Reading Scale

Beatrice Dubnow and Martin H. Jason

Purpose

To help measure elementary students' self-perceptions of their reading abilities.

Administration

1. Reproduce the scale.
2. Explain how students should mark their answers. Because words above the third-grade reading level were not included in the items, most students should be able to complete the scale independently. For younger or less able readers, read the items aloud.

Scoring and Interpretation

1. Students are given one point for each item to which they give an answer representing a positive self-perception. Use the key that follows.

1.	No	12.	Yes
2.	No	13.	Yes
3.	Yes	14.	No
4.	No	15.	Yes
5.	Yes	16.	Yes
6.	No	17.	No
7.	Yes	18.	Yes
8.	No	19.	No
9.	Yes	20.	No
10.	Yes	21.	Yes
11.	No	22.	Yes

2. The student's total score is a qualitative self-perception of his or her reading abilities.

3. Teachers can use the results to help plan intervention strategies.

Jason, M.H., & Dubnow, B. (1973). The relationship between self-perceptions of reading abilities and reading achievement. In W.H. MacGinitie (Ed.), *Assessment problems in reading* (pp. 96–101). Newark, DE: International Reading Association.

Self-Report Reading Scale

Please Print

Name _____ Boy ☐ Girl ☐

School _____

Room _____ Grade _____

Today's Date _____
 Year Month Day

Date of Birth _____
 Year Month Day

What to do: 1. These are sentences about reading.

2. Read each sentence and make an ☒ in the Yes or No box.

3. There are no right or wrong answers. Just mark the way you feel about each one.

1. I can do better in my other school work than I can in reading. Yes ☐ No ☐

2. There are too many hard words for me to learn in the stories I read. Yes ☐ No ☐

3. If I took a reading test, I would do all right on it. Yes ☐ No ☐

4. In school I wish I could be a much better reader than I am. Yes ☐ No ☐

5. I can help other pupils in my class to read because I'm a good reader. Yes ☐ No ☐

6. If reading gets too hard for me, I feel like not trying to read anymore. Yes ☐ No ☐

Jason, M.H., & Dubnow, B. (1973). The relationship between self-perceptions of reading abilities and reading achievement. In W.H. MacGinitie (Ed.), *Assessment problems in reading* (pp. 96–101). Newark, DE: International Reading Association.

7. Most of the time I can read the same books as well as the good readers. Yes ☐ No ☐

8. When I read in school, I worry a lot about how well I'm doing. Yes ☐ No ☐

9. Most of the time when I see a new word, I can sound it out by myself. Yes ☐ No ☐

10. I can read as well as the best readers. Yes ☐ No ☐

11. Most of the time I feel I need help when I read in school. Yes ☐ No ☐

12. If my teacher called on me to read to the class, I would do well. Yes ☐ No ☐

13. I can read as fast as the good readers. Yes ☐ No ☐

14. Most of the things I read in school are too hard. Yes ☐ No ☐

15. Pupils in my class think I'm a good reader. Yes ☐ No ☐

16. Most of the time I can finish my reading work. Yes ☐ No ☐

17. Most of the time I feel afraid to read to the class. Yes ☐ No ☐

18. I can read a long story as well as a short one. Yes ☐ No ☐

19. It's hard for me to answer questions about the main idea of a story. Yes ☐ No ☐

20. Most of the time I feel I will never be a good reader in school. Yes ☐ No ☐

21. My teacher thinks I'm a good reader. Yes ☐ No ☐

22. I know what most of the hard words mean when I read them. Yes ☐ No ☐

Jason, M.H., & Dubnow, B. (1973). The relationship between self-perceptions of reading abilities and reading achievement. In W.H. MacGinitie (Ed.), *Assessment problems in reading* (pp. 96–101). Newark, DE: International Reading Association.

Motivation to Read Profile: Conversational Interview

Linda B. Gambrell, Barbara Martin Palmer, Rose Marie Codling, and Susan Anders Mazzoni

Purpose

To qualitatively assess students' self-concepts as readers and the value they place on reading.

Administration

1. Reproduce the Conversational Interview so that you have a form for each student.

2. Choose in advance the section(s) or specific questions you want to ask from the Conversational Interview. Reviewing the information on students' Reading Surveys may provide information about additional questions that could be added to the interview.

3. Familiarize yourself with the basic questions provided in the interview prior to the interview session in order to establish a more conversational setting.

4. Select a quiet corner of the room and a calm period of the day for the interview.

5. Allow ample time for conducting the Conversational Interview.

6. Follow up on interesting comments and responses to gain a fuller understanding of students' reading experiences.

7. Record students' responses in as much detail as possible. If time and resources permit, you may want to audiotape answers to A1 and B1 to be transcribed after the interview for more in-depth analysis.

8. Enjoy this special time with each student!

Scoring and Interpretation

1. The interview explores three areas: 1) motivational factors related to the reading of narrative text, 2) information about informational reading, and 3) general factors related to reading motivation.

2. Use the students' responses along with the MRP Reading Survey to gain greater depth into students' reading experiences.

Gambrell, L.B., Palmer, B.M., Codling, R.M., & Mazzoni, S.A. (1996). Assessing reading motivation. *The Reading Teacher, 49*, 518–533.

Motivation to Read Profile: Conversational Profile

A. Emphasis: Narrative text

Suggested prompt (designed to engage student in a natural conversation): I have been reading a good book . . . I was talking with . . . about it last night. I enjoy talking about good stories and books that I've been reading. Today I'd like to hear about what you have been reading.

1. Tell me about the most interesting story or book you have read this week (or even last week). Take a few minutes to think about it. (Wait time.) Now, tell me about the book or story.

 Probes: What else can you tell me? Is there anything else? _____

2. How did you know or find out about this story? _____

 ❏ assigned ❏ in school

 ❏ chosen ❏ out of school

3. Why was this story interesting to you? _____

B. Emphasis: Informational text

Suggested prompt (designed to engage student in a natural conversation): Often we read to find out about something or to learn about something. We read for information. For example, I remember a student of mine . . . who read a lot of books about . . . to find out as much as he/she could about. . . . Now, I'd like to hear about some of the informational reading you have been doing.

Gambrell, L.B., Palmer, B.M., Codling, R.M., & Mazzoni, S.A. (1996). Assessing reading motivation. *The Reading Teacher, 49,* 518–533.

1. Think about something important that you learned recently, not from your teacher and not from television, but from a book or some other reading material. What did you read about? (Wait time.) Tell me about what you learned.

 Probes: What else could you tell me? Is there anything else? _____

2. How did you know or find out about this book/article? _____

 ❏ assigned ❏ in school

 ❏ chosen ❏ out of school

3. Why was this book (or article) important to you? _____

C. Emphasis: General reading

1. Did you read anything at home yesterday? _____ What? _____

2. Do you have any books at school (in your desk/storage area/locker/book bag) today that you are reading? _____ Tell me about them. _____

3. Tell me about your favorite author. _____

Gambrell, L.B., Palmer, B.M., Codling, R.M., & Mazzoni, S.A. (1996). Assessing reading motivation. *The Reading Teacher, 49,* 518–533.

4. What do you think you have to learn to be a better reader? _____

5. Do you know about any books right now that you'd like to read? Tell me about them. _____

6. How did you find out about these books? _____

7. What are some things that get you really excited about reading books? _____

Tell me about . . .

8. Who gets you really interested and excited about reading books? _____

Tell me more about what they do. _____

Gambrell, L.B., Palmer, B.M., Codling, R.M., & Mazzoni, S.A. (1996). Assessing reading motivation. *The Reading Teacher, 49*, 518–533.

What Are Some of Your Ideas About Reading?

Thomas H. Estes

Purpose

To acquire a quantitative idea of a student's attitude toward reading. The scale can be used with students in grades three through twelve.

Administration

1. Reproduce the sheet titled "What Are Some of Your Ideas About Reading?"
2. Assure students that their responses will not affect their grades or standing in the course.
3. Explain how students should mark their answers.
4. Read each of the statements aloud and permit students ample time to circle their responses.

Scoring and Interpretation

1. Assign numerical values to each of the 20 items as follows:

Type and Number of Item		*Numerical Values*				
		SA	A	U	D	SD
Negative: 1, 3, 4, 6, 8, 9,						
11, 12, 13, 16, 17, 20		1	2	3	4	5
Positive: 2, 5, 7, 10, 14,						
15, 18, 19		5	4	3	2	1

2. Add the numerical values for the positive statements and the negative statements. The student's total score is a quantitative reflection of his or her attitude toward reading. Scores above 60 indicate varying degrees of positive attitudes, and scores below 60 indicate varying degrees of negative attitudes.

3. By administering the scale on a pretest and posttest (September and May) basis, the teacher can note changes in attitude toward reading by subtracting the early score from the later one.

4. Consult the original article for further information on the construction of the attitude scale. Further validation of the scale can be found in Kenneth L. Dulin and Robert D. Chester, "A Validation Study of the Estes Attitude Scale," *Journal of Reading, 18*, 1974, 56–59.

Adapted from Estes, T.H. (1971). A scale to measure attitudes toward reading. *Journal of Reading, 15*, 135–138.

Name _____ Date _____

What Are Some of Your Ideas About Reading?

SA A U D SD 1. Reading is for learning but not for enjoyment.

SA A U D SD 2. Money spent on books is well spent.

SA A U D SD 3. There is nothing to be gained from reading books.

SA A U D SD 4. Books are a bore.

SA A U D SD 5. Reading is a good way to spend spare time.

SA A U D SD 6. Sharing books in class is a waste of time.

SA A U D SD 7. Reading turns me on.

SA A U D SD 8. Reading is only for students seeking good grades.

SA A U D SD 9. Books aren't usually good enough to finish.

SA A U D SD 10. Reading is rewarding to me.

SA A U D SD 11. Reading becomes boring after about an hour.

SA A U D SD 12. Most books are too long and dull.

SA A U D SD 13. Free reading doesn't teach anything.

SA A U D SD 14. There should be more time for free reading during the school day.

SA A U D SD 15. There are many books that I hope to read.

SA A U D SD 16. Books should not be read except for class requirements.

SA A U D SD 17. Reading is something I can do without.

SA A U D SD 18. A certain amount of summer vacation should be set aside for reading.

SA A U D SD 19. Books make good presents.

SA A U D SD 20. Reading is dull.

Adapted from Estes, T.H. (1971). A scale to measure attitudes toward reading. *Journal of Reading, 15,* 135–138.

Checklist for Student's Attitudes and Personal Reading

Student _____ Grade _____ Teacher _____

	Seldom			Sometimes			Often		
	Oct.	Feb.	May	Oct.	Feb.	May	Oct.	Feb.	May
1. Possesses printed materials not assigned									
2. Uses classroom library									
3. Checks out books from school library									
4. Voluntarily shares outside reading									
5. Talks with other students about reading									
6. Seems to have a favorite author									
7. Requests more reading about topics									
8. Uses reading to satisfy personal interests									
9. Reads for recreation									
10. Chooses reading when choices are given									
11. Reading reflects interests in _____									
12. Applies ideas from reading to his/her life									
13. Seems to enjoy reading									
14. Participates in classroom book club									
15. Participates in book exchange club									
16. Parents report reading at home									

From Johns, J.L. (1991). Literacy portfolios: A primer. *Illinois Reading Council Journal, 19*, 4–10. May be reproduced for non-commercial educational purposes.

CHAPTER

RESOURCES

Teacher Resources

- Phonemic Awareness: Books To Read Aloud
- Sound Boxes (for Strategy 1 in Section 2.10)

Phonemic Awareness: Books to Read Aloud

Aylesworth, J. *Old Black Fly*. New York: Scholastic, 1993.

This alphabet book uses rhythm and rhyme as it describes a bothersome fly that lands on things beginning with each letter of the alphabet.

Brown, M.W. *Four Fur Feet*. New York: Doubleday, 1993.

In this book, the student is drawn to the /f/ sound as the phrase "four fur feet" is repeated in every sentence as a furry animal walks around the world. The same pattern is used throughout the story.

Carter, D. *More Bugs in Boxes*. New York: Simon and Schuster, 1990.

This pop-up book contains a series of questions and answers about make-believe bugs that are found inside a variety of boxes. Both the questions and answers make use of alliteration: "What kind of bug is in the rosy red rectangle box? A bright blue big mouth bug."

Deming, A.G. *Who is Tapping at My Window?* New York: Penguin, 1994.

A young girl hears a tapping at her window and asks, "Who is there?" The farm animals each respond, "It's not I," and she discovers that it is the rain. The book is predictable in that each pair of animals rhymes (for example, dog/frog).

Geraghty, P. *Stop That Noise!* New York: Crown, 1992.

A mouse is annoyed with the many sounds of the forest. The animal and machine sounds make the book useful in drawing students' attention to the sounds in language.

Gordon, J. *Six Sleepy Sheep*. New York: Puffin Books, 1991.

The use of the /s/ sound throughout the book is useful for developing a letter-sound association.

Kuskin, K. *Roar and More*. New York: HarperTrophy, 1990.

This book contains many poems and pictures that portray the sounds that animals make. Both the use of rhyme and presentation of animal sounds draw students' attention to sounds.

Lear, E. *A Was Once an Apple Pie*. Cambridge, MA: Candlewick, 1997.

This alphabet book has nonsense rhymes that accompany silly pictures of words that begin with each letter of the alphabet. For example, "D was once a little doll, Dolly, Molly, Polly, Nolly, Nursy dolly."

Lewison, W. *Buzz Said the Bee*. New York: Scholastic, 1992.

A series of animals sit on top of one another in this story. Before each animal climbs on top of the next, it does something that rhymes with the animal it approaches. For example, "the pig takes a bow before sitting on the cow."

Most, B. *Cock-A-Doodle-Moo*. New York: Harcourt Brace, 1996.

A rooster loses his voice and asks the cow for help to wake all the animals in the barnyard. The cow's inability to crow like a rooster results in him saying different onsets instead of /c/ for cock, as well as moo for doo.

Otto, C. *Dinosaur Chase*. New York: HarperTrophy, 1991.

Both alliteration and rhyme are present in this simple, colorful book.

Parry, C. *Zoomerang-a-Boomerang: Poems to Make Your Belly Laugh*. New York: Puffin Books, 1991.

Practically all of the poems in this collection play with language, particularly through the use of predictable and humorous rhyme patterns.

Pomerantz, C. *If I Had a Paka*. New York: Mulberry, 1993.

Eleven languages are represented among the 12 poems included in this book. Attention is drawn to phonemes (sounds) when languages other than English are introduced. Rhyme and repetition are also included.

Sendak, M. *Alligators All Around: An Alphabet*. New York: HarperTrophy, 1990.

This book uses alliteration for each letter of the alphabet.

Westcott, N. *The Lady with the Alligator Purse*. Boston: Little, Brown, 1998.

This highly engaging book tells the story of Tim, whose mother put him in the bathtub to see if he could swim. The silly rhyme and rhythm have made it a well-loved children's song and book.

Adapted from Yopp, H.K. (1995). Read-aloud books for developing phonemic awareness: An annotated bibliography. *The Reading Teacher, 48,* 538–542.

Sound Boxes

Sound Boxes (continued)

Sound Boxes (continued)

Sound Boxes (continued)

Sound Boxes (continued)

CHAPTER 3

RESOURCES

Words for Use in Teaching Vowel Sounds

Short Sounds

a		e		i		o		u	
and	fat	bell	beg	is	it	sock	clock	rug	us
can	apple	red	slept	twin	dig	frog	stop	run	up
add	last	rest	sled	slid	hip	hog	pop	dug	dust
at	mad	pet	met	hill	tin	odd	hot	rut	rub
cat	fast	bed	help	brick	hit	mop	log	must	but
hand	glad	step	sell	his	big	hop	cot	sun	bus
dad	am	men	hen	did	will	pond	not	fun	bum
flag	bad	send	wet	milk	in	fog	dot	drum	duck
bag	had	pen	egg	rib	trip	pot	doll	tug	bug
fact	tan	bet	chest	drill	ill	lot	ox	struck	mud

Long Sounds

a		e		i		o		u	
fade	may	Pete	east	Mike	like	hose	note	use	flute
say	bake	three	see	hide	time	hope	poke	music	plume
tape	pay	eat	eve	bike	ripe	rose	open	cue	cute
same	rain	peep	free	pike	pile	note	over	mule	rule
pain	Jane	feed	jeep	dime	mice	boat	slope	tube	blue
take	tame	be	team	die	fine	robe	rode	fuel	rude
way	save	mean	beet	dine	light	home	row	clue	unit
wave	age	green	bean	five	ride	joke	nose	fuse	cube
ate	day	weed	she	side	pine	bone	rope	suit	brute
take	make	keep	seat	nice	pie	cone	stove	dual	tune

Rank Order of the 300 Most Common Words

the	up	make	right	food	body	money
of	said	now	should	under	end	become
and	out	way	small	always	hand	group
to	if	each	old	however	head	government
a	some	called	think	man	read	later
in	would	did	take	air	others	living
is	so	just	still	asked	year	change
that	people	after	place	both	since	days
it	them	water	find	being	against	animals
was	other	through	off	does	young	word
for	more	get	different	going	give	let
you	will	because	part	big	set	wanted
he	into	back	found	without	kind	across
on	your	where	us	looked	room	American
as	which	know	world	say	eyes	early
are	do	little	away	left	number	though
they	then	such	life	began	far	four
with	many	even	three	mother	person	face
be	these	much	went	during	city	best
his	no	our	those	tell	better	became
at	time	must	own	land	white	seen
or	been	before	help	next	side	himself
from	who	good	every	once	family	sure
had	like	too	here	need	night	energy
I	could	long	house	high	didn't	sun
not	has	me	might	last	country	second
have	him	years	between	until	name	feet
this	how	day	never	children	it's	really
but	than	used	home	along	ever	certain
by	two	work	thought	took	form	turned
were	may	any	put	together	usually	toward
one	only	go	again	sometimes	hard	parts
all	most	use	important	saw	knew	black
she	its	things	while	enough	today	ways
when	made	well	something	light	times	show
an	over	look	states	got	soon	means
their	see	another	don't	example	told	door
there	first	around	why	words	several	special
her	new	man	large	united	system	course
can	very	great	want	almost	state	known
we	my	same	few	father	upon	move
what	also	came	school	live	thing	yet
about	down	come	often	keep	earth	

Reprinted with permission from Zeno, S.M., Ivens, S.H., Millard, R.T., & Duvvuri, R. *The Educator's Word Frequency Guide.*
Copyright © 1995 by Touchstone Applied Science Associates (TASA), Inc.

Revised Dolch List

a	could	he	might	same	told
about	cut	heard	more	saw	too
across	did	help	most	say	took
after	didn't	her	much	see	toward
again	do	here	must	she	try
all	does	high	my	short	turn
always	done	him	near	should	two
am	don't	his	need	show	under
an	down	hold	never	six	up
and	draw	hot	next	small	upon
another	eat	how	new	so	us
any	enough	I	no	some	use
are	even	I'm	not	soon	very
around	every	if	now	start	walk
as	far	in	of	still	want
ask	fast	into	off	stop	warm
at	find	is	oh	take	was
away	first	it	old	tell	we
be	five	its	on	ten	well
because	for	just	once	than	went
been	found	keep	one	that	were
before	four	kind	only	the	what
began	from	know	open	their	when
best	full	last	or	them	where
better	gave	leave	other	then	which
big	get	left	our	there	while
black	give	let	out	these	white
blue	go	light	over	they	who
both	going	like	own	think	why
bring	gone	little	play	this	will
but	good	long	put	those	with
by	got	look	ran	thought	work
call	green	made	read	three	would
came	grow	make	red	through	yes
can	had	many	right	to	yet
close	hard	may	round	today	you
cold	has	me	run	together	your
come	have	mean	said		

The rationale and research for this list are described in Johns, J.L. (1981). The development of the revised Dolch list. *Illinois School Research and Development, 17*, 15–24.

Revised Dolch List
(Organized by Reader Level)

Preprimer		Primer		Grade 1		Grade 2	
a	look	about	on	after	long	across	near
and	make	all	one	again	made	always	need
are	me	around	out	am	many	because	once
at	my	ask	put	an	more	been	only
big	no	away	run	another	much	best	open
blue	not	but	saw	any	must	both	round
call	play	eat	say	as	never	close	same
can	ran	fast	she	be	next	done	short
come	red	from	show	before	off	draw	six
did	said	good	so	began	oh	enough	small
do	see	has	some	better	old	even	start
down	stop	him	soon	black	or	every	ten
for	that	his	take	bring	other	full	thought
get	the	into	then	by	our	grow	through
go	this	know	they	came	over	heard	today
green	to	let	too	cold	own	high	together
have	up	like	two	could	read	hot	toward
he	want	may	us	cut	right	I'm	turn
help	we	new	went	didn't	should	keep	upon
here	what	now	yes	does	still	leave	use
I	who	of	your	don't	tell	left	warm
in	will			far	than	mean	well
is	with			find	their	might	while
it	work			first	them	most	yet
little	you			five	there		
				found	these		
				four	think		
				gave	those		
				give	three		
				going	told		
				gone	took		
				got	try		
				had	under		
				hard	very		
				her	walk		
				hold	was		
				how	were		
				if	when		
				its	where		
				just	which		
				kind	white		
				last	why		
				light	would		

High-Frequency Nouns

air	girl	nothing
back	group	people
book	hand	place
boy	head	road
car	home	room
children	house	school
city	man	side
day	men	table
dog	money	thing
door	morning	time
eye	mother	top
face	Mr.	town
father	Mrs.	tree
feet	name	water
friend	night	way
		year

The development of this list is described in Johns, J.L. (1975). Dolch list of common nouns—A comparison. *The Reading Teacher, 28,* 338–340.

Alphabetized List of the 100 Words Used Most Frequently by Children in Their Writing

a	for	mother	there
about	from	my	they
after	get	no	things
all	go	not	think
am	got	now	this
an	had	of	time
and	have	on	to
are	he	one	too
around	her	or	two
as	him	our	up
at	his	out	us
back	home	over	very
be	house	people	was
because	I	put	we
but	if	said	well
by	in	saw	went
came	into	school	were
can	is	see	what
could	it	she	when
day	just	so	who
did	know	some	will
didn't	like	that	with
do	little	the	would
don't	man	them	you
down	me	then	your

From Hillerich, R.L. (1978). *A Writing Vocabulary of Elementary Children.* Springfield, IL: Charles C Thomas.

Word Patterns

Short *a* Sounds

-ab	-ack	-ad	-ag	-am	-amp	-an
cab	back	ad	bag	am	camp	an
dab	hack	bad	gag	dam	damp	ban
gab	jack	cad	hag	ham	lamp	can
jab	pack	dad	tag	jam	champ	fan
lab	rack	fad	lag	lamb	clamp	man
nab	sack	had	rag	clam	cramp	pan
tab	tack	lad	sag	cram	stamp	ran
blab	black	mad	tag	slam	tramp	tan
crab	slack	pad	wag	swam		van
drab	crack	sad	brag			clan
grab	track	clad	drag			plan
scab	shack	glad	flag			scan
slab	whack	shad	shag			span
stab	smack		snag			than
	snack		stag			
	stack					

-and	-ang	-ank	-ap	-ash	-ast	-at
and	bang	bank	cap	ash	cast	at
band	fang	rank	gap	bash	fast	bat
hand	gang	sank	lap	cash	last	cat
land	hang	tank	map	dash	mast	fat
sand	rang	yank	nap	gash	past	hat
gland	sang	blank	rap	hash	vast	mat
grand	tang	clank	sap	lash	blast	pat
stand	clang	plank	tap	mash		sat
	slang	crank	chap	rash		vat
		drank	clap	sash		brat
		frank	flap	clash		chat
		spank	slap	crash		flat
		thank	snap	smash		scat
			trap	stash		slat
				trash		that

-atch

catch
hatch
latch
match
patch
thatch

Short *e* Sounds

-eck	-ed	-eg	-ell	-en	-end	-ent
deck	bed	beg	bell	den	end	bent
heck	fed	egg	dell	hen	bend	dent
neck	led	keg	fell	men	lend	lent
peck	red	leg	sell	pen	mend	rent
check	wed	peg	tell	ten	send	sent
speck	bled		well	glen	blend	tent
	fled		yell	then	spend	went
	sled		quell	when	trend	spent
	shed		shell			
	sped		smell			
			spell			
			swell			

-ess	-est	-et
less	best	bet
mess	nest	get
bless	pest	jet
chess	rest	let
dress	test	met
	vest	net
	west	pet
	chest	set
	crest	wet
	quest	vet
		fret

Short *o* Sounds

-ob	-ock	-od	-og	-ong	-ot
cob	cock	cod	bog	bong	cot
fob	dock	hod	cog	gong	dot
gob	hock	nod	dog	long	got
job	lock	pod	fog	song	hot
rob	mock	rod	hog	tong	not
mob	pock	sod	jog	wrong	pot
sob	rock	clod	log	strong	rot
blob	sock	plod	clog		blot
slob	tock	shod	frog		clot
snob	clock		smog		plot
	flock				slot
	crock				shot
	frock				spot
	shock				trot
	smock				
	stock				

Short *i* Sounds

-ib	-ick	-id	-ift	-ig	-ill	-im
bib	kick	bid	gift	big	bill	dim
fib	lick	did	lift	dig	fill	him
rib	nick	hid	rift	fig	gill	rim
crib	pick	kid	sift	jig	hill	skim
	sick	lid	drift	pig	kill	slim
	tick	rid	shift	rig	mill	swim
	wick	grid	swift	wig	pill	trim
	brick	skid		brig	rill	whim
	trick	slid		swig	sill	
	chick				till	
	thick				will	
	click				chill	
	flick				drill	
	slick				grill	
	quick				quill	
	stick				spill	

-in	-ing	-ink	-ip	-ish	-it	-itch
in	bing	ink	dip	dish	it	itch
bin	ring	pink	hip	fish	bit	ditch
din	sing	sink	lip	wish	fit	pitch
fin	wing	wink	nip	swish	hit	witch
kin	bring	blink	rip		kit	stitch
pin	fling	slink	sip		lit	switch
sin	sting	stink	tip		pit	
tin	string	think	zip		sit	
win	swing		yip		wit	
chin	thing		chip		grit	
shin			ship		mitt	
thin			whip		quit	
grin			flip		slit	
skin			slip		skit	
spin			grip		spit	
twin			trip		twit	
			quip			
			skip			
			snip			

Short *u* Sounds

-ub	-uck	-ud	-uff	-ug	-ull	-um
cub	buck	bud	buff	bug	cull	bum
dub	duck	cud	cuff	dug	dull	gum
hub	luck	mud	huff	hug	gull	hum
nub	muck	stud	muff	jug	hull	mum
pub	puck	thud	puff	lug	lull	rum
rub	suck		bluff	mug	mull	sum
sub	tuck		gruff	pug	null	glum
tub	chuck		stuff	rug	skull	slum
club	shuck			tug		drum
grub	cluck			chug		scum
stub	pluck			thug		chum
	stuck			plug		
				slug		
				smug		

-ump	-un	-unch	-ung	-unk	-up	-ush
bump	bun	bunch	dung	bunk	up	gush
dump	fun	lunch	hung	dunk	cup	hush
hump	gun	punch	lung	hunk	pup	lush
jump	nun	brunch	rung	junk	sup	mush
lump	pun	crunch	sung	sunk		rush
pump	run		clung	chunk		blush
clump	sun		flung	drunk		flush
plump	shun		stung	flunk		plush
slump	spun		swung	skunk		slush
stump	stun					brush
thump						crush
						shush

-ust	-ut
bust	but
dust	cut
just	gut
lust	hut
must	jut
rust	nut
crust	rut
	shut

Long *a* Sounds

-ace	-ade	-age	-aid	-ail	-ain	-ale
ace	fade	age	aid	ail	gain	ale
face	jade	cage	laid	bail	main	dale
lace	lade	page	maid	fail	pain	hale
mace	made	rage	paid	hail	rain	kale
pace	wade	sage	raid	jail	vain	male
race	blade	wage	braid	mail	brain	pale
brace	glade	stage		nail	drain	sale
place	grade			pail	grain	tale
space	trade			rail	train	vale
	shade			sail	chain	scale
	spade			tail	plain	shale
				vail	slain	stale
				wail	stain	whale
				frail		
				quail		
				snail		
				trail		

-ame	-ane	-ape	-aste	-ate	-ave	-ay
came	cane	ape	baste	ate	cave	bay
dame	lane	cape	haste	date	gave	day
fame	mane	gape	paste	fate	nave	gay
game	pane	nape	taste	gate	pave	hay
lame	sane	rape	chaste	hate	rave	jay
name	vane	tape		late	save	lay
same	wane	drape		rate	brave	nay
tame	crane	grape		sate	crave	pay
blame		shape		crate	grave	ray
flame				grate	shave	say
frame				plate	slave	way
shame				skate		clay
				slate		play
				state		fray
						tray
						stay
						sway

-aze
daze
gaze
haze
maze
blaze
glaze
graze

Long *e* Sounds

-e	-ea	-each	-ead	-eak	-eal	-eam
be	pea	each	bead	beak	deal	beam
he	sea	beach	lead	leak	heal	ream
me	tea	peach	read	peak	meal	seam
we	flea	reach	plead	weak	peal	team
she	plea	teach		bleak	real	cream
		bleach		freak	seal	dream
				speak	veal	gleam
					zeal	
					steal	

-ean	-eat	-ee	-eed	-eek	-eel	-een
bean	eat	bee	deed	leek	eel	keen
dean	beat	fee	feed	meek	feel	seen
lean	feat	see	heed	peek	heel	teen
mean	heat	tee	need	reek	keel	green
wean	meat	wee	seed	seek	peel	queen
clean	neat	free	weed	week	reel	sheen
glean	peat	tree	bleed	cheek		
	seat	glee	breed	creek		
	cheat	thee	creed	sleek		
	cleat	three	freed			
	pleat		greed			
	treat		speed			
	wheat		steed			
			tweed			

-eep	-eet
beep	beet
deep	feet
jeep	meet
keep	fleet
peep	greet
seep	sheet
weep	sleet
creep	sweet
sheep	tweet
steep	
sweep	

Long *o* Sounds

-o	-oad	-oam	-oan	-oast	-oat	-obe
go	goad	foam	loan	boast	oat	lobe
no	load	loam	moan	coast	boat	robe
so	road	roam	roan	roast	coat	globe
	toad	groan		toast	goat	
					moat	
					bloat	
					float	
					gloat	

-ode	-oe	-oke	-old	-ole	-olt	-ome
ode	doe	coke	old	dole	bolt	dome
bode	foe	joke	bold	hole	colt	home
code	hoe	poke	cold	mole	dolt	Nome
mode	toe	woke	gold	pole	jolt	
rode	woe	yoke	hold	role	volt	
		bloke	mold	stole		
		choke	sold			
		smoke	told			
		spoke				

-one	-ope	-ose	-ost	-ote	-ow
bone	cope	hose	ghost	note	bow
cone	dope	nose	host	rote	low
lone	hope	pose	most	tote	mow
pone	mope	rose	post	vote	row
tone	rope	chose		quote	sow
zone	scope	those			tow
shone	slope	close			blow
stone					flow
					glow
					slow
					crow
					grow
					show
					snow

Long *u* Sounds

-use	-ute
use	cute
fuse	mute
muse	flute

Long *i* Sounds

-ice	-ide	-ie	-ife	-igh	-ight	-ike
lice	bide	die	knife	high	bright	bike
mice	hide	lie	life	nigh	fight	dike
nice	ride	pie	rife	sigh	flight	hike
rice	side	tie	wife	thigh	fright	like
vice	tide	vie			light	mike
slice	wide				might	pike
spice	bride				night	spike
twice	glide				plight	
	slide				right	
					sight	
					slight	
					tight	

-ild	-ile	-ime	-ind	-ine	-ipe	-ire
mild	file	dime	bind	dine	pipe	ire
wild	mile	lime	find	fine	ripe	dire
child	pile	time	hind	line	wipe	fire
	rile	chime	kind	mine	gripe	hire
	tile	crime	mind	nine	swipe	mire
	vile	grime	rind	pine	sire	
	smile	slime	wind	tine	tire	
	while		blind	vine	wire	
			grind	shine		
				spine		
				swine		
				thine		
				twine		
				whine		

-ite	-ive
bite	dive
kite	five
mite	hive
site	live
quite	chive
spite	drive
white	

Commonly Occurring Contractions

let's	haven't	they'd
didn't	aren't	you'll
it's	I'm	she'd
won't	he's	weren't
that's	we're	I'd
can't	you're	you've
wasn't	what's	you'd
isn't	there's	we'd
hadn't	she's	they'll
don't	wouldn't	we've
I'll	she'll	who'll
we'll	here's	he'd
I've	ain't	doesn't
he'll	couldn't	where's
hasn't	they're	they've

Compound Words

afternoon	everyone	pancake
airplane	everything	peanut
anybody	eyebrows	pinball
anyone	farmland	playground
applesauce	firecracker	playhouse
backbone	firefly	quarterback
backseat	firehouse	quicksand
barefoot	fireplace	railroad
barnyard	fishhook	rainbow
baseball	flashlight	raincoat
basketball	football	rattlesnake
bathtub	fullback	rollerblade
bedroom	goldfish	rowboat
beehive	grandmother	sailboat
billboard	grasshopper	sandpaper
birthday	hallway	skyscraper
birthplace	headlight	snowball
bookcase	headset	snowflake
bookmark	highchair	sometimes
campfire	highway	starfish
chalkboard	homesick	strawberry
checkerboard	horseshoe	sunrise
classroom	jellybean	sunset
cookbook	jellyfish	sunshine
copyright	keyboard	teenager
cowboy	mailbox	thunderstorm
cupcake	mailman	toothbrush
daydream	maybe	underline
deadline	motorcycle	uphill
doghouse	necktie	volleyball
downhill	neighborhood	waterfall
downtown	newspaper	watermelon
downstairs	notebook	whirlpool
dragonfly	oatmeal	wildlife
driveway	outlaw	without
drugstore	outside	wristband
earthquake	overboard	wristwatch

From Jerry L. Johns and Susan Davis Lenski, *Improving Reading: Strategies and Resources* (3rd ed.). Copyright © 2001 Kendall/Hunt Publishing Company (1-800-247-3458, ext. 5). May be reproduced for noncommercial educational purposes.

The Nifty Thrifty Fifty

Word	Prefix	Suffix or ending
antifreeze	anti	
beautiful		ful (y-i)
classify		ify
communities	com	es (y-i)
community	com	
composer	com	er
continuous	con	ous
conversation	con	tion
deodorize	de	ize
different		ent
discovery	dis	y
dishonest	dis	
electricity		ity
employee	em	ee
encouragement	en	ment
expensive	ex	ive
forecast	fore	
forgotten		en (double t)
governor		or
happiness		ness (y-i)
hopeless		less
illegal	il	
impossible	im	
impression	im	sion
independence	in	ence
international	inter	al
invasion	in	sion
irresponsible	ir	ible
midnight	mid	

(continues)

The Nifty Thrifty Fifty *(continued)*

Word	Prefix	Suffix or ending
misunderstand	mis	
musician		ian
nonliving	non	ing (drop e)
overpower	over	
performance	per	ance
prehistoric	pre	ic
prettier		er (y-i)
rearrange	re	
replacement	re	ment
richest		est
semifinal	semi	
signature		ture
submarine	sub	
supermarkets	super	s
swimming		ing (double m)
transportation	trans	tion
underweight	under	
unfinished	un	ed
unfriendly	un	ly
unpleasant	un	ant
valuable		able (drop e)

CHAPTER 4

RESOURCES

Recording a Student's Oral Reading Miscues

Substitutions

Jim saw *a̷* the boy.

Omissions

Poor little ~~Baby~~ Bear could not move from the tall tree.

Insertions

He strolled along the path and soon ^*he* was deep in the forest

Reversals

Are they twins?

Repetitions

A. Correcting a miscue

ⓒ *see*
Baby Bear did not know where
he was.

B. Abandoning a correct form

ⓐⓒ *along*
He stayed alone in the pine tree
all night

C. Unsuccessfully attempting to correct an
initial miscue *2. ha-*
ⓤⓒ *1. heavy*
He had slept hard all night.

D. Plain repetition
Jim saw a bear.

Additional Markings

A. Partial Words

res –
The hunters rescued the boys.

B. Nonword substitutions

$ frontmer
People on the frontier had shooting contests.

C. Punctuation ignored
. . . from same maple and oak trees⁄As Bill

D. Intonation
He played a record′ that was his favorite.

E. Word pronounced by examiner

℗
Men on the frontier often had shooting contests.

F. Dialect

ⓓ *goed*
He went home

G. Lip movement
place LM in margin

H. Finger pointing
place FP above word

I. Vocalization
place V in text

From Johns, J.L. (2001). *Basic Reading Inventory* (8th ed.). Dubuque, IA: Kendall/Hunt Publishing Company (1-800-247-3458, ext. 5). May be reproduced for noncommercial educational purposes.

Qualitative Summary of Miscues

Jerry L. Johns

MISCUE	TEXT	GRAPHIC SIMILARITY			CONTEXT		Self-Correction of Unacceptable Miscues
		Beginning	Middle	End	Acceptable	Unacceptable	
Column Total							
Number of Miscues Analyzed							
Percentage							

PREDICTION STRATEGY

Graphic Similarity

B M E

100%
90
80
70
60
50
40
30
20
10

____% ____% ____%

Miscues Acceptable in Context

100%
90
80
70
60
50
40
30
20
10

____%

CORRECTION STRATEGY

Unacceptable Miscues Self-Corrected

100%
90
80
70
60
50
40
30
20
10

____%

Structured Repeated Readings

The structured repeated readings strategy is useful with students who:

- read word by word.
- experience little success in reading.
- lack motivation.
- read very slowly.
- lack conversational qualities in oral reading.
- show little confidence in reading.
- say they can't read well.

Using Structured Repeated Readings

Follow these steps to apply the strategy.

1. Select a passage or story of 50 to 200 words at an appropriate level of difficulty for the student.

2. Have the student read the selection orally. Keep track of the time (in seconds) and miscues.

3. Record the time in seconds and number of miscues on a chart.

4. Ask the student to reread the same material silently.

5. Then have the student reread the selection orally to the teacher or aide. Chart the time and the number of miscues again.

6. Continue the procedure over a period of time until a rate of about 85 words per minute is achieved.

7. Repeat the strategy with a new selection.

Alternate Procedure

1. The student reads the selection along with a tape-recorded narration using earphones. (Caution: The rate of reading on the tape must match the student's ability to follow along.)

2. The student repeats step 1 until audio support is no longer needed.

3. The student begins the process outlined in the original procedure.

Example

This is how structured repeated readings worked with Tracy, a student experiencing difficulty in reading. The following six steps correspond to those in the original explanation.

1. The teacher chose a selection for Tracy to read. The selection contained 132 words.

2. Tracy read the selection orally to the teacher. She made 6 miscues and it took her 124 seconds. To convert seconds into rate, multiply the number of words in the selection by 60 and then divide by the time (in seconds) it takes the student to read the passage. For Tracy, the rate is 64 words per minute (wpm).

number of word		seconds required	
in selection	constant	for reading	rate
(132	× 60)	÷ 124	= 64 wpm

3. With Tracy's help, the teacher recorded the scores (6 miscues and 124 seconds) on the accompanying Reading Progress Chart.

4. Tracy practiced the same selection silently several times by herself.

5. Later, Tracy read the same selection to her teacher a second time. On this reading she made 5 miscues and took 100 seconds—quite an improvement over her first reading.

6. The procedure was repeated over a period of several days. By the third reading, Tracy achieved a rate of about 88 words per minute:

$$(132 \times 60) \div 90 = 88$$
$$7,920 \div 90 = 88$$

At this point, the teacher could have introduced a new passage, but Tracy wanted to try to improve her reading of the first passage even more. After some independent practice and three more readings, the result was a rate of 132 wpm ($7,920 \div 60 = 132$) with no miscues. Then Tracy felt she was ready to move on to a new passage.

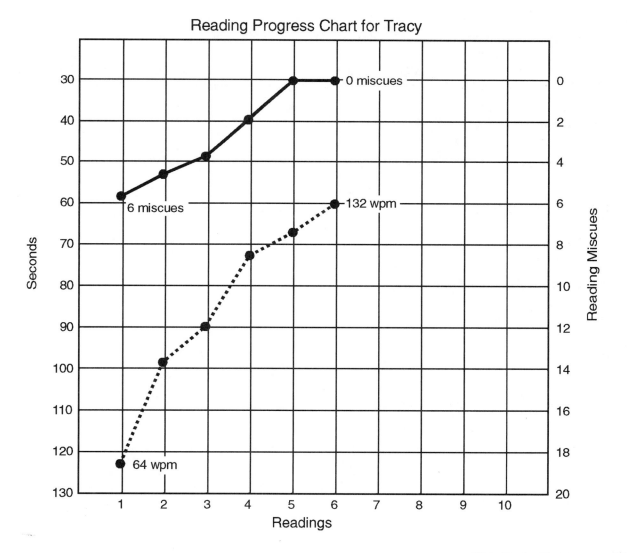

Reading Progress Chart for Tracy

Additional Comments

Notice that the Reading Progress Chart was set up to show visible evidence of gain. A blank chart is provided for teachers to duplicate and use with students for whom the procedure is appropriate. The chart is a real motivational device for most students. They enjoy watching their progress. The chart, however, should not be posted in the classroom without students' permission. Some students are private about their reading and may not wish for others to see their chart. It is recommended that the chart not be displayed in the classroom.

Comprehension is not the main focus of this strategy. However, comprehension questions can be asked or retellings completed after the initial and final readings to help assess improvement, or a different comprehension question can be posed after each rereading. As less attention is needed for decoding, more attention becomes available for comprehension. With greater fluency, the student can concentrate on the meaning of the selection.

Often the question of counting miscues arises. Should all miscues be recorded or only those significant ones that change meaning? Some teachers begin by counting all miscues and then move to discussing miscues with the student to determine those that are significant.

Remember the following guidelines.

- Repeated readings are a supplement to reading instruction.
- Some students respond more readily than others.
- The 85 wpm criterion isn't an absolute; use your judgment.
- Repeated readings focus on fluency and rate of reading.
- With increased fluency, students make fewer miscues and can focus more on comprehension.
- Encourage students to engage in multiple practice readings between each timed reading.

Reading Progress Chart for _____

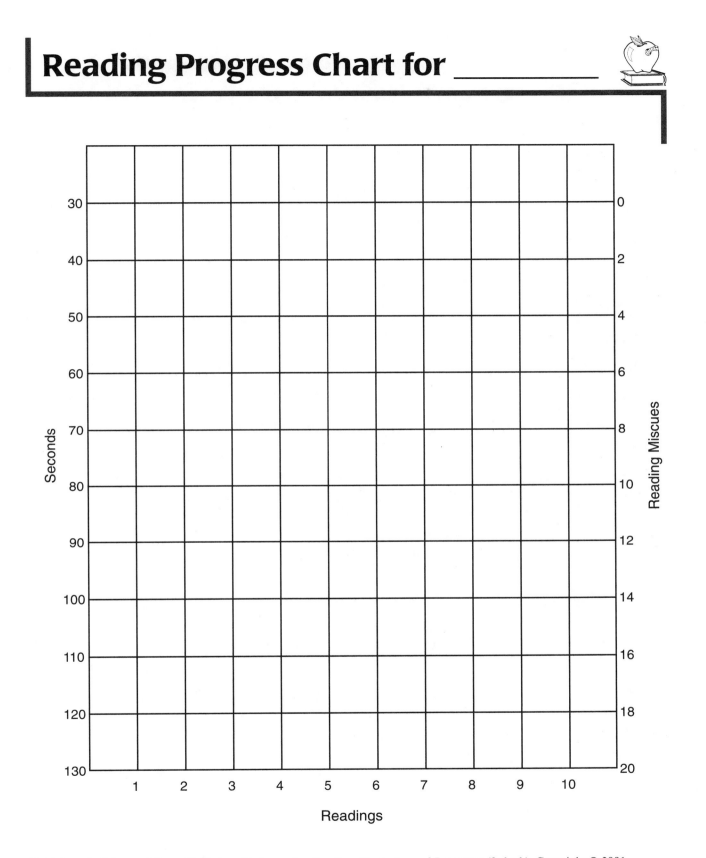

Seconds (left axis): 30, 40, 50, 60, 70, 80, 90, 100, 110, 120, 130

Reading Miscues (right axis): 0, 2, 4, 6, 8, 10, 12, 14, 16, 18, 20

Readings (bottom axis): 1, 2, 3, 4, 5, 6, 7, 8, 9, 10

Oral Reading Alternatives to Round-Robin Reading

Choral Reading. All students read text aloud together.

Glossing. The teacher models reading fluency by reading a selection slowly with expression. The teacher "glosses" by stopping to explain a word or phrase. Students listen, or listen and follow along with the printed text.

Official Announcer. Give each student the opportunity to be the official announcer by assigning a student each day to read announcements, student writings, and memos. Students may ask the teacher for assistance with the text before reading to the class.

Radio Program. A small group of students reads a play or radio script into a tape recorder for class presentations.

Overviewer. A student reads aloud titles, subheads, and vocabulary words before the class reads a selection.

Flash Cards. Using sight words, or vocabulary words on cards, students try to read the group of cards as rapidly and accurately as possible. Phrases can also be used.

Play Reading. Students read plays for class presentations.

Singing. Students read lyrics of a song before singing it.

Games. Many board games require students to read text as they play.

Formal Speech. Students write and read a persuasive or informational speech for the class.

Find the Answer. The teacher asks a question about a text. Students read the part of the text that includes the answer.

Joke of the Day. Students read aloud a joke or riddle for the class.

From Fry, E.B., Kress, J.E., & Fountoukidis, D.L. (1993). *The reading teacher's book of lists* (3rd ed.). Englewood Cliffs, NJ: Prentice-Hall.

Procedure for Determining Words Per Minute

	Example
1. Count or estimate words in selection.	150
2. Multiply by 60.	9000
3. This numeral becomes the dividend.	$\overline{)9000}$
4. Time the student's reading in seconds.	100
5. This numeral becomes the divisor.	$100\overline{)9000}$
6. Do the division.	$100\overline{)9000}^{\,90}$
7. The resulting numeral is the quotient, which is words per minute.	90

$$\begin{array}{r} 90 \text{ words per minute} \\ 100\overline{)9000} \\ \underline{900} \end{array}$$

Median Oral Reading Rates for Students in Grades Two through Five

Grade	Percentile	Fall WPM*	Winter WPM	Spring WPM
2	75	82	106	124
	50	53	78	94
	25	23	46	65
3	75	107	123	142
	50	79	93	114
	25	65	70	87
4	75	125	133	143
	50	99	112	118
	25	72	89	92
5	75	126	143	151
	50	105	118	128
	25	77	93	100

*Reported in words correct per minute

Note: These norms are based on over 7,000 students and provide words correct per minute. These norms are reported in the *Basic Reading Inventory* (Johns, 2001) from a study conducted by Hasbrouck, J.E., & Tindal, G. (1992). Curriculum-based oral reading fluency norms for students in grades 2 through 5. *Teaching Exceptional Children, 24,* 41–44.

Five-Point Fluency Scale for Reading

Level	Description
1	Reads almost entirely word by word; some long pauses between words
2	Reads mostly in 2-to-3 word phrases with some word by word; some evidence of punctuation
3	Reads mostly in phrases; little intonation; ignores some punctuation
4	Reads mostly in phrases; a little choppy at times; attends to punctuation
5	Reads fluently with good expression

CHAPTER 5

RESOURCES

Grades at Which to Introduce Common Prefixes

Prefix	Meaning	Example	Grade to Introduce +
un*	opposite	uncover	3
under	below	underdog	3
dis*	opposite	disapprove	4
re*	again	rewrite	4
re*	back	return	4
de	remove	defog	4
in (il, im, ir)*	opposite	inability	5
		illogical	
		improper	
		irregular	
in (im)*	in	invasion	5
pre	before	predawn	5
sub	under	submerge	5
inter	between	intercept	6
mis	bad or wrong	misapply	6
trans	across	transoceanic	7
en	in	encompass	7
super	very big, large	superhighway	8
anti	against	antisocial	8
fore	in front of/before	foretell	—
mid	middle	midday	—
non	opposite	nondirective	—
over	too much	overachieve	—
semi	half	semipro	—

* These prefixes account for 58% of all prefixed words.

+ The recommended grade level to initiate instruction is from Gunning (2000).

From White, T., Sowell, J., & Yanagihara, A. (1989). Teaching elementary students to use word-part clues. *The Reading Teacher, 42*, 302–308.

Fifteen Frequently Occurring Prefixes

Prefix	Meaning(s)
ab-	away, from, off
ad-	at, to, toward
be-	make, against, to a great degree
com-	with, together, in association
de-	separation, away, opposite of, reduce, from
dis-	opposite of, apart, away, not
en-	cause to be, put in or on
ex-	from, out of, former, apart, away
in-	into, in, within
in-	not
pre-	before in place, time, rank, order
pro-	before, forward, for, in favor of
re-	again, back
sub-	under, beneath, subordinate
in-	not, the opposite of, reversal

From Stauffer, R.G. (1969b). *Teaching reading as a thinking process.* New York: Harper & Row.

Affixes with Invariant Meanings

Combining Forms

anthropo-
auto-
biblio-
bio-
centro- (centri-)
cosmo-
heter- (hetero-)
homo-
hydro-
iso-
lith-
micro-
mono-
neuro-
omni-
pan-
penta-
phil- (philo-)
phono-
photo-
pneumo-
poly-
proto-
pseudo-
tele-
uni-

Prefixes

apo-
circum-
equi-
extra-
intra-
intro-
mal-
mis-
non-
syn-

Adjective Endings

-able (-ible, -ble)
-acious
-est
-ferous
-fic
-fold
-form
-ful
-genous
-less
-like
-most
-ous
-ose
-scopic
-wards
-wise

Noun Suffixes

-acity	-ism
-ana	-ist
-ance	-itis
-archy	-kin
-ard (-art)	-latry
-aster	-let
-ation (-tion, -ion)	-ment
-bility	-meter
-chrome	-metry
-cide	-mony
-cle	-ness
-cule	-ock
-dom	-ology
-ee	-phobia
-eer	-phore
-ence	-ric
-ery	-scope
-ess	-scopy
-far	-ship
-fication	-ster
-gram	-stress
-graph	-trix
-grapher	-tude
-graphy	-ty
-hood	-ule
-ics	
-ier	

From Deighton, L.C. (1959). *Vocabulary development in the classroom.* New York: Teachers College.

Suffixes and Endings Accounting for 87% of All Suffixed Words

Suffix	Examples
ed*	protected, acted
ing*	vanishing, painting
s/es*	authors, washes
al	national, informational
er/or	smaller, janitor
ible/able	possible, affordable
ion/tion	region, generation
ity	infinity, popularity
ly	slowly, friendly
ment	fulfillment, government
ness	likeness, kindness
y	rainy, discovery

*These suffixes or endings account for 65% of all suffixed words.

Twenty-Four Useful Suffixes

Suffix	Meaning(s)	Example
-able	capable of being	allowable
-age	act of	marriage
-al	have the nature of	causal
-an (-n, -ian)	one/who, relating to	librarian
-ance	state of being	brilliance
-ant	person or thing that acts	claimant
-ary	of or pertaining to	alimentary
-ate	cause to be	activate
-ence	state or quality of being	congruence
-ent	one who	recipient
-er	relating to	beater
-ful	having much, tending to	colorful
-ic (-etic)	pertaining to, resembling	heroic
-ical	of, like, pertaining to	monarchical
-ion (-tion, -ation)	act of, state, or condition	affirmation
-ish	having the nature of	dragonish
-ity (-ty)	quality, state, or condition of being	adaptability
-ive	tending or disposed to	meditative
-less	without, having no	aimless
-ment	state of being, act of	admonishment
-ness	quality, state, or condition of being	fairness
-or	person or thing that does	conqueror
-ous	having, abounding in	delirious
-y	pertaining to, causing	loamy

From Thorndike, E.L. (1941). *The teaching of English suffixes.* New York: Teachers College.

Homophones

air	beat	broach	core	eyelet
heir	beet	brooch	corps	islet
aisle	bell	bury	course	faint
isle	belle	berry	coarse	feint
all	bin	but	creek	fair
awl	been	butt	creak	fare
ant	birth	by	crews	faker
aunt	berth	buy	cruise	fakir
arc	blew	cannon	cue	fate
ark	bleu	canon	queue	fete
assent	bore	carrot	current	feet
ascent	boar	carat	currant	feat
ate	born	caret	dam	feign
eight	borne	karat	damn	fain
auger	bow	cask	dear	ferule
augur	beau	casque	deer	ferrule
aye	bow	cellar	desert	fir
eye	bough	seller	dessert	fur
bail	bowl	cheap	die	flee
bale	boll	cheep	dye	flea
ball	boy	chews	do	flew
bawl	buoy	choose	dew	flue
				flu
base	brake	choir	doe	
bass	break	quire	dough	flour
				flower
bate	braze	clime	dun	
bait	braise	climb	done	fold
				foaled
bazaar	bred	close	earn	
bizarre	bread	clothes	urn	fore
				four
bear	bridal	colonel	ewe	
bare	bridle	kernel	yew	foul
				fowl

Homophones *(continued)*

fourth	him	lo	morn	paws
forth	hymn	low	mourn	pause
frieze	hoard	load	muse	peak
frees	horde	lode	mews	pique
freeze				
	holy	lone	need	pearl
gate	wholly	loan	knead	purl
gait	holey		kneed	
		loot		peddle
gauge	horse	lute	night	pedal
gage	hoarse		knight	
		maid		peel
gnu	hour	made	no	peal
knew	our		know	
new		male		piece
	hue	mail	none	peace
great	hew		nun	
grate		mane		pier
	idle	main	not	peer
grown	idol		knot	
groan		marry		plane
	knows	merry	oar	plain
guild	nose		ore	
gild		maul	o'er	plum
	leaf	mall		plumb
guilt	lief		one	
gilt		maze	won	pole
	leak	maize		poll
hail	leek		oral	
hale		meet	aural	pray
	lee	meat		prey
hare	lea	mete	pair	
hair		mein	pear	rabbit
	led	mean	pare	rabbet
haul	lead			
hall		metal	pale	rack
	lesson	mettle	pail	wrack
heart	lessen			
hart		might	palate	racket
	liar	mite	pallet	racquet
heel	lyre			
heal		minor	pane	rain
he'll	liken	miner	pain	rein
	lichen			reign
here		moat	patients	
hear		mote	patience	raise
				raze

From Jerry L. Johns and Susan Davis Lenski, *Improving Reading: Strategies and Resources* (3rd ed.). Copyright © 2001 Kendall/Hunt Publishing Company (1-800-247-3458, ext. 5). May be reproduced for noncommercial educational purposes.

Homophones (continued)

rap	rung	shoe	sunny	two
wrap	wrung	shoo	sonny	to
				too
read	rye	skull	surf	
reed	wry	scull	serf	vale
				veil
real	sale	slay	surge	
reel	sail	sleigh	serge	vein
				vain
reck	seam	slight	tale	vane
wreck	seem	sleight	tail	
				wait
red	sear	so	taught	weight
read	seer	sew	taut	
	sere	sow		waste
right			tax	waist
write	see	soar	tacks	
	sea	sore		wave
rime			tea	waive
rhyme	seed	son	tee	
	cede	sun		way
ring			team	weigh
wring	seen	soul	teem	
	scene	sole		we
rock			tear	wee
roc	sell	stare	tare	
	cell	stair		wear
rode			there	ware
road	sense	stationery	they're	
	cense	stationary	their	week
roe				weak
row	sent	steak	the	
	cent	stake	thee	whole
roll	scent			hole
role		steal	threw	
	serial	steel	through	wood
root	cereal			would
route		step	throws	
	sight	steppe	throes	wreak
rows	site			reek
rose	cite	stoup	time	
		stoop	thyme	
rude	sign			
rood	sine	strait	toe	
		straight	tow	
ruff	signet			
rough	cygnet			

CHAPTER 6

RESOURCES

📖 Using Multiple Intelligences

📖 Elaborative Strategies Using the Multiple Intelligences

Using Multiple Intelligences

As you provide students with strategies to elaborate on text, you need to keep in mind that not all students think in the same ways. Each of us has preferred ways of thinking. Gardner (1993) has identified eight types of thinking which he calls intelligences. As you ask students to process text, try to give them a variety of options. You may have a strong verbal/linguistic intelligence and give assignments that fit that strength; your students may have other strengths. It is important, therefore, that you vary the types of activities you ask your students to accomplish. A general description for the intelligences follows (Eanes, 1997).

Learners with strong **verbal/linguistic** intelligence often:

- enjoy reading, writing, and speaking.
- enjoy research and report writing.
- recall names, places, dates, and details.
- prefer typing to writing.
- like books, periodicals, and recordings.
- enjoy storytelling and oral reading to share stories.
- enjoy creative writing, poetry, and joke telling.

Learners with strong **logical/mathematical** intelligence often:

- have good problem-solving and reasoning skills.
- like to formulate and answer logical questions.
- enjoy sorting, categorizing, and classifying.
- like to explore and analyze.
- like puzzles, mysteries, and riddles.
- like technology.
- are strong in math.

Learners with strong **visual/spatial** intelligence often:

- need visuals to understand new concepts.
- use a great deal of mental imagery.
- like to make and read maps, charts, and diagrams.
- enjoy mazes and puzzles.
- have a strong imagination.
- are good at designing, drawing, creating, and constructing.
- enjoy videos, photographs, slides, and multimedia.
- enjoy giving media presentations.

Learners with strong **body/kinesthetic** intelligence often:

- are good at physical activities.
- like to move around.
- like to touch things.
- use lots of gestures for communicating.
- enjoy hands-on learning.
- like to communicate through drama, dance, and movement.

Learners with strong **musical/rhythmic** intelligence often:

- enjoy listening and responding to music.
- recall melodies easily.
- notice things like pitch and rhythm.
- are highly aware of sounds in the environment.
- are fascinated by computerized sound systems.
- learn better while listening to certain types of music.
- love stories about music.

Learners with strong **interpersonal** intelligence often:

- have strong leadership skills.
- are very sociable and have good interpersonal skills.
- are good at organizing people.
- are good communicators.
- are good mediators and listeners.
- solve problems by talking through them.
- like discussion.
- enjoy interviewing and debating.
- learn best by talking to others.
- enjoy cooperative learning.

Learners with strong **intrapersonal** intelligence often:

- have a strong sense of self.
- are very self-confident.
- prefer working alone.
- have good instincts about strengths and abilities.
- pursue interests, dreams, and goals.
- seek help to pursue or achieve goals.
- like independent research projects.
- like cumulative writing projects.
- like to sit quietly.

Learners with strong **naturalistic** intelligence often:

- enjoy learning from nature.
- notice naturally-occurring patterns.
- like ecological issues.
- analyze natural situations.
- work in natural settings.
- learn from living things.

Elaborative Strategies Using the Multiple Intelligences

As you prepare reading instruction for your students, try to provide a variety of strategies that will appeal to students who have different strengths. You might want to vary your assignments over several weeks, or give students a choice of assignments. The following ideas would be appropriate for each of the eight different intelligences.

Verbal/Linguistic Intelligence

1. Tell or retell the story.
2. Respond to the story by drawing or writing.
3. Read related stories.
4. Write a story to go with a wordless picture book.
5. Model a new story on the one just read.
6. Create a comparison/contrast chart with another story by the same author.
7. Write a script for Readers' Theater.

Logical/Mathematical Intelligence

1. Sort objects related to the story.
2. Measure or graph distances related to the story.
3. Make a matrix using the characters in the story.
4. Create a map showing the setting.
5. Discuss the character's motivations and decide whether they are reasonable.
6. Plan an itinerary for places a character visited.

Visual/Spatial Intelligence

1. Visualize your favorite part of the story and draw it.
2. Design a cover for the book.
3. Recreate several illustrations.
4. Make a newspaper, magazine, or video ad for the story.
5. Imagine you are part of the plot and draw an image that portrays how you are feeling.

Body/Kinesthetic Intelligence

1. Role play the story.
2. Create a puppet show for the story.
3. Have a special day relating to the book. Dress like the characters.
4. Act out a sequence of events from the plot.
5. Invent a game from the story.

Musical/Rhythmic Intelligence

1. Write a jingle or rap having to do with something in the story.
2. During a shared reading, create actions to fit the plot.
3. Sing a song related to the story and add verses that fit the plot.
4. Put words relating to the story to an existing tune.
5. March in a parade while singing a song related to the story.

Interpersonal Intelligence

1. In groups, design something relating to a character in the story.
2. Work with a partner and write a different version of the story.
3. In literature groups, discuss the plot, setting, character, and problem for the story.
4. Discuss the problem of the story and decide in groups how to solve the problem in ways the character did not use.
5. Discuss a character in the story and try to convince group members that the character would or would not be a good friend to have.

Intrapersonal Intelligence

1. Have students write down all they want to know about the topic of the story.
2. Designate a day for students to wear or bring something related to the story.
3. Ask students to tell about something similar that happened to them.
4. Write about how students would feel and what they would do if they were a character in the story.
5. Ask students to write their memories of an event from the story as a diary entry.

Naturalistic Intelligence

1. Have students read about the natural environment.
2. Take students outside for silent reading.
3. Use examples from nature for word study.
4. Discuss ecological issues from books or novels.
5. Write class stories using settings in the natural world.

CHAPTER 7

Story Maps

- Story Map Using Story Grammar
- Story Map Showing Character Change
- Story Map Using Events
- Story Map Showing Attempts and Outcomes
- Story Map Using Chronological Events
- Story Map Showing Events
- Story Map Showing Story Elements

Story Frames

- Story Summary with One Character Included
- Important Idea or Plot
- Setting
- Character Analysis
- Character Comparison

Idea-Maps

- Main Idea-Map
- Compare-Contrast Idea-Map
- Description Idea-Map
- Sequence Idea-Map
- Problem-Solution Idea-Map
- Cause-Effect Idea-Map

Monitoring Reading Self-Check Lists

- Student Self-Check List
- What I Did While Reading
- Student Checklist

RESOURCES

Story Map Using Story Grammar

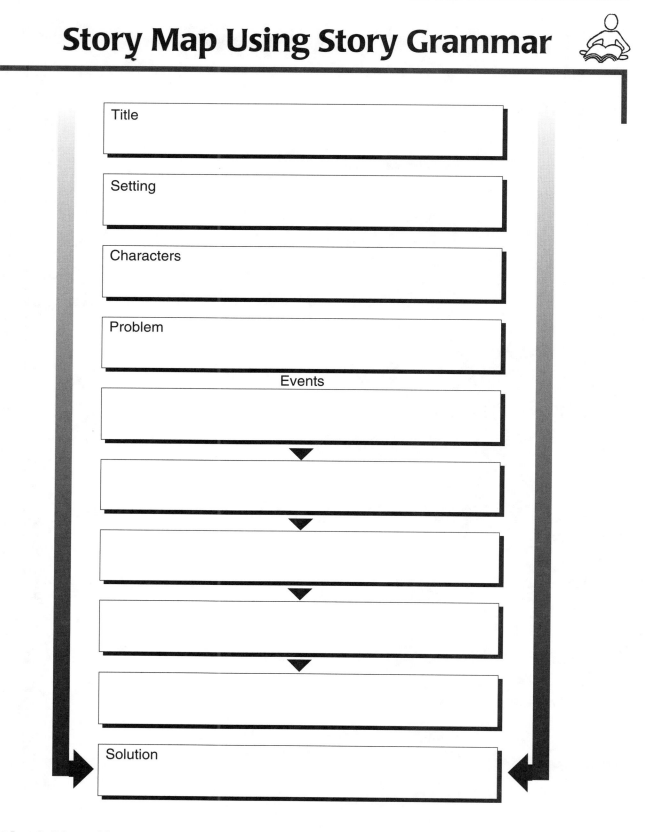

Title

Setting

Characters

Problem

Events

Solution

Story Map Showing Character Change

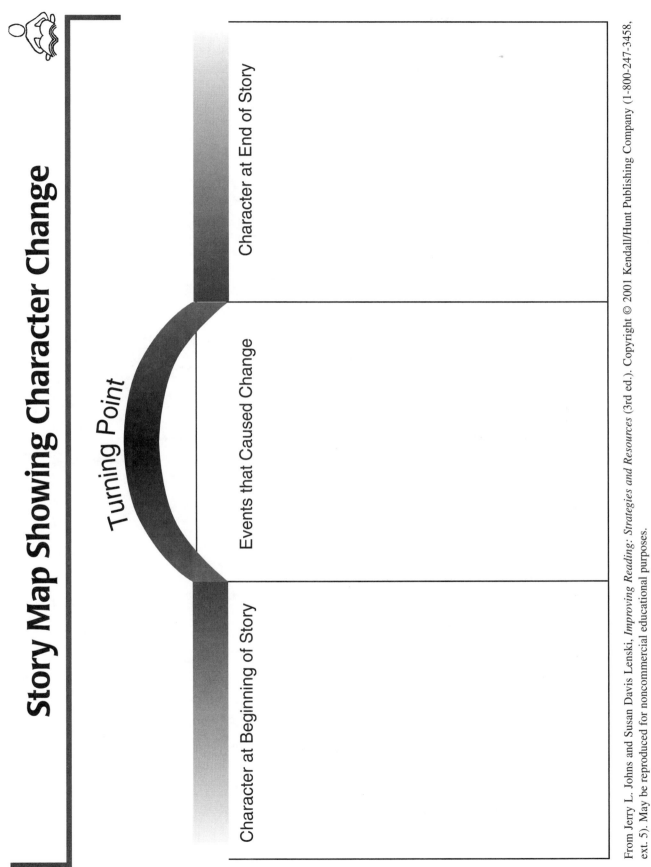

Turning Point

Character at Beginning of Story

Events that Caused Change

Character at End of Story

Story Map Using Events

Events Before the Story Is Told

Story Events

Events After the Story Is Told

Story Map Showing Attempts and Outcomes

Title

Setting

Characters

Goal

Problem

Attempts	Outcomes

Solution

Story Map Using Chronological Events

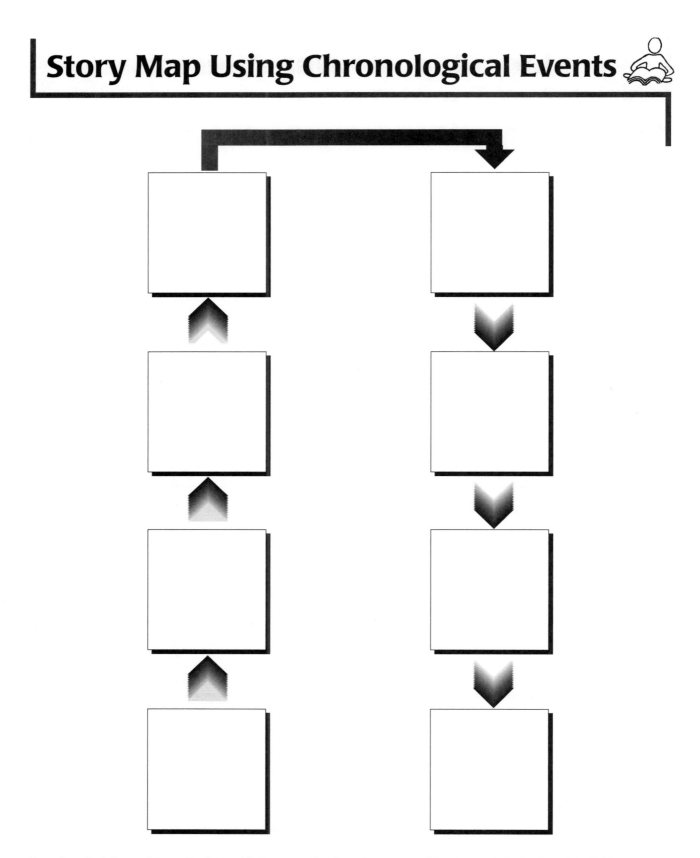

Story Map Showing Events

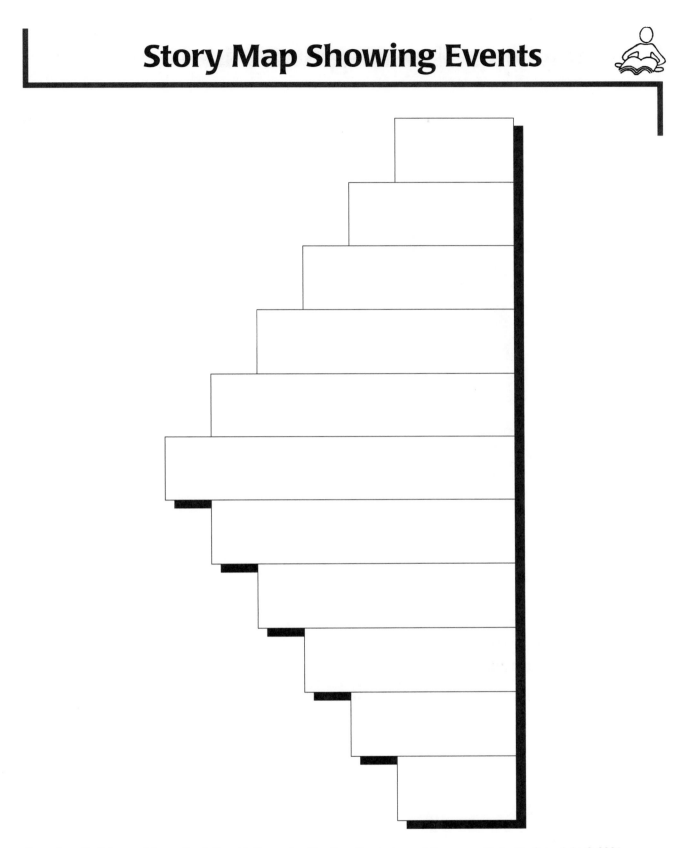

Story Map Showing Story Elements

Story Summary with One Character Included

Our story is about _____

_____.

_____ is an important character in the story.

_____ tried to _____

_____.

The story ends when _____

_____.

Name _____ Date _____

Important Idea or Plot

In this story the problem starts when _____

_____.

After that, _____.

Next, _____.

Then, _____.

The problem is finally solved when _____

_____.

The story ends _____

_____.

Setting

This story takes place_____.

I know this because the author uses the words "_____

_____."

Other clues that show when the story takes place _____

_____.

Character Analysis

_____ is an important character in our story.

_____ is important because _____

_____ .

Once he or she _____ .

Another time, _____ .

I think that _____
(character's name)

is _____
(character trait)

because _____ .

Character Comparison

_____ and _____
(characters' names)

are two characters in our story. _____ is
(character's name)

_____,
(character's trait)

while _____ is
(character's name)

_____.
(character's trait)

For instance, _____ tries to

and _____ tries to

_____.

_____ learns a lesson when
(character's name)

_____.

_____ also learns
(character's name)

that _____.

Main Idea-Map

Topic

Details

Main Idea Sentence

Compare-Contrast Idea-Map

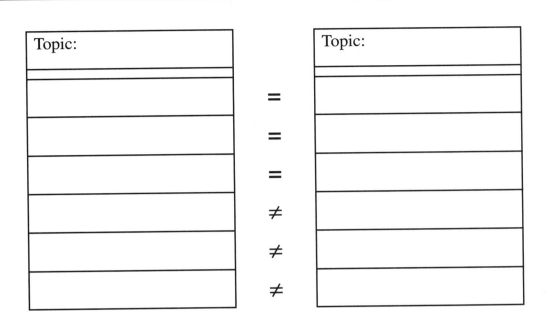

Topic: _____ = Topic: _____
 =
 =
 ≠
 ≠
 ≠

Description Idea-Map

Topic: _____

Sequence Idea-Map

Topic:

Problem-Solution Idea-Map

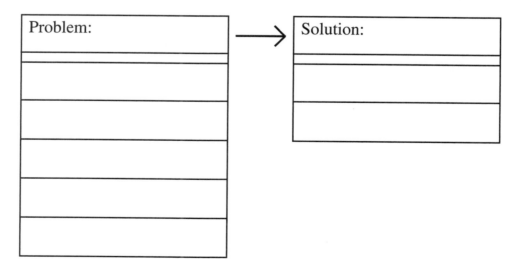

Problem:

Solution:

Name _____ Date _____

Cause-Effect Idea-Map

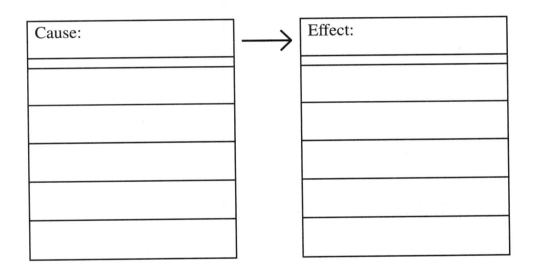

Cause: → Effect:

Name _____ Date _____

Student Self-Check List

	Yes	No
Before you began reading, did you		
1. Ask yourself what the reading was going to be about?	❏	❏
2. Think about what you already knew about the topic?	❏	❏
3. Make a prediction about the contents of the passage?	❏	❏
As you were reading, did you		
4. Know if you didn't understand something?	❏	❏
5. Stop and read again if you didn't understand?	❏	❏
6. Read ahead if you didn't know a word to see if you could figure it out from the words around it?	❏	❏
7. Try to put yourself in the story?	❏	❏
8. Check to see whether your prediction was correct?	❏	❏
9. Make a new prediction?	❏	❏
After you finished reading, did you		
10. Think about what the passage was mostly about?	❏	❏
11. Think about your predictions? Were they proven correct? Why or why not?	❏	❏
12. Think about how you might use the information in the future?	❏	❏

From Roberta L. Berglund and Richard J. Telfer.

Name _____ Date _____

What I Did While Reading

Here's my self-evaluation of what I did while I was reading _____
_____ (name of book or story).

I checked (✓) those things I did.

Strategies	Not Much	A Little	Most of the Time	Almost Always
Used text structure				
Made predictions				
Made pictures in my mind				
Found problems like hard words and not understanding				
Fixed problems by rereading, looking ahead, and checking the dictionary				
Summarized				
Asked myself questions				
Here are other strategies I used:				

From Davey, B. (1983). Think-aloud—Modeling the cognitive processes of reading comprehension. *Journal of Reading, 27*, 44–47.

Name _____ Grade _____ Date _____

Student Checklist

Please draw a face to show how you feel about the following sentences.

If you feel this way often, draw

If you feel this way sometimes, draw

If you feel this way never, draw

I like to find things out for myself. I am curious.
I like to read.
I understand what I read.
I try to figure out new words by myself.
I use what I already know.
I have lots of trouble with words.

CHAPTER

Parent Survey About Reading

Dear Parents,

Please take a few minutes and reflect on what you have observed about your child's reading at home. Your information can help me provide appropriate instruction to your child. I appreciate your help.

Sincerely,

Child's Name _____

Parent or Caregiver's Name _____

1. What strengths do you think your child has in reading?

2. Please list your child's interests.

3. What books or authors does your child like?

4. What concerns do you have about your child's reading?

5. What magazines, books, or newspapers do the adults in your home generally read?

6. What hobbies or interests does your family have?

No "LION" I've Been Trying

**This Special
Achievement Award
is being presented**

to _____

for _____

ROARING
SUCCESS
MEDAL

date

official signature

From Jerry L. Johns and Susan Davis Lenski, *Improving Reading: Strategies and Resources* (3rd ed.). Copyright © 2001 Kendall/Hunt Publishing Company (1-800-247-3458, ext. 5). May be reproduced for noncommercial educational purposes.

Reading Award Certificate

presented to

References

Adams, M.J. (1990a). *Beginning to read: Thinking and learning about print.* (A summary prepared by S.A. Stahl, J. Osborn, & F. Lear). Champaign: University of Illinois.

Adams, M.J. (1990b). *Beginning to read: Thinking and learning about print.* Cambridge, MA: MIT Press.

Agnew, M.L. (2000). DRAW: A motivational reading comprehension strategy for disaffected readers. *Journal of Adolescent & Adult Literacy, 46,* 574–576.

Alvermann, D. (1991). The discussion web: A graphic aid for learning across the curriculum. *The Reading Teacher, 45,* 92–99.

Alvermann, D.E., Moon, J.S., & Hagood, M.C. (1999). *Popular culture in the classroom: Teaching and researching critical media literacy.* Newark, DE: International Reading Association and Chicago, IL: National Reading Conference.

Ames, C. (1992). Classrooms: Goal, structures, and student motivation. *Journal of Educational Psychology, 84,* 261–271.

Anderson, R.S., & Speck, B. (2001). *Using technology in K–8 classrooms.* Upper Saddle River, NJ: Prentice Hall.

Armbruster, B.B. (1986). Using frames to organize expository text. Paper presented at the National Reading Conference, Austin, TX.

Baker, A.J. (2000). Parent involvement for the middle level years: Recommendations for schools. *Schools in the Middle, 6,* 27–30.

Ball, E.W., & Blachman, B.A. (1991). Does phonemic awareness training in kindergarten make a difference in early word recognition and developmental spelling? *Reading Research Quarterly, 26,* 49–66.

Bannatyne-Cugnet, J. (1994). *A prairie year.* Plattsburgh, NY: Tundra.

Base, Graeme. (1986). *Animalia.* New York: Harry N. Abrams.

Bauer, C.F. (1995). *The poetry break, An annotated anthology for introducing children to poetry.* New York: H.W. Wilson.

Bear, D.R., Invernizzi, M., Templeton, S., & Johnston, F. (2000). *Words their way: Word study for phonics, vocabulary, and spelling instruction.* Upper Saddle River, NJ: Prentice Hall.

Beck, I., & McKeown, M. (1991). Conditions of vocabulary acquisition. In R. Barr, M.L. Kamil, P. Mosenthal, and P.D. Pearson (Eds.), *Handbook of reading research* (Vol. II) (pp. 789–814). New York: Longman.

Bentin, S., & Leshem, H. (1993). On the interaction between phonological awareness and reading acquisition: It's a two-way street. *Annals of Dyslexia, 43,* 125–148.

Blachowicz, C.L.Z. (1986). Making connections: Alternatives to the vocabulary notebook. *Journal of Reading, 29,* 643–649.

Blachowicz, C.L.Z., & Fisher, P. (2000). Vocabulary instruction. In M.L. Kamil, P.B. Mosenthal, P.D. Pearson, & R. Barr (Eds.), *Handbook of reading research* (Vol. III) (pp. 503–523). Mahwah, NJ: Erlbaum.

Boning, T., & Boning, R. (1957). I'd rather read than . . . *The Reading Teacher, 10,* 196–200.

Boyton, S. (1983). *A is for angry: An animal and adjective alphabet.* New York: Workman.

Bradley, L., & Bryant, P. (1983). Categorizing sounds and learning to read: A causal connection. *Nature, 301,* 419–421.

Brozo, W.G., & Simpson, M.L. (1991). *Readers, teachers, learners: Expanding literacy in secondary schools.* New York: Macmillan.

Burnett, F.H. (1990). *The secret garden.* New York: Dell.

Camp, D.J., & Tompkins, G.E. (1990). The abecedarius: Soldier of literacy. *Childhood Education, 66,* 298–302.

Carlsen, G.R., & Sherrill, A. (1988). *Voices of readers: How we come to love books.* Urbana, IL: National Council of Teachers of English.

Chall, J.S. (1987). Two vocabularies for reading: Recognition and meaning. In M.G. McKeown & M.E. Curtis (Eds.), *The nature of vocabulary acquisition* (pp. 1–17). Hillsdale, NJ: Erlbaum.

Cicciarelli, J.T. (1997). *Parent letters for the primary grades.* Cypress, CA: Creative Teaching Press.

Clay, M.M. (1967). The reading behavior of five-year-old children: A research report. *New Zealand Journal of Educational Studies, 2,* 11–31.

Cleland, J.V. (1999). We-can charts: Building blocks for student-led conferences. *The Reading Teacher, 52,* 588–595.

Cole, J. (1990). *The magic school bus lost in the solar system.* New York: Scholastic.

Cole, J.E. (2000). *Intrinsic motivation to read: A case study of the literacy personalities of four second-grade readers.* Unpublished doctoral dissertation. DeKalb, IL: Northern Illinois University.

Colvin, C., & Schlosser, L.K. (1997/1998). Developing academic confidence to build literacy: What teachers can do. *Journal of Adolescent & Adult Literacy, 41,* 272–281.

Cramer, E.H. (1992). *Mental imagery and reading* (Literacy Series No. 1). Bloomington, IL: Illinois Reading Council.

Csikszentmihalyi, M. (1991). Literacy and intrinsic motivation. In S.R. Graubard (Ed.), *Literacy* (pp. 115–140). New York: Noonday.

Cummings, P. (1991). *Clean your room, Harvey Moon.* New York: Bradbury.

Cunningham, P.M. (1993). Action phonics. In M.W. Olson & S.P. Homan (Eds.), *Teacher to teacher: Strategies for the elementary classroom* (pp. 9–12). Newark, DE: International Reading Association.

Cunningham, P.M. (1995). *Phonics they use: Words for reading and writing* (2nd ed.). New York: HarperCollins.

Cunningham, P.M. (2000). *Phonics they use: Words for reading and writing* (3rd ed.). New York: Longman.

Cunningham, P.M., & Allington, R.L. (1999). *Classrooms that work: They can all read and write* (2nd ed.). New York: Addison Wesley.

Cunningham, P.M., & Cunningham, J.W. (1992). Making words: Enhancing the invented spelling-decoding connection. *The Reading Teacher, 46,* 106–107.

Cunningham, P.M., & Hall, D.P. (1994a). *Making big words: Multilevel, hands-on spelling and phonics activities.* Parsippany, NJ: Good Apple.

Cunningham, P.M., & Hall, D.P. (1994b). *Making words: Multilevel, hands-on, developmentally appropriate spelling and phonics activities.* Parsippany, NJ: Good Apple.

Cunningham, P.M., & Hall, D.P. (1997). *Making more words: Multilevel, hands-on phonics and spelling activities.* Torrence, CA: Good Apple.

Cunningham, P.M., & Hall, D.P. (1998). *Month by month phonics for upper grades: A second chance for struggling readers and students learning English.* Greensboro, NC: Carson-Dellosa.

Dale, E., & O'Rourke, J. (1971). *Techniques of teaching vocabulary.* Palo Alto, CA: Field Enterprises.

Davey, B. (1983). Think-aloud—Modeling the cognitive processes of reading comprehension. *Journal of Reading, 27,* 44–47.

Davey, B. (1986). Using textbook activity guides to help students learn from textbooks. *Journal of Reading, 29,* 489–494.

DeGenaro, J.J. (1993). Where there's a word, there's a vowel. In M.W. Olson & S.P. Homan (Eds.), *Teacher to teacher: Strategies for the elementary classroom* (p. 9). Newark, DE: International Reading Association.

Deighton, L.C. (1959). *Vocabulary development in the classroom.* New York: Teachers College.

Dowhower, S.L. (1999). Supporting a strategic stance in the classroom: A comprehension framework for helping teachers help students to be strategic. *The Reading Teacher, 52,* 672–688.

Duke, K. (1992). *Aunt Isabel tells a good one.* New York: Puffin.

Duke, N.K., & Stewart, B.B. (1997). Standards in action in a first-grade classroom: The purpose dimension. *The Reading Teacher, 51,* 228–237.

Dunn-Rankin, P. (1968). The similarity of lower-case letters in the English alphabet. *Journal of Verbal Learning and Verbal Behavior, 7,* 990–995.

Eanes, R. (1997). *Content area literacy.* New York: Delmar.

Edwards, P.A. (1995). Combining parents' and teachers' thoughts about storybook reading at home and school. In L.M. Morrow (Ed.), *Family literacy: Connections in schools and communities* (pp. 54–69). Newark, DE: International Reading Association.

Ehri, L., & Wilce, L. (1985). Movement into reading: Is the first stage of printed word learning visual or phonetic? *Reading Research Quarterly, 20,* 163–178.

Elkonin, D.B. (1973). USSR. In Downing, J. (Ed.), *Comparative reading: Cross-national studies of behavior and processes in reading and writing* (pp. 551–579). New York: Macmillan.

Elley, W.B. (1988). Vocabulary acquisition from listening to stories. *Reading Research Quarterly, 24,* 174–187.

Elting, M., & Folsom, M. (1980). *Q is for duck: An alphabet guessing game.* New York: Clarion.

Estes, T.H. (1971). A scale to measure attitudes toward reading. *Journal of Reading, 15,* 135–138.

Faltis, C.J. (2001). *Joinfostering: Teaching and learning in multilingual classrooms* (3rd ed.). Upper Saddle River, NJ: Prentice Hall.

Fields, M.V., & Spangler, K.L. (2000). *Let's begin reading right: A developmental approach to emergent literacy* (4th ed.). Upper Saddle River, NJ: Prentice Hall.

Fowler, G.L. (1982). Developing comprehension skills in primary students through the use of story frames. *The Reading Teacher, 36,* 176–179.

Fox, B.J. (1996). *Strategies for word identification.* Columbus, OH: Merrill.

Fox, B.J. (2000). *Word identification strategies* (2nd ed.). Upper Saddle River, NJ: Prentice Hall.

Fredericks, A.D., & Rasinski, T.V. (1990). Involving parents in the assessment process. *The Reading Teacher, 44,* 346–349.

Freeman, G., & Reynolds, E.G. (1980). Enriching basal reader lessons and semantic webbing. *The Reading Teacher, 33,* 677–684.

Fry, E.B., Kress, J.E., & Fountoukidis, D.L. (1993). *The reading teacher's book of lists* (3rd ed.). Englewood Cliffs, NJ: Prentice Hall.

Gambrell, L.B. (1996). Creating classroom cultures that foster reading motivation. *The Reading Teacher, 50,* 14–25.

Gambrell, L.B., & Jawitz, P.B. (1993). Mental imagery, text illustrations, and children's story comprehension and recall. *Reading Research Quarterly, 28,* 264–273.

Gambrell, L.B., Palmer, B.M., Codling, R.M., & Mazzoni, S.A. (1996). Assessing reading motivation. *The Reading Teacher, 49,* 518–533.

Gardner, H. (1993). *Multiple intelligences.* New York: BasicBooks.

Gillet, J.W., & Temple, C. (1990). *Understanding reading problems: Assessment and instruction* (3rd ed.). Glenview, IL: Scott Foresman.

Gillet, J.W., & Temple, C. (2000). *Understanding reading problems: Assessment and instruction* (4th ed.). New York: Longman.

Glazer, J.I. (2000). *Literature for young children* (4th ed.). Upper Saddle River, NJ: Prentice Hall.

Goldstein, A. (July 3, 2000). Paging all parents. *Time,* 47.

Goodman, K.S. (1996). *On reading.* Portsmouth, NH: Heinemann.

Goodman, Y.M., & Marek, A.M. (1996). *Retrospective miscue analysis: Revaluing readers and reading.* Katonah, NY: Richard C. Owen.

Grant, R. (1993). Strategic training for using text headings to improve students' processing of content. *Journal of Reading, 36,* 482–487.

Graves, M.F., Watts-Taffe, S.M., & Graves, B.B. (1999). *Essentials of elementary reading* (2nd ed.). Boston: Allyn and Bacon.

Greenlaw, J. (2001). *English language arts and reading on the internet. A resource for K–12 teachers.* Upper Saddle River, NJ: Prentice Hall.

Griffith, P.L., & Olson, M.W. (1992). Phonemic awareness helps beginning readers break the code. *The Reading Teacher, 45,* 516–523.

Gunning, T.G. (1996). *Creating reading instruction for all children* (2nd ed.). Boston: Allyn and Bacon.

Gunning, T.G. (1998). *Great books for beginning readers.* Boston: Allyn and Bacon.

Gunning, T.G. (2000). *Creating literacy instruction for all children* (3rd ed.). Needham Heights, MA: Allyn and Bacon.

Guthrie, J.T., & Wigfield, A. (2000). Engagement and motivation in reading. In M.L. Kamil, P.B. Mosenthal, P.D. Pearson, & R. Barr (Eds.), *Handbook of reading research* (Vol. III) (pp. 403–422). Mahwah, NJ: Erlbaum.

Guthrie, J.T., Wigfield, A., Metsala, J.L., & Cox, K.E. (1999). Motivational and cognitive predictors of text comprehension and reading amount. *Scientific Studies of Reading, 3,* 231–256.

Haggard, M.R. (1982). The vocabulary self-collection strategy: An active approach to word learning. *Journal of Reading, 27,* 203–207.

Hall, K.P. (Ed.). (1997). *Parent letters for the intermediate grades.* Cypress, CA: Creative Teaching Press.

Hammond, D. (1983). How your students can predict their way to reading comprehension. *Learning, 12,* 62–64.

Hansen, J. (1981). The effects of inference training and practice on young children's reading comprehension. *Reading Research Quarterly, 16,* 391–417.

Harmin, M. (1995). *Inspiring active learning.* Edwardsville, IL: Inspiring Strategy Institute.

Havill, J. (1990). *Jamaica-tag-along.* Boston, MA: Houghton Mifflin.

Hayes, D.A. (1989). Helping students GRASP the knack of writing summaries. *Journal of Reading, 33,* 96–101.

Heckelman, R.G. (1969). A neurological-impress method of remedial-reading instruction. *Academic Therapy Quarterly, 4,* 277–282.

Heimlich, J.E., & Pittleman, S.D. (1986). *Semantic mapping: Classroom applications.* Newark, DE: International Reading Association.

Henk, W.A., & Melnick, S.A. (1995). The reader self-perception scale (RSPS): A new tool for measuring how children feel about themselves as readers. *The Reading Teacher, 48,* 470–482.

Higgins, N., & Hess, L. (1999). Using electronic books to promote vocabulary development. *Journal of Research on Computing in Education, 31,* 425–430.

Hillerich, R.L. (1978). *A writing vocabulary of elementary children.* Springfield, IL: Charles C Thomas.

Hoban, T. (1989). *Of colors and things.* New York: Greenwillow.

Hohn, W., & Ehri, L. (1983). Do alphabet letters help prereaders acquire phonemic segmentation skills? *Journal of Educational Psychology, 75,* 752–762.

Hughey, J.B., & Slack, C. (2001). *Teaching children to write.* Upper Saddle River, NJ: Prentice Hall.

International Reading Association (1999). *Multiple methods of beginning reading instruction: A position statement of the International Reading Association.* Newark, DE: Author.

International Reading Association (2000). *Making a difference means making it different: Honoring children's rights to excellent reading instruction.* Newark, DE: Author.

Jason, M.H., & Dubnow, B. (1973). The relationship between self-perceptions of reading abilities and reading achievement. In W.H. MacGinitie (Ed.), *Assessment problems in reading* (pp. 96–101). Newark, DE: International Reading Association.

Jenkins, E. (1997). *Ella Jenkins song book for children.* New York: Oak Publications.

Jett-Simpson, M. (1989). *Adventuring with Books: A booklist for pre-K–grade 6.* Urbana, IL: National Council of Teachers of English.

Johns, J.L. (1975). Dolch list of common nouns—A comparison. *The Reading Teacher, 28,* 338–340.

Johns, J.L. (1977). Children's conceptions of a spoken word: A developmental study. *Reading World, 16,* 248–257.

Johns, J.L. (1980). First graders' concepts about print. *Reading Research Quarterly, 15,* 529–549.

Johns, J.L. (1981). The development of the revised Dolch list. *Illinois School Research and Development, 17,* 15–24.

Johns, J.L. (1991). Literacy portfolios: A primer. *Illinois Reading Council Journal, 19,* 4–10.

Johns, J.L. (2001). *Basic reading inventory* (8th ed.). Dubuque, IA: Kendall/Hunt.

Johnson, B., & Kaufman, B. (1999). *Project prevent workshop.* Des Plaines, IL: School District 62.

Johnson, D.D., & Pearson, P.D. (1984). *Teaching reading vocabulary* (2nd ed.). New York: Holt.

Klesius, J., Laframboise, K.L., & Gaier, M. (1998). Humorous literature: Motivation for reluctant readers. *Reading Research and Instruction, 37,* 253–261.

Kress, J. (1993). *The ESL teacher's book of lists.* Upper Saddle River, NJ: Prentice Hall.

Krows, J. (1993). My house. In *At my window.* Orlando, FL: Harcourt Brace Jovanovich.

Labbo, L. (2000). 12 things young children can do with a talking book in a classroom computer center. *The Reading Teacher, 53,* 542–546.

Lamberg, W.J., & Lamb, C.E. (1980). *Reading instruction in the content areas.* Geneva, IL: Houghton Mifflin.

Layne, S.L. (1996). *Vocabulary acquisition by fourth-grade students from listening to teachers' oral reading of novels.* Unpublished doctoral dissertation, Northern Illinois University, DeKalb.

Lehman, J.H. (1990). *The saga of Shakespeare Pintlewood and the great silver fountain pen.* Elgin, IL: Brotherstone Publishers.

L'Engle, M. (1962). *A wrinkle in time.* New York: Dell.

Lenski, S.D. (1999). The Directed Reading-Connected Activity (DR-CA): A strategy to promote connections across texts. *Journal of Reading Education, 24,* 9–12.

Lenski, S.D., & Johns, J.L. (2000). *Improving writing: Resources, strategies, and assessments.* Dubuque, IA: Kendall/Hunt.

Lenski, S.D., & Niersheimer, S.L. (in press). Strategy instruction from a sociocognitive perspective. *Reading & Writing Quarterly.*

Lima, C.W., & Lima, J.A. (1998). *A to zoo: Subject access to children's picture books* (5th ed.). New Providence, NJ: R.R. Bowker.

Lobel, A. (1970). *Frog and toad are friends.* New York: Harper and Row.

Lowry, L. (1993). *The giver.* New York: Bantam Doubleday Dell.

Lundberg, I., Frost, J., & Petersen, O.P. (1988). Effects of an extensive program for stimulating phonological awareness in preschool children. *Reading Research Quarterly, 23,* 264–284.

Manzo, A.V. (1969). The ReQuest procedure. *Journal of Reading, 13,* 123–126.

Manzo, A.V., & Manzo, U.C. (1993). *Literacy disorders: Holistic diagnosis and remediation.* New York: Harcourt Brace Jovanovich.

Martin, B., Jr. (1970). *Brown bear, brown bear.* New York: Holt.

Martin, B., Jr., & Archambault, J. (1989). *Chicka chicka boom boom.* New York: Simon and Schuster.

May, F.B. (1990). *Reading as communication* (3rd ed.). Columbus, OH: Merrill.

McCormick, S. (1995). *Instructing students who have literacy problems* (2nd ed.). Columbus, OH: Merrill.

McCormick, S. (1999). *Instructing students who have literacy problems* (3rd ed.). Upper Saddle River, NJ: Prentice Hall.

McGee, L.M., & Richgels, D.J. (1996). *Literacy's beginnings: Supporting young readers and writers* (2nd ed.). Boston: Allyn and Bacon.

McGinley, W.J., & Denner, P.R. (1987). Story impressions: A prereading/writing activity. *Journal of Reading, 31,* 248–253.

McKenna, M.C., and Kear, D.J. (1990). Measuring attitude toward reading: A new tool for teachers. *The Reading Teacher, 43,* 626–639.

McKenna, M.C., Kear, D.J., & Ellsworth, R.A. (1995). Children's attitudes toward reading: A national survey. *Reading Research Quarterly, 30,* 934–956.

McLoyd, V. (1979). The effects of extrinsic rewards of differential value on high and low intrinsic interest. *Child Development, 50,* 1010–1019.

McPhail, J.C., Pierson, J.M., Freeman, J.G., Goodman, J., & Ayappa, A. (2000). The role of interest in fostering sixth grade students' identities as competent learners. *Curriculum Inquiry, 30,* 43–69.

Meier, D.R. (2000). *Scribble scrabble: Learning to read and write; success with diverse teachers, children, and families.* New York: Teachers College Press.

Miles, B. (1995). *Hey! I'm reading.* New York: Scholastic.

Miller, W.H. (1995). *Alternative assessment techniques for reading & writing.* West Nyack, NY: The Center for Applied Research in Education.

Moore, D.M., & Moore, S.A. (1986). Possible sentences. In E.K. Dishner, T.W. Bean, J.E. Readence, & D.W. Moore (Eds.), *Reading in the content areas: Improving classroom instruction* (2nd ed.) (pp. 174–179). Dubuque, IA: Kendall/Hunt.

Moore, M. (1998). Using De Bono's thinking hats with BTN. *Practically Primary, 3,* 9–10.

Morningstar, J. (1999). Home response journals: Parents as informed contributors in their understanding of their child's literacy development. *The Reading Teacher, 52,* 690–697.

Morris, D., & Perney, J. (1984). Developmental spelling as a predictor of first-grade reading achievement. *The Elementary School Journal, 84,* 441–457.

Morrow, L.M. (1983). Home and school correlates of early interest in literature. *Journal of Educational Research, 76,* 221–230.

Musgrove, M. (1976). *Ashanti to Zulu: African traditions.* New York: Dial.

Nagy, W., & Anderson, R.C. (1984). How many words are there in printed school English? *Reading Research Quarterly, 19,* 304–330.

Nagy, W.E., & Scott, J.A. (2000). Vocabulary processes. In M.L. Kamil, P.B. Mosenthal, P.D. Pearson, & R. Barr (Eds.), *Handbook of reading research* (Vol. III) (pp. 269–284). Mahwah, NJ: Erlbaum.

National Reading Panel (2000). *Teaching children to read: An evidence-based assessment of the scientific research literature on reading and its implications for reading instruction.* Washington, DC: National Institute of Child Health & Human Development.

Numeroff, L.J. (1991). *If you give a moose a muffin.* New York: HarperCollins.

Numeroff, L.J. (1996). *If you give a mouse a cookie.* New York: HarperCollins.

Nurss, J., Hough, R.A., & Goodson, M.S. (1981). Prereading/language development in two day care centers. *Journal of Reading Behavior, 13,* 23–31.

O'Flahavan, J.F., Hartman, D.K., & Pearson, P.D. (1988). Teacher questioning and feedback practices: A twenty year perspective. In J.E. Readence & R.S. Baldwin (Eds.), *Dialogues in literacy research* (37th Yearbook of the National Reading Conference) (pp. 183–208). Chicago: National Reading Conference.

Ogle, D.M. (1989). The know, want to know, learn strategy. In K.D. Muth (Ed.), *Children's comprehension of text* (pp. 205–223). Newark, DE: International Reading Association.

Opitz, M.F. (1995). *Getting the most from predictable books.* New York: Scholastic.

Opitz, M.F. (2000). *Rhymes & reasons: Literature and language play for phonological awareness.* Portsmouth, NH: Heinemann.

Opitz, M.F., & Rasinski, T.V. (1998). *Good-bye round robin: Twenty-five effective oral reading strategies.* Portsmouth, NH: Heinemann.

Palinscar, A.S., & Brown, A.L. (1986). Interactive teaching to promote independent learning from text. *The Reading Teacher, 39,* 771–777.

Park, B. (1996). *Mick Harte was here.* New York: Scholastic.

Peek, M. (1985). *Mary wore her red dress and Henry wore his green sneakers.* New York: Clarion.

Pelham, D. (1990). *Sam's sandwich.* New York: Dutton.

Pinnell, G.S., & Fountas, I.C. (1998). *Word matters: Teaching phonics and spelling in the reading/writing classroom.* Portsmouth, NH: Heinemann.

Piper, W. (1953). *The little engine that could.* New York: Harper and Row.

Pittleman, S.D., Heimlich, J.E., Berglund, R.L., & French, M.P. (1991). *Semantic feature analysis: Classroom applications.* Newark, DE: International Reading Association.

Pressley, M. (2000). What should comprehension instruction be the instruction of? In M.L. Kamil, P.B. Mosenthal, P.D. Pearson, & R. Barr (Eds.), *Handbook of reading research* (Vol. III) (pp. 545–561). Mahwah, NJ: Erlbaum.

Purcell-Gates, V. (2000). Family literacy. In M.L. Kamil, P.B. Mosenthal, P.D. Pearson, & R. Barr (Eds.), *Handbook of reading research* (Vol. III) (pp. 853–870). Mahwah, NJ: Erlbaum.

Rabe, B. (1981). *The balancing girl.* New York: E.P. Dutton.

Raines, S.C., & Isbell, R. (1988, April). *An array of teaching ideas using wordless picture books.* Paper presented at the Annual Study Conference of the Association for Childhood Education International, Salt Lake City, UT.

Raphael, T.E. (1984). Teaching learners about sources of information for answering comprehension questions. *Journal of Reading, 27,* 303–311.

Rasinski, T., & Padak, N. (2000). *Effective reading strategies: Teaching children who find reading difficult* (2nd ed.). Upper Saddle River, NJ: Prentice Hall.

Rasinski, T.V., Padak, N.D., Linek, W.L., & Sturtevant, E. (1994). Effects of fluency development on urban second-grade readers. *Journal of Educational Research, 87,* 158–165.

Rawls, W. (1961). *Where the red fern grows*. New York: Doubleday.

Readence, J.E., Bean, T.W., & Baldwin, R.S. (1998). *Content area literacy* (6th ed.). Dubuque, IA: Kendall/Hunt.

Rhodes, L.K. (1981). I can read! Predictable books as resources for reading and writing instruction. *The Reading Teacher, 34*, 511–518.

Richards, J.C., & Gipe, J.P. (1993). Getting to know story characters: A strategy for young and at-risk readers. *The Reading Teacher, 47*, 78–79.

Richek, M.A., Caldwell, J.S., Jennings, J.H., & Lerner, J.W. (1996). *Reading problems: Assessment and teaching strategies* (3rd ed.). Boston: Allyn and Bacon.

Rinne, C.H. (1998). Motivating students is a percentage game. *Phi Delta Kappan, 79*, 620–627.

Roberts, B. (1992). The evolution of the young child's concept of word as a unit of spoken and written language. *Reading Research Quarterly, 27*, 124–138.

Roberts, E.P. (1999). Critical teacher thinking and imaginations: Uncovering two vocabulary strategies to increase comprehension. *Reading Horizons, 40*, 65–67.

Robinson, R.P. (1946). *Effective study*. New York: Harper and Row.

Roe, B.D., Stoodt, B.D., & Burns, P.C. (2001). *The content areas: Secondary school literacy instruction* (7th ed.). Boston: Houghton Mifflin.

Routman, R. (1991). *Invitations: Changing as teachers and learners K-12*. Portsmouth, NH: Heinemann.

Rubin, D. (1993). *A practical approach to teaching reading*. Needham Hts., MA: Allyn and Bacon.

Ruddell, M.R. (1993). *Teaching content reading and writing*. Needham Hts., MA: Allyn and Bacon.

Ruddell, R.B. (1974). *Reading-language instruction: Innovative practices*. Englewood Cliffs, NJ: Prentice Hall.

Rupley, W.H., Logan, J.W., & Nichols, W.D. (1998/1999). Vocabulary instruction in a balanced reading program. *The Reading Teacher, 52*, 336–346.

Ryan, R.M., & Deci, E.L. (2000). Self-determination theory and the facilitation of intrinsic motivation, social development, and well-being. *American Psychologist, 55*, 68–78.

Samuels, S.J. (1994). Toward a theory of automatic information processing in reading revisited. In R.B. Ruddell, M.R. Ruddell, & H. Singer (Eds.), *Theoretical models and processes of reading* (4th ed.) (pp. 816–837). Newark, DE: International Reading Association.

Sanacore, J. (2000). Promoting the lifetime reading habit in middle school students. *The Clearing House, 73*, 157–161.

Schmidt, B., & Buckley, M. (1991). Plot relationships chart. In J.M. Macon, D. Bewell, & M. Vogt (Eds.), *Responses to literature: Grades K-8* (pp. 7–8). Newark, DE: International Reading Association.

Schmitt, M.C. (1990). A questionnaire to measure children's awareness of strategic reading processes. *The Reading Teacher, 43*, 454–461.

Scieszka, J. (1989). *The true story of the 3 pigs by A. Wolf*. New York: Scholastic.

Seuss, Dr. (1965). *Hop on pop*. New York: Beginning Books.

Sherman, R., & Wright, G. (1999). Let's create a comic strip. *Reading Improvement, 36*, 66–72.

Sinatra, R. (1987). *Visual literacy connections to thinking, reading and writing*. Springfield, IL: Charles C Thomas.

Slattery, R. (2000a). *Working with onsets and rimes*. Manuscript in preparation.

Slattery, R. (2000b). *Developing phonemic awareness through invented spelling: A contextualized approach*. Manuscript submitted for publication, Northern Illinois University, DeKalb.

Smith, H.M., & Read, D. (1982). Teaching visual literacy through wordless picture books. *The Reading Teacher, 35*, 928–933.

Smolkin, L.B., & Yaden, D.B. (1992). O is for mouse: First encounters with the alphabet book. *Language Arts, 69*, 432–441.

Snow, C.E., Burns, S.M., & Griffin, P. (Eds.). (1998). *Preventing reading difficulties in young children*. Washington, DC: National Academy of Education.

Sobol, D.J. (1981). *Encyclopedia Brown's second record book of weird and wonderful facts*. New York: Dell.

Stanfill, S. (1978). The great American one-sentence summary. In O. Clapp (Ed.), *Classroom practices in teaching classroom English, 1977–1978* (pp. 47–49). Urbana, IL: National Council of Teachers of English.

Stanovich, K.E. (1991). Word recognition: Changing perspectives. In R. Barr, M.L. Kamil, P. Mosenthal, & P.D. Pearson (Eds.), *Handbook of reading research* (Vol. II) (pp. 418–452). New York: Longman.

Stanovich, K.E. (1993/1994). Romance and reality (Distinguished Educator Series). *The Reading Teacher, 47*, 280–291.

Stauffer, R.G. (1969a). *Directing reading maturity as a cognitive process*. New York: Harper and Row.

Stauffer, R.G. (1969b). *Teaching reading as a thinking process*. New York: Harper and Row.

Stephens, E.C., & Brown, J.E. (2000). *A handbook of content literacy strategies: 75 practical reading and writing ideas*. Norwood, MA: Christopher-Gordon.

Sternberg, R.J., & Powell, J.S. (1983). Comprehending verbal comprehension. *American Psychologist, 38,* 878–893.

Swindall, V., & Cantrell, J.R. (1999). Character interviews help bring literature to life. *The Reading Teacher, 53,* 23–25.

Taba, H. (1967). *Teacher's handbook for elementary social studies.* Reading, MA: Addison-Wesley.

Taylor, G. (1998). A discussion, not a report, if you please. *Journal of Adolescent and Adult Literacy, 41,* 561–563.

Thorndike, E.L. (1941). *The teaching of English suffixes.* New York: Teachers College.

Tompkins, G.E. (1998). *50 literacy strategies: Step by step.* Upper Saddle River, NJ: Prentice Hall.

Tompkins, G.E. (2000). *Teaching writing: Balancing process and product* (3rd ed.). Upper Saddle River, NJ: Prentice Hall.

Tompkins, G.E. (2001). *Literacy for the 21st century: A balanced approach* (2nd ed.). Upper Saddle River, NJ: Prentice Hall.

Tompkins, G.E., & Hoskisson, K. (1991). *Language arts: Content and teaching strategies.* New York: Macmillan.

Towell, J.H. (1999/2000). Motivating students through music and literature. *The Reading Teacher, 53,* 284–287.

Treiman, R., & Zukowski, A. (1991). Levels of phonological awareness. In S.A. Brady & D.P. Shankweiler (Eds.), *Phonological processes in literacy* (pp. 67–81). Hillsdale, NJ: Erlbaum.

Treiman, R., & Zukowski, A. (1996). Children's sensitivity to syllables, onsets, rimes, and phonemes. *Journal of Experimental Child Psychology, 61,* 193–215.

Tullock-Rhody, R., & Alexander, J.E. (1980). A scale for assessing attitudes toward reading in secondary schools. *Journal of Reading, 23,* 609–614.

Tumner, W.E., Herriman, M.L., & Nesdale, A.R. (1988). Metalinguistic abilities and beginning reading. *Reading Research Quarterly, 23,* 134–158.

Turkle, B. (1976). *Deep in the forest.* New York: Dutton.

Viorst, J. (1972). *Alexander and the terrible, horrible, no good, very bad day.* New York: Atheneum.

Waddell, M. (1975). *Owl babies.* Cambridge, MA: Candlewick Press.

Walker, B.J. (2000). *Diagnostic teaching of reading* (4th ed.). Upper Saddle River, NJ: Prentice Hall.

White, E.B. (1952). *Charlotte's web.* New York: Harper and Row.

White, T.G., Sowell, J., & Yanagihara, A. (1989). Teaching elementary students to use word-part clues. *The Reading Teacher, 42,* 302–308.

Wisendanger, K.D. (2001). *Strategies for literacy education.* Upper Saddle River, NJ: Prentice Hall.

Wigfield, A., Eccels, J.S., Yoon, K.S., Harold, R.D., Arbreton, A.J.A., Freedman-Doan, C., & Blumenfeld, P.C. (1997). Change in children's competence beliefs and subjective task values across the elementary school years: A 3-year study. *Journal of Educational Psychology, 89,* 451–469.

Wilder, L.I. (1932). *Little house in the big woods.* New York: Harper.

Wilson, P.T. (1988). *Let's think about reading and reading instruction: A primer for tutors and teachers.* Dubuque, IA: Kendall/Hunt.

Wilson, R.M., Hall, M., Leu, D.J., & Kinzer, C.K. (2001). *Phonics, phonemic awareness, and word analysis for teachers* (7th ed.). Upper Saddle River, NJ: Prentice Hall.

Wood, K. (1984). Probable passages: A writing strategy. *The Reading Teacher, 37,* 496–499.

Yopp, H. (1988). The validity and reliability of phonemic awareness tests. *Reading Research Quarterly, 23,* 159–177.

Yopp, H.K. (1995). A test for assessing phonemic awareness in young children. *The Reading Teacher, 49,* 20–29.

Yopp, R.H., & Yopp, H.K. (2000). Sharing informational text with young children. *The Reading Teacher, 53,* 410–419.

Zeno, S.M., Ivens, S.H., Millard, R.T., & Duvvuri, R. (1995). *The educator's word frequency guide.* Brewster, NY: Touchstone Applied Science.

Index

Figurative language, 258–59
File folders, of prior knowledge, 276–77
First person point of view, book list for, 337
Five by five strategy, word-solving skills, 431–32
Five-point fluency scale, 577
Fix-ups, monitoring, 366–72
Flexibility, in word identification, 179–83
Fluency, in oral reading, 185–209. *See also* Oral reading
Fluency, parents and, 435–40
 background, 435
 echo reading, 435–36
 practice activities, 440
 reading calendar, 439
 story-reading ideas, 437–38
 structured repeated readings, 570–73
Fluent readers, activities for, 492, 502
Four in a row, 153
Four square game, 266
FRED (acronym), 14
Frequently used words, list, 553
Friendly contract, motivation and, 61
FRISBEE (acronym), 14

G

Games (by name)
 Affix Stopped Me (The), 153
 Categories, 293
 Clues and Questions, 266
 Compound Word Dominoes, 152
 Consonant Rummy, 134
 Dictionary Detective, 174
 Envelope Alphabet, 172
 Find a Rhyme, 89
 Find Rhyming Words, 89
 Fish, 117
 Four in a Row, 153
 Four Square, 266
 Funny Questions, 80
 Get the Facts, 296–97
 Go Fish, 114
 Going to New York, 305
 Group Ball Toss, 152
 Group Me, 89
 How Is It Ordered, 304
 Letters and Names, 114
 Match, 114, 293
 One, Two, or Three, 153
 Palindromes, 265–66
 Pick Up, 134
 Picture Pairs, 79–80
 Pronounce a Word, 80
 Remember and Rhyme, 89
 Scramble, 304

 Tom Swifties, 265
 Tour the Zoo, 253
 Tricky Words, 117
 Twister, 152
 Wheel Spin, 153–54
 Wordo, 113
 Yes-No, 79
Games (by topic)
 comprehension, 293, 296–97
 dictionary, 172, 174, 253
 interest in words, 265–66
 main idea, 293
 phonics, 134
 sequence, 304–5
 structural analysis, 143–54
 vowels, 139
Gender/ethnic distribution, reading attitudes, 24
Genre charts, 54–56
Get the Facts game, 296–97
Getting to know my character, 314–16
Goalsetting, motivation and, 52–61
 challenging book calendar, 57–58
 daily reading record, 52–54
 genre charts, 54–56
Going to New York game, 305
GRAB (acronym), 14
Grades, for introducing prefixes, 580
Graphic organizers, 224–36
 cause-effect, 232
 chain of command, 225
 continuum, 226
 cycle, 227
 hierarchy, 229
 meaning vocabulary, 224–36
 nonfiction, 347–49
 overlapping concepts, 231
 parts of a concept, 233
 parts of a whole, 234
 priorities in descending order, 235
 relationships, 236
 time line, 230
 Venn diagram, 228
GRASP strategy, 376–78
GRINCH (acronym), 14
Group Ball Toss game, 152
Guide words, dictionary, 172–73

H

Harder ending activity, 156
Herringbone, text processing, 391–92
Hierarchy, graphic organizer, 229
Home/school literacies, 478–89
 background, 478
 cooking together, 484–85
 magazines for children, 486–87
 parent interest survey, 478–81

 practice activities, 488–89
 real reading at home, 482–84
Homework schedule, 475–76
Homework tips, 467–69
Homographs, 260–262
Homophones
 resource, 585–87
 vocabulary building with, 257–58
How Is It Ordered game, 304
Humor, and motivation, 29, 31
Humorous literature, list, 31

I

Idea-maps, 608–11
 cause-effect, 611
 compare-contrast, 609
 description, 609
 main, 608
 nonfiction, 351
 problem-solution, 610
 sequence, 610
Ideas about reading, resource, 534–35
Identification, of words. *See* Word identification
Important idea, story frames, 604
Index cards, reminders, 470
Inferences, comprehension and, 313–18
 background, 313
 character interviews, 317
 getting to know my character, 314–16
 practice activities, 318
 writer and me questions, 313–14
Inflectional endings, 143–44
Intelligence, 590–93
Interest chart, parents and schoolwork, 459–61
Interest inventory, 34–35
 resources, 522–23
Internet. *See* Technology resources *and* Web sites
Internet reading, parents and schoolwork, 464
Interpersonal intelligence, resource, 593
Intrapersonal intelligence, resource, 593
Inventory of experiences, 37

K

Knowledge rating guide, for meaning vocabulary, 215–16
Known words, prediction in context, 164–67
K-W-L, prior knowledge strategy, 278–80

L

Letter-sound correspondences, consonants, 129
Limited interests, motivation, 33–37
Line graphs, interpreting, 355–57
Linked synonyms, in context, 237
List-group-label system, meaning vocabulary, 219
Literacy, emergent, 63–123
Logical/mathematical intelligence, resource, 592
Long E, 137
Low confidence, and motivation, 42–50

M

Magazines for children, 486–87
Main idea search, 288–91
Main idea-maps, 608
Main point approach, for comprehension, 288–93
 finding main idea, 288–90
 games, 293
 main idea search, 288–91
 practice activities, 291–93
Making a book, parents and, 425–26
Making a picture, visualizing, 320–21
Making words, 141–42
Match game, 293
Meaning, unknown words and, 238
Meaning vocabulary, 214–36
 background, 214–15
 contextual redefinition, 217
 feature analysis, 219–20
 feature chart, 221
 graphic organizers, 224–36
 knowledge rating guide, 215–16
 list-group-label system, 219
 possible sentences, 216
 preview in context, 218
 self-collection, 216–17
 semantic mapping, 222
 word map, 223–24
Meaning-changing omissions, oral reading, 203
Meaning-changing substitutions, oral reading, 197–99
Median oral reading rates, 576
Memorization techniques, 405
Mental pictures, visualizing, 320
Microtheme, summarizing and, 378
Mind reader, 156
Miscues, in oral reading, 568
Miscues, qualitative summary of, resource, 569
Mnemonic devices, 406
Monitoring, 363–64
Mood music, motivation, 30

Motivation, 1–61
 attitude surveys, 18–28
 book talks, 38–39
 goalsetting and, 52–61
 humor and, 29, 31
 lack of, 4
 limited interests, 33–37
 low confidence and, 42–50
 mood music, 30
 negative attitude, 17
 overview, 2
 picture book songs, 29, 30
 popular culture, 39–40
 practice activities, 11–14
 profile, 6, 530–33
 reading survey, 6–10
 reinforcement activities, 32
 technology resources for, 3
 thumbs-up/thumbs-down strategy, 11–13
 vocabulary for comments, 15–16
Motivation, parents and, 449–58
 attitude scale, 449–51
 background, 449
 practice activities, 458
 reading aloud, 452–53
 reading aloud techniques, 453
 school success, 455
 self-esteem, 456–57
 teacher/parent communication, 454–55
Motivation to read profile, resource, 530–33
Motivational comments, 15–16
Multiple intelligences, resource, 590–93
 body/kinesthetic, 593
 interpersonal, 593
 intrapersonal, 593
 logical/mathematical, 592
 musical/rhythmic, 593
 naturalistic, 593
 verbal/linguistic, 592
 visual/spatial, 592
Music, mood, 30
Musical/rhythmic intelligence, resource, 593
My Ideas about Reading, resource, 525

N

Narrative passages, retelling, 390
Narrative text, fiction, 337–39
Naturalistic intelligence, resource, 593
Negative attitude, motivation and, 17
News about Me strategy, 35–36
Nifty Thrifty Fifty, 145–46
 resource, 564–65
NIM (Neurological Impress Method), for oral reading, 192

No "Lion" I've Been Trying award, 617
Nonfiction text structure, 346–52
 background, 346
 expository text, 350–51
 graphic organizers, 347–49
 idea-mapping, 351
 organizational patterns of, 346
 practice activities, 352
 probable passages, 349–50
Nonmeaning-changing omissions, oral reading, 204
Nonmeaning-changing substitutions, oral reading, 199
Nonword substitutions, oral reading, 200–201
Norms, for attitude survey, 24
Nouns, high-frequency, resource, 552

O

Odd word out, 102
Older readers and oral reading, 191
Omniscient point of view, book list for, 337
One, Two, or Three game, 153
Onsets, 96–101
 blending, 98
 defined, 96
 practice activities, 100–101
 segmenting, 97
 show and tell, 98–100
Open-minded portraits, visualizing, 325–26
Opinion, student, 11
Oral language, 66–68
 perspective and strategies, 66–68
 promoting, 67
Oral language, promoting, 67–68
Oral reading, 185–209
 alternatives to round-robin reading, 574
 as assessment, 186–87
 background, excessive use of, 206
 dialects, 208–9
 fluency of, 189–91
 functional situations for, 207
 meaning-changing omissions, 203
 meaning-changing substitutions, 197–99
 median rates for grades 2–5, 576
 NIM procedure, 192
 nonmeaning-changing omissions, 204
 nonmeaning-changing substitutions, 199
 nonword substitutions, 200–201
 older readers and, 191
 opportunities for, 207–8

median oral reading rates, 576

practice activities, 361–62

Reading role models, 5

Reading self-check list, resource, 612–14

Reading strategy questions, 373

Reading survey, motivation, 6–10

Real reading at home, parents and, 482–84

References, in text, 619–625

Reinforcement activities. *See* Practice activities *under individual topics*

Relationships, graphic organizer, 236

Reluctant readers, defined, 4

Remembering, 404–10

background, 404

DRAW strategy, 406

memorization techniques, 405

mnemonic devices, 406

practice activities, 410

reaction guide, 407–9

Repeated readings, structured, 570–72

Repetition

book list for, 337

story element, 336, 338

of words and phrases, oral reading, 202

Retelling, 390–91

expository passages, 390–91

narrative passages, 390

text processing, 390–91

Reversals, of letters and words, 115–17

games, 117

Rhody attitude assessment, secondary reading, 27–28

administration, 27

purpose, 27

scoring and interpretation, 27

test, 28

Rhyme/ending combination, 156

Rhyming, beginning reading and, 86–89

discriminating activities, 87–88

games, 89

listening activities, 86–87

producing activities, 88–89

reciting activities, 87

RIBET (acronym), 14

Rime, defined, 96

RINGO (acronym), 14

RIOT (acronym), 14

RIP (acronym), 14

Role models, reading, 5

Round-robin reading, alternatives to, resource, 574

S

SAFARI (acronym), 14

Saga of Shakespeare Pintlewood, 369–71

Sample story, monitoring, 369–71

School success, parents and, 455

Schoolwork, parents and, 467–77

assignment sheet, 470–72

background, 467

homework schedule, 475–76

homework tips, 467–69

practice activities, 477

test-preparation checklist, 473–74

Scoring, attitude survey, 24–27

Scramble game, 304

SCROL strategy, 271

Secondary reading, Rhody attitude assessment, 27–28

Self-collection, meaning vocabulary, 216–17

Self-esteem, parents and, 456–57

Self-perception scale, 42–47

Self-report reading scale, resource, 527–29

Semantic mapping, meaning vocabulary, 222

Sense of story, 118–23

Sentence completion, resource, 523

Sequence, in comprehension, 298–305

activity list, 300–302

background, 298

games, 304–5

idea-maps, 610

pattern of, 348

practice activities, 302–4

sequencing, 298–300

Sequencing, 298–300

Sesquipedalian words, 256–57

Setting

story element, 336, 338

story frames, 605

Short I, 136–37

Show and tell, 98–100

Sight vocabulary, 161–63

background, 161

practice activities, 162–63

sight words, 162

total, 161

Sight words, basic, 155–60

background, 155

explicit instruction, 157

pattern books, 157–58

practice activities, 158–60

word wall, 156–57

Songs, picture books, 30

Sound boxes, resource, 539–45

Sound to word matching, 102

Sound wheel, word-solving skills, 429–30

Spanish dialect, 208

Spelling, 109–10

developmental stages of, 110

phonemic principles of, 109–10

SQ3R strategy, 271–74

SQUIRT (acronym), 14

SSR (acronyms), 14

Story, sense of, in beginning reading, 118–23

structure, 119–23

Story, seven main elements of, 336

story maps, 602

Story frames, 603–7

character analysis, 606

character comparison, 607

fiction, 339–40

important idea, 604

plot, 604

setting, 605

summary with one character, 595

Story grammar, 596

Story impressions, predictions, 309

Story maps, resource, 596–602

attempts, 599

character change, 597

chronological events, 600

fiction, 339

outcomes, 599

showing events, 601

story elements, 602

story grammar, 596

using events, 598

Story pyramid, fiction, 340–42

Story-reading ideas, 437–38, 443–44

fluency, 437–38

Storytelling, oral reading, 207

Structural analysis, 143–54

affixes, 146

background, 143

compound words, 147

contractions, 146–47

games, 152–54

inflectional endings, 143–44

nifty thrifty fifty, 145–46

polysyllabic words, 147–48

practice activities, 149–51

syllabication, 148

word identification, 143–54

Structure, story, 119–23

practice activities, 122–23

predicting, 120–21

Structured repeated readings, 570–72

Student self-check list, 612–14

Student writing publication, parents and, 424

Suffixes, resource, 583–84

Summarizing, of ideas, 375–79

background, 375

GRASP strategy, 376–78

microtheme, 378